Architecture and the Urban in Spanish Film

Architecture and the Urban in Spanish Film

EDITED BY

Susan Larson

intellect

Bristol, UK / Chicago, USA

First published in the UK in 2021 by
Intellect, The Mill, Parnall Road, Fishponds, Bristol, BS16 3JG, UK

First published in the USA in 2021 by
Intellect, The University of Chicago Press, 1427 E. 60th Street,
Chicago, IL 60637, USA

A catalogue record for this book is available from the British Library.

Copy editor: Newgen KnowledgeWorks
Cover designer: Alex Szumlas
Cover image: Photograph of Emilio Ruiz on the set of Operación Ogro (1979).
Used with permission of the Filmoteca Española and the family of Emilio Ruiz.
Frontispiece image: Pedro Almodóvar (dir.), *Mujeres al borde*, 1988. Spain.
© El Deseo
Production manager: Jessica Lovett
Typesetter: Newgen KnowledgeWorks

Print ISBN 978-1-78938-489-5
ePDF ISBN 978-1-78938-490-1
ePUB ISBN 978-1-78938-491-8

Printed and bound by Page Brothers

This is a peer-reviewed publication.

Contents

Figures

Acknowledgments

Many people on both sides of the Atlantic worked together on this book, and I sincerely thank all of the contributors for the enthusiasm and intellectual generosity they demonstrated from the very beginning of the project. This volume is also indebted to the anonymous external reviewers for sharing their time and expertise with us. Their insight and recommendations made this an even stronger collection of essays.

This volume would not have been possible without the resources of the Filmoteca Española (Spanish National Film Archive) of Spain's Ministry of Culture and the Filmoteca's outstanding team of librarians who helped me locate rare images and provided answers to questions about Spain's complex and incomplete film history. A special thanks goes to the indefatigable Trinidad del Río Sánchez and the always gracious support of José Luis Estarrona, Julia Carrasco, Magdalena Rodríguez Rubio and Anabel Bueno. I also am grateful to Rosa Ruiz González, who generously granted us permission to include the image of her father taken during the construction of the sets for *Operación Ogro* as the starting point for this publication.

Eva Woods Peiró, Jeff Zamostny, Julia Hernández de León, Matthew Feinberg, Steve Marsh, Patricia Keller, Leigh Mercer, Benjamin Fraser, David George, Stephen Luis Vilaseca and Marga Lobo will recognize that some of the ideas developed in this book are the result of long-standing conversations about film, space and Spanish history that began decades ago. The hours I have spent talking about Spanish film with Gema Vela, David Foshee and Andrew Cosper have allowed me to articulate and develop my ideas in recent years, and I will be forever grateful for having such intelligent collaborators. Gema Vela's technical expertise and support were key to preparing this manuscript in this brave new digital world. I am also grateful for the opportunity to have worked with Jessica Lovett and the production team at Intellect Books and Silvia Benvenuto on the index. They were a key source of creativity and encouragement throughout the production process.

One of the primary goals of this volume was to bring together film scholars and historians based in Spain with Anglo-American academics researching Spanish film in order to create a diverse and stimulating exchange of ideas and methodologies. This meant, of course, that many hours were invested in the translation of the chapters originally written in Spanish. This work was undertaken by a fantastic team of graduate students at Texas Tech University that included Dania Al-Barghuthi, Zachary Brandner, Maya Edwards, David Foshee, Robin Tipperman and Consuelo del Val.

Essential support for this volume was provided by the Texas Tech University College of Arts & Sciences, the Charles B. Qualia Endowment Fund and Carmen Pereira, chair of the Department of Classical and Modern Languages and Literatures of Texas Tech University.

Introduction: Architecture, the Urban and the Critical Possibilities of Spanish Film Studies

Susan Larson, Texas Tech University

I felt like I had stepped into another time-space dimension when, looking for something else entirely in the Filmoteca Española (Spanish National Film Archives) in Madrid, I first ran across the film set captured in the image on the cover of the volume you hold in your hands. Gathering dust in a corner of a chaotic storage space full of unlabeled movie cameras, boxes of handbills and other remnants of Spanish film history I was surprised when I ran across the meticulously crafted street used in the most iconic film shots of director Gillo Pontecorvo's 1979 Spanish and Italian coproduction *Operación Ogro*. The film was named for the attack planned by four members of the separatist group ETA against Luis Carrero Blanco, Prime Minister of Spain from 1973 until his death and the named successor to *caudillo* Francisco Franco. Carrero Blanco was the living incarnation of what seemed in the early 1970s to be the threat of an endless continuation of the repressive military dictatorship that had been in place in Spain since 1939, and his assassination is a watershed moment in the Spanish transition to democracy that would begin in earnest (albeit with fits and starts) after the death of Franco in 1975.

The screenplay for *Operación Ogro* relied heavily on the 1974 book of the same name written by Eva Forest (writing under the pseudonym Julen Agirre), who was one of the most widely known and polemical symbols of the resistance to the Franco regime. Forest's account described how an ETA commando group, posing as sculpture students, rented the basement apartment of Calle de Claudio Coello 104, a location on the route that Carrero Blanco regularly took to go to mass at the San Francisco de Borja Church. It took them five months to dig a tunnel under the street and then to pack it with 80 kg of explosives. On 20 December, according to

FIGURE I.1: Photograph of Emilio Ruiz on the set of *Operación Ogro* (1979). Used with permission of the Filmoteca Española and the family of Emilio Ruiz.

Forest's account, three members of the group, disguised as electricians, set off the bomb just as Carrero Blanco's Dodge Dart passed by on the street overhead. The explosion was so powerful that it sent the car 20 m into the air, over the top of a five-story building, crashing down on the second story balcony of a nearby Jesuit school. Carrero Blanco survived the blast but died shortly thereafter. His bodyguard and driver were killed instantly. The 'electricians' escaped in the ensuing chaos by sounding the alarm about a supposed gas leak and were never taken to trial.

Inside the model of the Calle de Claudio Coello in the Filmoteca are two versions of the Dodge Dart: one in pristine condition and the other of the car destroyed and mangled after the bombing. The impact of stumbling by mistake upon this side-by-side, seemingly simultaneous 'before and after' miniature chronotope of an event that altered the course of Spanish history is powerful. I had to resist the inexplicable urge to physically place myself inside the set and to pick up the before and after toy-sized vehicles, one in each hand, in order to think through this moment in history as well as to fully appreciate first-hand and close-up the startling realism of the miniature set itself. As film spectators we know of course that film sets are not real, but these smaller-than-life models force us to come face to face with the remarkable artistry that goes into the making of cinematic images of the built environment and to become hyper-conscious of the manipulation of scale, perspective and movement involved in the work undertaken by the oftentimes hundreds of people involved in making a film.

When I found the emblematic image that graces the cover of this volume (see Figure I.1) I was not surprised to find that someone else had had this same urge to place himself at the center of this pivotal point in the time-space continuum of Spanish history. The man in this photograph crouched deep inside the very same small-scale model with Carrero Blanco's pre-explosion Dodge Dart in his hands is none other than the film set designer himself, Emilio Ruiz del Río (1923–2007). Emilio Ruiz was a towering presence in the Spanish film industry but receives very little attention in Spanish film history and criticism, much like the internationally renowned Spanish special effects and set design pioneer Segundo Chomón (1871–1929), born a century earlier. Both filmmakers worked literally behind the scenes on a great number of Spanish films and were subsequently in high demand in other international centers of film production (Chomón in Paris, Ruiz in Hollywood, Bollywood and other parts of the world) for their innovative design and use of new visual technologies to create increasingly sophisticated and expansive film images. Ruiz's career lasted more than 60 years, during which he was responsible for the miniature models, set designs and special effects of more than 450 films (see Monleón [2008] for an excellent documentary film about Ruiz's career and Ruiz's [1996] autobiography *Rodando por el mundo*). He began his career as the set painter for the historical scenes and landscapes of nationalist propaganda films such as Juan de Orduña's *Locura de amor* (1948) and *Alba de América* (1951). Toward the end of his life he continued to work with Spanish film directors such as David and Fernando Trueba and Álex de la Iglesia but also made a name for himself internationally, playing an active role in the production and design teams of films such as Orson Welles's *Mr. Arkadin* (1955), Stanley Kubrick's *Spartacus* (1960), George Cuckor's *Travels with My Aunt* (1960) and David Lynch's *Dune* (1984). One of the last films he worked on was Guillermo del Toro's visually stunning *Pan's Labyrinth* (2006).

Ruiz was in high demand in large part because he was a world-class matte painter of crowds and mountains, but he was a true master of making nondescript buildings into far-away exotic places. Before our current era of computer-generated 3-D environments, matte painters represented a landscape, set or distant location that allowed filmmakers to create the illusion of an environment that was not present in the filming location. Historically, these artists worked with film technicians to combine a matte-painted image (usually on glass, but sometimes on other materials) with live-action footage (see Figure I.2). Ruiz was the undisputed master of using imagery to manipulate time and space throughout much of Spain's twentieth-century film history, creating environments that would otherwise be impossible or too expensive to film.

FIGURE I.2: Still of aluminum cutout painting of Emilio Ruiz recreating nineteenth-century Madrid for the television series *Fortunata and Jacinta* (1979) (Directed by Mario Camus).

This image of Emilio Ruiz sitting inside his own model of the Calle de Claudio Coello for *Operación Ogro* exemplifies what compelled me to put together this volume. *Architecture and the Urban in Spanish Film* is meant to make us think about what goes on between and behind the scenes (the sets, of course, but also screenwriting, editing, sound and cinematography) to create cinematic space. Film is simultaneously thrilling and dangerous because it constructs, simulates and activates urban settings and the architectural structures of the built environment in ways that ignite the imagination and inspire us to make connections to other ideas, to other times and to other spaces that may or may not have even existed at all.

Ours is an interesting moment in history to stop and reflect on what film means, in Spain and elsewhere. A combination of factors – the death of the studio system, the rise of streaming platforms, the closing of hundreds of movie theaters, the weakening of the concept of a national cinema and the democratization of access to the equipment necessary to make films – all of these factors change the way movies are made, distributed and how they are woven into our imaginations and everyday lives. Reflecting on this current state of affairs, James Tweedie asks the following series of pertinent questions regarding urban space and the state of film today in his discussion of the implications for film criticism of Alain Badiou's *Being and Event* (2005):

> is film primarily a storytelling medium or a mechanized recording of reality? Is it an apparatus best understood as linked to the other machinery of modernity or more of a prosthetic extension of the human gaze? Is it one node among many in a network of opinion-shaping media or does it create unique occasions when urban populations gather and discover communities like and unlike themselves?
>
> (Tweedie 2012: 120)

Both filmmaking and writing about cinema often begin by posing these fundamental questions and the answers usually depend on one's repertoire of critical concepts.

There is a long tradition of Spanish film criticism in the Anglo-American academy that talks at cross-purposes with the criticism of scholars from Spain. There are also a great number of exceptional film critics and historians in Spain whose work has rarely if ever appeared in English. Further contributing to the fragmentation of Spanish film studies and the study of urban film in particular, the topic is approached by researchers housed in a variety of departments that range from film studies to architecture, urban studies, cultural studies, art history, philosophy and literature, and each discipline often speaks its own hermetic language and relies on its own set of assumptions. Juan Egea has come up with the innovative and productive *portmanteau* 'Filmspanism' in his effort to trace the development of the study of Spanish cinema since its foundational texts in order to ascertain the set of concerns and research methods that have culminated in what he calls 'a sustained intellectual engagement with the idea of national cinema, whether to affirm its existence, question it, or open it up to translational or even postnational imaginaries' (Egea 2021: 1). Steve Marsh takes this reconsideration of both cinematic form and the national geographical imaginary even further in his work on largely neglected and experimental film that 'points to the plurality of affiliations at work within the territorial space known as Spain, the otherness that dwells within its frontiers as well as that which seeps beyond them' for the purpose of envisioning a Spanish film studies that 'mobilizes [...] the politics of global filmic practice and its materialities beyond the sterile confines of the nation' (Marsh 2021: 1). *Architecture and the Urban in Spanish Film* has been inspired by recent directions in the field such as these and hopes to create a productive dialogue as we break through some of these national and disciplinary divides.

One of the strengths of a volume of essays such as this one is that it brings together a group of film scholars who have been thinking about how to answer the same set of questions from different perspectives. These essays, taken together, capture a diverse but occasionally overlapping set of methodologies and themes. Some of the shared concerns that emerge from this volume include (1) how to approach the reciprocal relationship between the architectural and the urban in cinema; (2) the ways cinema as a new technology reshaped how cities and buildings were built and inhabited in the era of modernization; (3) the question of the mobile gaze; (4) film's role in the shifting relationship between the interior and exterior and the private and the public; (5) the role of film in everyday life; (6) cinematic critiques of monumentality and the construction of historical memory for a variety of viewing publics; and (7) last but not least, the impact of the digital and the virtual on filmmaking and spectatorship. In what remains of this Introduction we will walk through each one of these nodes that, taken together, create a network of meanings and future interpretive possibilities.

The relationship between architecture and film is a singular one. By approaching architectural space through different angles and framings, using close-ups and panoramic views, the mobile film camera makes it possible to see familiar buildings in new ways. Film enables our eyes and minds to visit spaces that are inaccessible to us and gives us vivid experiences of architecture that no longer exists as well as imaginary visions of buildings that could be in the future. To think about modern architecture, one has to pass back and forth between the question of space and the question of representation. This does not mean abandoning the traditional architectural object, the building. It means looking at it much more closely than before, but in a different way – usually, thanks to film, in a way that closely connects the buildings to mass culture, everyday life and human involvement in the creation of social space. As Beatriz Colomina explains in *Privacy and Publicity: Modern Architecture as Mass Media*, modern architecture is never fixed but always in motion, just like film and the city itself.

> Crowds, shoppers in a department store, railroad travelers and the inhabitants of Le Corbusier's houses have in common with movie viewers that they cannot fix (arrest) the image. Like the movie viewers that [Walter] Benjamin describes ('no sooner has his eye grasped a scene than it is already changed'), they inhabit a space that is neither inside nor outside, public nor private (in the traditional understanding of these terms). (Colomina 1994: 6)

Colomina argues that modernity coincides with the publicity of the private. It is in Le Corbusier's architecture, for this critic, where one can first begin to see the impact of new building technologies on the way the world is seen both from within and without the private home. The way urban citizens experience space actually changes in the modern era in the sense that walls that define domestic space are dematerialized or thinned down thanks to new building technologies, replaced by large glass windows that come to redefine space. The house becomes a device to see the world, a mechanism for viewing. The modern transformation of the house produces a space defined by a wall of 'moving' images. For Colomina, modern architecture's spaces are the spaces of media, of publicity. 'To be "inside" this space is only to see. To be "outside" is to be part of the image, to be seen' (Colomina 1994: 11). The modern city, then, longer has so much to do with public space in the traditional sense of a public forum, a square or the crowd. Colomina argues that modernity is an experience of constantly shifting boundaries and that architecture is increasingly organized by the way we think about the relationships between inside and outside, private and public. With modernity there is a shift in these relationships, a displacement of the traditional sense of an outside, an enclosed space, established in clear opposition to the outside. This revolutionary concept that infiltrates into our experience of everyday life asks us to consider how boundaries are shifting in the modern age and how this shifting takes place everywhere: in the city, of course, but also in all the technologies that define the space of the city: the trolleys, newspapers, photography, electricity, print advertisements, reinforced concrete, glass, the telegraph, radio and, of course, film. Each is a mechanism of spatial disruption and revolution.

The work of urban historian Lewis Mumford is frequently the go-to for anyone looking for a definition of the city. Back in 1937, Mumford wrote that

> the essential physical means of a city's existence are the fixed site, the durable shelter, the permanent facilities for assembly, interchange and storage; the essential social means are the social division of labor, which serves not merely the economic life but the cultural process. The city in its complete sense, then, is a geographic plexus, an economic organization, an institutional process, a theater of social action, and an aesthetic symbol of collective unity. The city fosters art and is art; the city creates the theater and is the theater. It is in the city, the city as theater, that man's more purposive activities are focused, and work out, through conflicting and co-operating personalities, events, groups into more significant culminations.
>
> (Mumford 2011: 92)

A city requires a fixed (albeit expanding) geographical limit, buildings for shelter and the storage and exchange of goods, and a centered network for economic control including the division of labor. But the city is not simply a measurable, empty spatial container, according to Mumford. It is a theater of social action and a symbol of collective unity engulfed in an endless process of constant change and contestation between its actors.

The city is not the urban, however, and this distinction is an important one. For a tried and true definition of the urban, one need only go to Henri Lefebvre's 1968 book *Le droit à la ville*, in which the French philosopher famously explains how all aspects of the modern city (political, social, economic, cultural) underwent a radical shift in the nineteenth century. As Benjamin Fraser puts it,

> Lefebvre frames the nineteenth century as that time when the notion of cityspace as an exchange value begins to trump the city as use-value. In that context, bourgeois planners ultimately failed to create an urban reality for users and instead produced the city as a site for exploitation by capitalist speculators, builders and technicians. (Fraser 2015: 31)

Lefebvre's call for an urban revolution grew out of the urgent need to reclaim the use value of cities: something that had been significantly eroded by the alienation that city dwellers experienced both within their urban environments and at the hands of their fellow citizens. Why have Lefebvre's ideas about the city and urban space had such an impact on urban studies and cultural geography in recent years? It has something to do with how he presents the revolutionary potential of urban space as a site of encounter and a realm of possibility for enacting significant social change for all citizens. Film has historically had an important role to play in creating this realm of possibility since as a form of mass culture it is broadly accessible and able to engage in social criticism by imagining a wide variety of urban spaces that allow us to consider imaginary futures that are different from the ones in which we currently live, even if it is for a fleeting moment.

How does a film impact the viewer, and what are the representational politics of the seventh art? What are the relationships between film and how we perceive and make decisions about how we should live in our collective urban environment? How does film help us to think through what is real and what is not? How have these basic questions played out in Spanish films themselves and Spanish film criticism in particular? The essays in this volume all work toward coming to terms with these key questions from a variety of disciplinary vantage points.

Architecture and the Urban

> *Film's undoubted ancestor […] is – architecture.*
> Sergei M. Eisenstein, 'Montage and architecture'

This volume begins with Benjamin Fraser's essay 'Architecture, Urbanistic Ideology and the Poetic-Analytic Documentary Mode in *Mercado de futuros* (2011) by Mercedes Álvarez', where he builds on his previously mentioned work on the urban and film as a way of bringing together the real and the symbolic by exploring the interconnected themes of space, architecture and urban form in a film belonging to the Barcelona-based tradition of the *documental de creación*. In her careful selection, composition and editing of everyday urban scenes, Álvarez undermines the notion of Barcelona as a spectacular city and questions what Lefebvre (1995) defined as the 'triumphant and triumphalist' discourse of modernity. Fraser describes the director's indirect and poetic style that makes the spectator complicit in the spectacularization of a beautiful urban form, only to subsequently challenge the viewer to peer critically under the surface to 'return space to time'.

Likewise, Jorge Gorostiza's 'Establishing Shots as Urban Blueprints in Spanish Feature Films' brings together architecture and the urban by beginning with a discussion of the Spanish term *plano de situación*, a word with a double meaning in Spanish. It denotes the initial blueprint for every architectural project and most urban plans, but it can also be used when talking about a film's opening shot which often similarly provides sweeping views of the landscape of the city and a general blueprint of how and where the plot is going to be developed. The morphology of cities that do not exist helps us understand how real urban communities work and vice versa, argues Gorostiza, and his essay is a treasure trove of iconic opening shots of Spanish films and how they set up expectations for film viewers that may or may not be entirely consistent with a film's action and plot.

Mobility

> *The (im)mobile film spectator moves across an imaginary path, traversing multiple sites and times. Her fictional navigation connects distant moments and far-apart places. Film inherits the possibility of such a spectatorial voyage from the architectural field, for the person who wanders through a building or a site also absorbs and connects visual spaces.*
>
> Giuliana Bruno, 'Motion and emotion: Film and the urban fabric'

> *Space [...] exists in a social sense only for activity – for (and by virtue of) walking [...] or traveling.*
>
> Henri Lefebvre, *Le droit à la ville*

In the nineteenth century, machines that changed the measure of space and time (machines of mobility, such as trains, steamships, bicycles, and later automobiles and airplanes) changed the relationship between sight and bodily movement.

A variety of architectural forms also emerged which facilitated and encouraged a pedestrian mobilized gaze (exhibition halls, winter gardens, arcades, department stores, museums and later escalators and elevators). Technological advances in the uses of iron and glass changed the temporal concept of the seasonal just as museums changed the relation to the past. Coinciding with the new mobilities made possible by changes in transportation, architecture and urban planning, photography brought with it a virtual gaze, which brought the past to the present, the distant to the near, the miniscule to the enlargement. Machines of virtual transport (the panorama, the diorama and, later, the cinema) extended the virtual gaze of photography to provide virtual mobility. Film scholar Anne Friedberg argues that it is the increased centrality of the mobilized and virtual gaze to everyday life that ushered us into the postmodern age. She argues that thanks to what she calls a mobilized 'virtual' gaze (Friedberg 1993: 2), spatiotemporal displacements are now as much a part of the public sphere as they are of the private. The boundaries between public and private, already fragile, have been fully eroded. The *mobilized* gaze has a history, she argues, which begins well before the cinema and is rooted in other cultural activities that involve walking and travel. The virtual gaze, in fact, has a history rooted in all forms of visual representation since the cave painting, but is produced most dramatically by photography. It is cinema, then, that developed as an apparatus that combined the *mobile* with the *virtual*, granting cinema spectatorship with the power to forever change such basic concepts as the *present* and the *real*. Friedberg argues that the imaginary *flânerie* of film spectatorship offered a spatially mobilized visuality, for sure, but that it also, and perhaps more importantly, offered a new temporal mobility as well.

In 'The Rhythm of the Modern City: Traffic and Mobility in Spanish Film, 1896–1939', Nuria Rodríguez-Martín expertly illuminates these changes as they play out in Spanish film and urban space through her approach to both documentary and feature films from the first third of the twentieth century by showing how more than one hundred years ago the experience of time-space compression was understood and explained to filmgoers in Spain. The electrification of the first urban streetcars in 1900, together with the impact of automobiles and the more scientifically based management of urban traffic caused Madrid to look and act more like other large metropolitan areas and some sectors of urban society bemoaned the loss of what was often called the 'traditional' Spanish city. As the city outgrew its physical limits again and again, it absorbed municipalities such as Chamartín de la Rosa, Vallecas and Fuencarral and forced the city to think of itself as a metropolitan region and more than just an overgrown historical city center, subsequently demanding a new way of imagining the city as a network to allow for the flow of people and goods. This chapter traces the debates in the popular press between different sectors of Madrid's population as the capital city's identity was rapidly changing in the name of modernity.

David Foshee's contribution 'Childhood Spectacle, Modernity and Madrid as a Dystopic City: Luis Lucia's *Cerca de la ciudad* (1952)' zooms in from the panoramic, historical view provided by Rodríguez-Martín through its focus on the possibilities and obstacles for physical and class mobility of children in Francoist film of the 1950s. While most scholarly attention has until now been paid to the child's role in the creation of historical memory during the Franco years, this essay focuses on the cultural geographies of urban spectacle, drawing on the work of cultural geographer Cindi Katz to talk about the child as urban accumulation strategy, the child as ornamentation and the child as waste in a film that shows children moving constantly between the urban center and the surrounding suburbs, both of which are portrayed as heartless spaces structured by predatory capital.

In Franco-era films of the 1950s, urban citizens are seen as moving on foot, in buses, cars and trolleys through the streets and alleys of the rapidly growing metropolis. Tom Whittaker's innovative approach to urban mobility focuses not on the horizontal, however, but on the vertical in his 'Elevators and the Poetics of Vertical Mobility in Spanish Film', arguing that there is a need in film criticism of the urban to pay more attention to the kinds of mundane spaces that are too often taken for granted but are essential to the spatial materiality of everyday life. Elevators are transitional spaces between streets and apartments, between the public sphere and the domestic, and as such provide the filmmaker with a set of immensely meaningful opportunities to comment on the oftentimes uneven and contradictory processes of Spain's urban modernization. The relationship between verticality and social hierarchy; the presence of broken elevators as an indication of failed urban projects; and the use of elevators to create small incubators of social tension and fear through involuntary confrontation and contact: seen together, elevators in Spanish film often illuminate the cultural anxieties that were experienced as cities became significantly more dense and vertical after the 1950s.

Surface Tensions

> *Film is a panoramic wallpaper.*
>
> Giuliana Bruno, *Atlas of Emotion: Journeys in Art, Architecture and Film*

Giuliana Bruno's assertion in 'Architecture and the moving image' is that in the contemporary era, 'our walls are becoming more like light spaces, and they are at times even turning into screens', just as the visual architecture of our times is 'becoming increasingly fluid and mobile' (Bruno 2018: 46). In Juli Highfill's contribution 'An Archi-Texture of Pleasure: The *Verbena*, the *Modistilla* and the *Mantón de Manila* in *Rosa de Madrid* (1927)', cinema becomes an inhabitable space, a mode of dwelling and a kind of 'living architexture', to once again use a term coined by Giuliana Bruno (2014: 26). Highfill considers cinematic interventions in the fledgling leisure industries that were creating new urban spaces in Madrid during the first decades of the twentieth century, most notably the *verbenas* (street fairs), festive events that filled the streets in honor of the capital city's patron saints. Scenes of *verbenas* with their myriad diversions and traditional motifs figure prominently in Spanish cinema of the 1920s and 1930s. In films such as *La Revoltosa* (1924), *La condesa María* (1928), *Gigantes y cabezudos* (1926), *La hija de Juan Simón* (1935) and *La Verbena de la Paloma* (1935), Highfill argues, the architecture of pleasure that moved bodies through space found its analog in motion pictures that likewise 'moved' their spectators, providing the thrills and chills of on-screen adventure and romance. Through a careful analysis of the urban spaces in the 1927 silent film *Rosa de Madrid,* Highfill shows how the modernization of the archetype of the *modistilla* is resituated in the vibrant commercial culture of the 1920s. During a time of vertiginous social change, *Rosa de Madrid* marshaled the affective power of cinema – its unique capacity to manufacture feeling – and invited its viewers to belong to this new 'archi-texture' of urban life and to embrace its liberatory possibilities, even if only for a few moments during the film-going experience.

El verdugo (*The Executioner*, 1963) is emblematic of Luis García Berlanga's films made during Spain's period of economic liberalization under the Franco dictatorship, from the politics of new public housing projects to social and moral conflicts caused by the country's opening up to tourism. Patricia Keller's essay 'Surface Tension and Utopian Underworlds: Orpheus and the Executioner in Luis García Berlanga's *El verdugo* (1963)' teases out Bruno's ideas about surface, depth and materiality in order to explore how the diverse spaces that comprise Berlanga's classic film – the prison, the apartment, the dream home, the construction site, the bedroom, the church, the city hall, the airport and the island – form an intricate network of social, political, cultural, countercultural, sexual, affective, architectural and cinematic economies. Keller's argument hinges on her consideration of a statement of Víctor Erice's in his essay 'Writing Cinema, Thinking Cinema' that '[c]inema authorizes Orpheus to look back without letting Eurydice die' (Erice 2000: 269). She finds this to be an apt way to describe how Berlanga looks into the past with a critical, contemplative gaze that somehow avoids falling into the kind of nostalgia so common in Spanish film of the 1960s, when Spain's past was frequently simplified, sanitized and rewritten in ways that did not allow for much critical reflection.

The Everyday

> *Anyone [can] observe how much more easily [...] architecture can be grasped in photography than in reality.*
>
> Walter Benjamin, 'A small history of photography'

Walter Benjamin's idea that architecture cannot be fully grasped without the aid of some form of visual technology is an immensely evocative one for the essays in this volume that explore the (in)capacity of film and film spectators to understand their urban constructed environments from any one individual vantage point. What are the concepts that the urban planners and architects have in mind when they design their cities and buildings, roads and parks? What is the meaning of the significant and inevitable gap between these modern, rational plans and the chaos and contingency of everyday life? How do real people adapt the official urban spaces of modernity for their own purposes? What are the politics of representing these everyday urban spaces in Spanish film? Architects and film historians Josefina González Cubero and Alba Zarza-Arribas propose several strategies to answer these questions in their essay 'Mediating Everyday Life: Domestic Architecture in Spanish Film'. This essay offers the reader an immensely informative history of the representation of interior, domestic space in Spain since the late nineteenth century, when these spaces were largely modeled on the theatrical traditions on which film drew heavily in its early years. With Francisco Elías's 1929 *El misterio de la Puerta del Sol*, however, the new technologies of sound and aerial photography would forever change the relationship between the way that domestic interior and the more public exterior urban spaces would be represented and understood. González Cubero and Zarza-Arribas weave together Spanish film history, architectural criticism and ever-changing needs for housing to explain the role of film in the shaping of the urban experience.

If González Cubero and Zarza-Arribas trace the roots of early filmic interiors to theater, Emeterio Diez Puertas and María de Arana Aroca remind us that theater is the source of many aspects of the structure of film narrative itself in their essay 'Through the Looking Glass: Images of the Ordinary World in Oscar-Nominated Spanish Cinema'. This essay takes a transatlantic approach to the understanding of discussions of everyday Spanish life in films that over the years have had an international audience thanks to their being included in the 'Best Foreign Language Film' category for the Hollywood-based Academy Awards. This approach is reciprocal in nature in that it unearths what type of daily life these particular Spanish films want to get across to an international audience, while at the same time it reveals the strategies the films use to invite spectators to 'cross through the looking glass' in order to enter the Spanish spatial imaginary. Using

Bakhtin's concept of the *chronotope* and paying particular attention not only to the films but to the actual screenplays on which they are based, Diez Puertas and Arana Aroca explain how the architectural and urban spaces the filmmakers create are ephemeral portals and that every film has its own particular way of providing the viewer with an architectural code of recognition, transformation and spatial construction.

Memory and the Monumental

> *Starting itself as a chance accumulation of relics, with no more rhyme or reason than the city itself, the museum at last presents itself to us as a means of selectively preserving the memorials of culture. What cannot be kept in existence in material form we may now measure in photography in still and moving pictures.*
>
> Lewis Mumford, 'The death of the monument'

Every national cinema is central to the creation of shared ideas about a country's identity and cities are invariably used as spectacles to undergird and justify political ideologies. The stark incongruity between the escapism of the many films made in Spain after the Civil War and the harsh realities of every life for the vast majority of Spaniards during the 1940s (known as the 'años del hambre' [years of hunger]), however, made any kind of cultural justification of the dictatorship harder and harder to maintain, especially after 1945 when Franco lost his fascist allies in Germany and Italy. According to data collected by Spain's Delegación Nacional de Sindicatos, in 1955 the number of *chabolas* (self-constructed, substandard housing or shacks) and caves in which some of Madrid's inhabitants lived rose above 18,000. The number of families renting individual rooms in larger homes with access to a kitchen reached around 20,000; the number of families living on abandoned farm land, according to the municipal count, reached around 5,000; the number of families involved in eviction proceedings as a result of the changes brought about by the new Ley de Arrendamientos Urbanos reached an estimated 7,000; the families that had since 1936 been living in public buildings such as slaughterhouses, bathhouses and schools, for example, hovered around 10,00 and, last but not least, it is estimated that around 10,000 families were living in temporary homes in short-term pension houses, hostels and other types of emergency housing. All of these added up to some 60,000 units that needed to be added to the city's housing offerings in order for life to return to some sense of pre-war normalcy. These numbers are very low, of course, because they do not begin to take into account the number of housing units required to accommodate the great demographic shift of migration from the countryside to the city that took place after the war.

Against this grim urban reality, how does one understand a filmmaker like José Antonio Nieves Conde, a Falangist whose films with strong neorealist tendencies were radically altered by the Francoist censors for being too critical of the economic injustices inherent to daily urban life after the Spanish Civil War? Many film critics have asked this question and the essay 'Who and What was José Antonio Nieves Conde Criticizing in the Film *El inquilino* (1957)?' co-authored by Susan Larson and Carlos Sambricio looks for an answer by considering a seemingly inconsequential screenplay written by Alfredo Marquerie in 1955 for the documentary film *Obra Sindical del Hogar* commissioned by the Delegación Nacional de Sindicatos, which was responsible for organizing all of the industrial workers in Spain during the Franco regime. The plot of *El inquilino* is remarkably similar to the narrative outlined in this 1955 screenplay and includes the pious, moralizing statements of the Obra Sindical that were put to such humorous use in the feature film two years later. The purpose of this 1955 documentary was to reinforce the confidence of Spanish workers in the state and its official workers' unions. Nieves Condes's feature film, however, ultimately undermined the ideology and project of Franco's housing policies. What Nieves Conde did not know, however, is that the regime would get the last laugh. Just a few months after the release of *El inquilino*, Spain's Minister of Housing, José Luis de Arrese, would almost single-handedly transfer the capacity to satisfy the urgent demand for public housing to the private sector.

Film scholar Vicente Sánchez-Biosca, calling himself a 'discourse archeologist', explores the dialectic between modernization and the capital of Spain that the Franco regime was still struggling to memorialize decades after the end of the Spanish Civil War. His essay 'Madrid 1964: Icon of Modernity or City of Memory? A Look at the "Details"' looks at images and voice-overs from three very different films made in the 1960s about Madrid. The emphasis is not on the narrative of the films themselves but instead on certain 'details' expressed in the voice-overs and initial shots of each film. Drawing on the concept of the 'detail' put forward by art historian Daniel Arasse in his discussion of painting, Sánchez-Biosca looks at these details as 'manifested as gaps' or small instances of resistance in relation to the overall meaning of the film. Because these details are necessarily partial and incomplete, they provide the opportunity to create flashes of meaning that are either indifferent or contrary to the overall ideologies of these films that were meant to convince filmgoers of the seamless discourse of nationalist power that the Franco regime so eagerly sought to create and uphold. This nationalist ideological project was growing more difficult to sustain in the mid-1960s when the capital city of Madrid was experiencing a significant student protest movement at the same time as it was being outfitted for the celebration of the so-called 25 Years of Peace, a massive campaign devised by the Minister of Information and Tourism Manuel Fraga Iribarne with the purpose of highlighting the achievements of the regime since the victory of 1939.

Samuel Amago's 'Making Madrid Plastic: Waste and Space in Pedro Almodóvar's Post-*movida* Films' jumps ahead in time to tease out how the capital city's regional authorities worked to forge a new identity that would distinguish the city from its historical association with the Franco dictatorship. This was ultimately a failed and incomplete project that never entirely broke its connections to its Francoist past, however. Amago argues that Pedro Almodóvar's films from the 1980s are part of a broader political and closely associated cultural project to transform the city's lived environment into an ahistorical place that would open the door to more aggressive capital investment and urban transformation. Looking closely at the themes of trash, waste and disposal in political discourse and public service announcements in Spain after the death of Franco, Amago connects these working vocabularies to the cultural and symbolic processes by which the entire country sought to sanitize its public spaces by removing monuments to Franco and key figures in the regime. These plastic lifeworlds of post-*movida* Madrid were a prefiguration of the increasingly neoliberal city to come.

The Virtual

> *Three modes of external control have historically stifled the creative process of a filmmaker: political, financial and technological. Today with the digital revolution, the camera will bypass all such controls and be placed squarely at the disposal of the artist.*
>
> Samira Makhmalbaf, 'The digital revolution and the future cinema'

Films were once created by a strip of celluloid physically moving through a camera and film projector. Today the moving image is most commonly generated by digital technology whose algorithmic calculations are invisible to the naked eye and the nature of whose 'indexical' trace of physical reality continues to provoke debate among scholars. Only film spectators of a certain age remember the click-click-clicking mechanical whir associated with watching a film on a 35-mm projector and how an error on the part of a projectionist (a bulb too close to the film strip or placing a reel out of order) would remind the movie-going public of just how fragile, volatile and even combustible film as a material object could be.

The ontological status of the silent digital images that film viewers see now is just as uncertain, of course, and an amalgam of conventional cinematography and computer-generated and otherwise manipulated imagery. Yet despite – perhaps because of – the myriad possibilities enabled by digital technology, analog photography and previous film technologies continue to inspire art photographers and filmmakers and suggest that the reports of the death of celluloid photography and moving images are premature. If we have learned anything about the emergence of new media, it is that they will converge and overlap with previous technologies. People lived among and filtered through multiple media one hundred years ago, and this is also the case for us in the twenty-first century. Yet to what extent our digital cinematography, ever-present webcams and nonindexical media such as global positioning systems (GPS) augment human vision or enable the cognitive advances championed by film critics such as Dziga Vertov and Jean Esptein is far from certain.

Although we may quantitatively see much more than we have in the past, do we actually know and understand more about ourselves and the world in motion around us? Leigh Mercer's contribution to this volume, 'Uncanny Urbanism and Generational Shifts in Carlos Marques Marcet's *10.000km* and *Anchor and Hope*' confronts these questions directly. Online apps and computer screens connect the young lovers located in Barcelona and Los Angeles in *10.000km* and in the film's mise en scène, the cityscape of Los Angeles is only revealed through virtual photo sharing, Google Street View, and Facebook posts. This is in stark contrast with the urban environment of Barcelona that is hyper-present in its almost complete absence from the film, with the exception of one crucial exterior balcony scene roughly halfway through the film, raising questions about the possibility of maintaining human relationships while deprived of sensorial connection in real space. By mining the virtual screens of contemporary urbanism or the alternative and neglected urban remnants of an industrial past that linger in the present day, the film problematizes the seamless relationship between urbanism and cinema in a way that effectively captures our own twenty-first-century moment. The postindustrial landscapes of boat canals become the strangely outside-of-time mise en scène (and significantly in this case, soundscapes) to explore the generational sea change portrayed in Marcet's *Anchor and Hope,* a film that explores what parenthood looks like for a present-day generation of thirty-somethings who are questioning the inherited structures of the traditional western family in the era of late capitalism. Mercer's discussion of Marcet's films points to a new twenty-first century use of urban film where the city is always either mediated or purposefully at a remove. Instead of a scaffolding for cinema or a counterpart held in tension with the cinematic, urban elements in both of Marques Marcet's films place viewers in the realm of the uncanny, where the familiar is made strange.

Stephen Luis Vilaseca's 'Dead to Capitalism: Zombified Territory and Junkie Spaces in *Cabanyal Z*, or How to Unleash Monstrous Creativity in the Urban' analyzes how the digital is not only thematic or part of the mediatized understanding of urban space, but key to the creation and distribution of a cinema as a collective political project. Supported largely by crowd-source funding, this participatory video takes the power of filmmaking out of the hands of the trained specialist or auteur and puts it into the hands of people who have something to say about their first-hand experience of consumption-based strategies of urban growth and design. The creators of the ten-episode series *Cabanyal Z*, Gerardo J. Nuñez and Joan Alamar, inspired by street artists, took advantage of spaces in the city in order to reflect on the city itself. Urban space becomes art, and the city itself became a cocreator of its artistic content when the thirteen-minute episodes were projected onto the walls of buildings in the Cabanyal neighborhood in Valencia where the project was born and filmed. This political project subsequently took on a longer, digital life when it became a Facebook page, a Twitter account, a YouTube channel and a WordPress blog. The repeated message underlying this grassroots, collaborative video project depicting the gentrification of a working-class neighborhood in Valencia in terms of a battle between zombies and other monsters is that if we embrace what Vilaseca calls 'zombie thought', if we 'rip out our bodily organs that function according to the logic of capital' (evoking Deleuze and Guattari's *A Thousand Plateaus*), we will be open to a new, different, more open logic that is more in tune with the needs and demands of our immediate environment.

As I conclude this introduction I am compelled to circle back to the image with which my text began and my consideration of the work of Spanish set designer Emilio Ruiz. Only if you look very carefully can you see the dust and rough construction of the delicate wooden platform and wrinkled rug on which Emilio Ruiz kneels inside his recreation of the Calle de Claudio Coello. The constructed nature of the street in miniature seeps in at the edges of what at first glance looks like a real street. The contrast of scale between the body of the actual set designer and the street he has (re)created captures the power of film to reshape urban space and to play with space and time in enormously empowering ways. I would argue that the power of urban film lies not in its ability to represent reality as it is or as it could be, however. It is at its best when it points us to the cracks in official discourses of how and why cities and buildings are conceived, constructed, lived and remembered. Through the shared, collective, social experience of film and the subsequent preservation of its history in the form of archives and criticism the monumental becomes the everyday and the everyday takes on a weight and importance that might otherwise have been lost.

REFERENCES

Badiou, Alain (2005), *Being and Event* (trans. Oliver Feltham), New York: Continuum.

Bruno, Giuliana (2002), *Atlas of Emotion: Journeys in Art, Architecture and Film*, New York: Verso.

Bruno, Guiliana (2008), 'Motion and emotion: Film and the urban fabric', in A. Webber and E. Wilson (eds), *Cities in Transition: The Moving Image and the Modern Metropolis*, London: Wallflower Press, pp. 14–28.

Bruno, Giuliana (2014), *Surface: Matters of Aesthetics, Materiality, and Media*, Chicago: University of Chicago Press.

Bruno, Giuliana (2018), 'Architecture and the moving image: A haptic journey from pre- to post-cinema', *La Furia Umana*, 34, http://www.lafuriaumana.it/index.php/67-archive/lfu-34/781-giuliana-bruno-architecture-and-the-moving-image-a-haptic-journey-from-pre-to-post-cinema. Accessed 8 June 2019.

Colomina, Beatriz (1994), *Privacy and Publicity: Modern Architecture as Mass Media*, Cambridge, MA: MIT Press.

Egea, Juan (2021), *Filmspanism: A Critical Companion to the Study of Spanish Cinema*, London and New York: Routledge.

Eisenstein, Sergei M. ([1938] 1989), 'Montage and architecture', Introduction by Yve-Alain Bois, *Assemblage*, 41, pp. 110–31.

Erice, Víctor (2000), 'Writing cinema, thinking cinema' (trans. Guys Wood and Julie Croy), in Linda C. Ehrlich (ed.), *The Cinema of Víctor Erice: An Open Window*, Lanham, MD: Scarecrow Press, pp. 267–69.

Fraser, Benjamin (2015), *Toward an Urban Cultural Studies: Henri Lefebvre and the Humanities*, New York: Palgrave Macmillan.

Friedberg, Anne (1993), *Window Shopping: Cinema and the Postmodern*, Berkeley: University of California Press.

Lefebvre, Henri (1968), *Le droit à la ville*, Paris: Anthropos.

Makhmalbaf, Samira (2014), 'The digital revolution and the future cinema', in S. MacKenzie (ed.), *Film Manifestos and Global Cinema Cultures: A Critical Anthology*, Berkeley: University of California Press, pp. 580–85.

Marsh, Steven (2020), *Spanish Cinema Against Itself: Cosmopolitanism, Experimentation, Militancy*, Bloomington: Indiana University Press.

Monleón, Sigfrido (2008), *El ultimo truco*, Spain: A. Santana, I. Uribe and Ariete-Ariane Films.

Mumford, Lewis (1937), 'The death of the monument', in N. Gabo and B. Nicholson (eds), *Circle: International Survey of Constructivist Art*, New York: Faber and Faber, pp. 263–70.

Mumford, Lewis ([1937] 2011), 'What is a city?', in R. T. LeGates an F. Stout (eds), *The City Reader*, 5th ed., New York: Routledge, pp. 91–95.

Ruiz del Río, Emilio (1996), *Rodando por el mundo. Mis recuerdos y mis trucajes cinematográficos*, Madrid: Asociación de Amigos del Cine Expermiental de Madrid.

Tweedie, James (2012), 'The event of cinema: Alain Badiou and media studies', *Cultural Critique*, 82, pp. 95–127.

PART 1

ARCHITECTURE AND THE URBAN

1

Architecture, Urbanistic Ideology and the Poetic-Analytic Documentary Mode in *Mercado de futuros* (2011) by Mercedes Álvarez

Benjamin Fraser, University of Arizona

> *Mercado de futuros quería ser sólo una cosa: un retrato cinematográfico sobre el mercado de la vivienda. El caso español constituía un buen ejemplo. La fiebre inmobiliaria, agudizada durante la última década, había transformado como nunca las ciudades, sus centros y periferias, había mordido sin piedad el paisaje y había convertido la costa del levante español en la mayor conurbación del mundo.*
>
> Mercedes Álvarez and Arturo Redin, 'Escribir el espacio, habitar el lenguaje'[1]

Mercado de futuros (Futures Market) (2011), the second full-length film directed by Mercedes Álvarez (Soria, 1966–present), is many things. First, it is a stunning artistic product that engages the visual sense in order to explore the theme of the crisis in Spain. In this respect, it is a complement to other post-15M works of visual art: for example, the performance piece *Los encargados* (2011), staged by Santiago Sierra and Jorge Galindo in Madrid's Gran Vía, and the 15M graphic novel *Lo que (me) está pasando: diarios de un joven emperdedor* (2015), created by comics artist Miguel Brieva.[2] Second, understood as a critical text in its own right – thus irreducible to the medium through which this critique is carried out – the film complements wider interest in thinking through the root causes and persisting consequences of the crisis in Spain. The film synthesizes and comments on economic, political, social and aesthetic discourse, exploring the same issues brought to light in the 15M dossier organized by Bryan Cameron and published in the *Journal of Spanish Cultural Studies* (2014), in Jon Snyder's *Poetics of Opposition in Contemporary Spain: Politics and the Work of Urban Culture* (2015) and in Luis Moreno-Caballud's *Cultures of Anyone* (2015), for example. It also builds on a tradition of cultural studies approaches to Barcelona's urban culture (Balibrea 2017; Bou and Subirana 2017; Degen 2008; Epps 2001, 2002; Illas 2012; Mercer 2013; Resina 2008; Vilaseca 2013). And third, it is a visual, critical text that reflects deeply on the urban phenomenon. What arguably makes *Mercado de futuros* a masterpiece is the emphasis that Álvarez places on interconnected themes of space, architecture and urban form. The result is a filmic challenge to the urbanistic ideology that continues to drive the production of space in the contemporary city.

The first section of this chapter, 'The Documentary of Creation: Architectural Coordinates and Urban Context', introduces the readers to Álvarez's work as a director and sets the coordinates for the analysis to follow. Striving to be concise, rather than precise, it introduces the cinematic genre of the documentary of creation as well as key details of the film's aesthetics, content and organization. The second section, 'The Poetic-Analytic Mode as Vehicle for and Critique of Capitalist-Urbanistic Ideology', articulates the value of the film's explicit urbanization of capitalist political economy. In line with the work of Henri Lefebvre, David Harvey and Barcelona-based urban theorist Manuel Delgado Ruiz, I assert the fundamental role played by urbanism and urbanistic ideology in capitalism's reproduction of city space since the nineteenth century. I take as my starting point the idea that the housing bubble is a contemporary – and specifically urban – manifestation of the periodic crises inherent to advanced capitalism (Harvey 2012; Lefebvre 1976, 1991), and instead I devote more time to analyzing key sequences from the film in light of Álvarez's visual poetics of representation. This section also references the classifications of documentary modality theorized by Bill Nichols (1991, 2001). Whereas Nichols describes how the poetic mode has often been seen as incompatible with politics, I explore how Álvarez uses its key tropes precisely as an analytic attack on the ideology of urbanized capitalism. It is here that the director portrays and politicizes urban architecture – within capitalistic, neoliberal contexts – as a surface. The visual allure of architecture in *Mercado de futuros* is depicted as the façade for a more crass and triumphalist urban modernity.

The Documentary of Creation: Architectural Coordinates and Urban Context

Mercado de futuros has received awards at the Premio Miradas Nuevas del Festival de Hyon, Vissions du Réel, the Premio 'Navaja de Buñuel' Película Revelación,

TVE, the Premio Mejor Documental, Festival de Cine de Nantes, Francia, and the Mención Especial de Jurado, Festival Internacional de Cine de Buenos Aires – all in 2011. Beyond its own merits, the film is also important on account of its director's connection with the tradition of the *documental de creación* in Spain. Many point to Joaquim Jordà's film *Mones com la Becky* (1999) as the origin of this form of cinematic expression, also emphasizing a debt owed to his work with the Escuela de Barcelona dating back to the second half of the 1960s (e.g. Riambau 2010: 11).[3] What is certain is that at the end of 1998, the Universitat Autònoma de Barcelona inaugurated the Máster en Teoría y Práctica del Documental Creativo (Viveros y Català 2010: 123), and the Máster en Documental de Creación program began at the Universitat Pompeu Fabra (UPF). Notably, 'La UPF, durante muchos años, no solo lideró el resurgir del documental en Cataluña, propició el surgimiento de autores que debutaban en el campo de la no-ficción' (For many years, the UPF did not only lead the resurgence of documentary film in Catalonia but promoted the emergence of authors that made their debut in the field of nonfiction film) (De Pozo and Oroz 2010: 67). Álvarez was among the first students in the program, along with other notable figures such as Isaki Lacuesta and Ariadna Pujol (see De Pozo and Oroz 2010: 68).

Like director Abel García Roure (*Una cierta verdad* [2008], see Fraser 2016), Álvarez had been a member of the team working with José Luis Guerín (Balló 2010: 108–09). Specifically, she was the *montadora*/editor on Guerín's film *En construcción* (Balló 2010: 113). Her first film project as director was *El cielo gira* (2004). Reduced to its barest content, this film explores the dwindling rural population of the small town Aldealseñor in Soria. Yet Álvarez uses this basic premise, along with paintings of Pello Azketa, an artist who is losing his sight, to forge a cinematic meditation on temporality, disappearance and human landscape. As Jordi Balló notes, this first full-length film is concordant with the broader aims of the *documental de creación*, in that, 'Con *El cielo gira* se ratificaba que la frontera entre documental y ficción era solo una cuestión nominal y de dramaturgia, y que en este cine de lo real anidaba una nueva poética y un nuevo sentido de la emoción' (*El cielo gira* confirmed that the boundary between documentary and fiction film was only a nominal matter of production and that this *cine de lo real* [real film] had a new poetics and a new sense of emotion) (Balló 2010: 115).[4] Themes of spatiality, time and memory were already interconnected in *El cielo gira*, and they were implicated in its critical success. Yet, as noted by critic Javier Serrano, in the director's sophomore effort these themes are notably and more directly urbanized.

With her second full-length film, Álvarez continues to question the border between documentary and fiction and to explore the way emotions are implicated in space/place. By effectively urbanizing *El cielo gira*'s cinematic insights regarding time, memory and loss, *Mercado de futuros* contributes to an urban subtradition of the *documental de creación*. Two figures are obligatory references for understanding what she accomplishes with this effort. Álvarez has been inspired by her mentor Víctor Erice's *El sol del membrillo* (1991) and is following closely in the footsteps of José Luis Guerín's *En construcción* (2001).[5] These two films played with documentary approaches to urban themes, and both were in dialogue with a poetic mode of urban representation.[6] Yet *Mercado de futuros* pushes both of these dimensions of the director's work to an extreme impossible in those earlier films. To explain: running through Erice's undoubtedly complex film there is also a more easily digestible biographical focus. The centrality of painter Antonio López García's artistic process to *El sol del membrillo* is a device that quite naturally supports the introduction of philosophical themes and subtly induces a poetic response in the spectator. Likewise, Guerín's challenging film centers on easily recognizable and iconic spaces that have long proven central to Barcelona's shifting identity as a global city. It is notable that *Mercado de futuros* does not rely on either of those advantages. Instead, the director has accepted the challenge of building a philosophical, poetic and urban narrative from scratch.

The film is defined by and constructed through a series of tensions. It is both inaccessible and inviting, conceptual and topical. At the beginning of the film, after a section of animation that is worthy of critical attention in its own right, a voice-over by Álvarez outlines the contemplative agenda for the film:

> Una noche, hace más de dos mil años, el poeta griego Simonides de Ceos acudía a una casa con más de veinte invitados. Durante la cena, mientras Simonides se ausentaba unos momentos, se hundió el techo de la casa, sepultando a todos los habitantes. Los cadáveres quedaron tan destrozados que nadie podía identificarlos. Pero Simonides sí pudo hacerlo. Porque recordaba el lugar exacto donde estaba sentado cada uno de los invitados. Se dice que Simonides inventó el arte de la memoria, y que fue utilizado durante siglos. Pero ese arte carece, desde hace mucho, de la más mínima importancia.[7]
>
> (Álvarez 2011)

There is a coldness to this introductory voice-over, as the director cultivates the appropriate philosophical distance for conducting a clinical investigation of contemporary urban society. The delivery of her words is decidedly dispassionate. Yet the subject matter is markedly familiar and even quotidian. The director's dispassionate tone and her verbal text's emphasis on the aporias of time – that is, notions of lack, forgetting, negligence – is reinforced by the still image of an empty white wall where a picture once hung. The scene that follows captures the clearing out of a house. It emphasizes common objects, wall-hangings, paintings and furniture that, in the poetic mode of filmmaking, can be seen as repositories for the emotional connections that saturate our living environments. The belongings of the former inhabitants are thus revealed to be residue from the routine projection of human emotions onto architectural space. This is a primary tension established throughout the film – the coldness of a 'pure' architecture versus the warmth of human relationships that imbue space with social meaning. We invest spaces, architectural forms and objects with significance, humanizing and personalizing them; yet this significance is destined to fade – particularly if we are inattentive to it over time. *Mercado de futuros* has been carefully shot and structured to convey that this is very much the case. We do indeed forget what has come before.

Related to this theme, Álvarez provides us with a somewhat routine cinematic memory exercise in *Mercado de futuros*. Though subtle, and perhaps easily forgotten, a doll figurine from this opening sequence of a house being cleared reappears meaningfully toward the end of the final lengthy flea-market sequence. This final sequence is filmed in the market Els Encants, located at the Plaça de les Glòries Catalanes, which is nestled near a highway exchange, and not far from the shadow of the Torre Agbar. As Manuel Delgado Ruiz writes in *La ciudad mentirosa: fraude y miseria del 'modelo Barcelona'*, juxtaposing the flea market and the tower designed by French starchitect Jean Nouvel specifically, 'cada mañana se reunían centenares de inmigrantes sin trabajo, de vagabundos y de otros miserables que compraban y vendían en un enorme bazar surgido espontáneamente, donde se podía encontrar todo tipo de objetos recogidos de los contenedores de basuras' (every morning hundreds of immigrants without jobs, homeless and other poor folks met in a huge and improvised flea market where all kinds of objects gathered from garbage dumpsters were bought and sold) (Delgado Ruiz 2007a: 51). Delgado's prose scene acquires cinematic form in lengthy sequences from *Mercado de futuros* featuring Els Encants, with a view to both the highway and the Torre Agbar (see Figure 1.1). The doll reappears in this context in the film's late sequences, and viewers may or may not remember it from the beginning of the film. Yet it is a reminder of our routine (in)attention to the emotional connections we forge with the object world. The doll symbolizes the emotional connections to space, place and other social objects, a use-value that is subjugated to the exchange economy. This prop's association with domestic family life and the use-value space of the home is important to its cinematic meaning. Its reappearance challenges viewers to confront their own levels of attentiveness or inattentiveness. Like those emotional connections symbolized and enacted by the doll, our emotional connections with place itself are similarly vulnerable to fading away, becoming less significant to us and losing their sustained social import and use-value.

Mercado de futuros is ultimately about the devaluation of emotion, belonging and connection to place in a market context that privileges exchange over use. Importantly, the film makes the case that both the object world and the urban built

FIGURE 1.1: Els Encants with view to highway and Torre Agbar. Mercedes Álvarez (dir.), *Mercado de futuros*, 2011. Spain. © IB Cinema.

environment are similarly positioned in the market as commodities. In texts such as *Introduction to Modernity* (1995), *Writings on Cities* (containing *The Right to the City*) (1996), and *The Urban Revolution* (2003), Henri Lefebvre charts the development of urban modernity from the nineteenth century as the period in which the city itself becomes a commodity. Delgado's own urban critique is explicitly indebted to Lefebvre's work as revealed in overt references from *El animal público* (1999), *Memoria y lugar* (2001) and *Sociedades movedizas* (2007b). *La ciudad mentirosa* in particular can be seen as applying Lefebvrian insights on the capitalist production of space to the urban context of Barcelona. In the introduction, titled 'La ciudad-negocio', Delgado writes:

> Quien ansía ocupar Barcelona y avasallarla es, hoy, un capitalismo financiero internacional que ha descubierto en el territorio una fuente de enriquecimiento y que aspira a convertir la capital catalana en un artículo de consumo con una sociedad humana dentro. Por supuesto, ése es un fenómeno que afecta a otras muchas ciudades del mundo, todas ellas objeto de recalificaciones masivas al servicio de los intereses de las grandes corporaciones multinacionales.[8]
>
> (Delgado Ruiz 2007a: 11)

Álvarez's cinematic critique effectively carries the insights offered by Lefebvre and Delgado to the screen. While the director seems to be shooting only in

Barcelona, her integration of speculative real estate projects and futures markets proves to be in line with Delgado's point that the Catalonian capital is immersed in a global system of exchange. The appearance of the Torre Agbar – which notably also appears on the dust jacket for Delgado's *La ciudad mentirosa* – anchors the film in the uneven geographical development of Barcelona. Yet also prominent are a range of other global spaces that appear indirectly – for example, through a preponderance of urban images and architectural models. Capitalist speculation is specifically urbanized through the representation of global real estate investments, including properties located in Dubai and Budapest. Álvarez complements the notion of place as a commodity by showcasing a variety of activities linking the city with business: not only real estate fairs (Barcelona Meeting Point and Salón Inmobiliario de Madrid) and a brokerage company (Bolsa de Ahorro Corporación) but also a convention dedicated to leadership (Expomanagement).

It is interesting that some existing scholarship on the film has downplayed the relationship of the urban form to capitalist speculation, effectively ignoring the role of the city as a prioritized commodity since the nineteenth century. For example, studies by Manuel de la Fuente (2017) and Isabel Estrada (2017), though valuable contributions noting the importance of *Mercado de futuros*, nonetheless fail to address architecture or the urban in sufficient depth. These accounts prefer to focus on the film's relevance to what comes across as essentially a political-economic crisis. While astute, these analyses tend to recapitulate broader trends in traditional economics in which the crucial role of urban environments in strategies of capital accumulation is overlooked. Even Marxian traditions are not immune from this tendency to take the city as the mere setting or backdrop for contemporary capitalism rather than a key commodity in and of itself (see Harvey 2012). That is, in addition to being the backdrop for the continuing exploitation of labor by capital, the urban landscape is both a product of capitalism (the result of speculative activity) and also its key generative component (a producer of exchange-value). The next section builds on insights from an article by Mercè Picornell (2017), who gives a bit more attention to the relationship constructed in the film between political economy and architectural and urban form. While being more explicit about the film's critique of capitalistic-urbanistic ideology, it is also crucial to understand how Álvarez exploits the poetic mode of documentary filmmaking.

The Poetic-Analytic Mode as Vehicle for and Critique of Capitalist-Urbanistic Ideology

This section attends to the way in which the ideology of urbanism manifests itself in the film's content and form and how this urbanistic perspective is handled by the director's critique. The documentary of creation's erosion of the border between fiction and documentary is itself important for the film, given the director's intent to push viewers to question values attributed to contemporary urbanism and its capitalistic ideology. In her careful selection, composition and editing of everyday urban scenes, Álvarez undermines the notion of Barcelona as a spectacular city and at once questions what Lefebvre (1995) defined as the 'triumphant and triumphalist' discourse of urban modernity. In doing so, she implicitly dialogues with a tradition of criticism that has critiqued Barcelona's reputation as a global city (Delgado Ruiz 2007a, 2007b; McNeill 1999, 2002; Degen 2000, 2004a, 2004b, 2008). In this case, the director advances trenchant critiques of neoliberal capitalism's colonization of urban space (Delgado Ruiz 1999, 2007b, 2010; Lefebvre 1973, 1991, 1996, 2003). In order to understand how *Mercado de futuros* accomplishes this, it is first necessary to underscore her adaptation of what Bill Nichols calls the poetic mode of documentary filmmaking.[9]

Mercado de futuros showcases various elements of the poetic mode. Perhaps most overtly – as introduced above in the first section – is 'the Voice of God commentator, whom we hear speaking in a voice-over but do not see' (Nichols 2001: 13).[10] Yet simultaneously the film provides evidence of a poetic mode variant that seeks to 'hint and suggest rather than declare or explain', a tendency where 'the point of view becomes implicit' (Nichols 2001: 48). This mode characteristically 'emphasizes visual associations, tonal or rhythmic qualities, descriptive passages, and formal organization' (Nichols 2001: 33), stressing 'mood, tone, and affect much more than displays of knowledge or acts of persuasion' (Nichols 2001: 103). Yet while it is quite often used without overt political intention – an example would be *Berlin: Symphony of a City* (Walter Ruttman 1927) – the poetic mode at times can be effectively combined with an analytic directorial voice – as illustrated in the example of *Man with a Movie Camera* (Dziga Vertov 1929) (both examples from Nichols 2001: 90). Beyond the poetic mode, of course, *Mercado de futuros* also blends elements of expository, observational and reflexive filmmaking, but stops short of demonstrating the director's need to 'intervene and interact'. Thus what Nichols calls 'the veil of illusory absence' is not 'shorn away' – as in the interactive mode of documentary film – but rather emphasized as a formal complement to Álvarez's interrogation of what has been lost in modern urban life. Her approach is poetic, mediated, but somewhat indirect; her style is thus more philosophical than interventionist. The effect is to preserve a visual sense of the seductiveness of urban power while nonetheless calling upon the mind to eviscerate its concomitant ideology.

It is worth asking why the poetic mode is seemingly incompatible with politics. Must that always be the case? And why is it a particularly apt mode for Álvarez in *Mercado de futuros*? What is perhaps most interesting in this regard is the posture of Álvarez's film concerning the figure of the worker or, by extension, a figure similarly contrasted with the class interests implicit in the capitalist city, the urbanite. Historically, the poetic and expository modes of documentary filmmaking represented such figures 'within an ethics of social concern and charitable empathy' and thus 'denied the worker a sense of equal status with the filmmaker' (Nichols 2001: 140). If one were to divide the film into two sections, admittedly a somewhat arbitrary division, this comment would prove somewhat informative regarding the first section. It would be even more accurate to say that the film's first section largely avoids depicting the worker or urbanite at all until its second half.

Some of the film's most striking poetic-analytic scenes occur in the first half of the film and either neglect the human form, limit its significance or subjugate it to the engine of capitalist-urbanistic production. There are still-camera images that capture ruins of the built environment that lack any human figure whatsoever (see figure 1 in Picornell 2017: 186). Or else the human figures that do appear are immobilized, seated in outdoor chairs and – their faces hidden from viewers – stripped of their human attributes (see the image in Serrano 2012). Such urbanites are somehow anesthetized to the ideological nature of the urban form and have effectively been turned into just another object in the built environment. The shot of businessmen immobilized in individual massage chairs is similarly evocative (see figure 4 in Picornell 2017: 189). This is one of the most absurdly powerful images in *Mercado de futuros* precisely because it illustrates so concisely – with no need for voice-over – how human beings have become anesthetized, via consumption, into a slumber of critical intellect.

Similar in this regard are the upper-middle class functionaries who in practice sustain the capitalistic-urbanistic machine. That is, the day-to-day business work of these professionals contributes fundamentally to the accumulation of capital in a small number of hands. Because of the nature of the work in which they engage, even if they are not themselves capitalists, these workers thus become indistinguishable from capitalist accumulation in practice. One memorable shot of such a white-collar professional shows a man in jacket and tie working on a laptop against the background of what might seem an idealized urbanized coastline (see figure 2 in Picornell 2017: 186).[11] The physical distance of this figure from the spectacularized urban image making up the background recapitulates a social distancing. Symbolically, he represents the disproportionate (and disproportionately patriarchal) social power enjoyed by the European planning class (i.e. Baron Haussmann in Paris and Ildefons Cerdà in Barcelona). Cinematically, he embodies the idea advanced by Richard Sennett that the 'visual technology of power' employed by modern urban planners 'alienated them, too, from their own work' (Sennett 1992: 61). Poetically and critically, he becomes in the viewer's imagination a servant to the capitalist production of space.

Overall, there is a poetic if grotesque beauty to the image of the city in *Mercado de futuros*. There is no question that this is a beautiful film. The generalized emphasis of the poetic mode on concerns such as mood, tone, rhythm and affect can be observed continually. As De la Fuente reflects, 'all the characters move like automatons in a beautiful but empty environment' (De la Fuente 2017: 189). At least initially, in what might be called the first half of the film, the director's artful choices of compositional framing and the lingering gaze of the camera seem to intentionally treat the urban form as an aesthetic object. Yet there are nonetheless wonderful moments when the superficial, slick, bird's-eye view, or two-dimensional image of the modern city is undermined to showcase the role of labor in its production.

One such scene (also discussed by Picornell) presents an entire indoor wall in what could be in a conference center or shopping mall that bears the image of a triumphantly urban scene. After the still camera lingers a moment on the urban image, a door opens in the wallpapered urban image and an employee steps out of an office, walking the length of the wall. This moment reveals, in symbolic terms, that behind the aesthetic splendor of the modern urban form there is human activity shaping the architectural landscape, which while it appears to be already given is of course the result of social labor. The surface – of the wall, and of urban architecture by extension – is only an illusion constructed in the interests of those who would profit from the image of the city as an exchange-value.

As this example in particular drives home, the film demonstrates a tendency to aestheticize urban form and then politically undermine this aestheticization in subtle ways. As Picornell has argued, 'the use of the cinematographic *trompe-l'oeil* encourages spectators to question what they see, to look beyond surface appearance' (Picornell 2017: 185, 189).[12] Tying this back to the classifications made by Nichols, the hybrid poetic-analytic documentary mode becomes for Álvarez an apt method for creating a conflict in her film's viewers. As cinematic spectators appreciating the beauty of the film's composition and architectural images, we become complicit in the spectacularization of urban form and somewhat anesthetized to urban conflict. Simply put, the splendor of photographic composition and cinematic montage in *Mercado de futuros* is entrancing. Yet at the same time, Álvarez challenges and encourages us to do the work of peering under the surface and returning space to time. In the process, she vindicates a form of urban memory that our wider society has neglected and that we may collectively choose to recapture at any moment whatsoever.

As the film moves through its second half, the figure of the worker/urbanite comes more clearly into view. Álvarez spends more time with Jesús, a second-hand object collector who works in the flea market known as Els Encants. In light of comments made by Nichols, this can be seen as a correction of the poetic mode's historical marginalization of the worker. The director allows Jesús significant on-screen time, with no voice-over. He progressively acquires a privileged position in the film and in the viewer's consciousness. This gradual shift needs to be understood in relationship to the film's development of the trope of surface and depth as it relates to the urban phenomenon. Here Álvarez shifts from the architectural aspects of the built environment to the immersive urban social context inhabited by the individual city dweller.

Jesús sits at a market stall that is in reality a large container. The container is overflowing with used, discarded objects to such a degree that he must sit out in front of it. As Jesús speaks with one flea-market visitor after the next, it becomes increasingly clear that he has littl to no desire to sell any of his wares. At times, he mentions that he probably has the item that is being requested, but is unable (or unwilling) to retrieve it. Thematically, these sequences effectively function as a cinematic return of the commodity from exchange-value to use-value. The goods in Jesús's container are useful to him not because he makes money off of them, but rather because they serve him as prompts for social interaction. The fact that Els Encants is shown in physical proximity to the Torre Agbar and the highway interchange of the Plaça de les Glòries Catalanes keeps viewers cognizant of the spectacular architectural image of Barcelona even as they spend time with one of the city's most forgotten urbanites.

These scenes centering on Jesús are also important in terms of their mise en scène. Here the items with potential exchange-value are hidden from view, and it is the human figure that is prioritized visually. Jesús is positioned in front of the goods and not behind them. The juxtaposition of this scene with the one discussed above – where a man exits from the hidden office door – could not be more clear. Although in that scene, the slick image hides the real human work, here, by contrast, use-value triumphs over exchange-value. As this juxtaposition illustrates, the film has shifted from surface to depth. Whereas before it foregrounded the surfaces of buildings and the exchange economy, now it highlights the individual urban dweller and the use-value of time. This is simultaneously a shift in scale, from the architecture and built environment of the monumental city toward the personal scale and the deep time of those who inhabit place. The camera and editing allow viewers to dwell with Jesús, and in doing so they shift from the presentation of the passive, immobilized human figure as part of a commodified urban world toward a form of human sociality that has been systematically neglected.

These final scenes of *Mercado de futuros* contrast with the cold, if contemplative, voice-over of the film's beginning and return viewers to the association between human warmth and what the modern city should be. The doll from the beginning of the film also reappears, a subtle but poignant reminder of our emotional human connections with the object world, and potentially also with the architectural form of the city. Álvarez arguably employs both Jesús and the doll to hammer home the central idea of the film, which is this: it is only our memory – of human connections, of an urban form of life not yet completely colonized by exchange-value – that can push our action to stem the tide of the dehumanizing consequences of capitalist-urbanistic ideology.

NOTES

1. '*Mercado de futuros* wanted to be just one thing: a cinematographic portrait of the housing market. The Spanish situation served as a good example. The real estate fever intensified during the last decade, transformed cities, its downtowns and peripheries like never before. It took a merciless bite out of the landscape of the eastern coast of Spain in the biggest conurbation in the world' (Mercedes Álvarez and Arturo Redin, 'Escribir el espacio, habitar el lenguaje', 2011, *Mercado de futuros* press kit; cited in Castanon-Akrami [2014: 249–50]).
2. On Miguel Brieva, see Fraser (2018); on Sierra and Galindo, see Snyder (2015).
3. Admitting, too, the importance of José Luis Guerín's *Innisfree* (1990) (Riambau 2010: 30).
4. He continues: 'Álvarez logró un filme casi milagroso, fruto de la paciencia, de la estancia en el lugar y de su capacidad para hacer aflorar cinematográficamente la génesis de un mundo' (Balló 2010: 113). Note that García Roure was the assistant director on Álvarez's first film (Balló 2010: 113).
5. Critics have noted her admiration for Víctor Erice (Torreiro 2010: 48, and vice-versa (Erice 2005), in addition to her film's resonance with Guerín's aesthetics (see Torreiro 2010: 46, also De Pozo and Oroz 2010: 69).
6. On *En construcción*, see Loxham (2006); on *El sol del membrillo*, see Fraser (2010: 177–87).
7. 'One evening, more than two thousand years ago, the Greek poet Simonides of Ceos visited a house with more than twenty guests. During supper, while Simonides was momentarily absent, the roof of the house collapsed and buried all of its residents. The corpses were so damaged that no one could identify them. However, Simonides could because he remembered the exact place where each one of the guests were sitting. They say that Simonides invented the art of memory and that it was used during centuries. But that kind of art has not had, for the longest time, any importance at all.'
8. 'The international financial capitalism that nowadays wishes to occupy and dominate Barcelona has discovered in this territory a source of wealth that aims to transform the Catalan capital into a commodity with a human society inside. Certainly, this is a trend that affects many other cities in the world, where all of them are the object of massive reclassifications that serve the interests of large multinational corporations.'
9. Note that Nichols categorizes modes of documentary filmmaking in *Representing Reality* (1991), but that the poetic mode was added later in his *Introduction to Documentary* (2001).

10. Nichols continues, noting that '[t]his anonymous but surrogate voice arose in the 1930s as a convenient way to describe a situation or problem, present an argument, propose a solution, and sometimes to evoke a poetic tone or mood [...] a poetic tone that made the transmission of information secondary to the construction of a deferential, somewhat romanticized mood' (Nichols 2001: 13–14).
11. Picornell notes the presence of 'carteles y maquetas como paisajes' (posters and scale models as landscapes) (Picornell 2017: 186, labeled figure 2), but does not sufficiently explore how these are used filmically or symbolically.
12. 'El uso del *trompe l'oeil*, un mecanismo que permite a Álvarez dibujar fisuras en la superficie de la hiperrealidad' (Picornell 2017: 185); 'El uso de formas diversas de *trompe-l'oeil* cinematográfico sirve para situar al espectador en una posición interrogante, desde donde puede aprender a mirar más allá de la superficie de lo que el poder – económico, político, periodístico – le pone ante los ojos' (the use of the cinematographic *trompe l'oeil* encourages spectators to question what they see, to look beyond surface of what power – economical, political, journalistic – put before their eyes) (Picornell 2017: 189).

REFERENCES

Álvarez, Mercedes (2011), *Mercado de futuros*, Spain: IB Cinema.

Balibrea, Mari Paz (2017), *The Global Cultural Capital: Addressing the Citizen and Producing the City in Barcelona*, London: Palgrave Macmillan.

Balló, Jordi (2010), 'Cronología de una transmisión (El Máster de Documental de la UPF)', in C. Torreiro (ed.), *Realidad y creación en el cine de no-ficción (El documental catalán contemporáneo, 1995–2010)*, Madrid: Cátedra, pp. 105–21.

Bou, Enric and Subirana, Jaume (eds) (2017), *The Barcelona Reader: Cultural Readings of a City*, Liverpool: Liverpool University Press.

Cameron, Bryan (ed.) (2014), 'Spain in crisis: 15-M and the culture of indignation', *Journal of Spanish Cultural Studies*, 15:1–2, pp. 1–275.

Castanon-Akrami, Brice (2014), '*Mercado de futuros* (2011) de Mercedes Álvarez ou la société du Spectacle et la crise du développement', in E. Fisbach and P. Rabaté (eds), *Actes choisis du colloque de Strasbourg 'Crise(s) dans le monde ibérique et ibéro-américain'*, *Hispanismes*, 4, pp. 248–60, http://www.hispanistes.org/images/PDF/HispanismeS/Hispanismes_4/19-shf%20hispanismes%204%20castanon%20brice.pdf. Accessed 3 March 2018.

Degen, Monica M. (2004a), 'Barcelona's games: The Olympics, urban design and glocal tourism', in J. Urry and M. Sheller (eds), *Tourism Mobilities: Places to Play, Places in Play*, London: Routledge, pp. 131–42.

Degen, Monica M. (2004b), 'Passejant per la passarel·la global: Ciutats i turisme urbà', *Transversal*, 23, pp. 30–32.

Degen, Monica M. (2008), *Sensing Cities: Regenerating Public Life in Barcelona and Manchester*, London and New York: Routledge.

De la Fuente, Manuel (2017), 'Documenting the indignation: Responses to the 2008 financial crisis in contemporary Spanish cinema', *Romance Quarterly*, 64:4, pp. 185–95.

Delgado Ruiz, Manuel (1999), *El animal público*, Barcelona: Anagrama.

Delgado Ruiz, Manuel (2001), *Memoria y lugar. El espacio público como crisis de significado*, Valencia: Ediciones Generales de la Construcción.

Delgado Ruiz, Manuel (2007a), *La ciudad mentirosa: Fraude y miseria del 'modelo Barcelona'*, Madrid: Catarata.

Delgado Ruiz, Manuel (2007b), *Sociedades movedizas: Pasos hacia una antropología de las calles*, Barcelona: Anagrama.

Delgado Ruiz, Manuel (2010), 'La ciudad levantada: la barricada y otras transformaciones radicales del espacio urbano', in *Hacia un urbanismo alternativo* (Architectonics, Mind, Land & Society 19/20), Barcelona: UPC, pp. 137–53.

Delgado Ruiz, Manuel (2011), *El espacio público como ideología*, Madrid: Catarata.

De Pozo, Gonzalo and Oroz, Elena (2010), 'Centralización y dispersión (Dos movimientos para cartografiar la "especificidad" del documental producido en Cataluña en la última década)', in C. Torreiro (ed.), *Realidad y creación en el cine de no-ficción (El documental catalán contemporáneo, 1995–2010)*, Madrid: Cátedra, pp. 61–86.

Epps, Brad (2001), 'Modern spaces: Building Barcelona', in J. R. Resina (ed.), *Iberian Cities*, New York and London: Routledge, pp. 148–97.

Epps, Brad (2002), 'Barcelona and the projection of Cataluña', *Arizona Journal of Hispanic Cultural Studies*, 6, pp. 191–287.

Erice, Víctor (2005), 'A propósito de *El cielo gira*', *El País*, 13 May, https://elpais.com/diario/2005/05/13/cine/1115935209_850215.html. Accessed 3 March 2018.

Estrada, Isabel (2017), '"Democrazy" in Spain: Cinema and new forms of social life in the twenty-first century', *MLN*, 132:2, pp. 386–406.

Fraser, Benjamin (2010), 'Encounters with Bergson(ism) in Spain: Reconciling Philosophy, Literature, Film and Urban Space', *Studies in Romance Languages and Literatures*, #295, Chapel Hill, NC: University of North Carolina.

Fraser, Benjamin (2015), *Toward an Urban Cultural Studies: Henri Lefebvre and the Humanities*, New York: Palgrave.

Fraser, Benjamin (2016), 'Battling voices: Schizophrenia as social relation in Abel García Roure's *Una cierta verdad* [A Certain Truth] (2008)', *Disability Studies Quarterly*, 36:2, n.pag.

Fraser, Benjamin (2018), 'Miguel Brieva, *quincemayista*: Art, politics and comics form in the 15-M graphic novel *Lo que (me) está pasando* (2015)', *Transmodernity: Journal of Peripheral Cultural Production of the Luso-Hispanic World*, 8:1, pp. 42–62.

Harvey, David (2012), *Rebel Cities*, London and New York: Verso.

Illas, Edgar (2012), *Thinking Barcelona: Ideologies of a Global City*, Liverpool: Liverpool University Press.

Lefebvre, Henri ([1973] 1976), *The Survival of Capitalism* (trans. Frank Bryant), London: Allison & Busby.

Lefebvre, Henri (1991), *The Production of Space* (trans. D. Nicholson-Smith), Oxford and Cambridge, MA: Blackwell.

Lefebvre, Henri ([1962] 1995), *Introduction to Modernity* (trans. J. Moore), London: New York: Verso.

Lefebvre, Henri ([1968] 1996), *The Right to the City*, in E. Kofman and E. Lebas (trans. and eds), *Writings on Cities*, Malden, MA, Oxford and Carlton: Blackwell, pp. 63–181.

Lefebvre, Henri ([1970] 2003), *The Urban Revolution* (trans. R. Bononno), Minneapolis: University of Minnesota Press.

Loxham, Abigail (2006), 'Barcelona under construction: The democratic potential of touch and vision in city cinema as depicted in *En construcción* (2001)', *Studies in Hispanic Cinemas*, 3:1, pp. 35–48.

McNeill, Donald (1999), *Urban Change and the European Left: Tales from the New Barcelona*, London and New York: Routledge.

McNeill, Donald (2002), 'Barcelona: Urban identity 1992–2002', *Arizona Journal of Hispanic Cultural Studies*, 6, pp. 245–62.

Mercer, Leigh (2013), *Urbanism and Urbanity: The Spanish Bourgeois Novel and Contemporary Customs* (1845–1925), Lanham, MD: Bucknell University Press.

Moreno-Caballud, Luis (2015), *Cultures of Anyone: Studies on Cultural Democratization in the Spanish Neoliberal Crisis*, Liverpool: Liverpool University Press.

Nichols, Bill (1991), *Representing Reality: Issues and Concepts in Documentary*, Bloomington: Indiana University Press.

Nichols, Bill (2001), *Introduction to Documentary*, Bloomington: Indiana University Press.

Picornell, Mercè (2017), 'Abriendo fisuras en el escenario de lo hyperreal: una lectura del documental Mercado de futuros de Mercedes Álvarez', *Confluencia: Revista Hispánica de Cultura y Literatura*, 32:2, pp. 178–91.

Resina, Joan Ramon (2008), *Barcelona's Vocation of Modernity: Rise and Decline of an Urban Image*, Stanford: Stanford University Press.

Riambau, Esteve (2010), 'Cuando los monos aún no eran como Becky (El documental catalán antes de 1999)', in C. Torreiro (ed.), *Realidad y creación en el cine de no-ficción (El documental catalán contemporáneo, 1995–2010)*, Madrid: Cátedra, pp. 11–31.

Sennett, Richard (1992), *The Conscience of the Eye: The Design and Social Life of Cities*, New York and London: W. W. Norton.

Serrano, Javier (2012), '*Mercado de futuros*, entre el suelo y el humo', *La República Cultural*, 19 March, https://larepublicacultural.es/article5533.html. Accessed 3 March 2018.

Torreiro, Casimiro (2010), 'De tendencias y autores (La configuración artística del documental catalán contemporáneo)', in C. Torreiro (ed.), *Realidad y creación en el cine de no-ficción (El documental catalán contemporáneo, 1995–2010)*, Madrid: Cátedra, pp. 33–59.

Vilaseca, Stephen (2013), *Barcelonan Okupas: Squatter Power!*, Lanham, MD: Fairleigh Dickinson University Press.

Viveros, Carmen and Català, Josep M. (2010), 'La nueva ecología del documental (El Máster de Documental Creativo de la UAB)', in C. Torreiro (ed.), *Realidad y creación en el cine de no-ficción (El documental catalán contemporáneo, 1995–2010)*, Madrid: Cátedra, pp. 123–41.

2

Establishing Shots as Urban Blueprints in Spanish Feature Films

Jorge Gorostiza, Academy of Fine Arts, Canary Islands

In Spanish, the architectural term *plano de situación* ('situational map') refers to the initial blueprint for every architectural project and most urban plans. This *plano* consists of a visualization of where the newly built or renovated buildings will be situated, the layout of the zone that will be planned, and provides a sense of scale in relation to the rest of the surrounding urban area. There is a close relationship between this architectural term and the film term, since in Spanish *plano de situación* also refers to a film's opening shot, which also characteristically provides sweeping views of the landscape of a city and a general blueprint of where the plot is going to be developed.

These initial blueprints or establishing shots in urban films are important. As Santos Zunzunegui writes,

> they contain information that will play a role, that will impart a space-time framework to the images that will come next. Even before the narrative itself gets underway, these shots invite us to evoke a kind of double sense of what will underline the story that is going to be developed.
>
> (Zunzunegui 1996: 20)[1]

Opening shots of movies are also important because they serve as documents of the morphologies of Spanish cities of the past while simultaneously exposing the worldviews of the film directors that are not always entirely consistent with the great variety of real-life urban experiences and problems.

Point of View

It is common for aerial photographs to accompany the initial blueprints of an architectural project, especially in this era when Google Maps makes them so accessible. The closest you can get to a blueprint of a city is a view from above and, in fact, many architectural blueprints are made thanks to photos obtained with special cameras for topographical work that are fixed on airplanes. Many Spanish movies begin with shots taken by cameras attached to airplanes in order to show cities from above. *¡Viva Madrid que es mi pueblo!* (Fernando Delgado 1928) is the first Spanish film that features aerial photography. It begins with a shot of a globe, then focuses on a map of Spain, followed by a map of the province of Madrid with a woman's finger pointing to the capital. The subsequent aerial shot flies over the Plaza de Cibeles, continues over the Calle de Alcalá and finally passes over the Gran Vía. The camera shifts the scale from the planetary to the cartographic, leaving behind the technologies of the past to implement more modern scientific knowledge. A similar but temporally reversed trajectory occurs in the later film *Trío de damas* (Pedro Lazaga 1960) in which the camera in flight follows the Paseo de Recoletos, reaches Cibeles Fountain and then circles the monument several times, leaving us with the decidedly premodern figure of Cybil, 'mother of the gods', according to Greek mythology. Another aerial pass over the city whose shots skillfully combine to create a rich meaning occurs in *Buenos días, condesita* (Luis César Amadori 1967). The film begins with a full view of Pedro Teixeira's 1656 map of Madrid, then zooms in on the Plaza Mayor. The subsequent shot is of the Plaza Mayor from the air; the camera turns and heads toward the south, pauses above the Calle de los Estudios, passes over the Plaza de Cascorro and Calle Ribera de Curtidores and settles into a street-level shot of El Rastro, where the protagonist, known as *la condesita* ('the little countess'), works selling records. The initial shot of the Teixeria map gives the protagonist (even if parodically) the appearance of a pedigree and nobility underlined by her nickname, while at the same time aerial views make a statement about with the reality of a more popular, *castizo* Madrid.

Aerial shots establishing the nature of the urban environment in Spanish film do not necessarily have to be touristic, iconic or monumental. In *Una gota de sangre para morir amando* (Eloy de la Iglesia 1973), for example, in one shot the camera flies above the area surrounding the Hospital Universitario La Paz,[2] which was at that time an isolated structure surrounded by empty lots of land. The building appears like a disturbing monster stranded in a wasteland. Another movie that starts with an arresting aerial shot that adds great meaning to a film's urban location is *27 horas* (Montxo Armendáriz 1986) that starts from the sea and progressively draws closer to the La Concha beach in San Sebastián, coming to a stop with a shot of a watchtower that reads seven o'clock, dramatically indicating the time and place where the action is about to begin.

There is typically more than one aerial shot at the beginning of films. There are various consecutive aerial shots, for example, in *Los palomos* (Fernando Fernán Gómez 1964), in which the Ministerio del Aire (headquarters of the Ministry of the Air Force) and the Plaza de España, filmed under a blanket of snow in this case, stand in as representing the city as a whole and also provide additional information about the time of year when the action will take place. The Edificio España and Torre de Madrid buildings, situated in the Plaza de Esapña, were the tallest structures in Spain at that time and were powerful symbols of modernity. These same buildings are also seen from the air in *En septiembre* (Jaime de Armiñán 1982), which also features the 'Nuevos Ministerios' and Azca sections of the Madrid.[3] Following the Paseo de la Castellana (the city's North-South axis and another symbol of modernity in the capital) to arrive at the intersection of Pinar and López de Hoyos streets, the camera eventually focuses its attention on a four-story mansion that houses a school where the protagonists studied that is under threat of demolition.

In *La joven casada* (Mario Camus 1975), another Madrid-based film, we have an aerial view of the Chamartín train station, followed by Retiro Park and ultimately, the blocks of multifamily housing where the main characters live. The station is understood at the beginning of the film to be the entrance to the city, but by the end of the film this same station is the means by which the protagonist flees the capital. This kind of beginning has also been employed in films about a variety of other cities. See, for example, *Barcelona Sur* (Jordi Cadena 1981) in which the camera seemingly soars over that city, featuring bird's-eye views of the monument to Christopher Columbus, against the backdrop of ships moored at the dock and the port's massive warehouses.

One historically significant film that includes a particularly extensive number of aerial shots at the beginning is *Las chicas de la Cruz Roja* (Rafael J. Salvia 1958). It starts with the Puerta de Alcalá and passes over an exhaustive list of recognizable icons of the city, including the Plaza de Cibeles, the Edificio España and Torre de Madrid in the Plaza de España, the Gran Vía, the Plaza del Callao, the Santiago Bernabeu soccer stadium, the Zarzuela Horsetrack, the Ministry of the Air Force, the Royal Palace in the Plaza de Oriente, the Plaza de Ramón y Cajal in the Ciudad Universitaria, again through the Plaza de España, the manmade lake of Retiro Park, Santiago Bernabeu again, the Ciudad Universitaria again, featuring the Escuela Técnica Superior de Ingenieros Industriales, the Colegio Mayor Guadalupe, the Plaza de Neptuno, the Castellana, the Plaza del Callao and finally returning to the Puerta de Alcalá again. As we can observe, the route taken by the camera is not a logical one connecting contiguous urban spaces. It is random, with the editing alternating between known monuments with spaces dedicated to popular entertainment and leisure such the racetrack and the stadium, and even repeating iconic places such as the Plaza del Callao and la Puerta de Alcalá which open and close this extended panoramic sequence.

Most aerial shots take place during daytime, but some others have also been used when the day comes to an end. One notable example is *El disputado voto del señor Cayo* (Antonio Giménez-Rico 1986) which begins filming decidedly nonmonumental architecture of little importance until the camera arrives at the Congreso de los Diputados (the location of the lower branch of Spain's legislature), where the plot begins. Establishing shots that feature a sunrise over Madrid can be found in *El vuelo de la Paloma* (José Luis García Sánchez 1989) which begins with the Torre Picasso on the Castellana, passing by the Casa Sindical (the Union Building, currently the headquarters of the Ministry of Health, Consumption and Social Welfare) in the Paseo del Prado, then landing in the Puerta de Alcalá precisely when the movie's title is superimposed onto the image. The aerial footage continues to the Torrespaña known as *el pirulí* (popularly named after a lollipop sold in the 1960s), the Plaza de Cibeles, Puerta del Sol, Plaza Mayor, the Calle Segovia Viaduct, the Royal Palace and finally, the Plaza del Conde de Barajas where the movie takes place. The purpose of this extensive aerial tour is to feature a series of monuments and familiar buildings, without a logical route, since the last plaza mentioned is located very close to the Plaza Mayor. Nighttime opening shots are not quite as common, but have occasionally been employed. One recent and notable example can be found in *Rumbos* (Manuel Burló Moreno 2016), which begins with the camera flying over Barcelona and capturing the Montjuic Telecommunications Tower and the Arts Hotel.

In order to capture the city from above, cameras are often employed from the tops of tall buildings. Many Spanish films begin with panoramic shots, like the one moving from right to left at the beginning of *El tigre de Chamberí* (Pedro Luis Ramírez 1957), in which the back of the Real Academia Española building is juxtaposed with the front of the Church of San Jerónimo el Real, buildings in an area with no relation whatsoever to the Chamberí neighborhood of the title. *Las muchachas de azul* (Pedro Lazaga 1957) begins with another panorama in the same vein from the Edificio España that pans from southwest to southeast, showing the Plaza de España, the Royal Palace and the Gran Vía. This is followed by another, similar sequence from the same building – this time from the northeast to the northwest, which ends by capturing the emblematic Arco de la Victoria, an imposing structure built in the Moncloa district of Madrid at the behest of Francisco Franco in 1936. Likewise, in *La ironía del dinero/Bonjour la chance* (Edgar Neville and Guy Lefranc 1957), there is another exceptional panoramic shot from the Edificio España from left to right, scanning the Royal Palace and the

Plaza de España while the narrator's voice-over informs the spectators that 'What you see down below is Madrid and those moving dots are Madrid's citizens, and those other dots moving even faster and passing through the dots moving more slowly are the cars, which, having paid a hefty fee, joyfully go hunting. Madrid is so beautiful! How beautiful cities are when seen from above!' (Edgar Neville and Guy Lefranc 1957),[4] the narrator jokes, celebrating the privileged point of view of the camera.

La chica del gato (Ramón Quadreny 1943) begins with a panoramic shot from right to left showing the Royal Palace in the Plaza de Oriente and the Opera House. Many years later, at the beginning of *Los nuevos españoles* (Roberto Bodegas 1974), a similar shot was taken by a camera located to the north of these buildings, creating a different effect by showing the same location but going in the opposite direction, portraying the Opera House in a different way than in *La chica del gato*. One sees the same urban landscape, but the buildings have been renovated. There are effective and notable panoramic shots from left to right at the beginning of *Solos en la madrugada* (José Luis Garci 1978) showing the Plaza del Emperador Carlos V and an overpass popularly called the Scalextrix de Atocha which, by the time the film was released, had been demolished. It is also seen at the beginning of *La que arman las mujeres* (Fernando Merino 1969) and once again at the beginning of *Adiós con el corazón* (José Luis García Sánchez 2000) from a building in the Plaza de los Cubos that pans Princesa Street until arriving at the Plaza Cristino Maroto. Panoramic shots that create significant meaning about other Spanish cities are also found in films such as *Fulano y mengano* (Joaquín Luis Romero Marchent 1959), where the camera pans from left to right from the Monasterio de Santa María del Parral, showing the skyline of the city of Segovia with its famous cathedral and ending with a shot of the Alcázar.[5] Fixed shots from above also anchor in place films such as *Solo química* (Alfonso Albacete 2015) in which Barcelona's Torre Glòries, the Hotel Arts, the Cathedral, the World Trade Center, the Columbus monument with a billboard underneath that reads 'La Rambla' and finally the Rambla itself are all displayed. Memorable shots from the beginning of *Entre tinieblas* (Pedro Almodóvar 1983) capture a night scene through the use of time-lapse photography. This same process was used years earlier to great effect in the low-angle establishing shots of *Más bonita que ninguna* (Luis César Amadori 1965), through a camera placed on the sidewalk at the start of the Gran Vía at the intersection with the Calle de Alcalá, while night falls.

Cameras are also frequently positioned in the hilly or mountainous areas surrounding the cities, providing an urban view from the periphery. One such panoramic shot can be found in *El Litri y su sombra* (Rafael Gil 1959) of Huelva, *El pico* (Eloy de la Iglesia 1983) of Bilbao, *La ciudad no es para mí* (Pedro Lazaga 1966) of Madrid, *Pasaje a Venezuela* (Rafael J. Salvia 1956) of Barcelona from

Monjuic and of Málaga in *Malvaloca* (Benito Perojo 1926), a film first whose first intertitle proclaims that 'Málaga [...] is the beauty of beauties, and pride of the land of Andalusia' (Perojo 1926).[6]

Cities can also be displayed from ground level, situating the camera from a human's point of view, which is also used on occasion to create panoramic shots. These shots can range from the pans from right to left at the beginning of *Crimen imperfecto* (Fernando Fernán Gómez 1970) and those that move vertically found in *Día tras día* (Antonio del Amo 1951) from the top of the statue of Eloy Gonzalo to the stalls of the Rastro, and in *Taxi* (Carlos Saura 2004) from the Metrópolis building that marks the beginning of the Gran Vía, with a clock in the background indicating the time of 2:03 in the afternoon, when the street is full of traffic and pedestrians. There are also panoramic shots that are combined with zooms as in *El alegre divorciado* (Pedro Lazaga 1976) which captures the Plaza de Cibeles, which is followed by a backwards zoom showing the Puerta de Alcalá, then a panoramic shot from right to left goes to the Gran Vía and the Metrópolis building, where yet another zoom frames the monument on its pedestal, thus managing to capture these two emblematic spaces of the capital in just one shot.

The noncentral neighborhoods of the city have also consistently been displayed in this way in Spanish film. For example, the panoramic shot from right to left reveals a public housing block in the Madrid neighborhood of San Pascual in *Colegas* (Eloy de la Iglesia 1982); the panoramic view from the Calle Guipúzcoa in the Barcelona neighborhood of Sant Martí that finishes with a frame of the Cine Levante in *A sangre fría* (Juan Bosch 1959); and another similar shot in the same vein of the Parque de Lisboa in *Duerme, duerme, mi amor* (Francisco Regueiro 1975).

Another vantage point from which to introduce the city to the viewer in a film's first moments is from a moving vehicle, as in *El pobre García* (Tony Leblanc 1961), *F.E.N.* (Antonio Hernández 1980) and *Solos en la madrugada* – all of which begin with the mobile camera leaving a tunnel before rising to street level at the Puerta de Alcalá. Other noteworthy examples include the entrance into Madrid at the beginning of *Trampa para Carolina* (Pedro Lazaga 1961) by way of the Carretera de La Coruña, by the aforementioned Arco del Triunfo, and turning left toward the Avenida de los Reyes Católicos. The shot then jumps to the area surrounding the Puerta de Toledo, where the action of the movie takes place far from any of these spaces.

In all of these examples, the camera is in motion, whether attached to an airplane or swiveling with stationary panoramic shots. The camera can also, however, create the sense of mobility by moving over still images. At the beginning of *Cerca de las estrellas* (César Fernáez Ardavín 1962), there is a panoramic shot from left to right of a view of the city obtained from a rooftop or in *Hacienda somos casi*

FIGURE 2.1: José María Nunes (dir.), *Mañana*, 1957. Spain. © Mercury Films.

todos (Mariano Ozores 1988) where it moves over some aerial photographs of the Manga del Mar Menor in Murcia, but the camera can also remain completely immobile, as we see at the beginning of *Mañana* (José María Nunes 1957) which consists of a series of nighttime photographs of Barcelona.

Taking into account all of these examples, it is possible to make a three-part classification of how cities are portrayed at the beginnings of movies. The first category depends on the point of view, which can be from the ground level or from above, but can be further subdivided according to where the camera has been placed: on airplanes, buildings, hills or vehicles. The second category to consider is the movement or lack of movement of the point of view. The third is the moment chosen to show the city, whether it be during the daytime, nighttime or in between, at dawn or dusk.

Descriptions

Spanish movies often begin with a mixture of texts that complement the images. For example, the first intertitle of the silent film *Alma de Dios* (Manuel Noriega

1923) reads 'Madrid. A heroic town that exudes progress under a blazing sun that brightens and makes the soul of Spain happy.'[7] In the background, there is a panoramic shot featuring the Puerta de Alcalá and the Plaza de Cibeles from the camera positioned on the Banco de España building. This is followed by another shot of the Neptune Fountain, also from above, surrounded by empty streets, and another intertitle appears: 'Trade and industry bring life and movement to its wide streets.'[8] The Puerta del Sol is then featured, accompanied by the following text: 'Preserving its old plazas and streets.'[9] The Plaza Mayor is next: 'With its old corners filled with ambiance',[10] showing the Rastro, with its monumentality going hand in hand with tradition. A few years later, in *¡Viva Madrid que es mi pueblo!* there is an intertitle announcing thus: 'In Madrid, like elsewhere, there are "things" that are just right',[11] and the camera captures the Puerta de Alcalá, the Correos building from the Paseo del Prado, the Banco Central building on Alcalá Street followed by the start of the Gran Vía at its intersection with Alcalá, in a panoramic shot from left to right until there is a shot framing the Church of San José, the Correos building again, but this time from the Calle de Alcalá, then the Royal Palace. The next intertitle says: 'and [...] of course. Many things that are bad',[12] whereby the camera shows various slums. To accompany the 'good businesses'[13] text, the camera points us to the Grandes Almacenes Madrid-París and the Almacenes Rodríguez buildings, both located along the Gran Vía. Immediately following the intertitle mentioning 'and bad businesses',[14] the camera captures the Rastro.

These two silent films incorporate the buildings and monuments that will continue to be shown in almost all of the establishing shots of subsequent Spanish productions for years to come. While the texts (intertitles and then, in the sound era, a narrator's voice) are almost invariably descriptive and glowing with praise, perhaps the one exception is the sincerity with which the movie directed by Delgado addresses the inhumane housing conditions of the city's poor citizens. The simple fact of putting these neighborhoods on screen does not necessarily imply a social critique, however. Sometimes this is done for a *costumbrista* effect,[15] like in *La revoltosa* (Florián Rey 1924) in which, after showing the Puerta de Toledo and the monastery of San Antonio de la Florida, the following intertitle appears: 'Madrid's low neighborhoods have made their way into literature and theater through writers in love with the town's picturesque customs and have an odd way of expressing themselves.'[16] Then there are certain contradictions, for example, in *El negro que tenía el alma blanca – Le danseur de jazz* (Benito Perojo 1927) whose first intertitle reads: 'In a popular neighborhood of Madrid',[17] but the Puerta del Sol is featured followed by Alcalá Street where it crosses the Gran Vía, and these most definitely cannot be considered popular neighborhoods by any stretch of the imagination.

The voice-overs of the films made during the Franco regime are generally much more triumphalist and covers up the social reality of the time. For example, the one from *Así es Madrid* (Luis Marquina 1953) begins after we hear a *chotis*[18] with lyrics mentioning the Royal Theater, Retiro Park, the Columbus monument and the neighborhoods of Ventas y Lavapiés. The voice-over says: 'Yes, that's how Madrid is, the Ciudad Universitaria, the Plaza Mayor [...] It's modern, it's old, it has money, distinction, and personality, like no other.'[19] When modern Madrid is mentioned, the Edificio España appears, which is often one of the most paradigmatic symbols of modernity in Spanish cinema of the time. Some voice-overs attempt to be more poetic. In *El Litri y su sombra*, a panoramic shot moves from left to right from the top of a hill as the voice-over tells us that

> more than a century ago, the city of Huelva was very different from what it is today. Nevertheless, there was something there that is still with us today and that will last forever. The shimmering salt mines that reflect the sky, the dazzling white of its scattered houses, the towers and bells of its small churches.[20]

This text was written by Agustín de Foxá, one of the authors of the lyrics to the Falangist hymn 'Cara al sol'.

The iconic monuments of each city are symbolic and work together to create cues that point the spectator to where the action of the film is going to take place. The cathedral of Santiago de Compostela, for example, in *La casa de la Troya* (Alejandro Pérez Lugín 1924), the basilica of Pilar of Zaragoza in *Nobleza baturra* (Florián Rey 1935), the Segovia aqueduct in *Fulano y mengano* and the Hanging Houses of Cuenca in *¡Qué tía la CIA!* (Mariano Ozores 1985): there are cities with several of these monuments, like Seville with the Giralda that appears at the beginning of *Currito de la Cruz* (Alejandro Pérez Lugín 1926) whose first intertitle reads: 'Dedicated to the Giralda'[21] The building's tower is seen from afar, followed by the intertitle '[an] expression of Seville that with its Art, its Beauty, and its Kindness, constantly rises to the heavens'.[22] There is a vertical panoramic shot that draws the eye to the heavens. Another Sevillian monument is the Torre del Oro, seen in *La reina mora* (Eusebio Fernández Ardavín 1937), where a panoramic shot begins from right to left showing the Guadalquivir River followed by another shot in the opposite direction from the Triana bridge. These two towers are also seen together at the beginning of *El frente de los suspiros* (Juan de Orduña 1942).

Texts frequently emphasize the meanings of monuments in cinema. In *Historias de Madrid* (Ramón Comas 1958), for example, the film begins with a voice-over saying, 'This is La Cibeles, one of the most beautiful and crowded plazas in Madrid, and that woman there in the center is a handmaid.'[23] The voice-over then mentions a man in the street and continues: 'Curiosity is a very feminine defect and I decided to follow him, I would have liked to know what he thought of me. Surely for him I was only that: La Cibeles.'[24] The statue itself is so important that while the voice-over narrates the story while following the protagonist, it is seemingly taking the place of the camera and, therefore, of the viewer, who identifies with the monument. This same monument is mentioned in the initial voice-over of *Cerca de la ciudad* (Luis Lucia 1952): 'No, there is no presentation title for now, because, first, we have to make an important clarification, our primary purpose was to make a documentary about Madrid. Day was dawning, when the camera began to work and look at the first shot: Cibeles, of course!'[25] The fountain is a symbol of Madrid and in this instance comes off as being a joke or formulaic cliché. After several more shots, the text mentions other views of the capital:

> Then we devote ourselves to collecting famous views of Madrid from characteristic angles. We were extracting the pure essence of an urban documentary in a series of frames that afterwards turned out to be too postcard-like, but all joking aside, Madrid is beautiful, really! What a great capital![26]

During this commentary, the film spectators have seen the Puerta de Alcalá, the Royal Palace, the Plaza de España, the Medical School of the Ciudad Universitaria, the Aqueduct, the Palacio de las Cortes and the Prado Museum, all of this prior to following a story that takes place almost entirely in one of its most degraded areas at the time, the Pozo del Tío Raimundo, a peripheral, poorly connected neighborhood with substandard housing where the residents notoriously suffer due to poor living conditions.

Urban infrastructure, on the other hand, is the subject of the commentary that opens *El hincha* (José María Elorieta 1958):

> Here there is a great city. Perceived from a certain distance it creates the impression of a modern paradise where peace and tranquility coexist. Nevertheless, in this city, just as in all great cities, there is a complicated system of arteries through which circulates a veritable flow of human life driven by the great engine of our time, which is being in a hurry.[27]

The camera captures the Gran Vía and the commentary continues: 'Those time-saving machines we call automobiles pass by incessantly in all directions and make up the motorized battalion of an army of civilians, and here is the infantry.'[28] With this phrase, a pedestrian crosswalk is shot from above, 'the suffering city, whose body parts are known as pedestrians, in a group of course, one by one dares to call out to another'.[29] From high up some people are shown leaving a building: 'More pedestrians, but these wanted to arrive earlier, so they have taken he trouble to go via the subway.' There is a shot of the Red de San Luis on the Gran Vía,[30] and the voice-over continues to comment on the ebb and flow of traffic and people, pointing out that 'here there is another mode of transportation for the nonmotorized citizens, it has a beautiful name full of warlike resonance: trolleybus, and it, too, is a son of the mad rush that sometimes forgets he has a mother'.[31] The voice-over praises the modernity of the Spanish city by focusing on the means of transport and the streets on which they run.

The streets also have been protagonists of many cinematic opening comments. For example, in *Mañana*, the voice of the protagonist is heard on-screen, as a young man walks the streets at night exclaiming thus: 'How beautiful the street is! And the night! And how happy I am when I can walk around by myself or run or shout: Hey, street! How beautiful you are! How I like the street at night.'[32] The city is celebrated by one of its inhabitants in this case, but removes some of the drama by lending the city a highly poetic aura, avoiding all criticism of the establishment. Something very similar occurs in the first moments of *Mi calle* (Edgar Neville 1960):

> This is my street, neither very modern nor very old, an ordinary street in Madrid from the last century, much like hundreds of others. I am going to tell you the story of almost half a century of the world reduced to the faint echo with which world events used to reach my street. This street is too old to be concerned about what goes on down the road a piece.[33]

A confined and nondescript urban enclave, the space of the street described in the film's first moments becomes the protagonist of the local story of its inhabitants, which turns its back on more global problems.

In addition to the monuments, the infrastructure and the streets, the everyday buildings are also mentioned, for example, in *Acompáñame* (Luis César Amadori 1966): 'A happy, welcoming, and modern city, with long rows of identical houses, similar blocks of houses',[34] while social housing blocks of varying heights and sizes are shot, until a panoramic shot captures from top to bottom a two-storey chalet and its front garden. 'Nevertheless, houses like this one can still be found, houses with personality that do not look like any other.'[35] Films expertly capture the wide gap between the modernity of the new, large-scale housing blocks and the old, traditional housing, setting the stage for the period in Spain's history known as *desarrollismo*.[36]

FIGURE 2.2: José María Elorieta (dir.), *El hincha*, 1958. Spain. © Ansara Films.

The Fictional City

A cinematic city that does not exist often stands in for all of the cities that exist. Fictional cities created through film have an advantage: their morphology helps us understand how real communities are interpreted on screen, many times better and in a more universal way than when a movie revolves around a real city. What is more, filmmakers have more freedom when showing a fictitious city than when they are tied to a real one since they can make more generalizations and have greater freedom, turning their work into what I have called elsewhere 'archetypical urban representations that allow us to know how current cities are visualized and also what their formal influence has been like in the real world' (Gorostiza 2016: 12).[37]

Imagined cities have been featured during the beginning of many Spanish movies. Perhaps the most well-known is the one from *Calle Mayor* (Juan Antonio Bardem 1956), a film that starts with a voice-over:

> Come, the day is dawning, the last bat is finishing his rounds and far away the first train of the morning is happily whistling. Down below is the city. A small provincial town. Any city, in any province of any country. The story that is about to begin has no precise geographic coordinates, people don't have any particular hair color or style of housing, no particular advertisements on the walls or a specific way of smiling and talking. None of this is a flag that envelops all of these men and women who are going to start to live right in front of us.[38]

The opening panoramic shots, meanwhile, capture Cuenca from above. Afterwards, there is a shot of Portales Street and the Cathedral of Santa María la Redonda in Logroño. The outdoor scenes were shot in those two cities and in Palencia, which means that several different cities were used as locations for the action of the film. This creates a geographically dispersed situation, resulting in 'what, effectively, could happen in any city of any province, but having achieved this generalization, which was of interest to the director in order to demonstrate that these situations occurred in every provincial town'[39] (Gorostiza 2006: 130). The only important thing in terms of location is that it is clear that the country where the action occurs is Francoist Spain.

Barcelona was often chosen as a place to film fictional, nonexistent cities that stood in for all cities. *Hay un camino a la derecha* (Francisco Rovira Beleta 1953) starts with a panoramic shot from right to left of the city from Montjuic, while

FIGURE 2.3: Juan Antonio Bardem (dir.), *Calle Mayor*, 1956. Spain. © Iberia Films.

FIGURE 2.4: Francisco Rovira Beleta (dir.), *Hay un camino a la derecha*, 1953. Spain. © Mercury Films.

a voice-over explains the following: 'This is a great neighborhood similar to all great neighborhoods and like them, made up of a multitude of people involved in the fight of everyday life with their joys and their sorrows, their triumphs and their failures'[40] followed by another panoramic shot in the opposite direction, showing the port.

At the beginning of *Cerca de las estrellas*, the voice-over states '[h]ere is a page of Life, the story of the Sunday of a working-class family from my country, which could happen, and perhaps does happen, in any city, on any day'.[41] *Sin la sonrisa de Dios – Senza sorriso* (Julio Salvador 1955) is another notable example, at the beginning of which, while the city is framed from above, a voice-over is heard: 'Here is a small portion of what man calls a great city, it does not matter which one. Viewed from a distance all cities look alike, a never-ending series of buildings that are grouped so tightly together, one could say they are placed on top of each other.'[42] Accompanying establishing shots with the camera situated on the ground, the voice-over says '[a]s we approach, we discover its streets, its great avenues, bridges, plazas and walkways, where man has always enjoyed looking for the most varied forms of light and color. Around these

FIGURE 2.5: Julio Salvador (dir.), *Sin la sonrisa de Dios*, 1955. Spain. © Mercury Films.

arteries, majestic blocks of buildings, monuments and architectural jewels are constructed.'[43] Gaudí's Sagrada Familia appears, 'which marks and distinguishes the character of a great city'.[44]

The Plaza de España is shown and the entrance of the Feria, 'but when examined closely, they start to look very much alike, the brick cells of their stories are almost identical, like the challenges posed to its inhabitants'.[45] The camera captures tall buildings from below. 'And what matters most',[46] the voice-over explains as a panoramic shot starts from right to left from Montjuic similar to the one from *Hay un camino a la derecha*, 'whether it's to the north or whether it's to the south, every city has its ugly neighborhood'.[47] There is a shot of a modest street, 'a neighborhood with narrow, smelly alleys where the sunlight barely reaches, a neighborhood with miserable housing, where there is not enough air to breathe, inhabited by humble people who are obliged to coexist with delinquency and immorality'.[48] The commentator continues talking about the neighborhood's inhabitants, and above all the children, who live their lives in the street:

> the children are abandoned to their own impulses, without the supervision of parents who send them to the street without realizing that the street can turn them into criminals; children who grow up bored and disappointed, with nothing to live for other than desensitizing themselves further. They are the first victims of the neighborhood, of that sad neighborhood without even a single hint of something beautiful, as if it were even lacking the consolation of a smile from God.[49]

The street that was a beautiful place in *Mañana* and a support system in *Mi calle*, here is 'the cradle of vice'[50] as it is in any city, despite the occasional appearance of the Sagrada Familia, the symbol of Barcelona. It could seem that *Sin la sonrisa de Dios* is a form of social criticism, like *Calle Mayor*, but this is not the case, because the film does not dwell on who should take political responsibility for this situation but on the inhabitants of the bad neighborhood themselves, using an insulting euphemism to refer to neighborhoods of people abandoned by society. The troubled parts of the city in this film are seen as inevitable, as they supposedly are in all cities, and therefore the only solution is an unlikely 'smile of God'.

City spaces on the silver screen, especially if they contain iconic monuments, are usually seen again and again and function as synecdoches of the city as a whole. But even when the same location appears in different movies, each appearance is distinct because the plot of each film, framed within a specific historic moment and stemming from a particular ideology, modifies the meaning of each filmed urban environment. This transformative capacity is one of the most important characteristics of the city, which is one of the most contested and fascinating things ever created. The urban is a complex space that is formally captured by film's moving images that allow us to detect the city's problems and consider ways to correct them. In conclusion, the situational maps that one finds in architectural plans are unable go into great detail about the nature of the actual buildings that will be erected, but their importance lies in the fact that they do indicate where they will be constructed and they lay out a lot's spatial limits and environmental conditions. Something similar happens in the opening shots of feature films. They 'take place', so to speak, before the plot and character development begin and frame what happens in the rest of film. One can categorize how these opening shots of urban space function in feature films by their point of view. Most of these shots are panoramic views containing vast amounts of urban space, and these views have been frequently accompanied by voice-overs that serve to create certain meanings subsequently associated with both real and imagined cities, which are usually made of up of a creative compendium of cities that actually do exist in the real world. The aim of this chapter, therefore, has been to explain how and why opening shots of urban feature films are complex and diverse in their points of view and how they set the stage for urban films in general.

Translated by Robin Tipperman.

NOTES

1. 'contienen información llamada a desempeñar un papel, a otorgar un marco espacio – temporal a las imágenes que vendrán a continuación. Previamente al origen propiamente dicho del relato se nos invita a movilizar un doble saber que va a servir de base a la historia que se va a desarrollar'.
2. Translator's Note: The Hospital Universitario La Paz, today Madrid's largest hospital, was constructed in 1964 in what is now known as the Fuencarral-El Pardo district. It holds symbolic significance as the hospital where General Francisco Franco, who was the Spanish authoritarian head of state for 39 years, died at the age of 82 after spending five weeks there.
3. Translator's Note: Nuevos Ministerios is the name of a centrally located government complex delimited by the Paseo de la Castellana, Raimundo Fernández Villaverde Street, Agustín de Betancourt and the San Juan de la Cruz Square. AZCA is the acronym for Asociación Mixta de Compensación de la Manzana A de la Zona Comercial de la Avenida del Generalísmo and refers to the financial district in central Madrid.
4. 'Aquello que se ve allá abajo es Madrid y aquellos puntos que se mueven son los madrileños, y aquellos otros puntos que se mueven más deprisa y que pasan por encima de los puntos que se mueven más despacio, son los automóviles, que habiendo pagado un fondo de retorno serio practican la caza con la mayor alegría. ¡Qué bonito es Madrid! ¡Qué bonitas son generalmente las ciudades vistas desde lo alto!'
5. Translator's Note: The Alcázar is Toledo's most iconic building and symbol of Spanish nationalism since the colonial period, where in 1521 Hernán Cortés was received by Charles I after the conquest of the Aztecs.
6. 'Málaga [...] bella entre la bellas, orgullo de la tierra andaluza.'
7. 'Madrid. La Villa heroica que da la fuerte impresión de su progreso bajo un sol esplendoroso que vivifica y alegra el alma de España.'
8. 'El comercio y la industria llenan de vida y de movimiento sus amplias vías.'
9. 'Conservando sus antiguas plazas y calles.'
10. 'y sus viejos rincones llenos de ambiente'.
11. 'en Madrid, como en todas partes, hay 'cosas' que están bien'.
12. 'y [...] claro. Muchas que están mal'.
13. 'buenos comercios'.
14. 'y malos comercios'.

15. Translator's Note: *Costumbrismo* in the Hispanic tradition is the nineteenth-century literary or pictorial representation of everyday life, mannerisms and customs. Unlike realism, it does not usually offer any overt social criticism.
16. 'El Madrid de los barrios bajos ha pasado a la literatura y al teatro al través de escritores enamorados de las pintorescas costumbres y del peculiar modo de expresarse del pueblo.'
17. 'En un barrio popular de Madrid'.
18. Translator's Note: In Madrid, the 'chotis' (originally *schottische*, a country dance performed in pairs) is considered the most typical of the city's dances since it has been danced at all of the city's popular festivals since the nineteenth century.
19. 'Sí, así es Madrid, la Ciudad Universitaria, la Plaza Mayor [...] Es moderno, es antiguo, tiene como ninguna capital, sello y personalidad.'
20. 'hace más de un siglo, la ciudad de Huelva era muy distinta a lo que hoy es, sin embargo, algo tenía que la de hoy también tiene y que perdurará eternamente, las salinas espejeantes donde se refleja el cielo, el blanco deslumbrador de su desparramado caserío, las torres y las campanas de sus iglesias pequeñas.'
21. 'Dedicatoria: A la Giralda'.
22. 'expresión de Sevilla que con su Arte, su Belleza, y su Bondad, se eleva constantemente al cielo'.
23. Esta es la Cibeles, una de las plazas más bonitas y concurridas de Madrid, y esa que hay en el centro es una servidora.'
24. 'La curiosidad es un defecto muy femenino y decidí seguirle, me hubiera gustado saber qué pensaba de mí, seguramente yo solo era para él eso: La Cibeles.'
25. No, no. No hay títulos de presentación por ahora porque antes tenemos que hacer una aclaración importante. Nuestro primer propósito fue rodar un documental sobre Madrid. Estaba amaneciendo cuando la cámara comenzó a funcionar. Y ven ustedes el primer plano [...] La Cibeles, ¡cómo no!'
26. 'Después nos consagramos a coleccionar perspectivas famosas de Madrid en ángulos característicos. Estábamos extrayendo la esencia pura de un documental urbano en una serie de encuadres que luego nos resultaron demasiado de tarjeta postal, pero bromas aparte, ¡Es bonito Madrid, verdad! ¡Qué gran capital!'
27. 'Aquí hay una gran ciudad, contemplada a cierta distancia da la impresión de un moderno paraíso en el que anidan la paz y el sosiego, sin embargo, en esta como en todas las grandes ciudades, hay un complicado sistema arterial y por él circula un verdadero torrente de vida humana impulsada por el gran motor de nuestra época, la prisa.'
28. 'Incesantemente pasan en todas direcciones esas máquinas de ahorrar minutos que se llaman automóviles y que forman el batallón motorizado del ejército ciudadano, y aquí está la infantería.'
29. 'el sufrido cuerpo cuyos componentes se les llama peatones, en grupo claro, uno a uno cualquiera se atreve a llamarse'.

30. Translator's Note: The Red the San Luis is a transportation hub formed at the end of the Calle Montera, where the Gran Vía meets Fuencarral and Hortaleza Streets.
31. 'más peatones, estos para llegar antes tomaron sus medidas por eso han cogido el Metro' se ve la Red de San Luis, en la Gran Vía, 'Aquí hay otro medio de transporte para los ciudadanos no motorizados, tiene un bello nombre lleno de resonancias bélicas: trolebús, y es también un hijo de la prisa que más de una vez se olvida de que tiene madre.'
32. '¡Qué bonita es la calle! ¡Y la noche!, y qué feliz soy yo cuando puedo pasear solo o correr o gritar: ¡Eh, calle! ¡Qué bonita eres! Cómo me gusta la calle y la noche.'
33. 'esta es mi calle, ni muy moderna, ni muy antigua, una calle corriente del Madrid del siglo pasado como hay varios centenares. Os voy a contar la historia de casi medio siglo del mundo reducida al débil eco con que los sucesos mundiales llegaban a mi calle. Esta calle tiene demasiada solera, es demasiado vieja para que le preocupe lo que ocurre un poco más allá'.
34. 'una ciudad alegre, acogedora, moderna, largas filas de casas iguales, bloques de pisos iguales'.
35. 'Sin embargo, aún pueden encontrarse y diferenciarse casas como esta, con personalidad, que no se parecen a ninguna otra.'
36. Translator's Note: Francoist *desarrollismo* (often translated in the press and subsequent academic scholarship in English as the 'Spanish economic miracle', was initiated in 1959 by technocrats (most of whom belonged to the Opus Dei) who replaced the previous Falangist political guard. *Desarrollismo* resulted in the creation of a larger middle class marked by a high degree of depoliticization that historians and sociologists have termed 'franquismo sociológico'. This period of rapid industrialization ended in approximately 1974, but only after Spain had experienced the second highest growth rate in the world, after that of Japan.
37. 'representaciones urbanas arquetípicas que sirven para saber cómo se visualizan las ciudades actuales y también cómo ha sido su influencia formal en lo real'.
38. 'Ven, está amaneciendo, el último murciélago termina su ronda y lejos pita alegremente el primer tren de la mañana, allí abajo está la ciudad. Una pequeña ciudad de provincias. Una ciudad cualquiera, en cualquier provincia de cualquier país. La historia que está a punto de comenzar no tiene unas coordenadas geográficas precisas, el color del pelo o la forma de las casas, los anuncios en las paredes o una manera determinada de sonreír y hablar, no deben ser forzosamente una bandera concreta para envolver a estos hombres y mujeres que van a empezar a vivir delante de nosotros.'
39. 'efectivamente, pueda suceder en cualquier ciudad de cualquier provincia, pero aún habiendo logrado esta generalización, que interesaba al director para demostrar que estas situaciones ocurrían en todas las urbes provincianas'.
40. 'Esta es una gran población semejante a todas las grandes poblaciones y como ellas, la suma de una multitud de seres lanzados a la lucha con sus alegrías y sus penas, sus triunfos y sus fracasos.'

41. 'he aquí una página de la Vida, la historia de un domingo de una familia obrera de mi país, que pudo ocurrir, y quizás ocurra, en cualquier ciudad, un día cualquiera'.
42. 'He aquí una ligera muestra de lo que el hombre llama una gran ciudad, no importa cuál. Vistas desde lejos todas las ciudades se parecen, una serie interminable de edificios tan agrupados que se diría están superpuestos.'
43. 'Al acercarnos, descubrimos sus calles, sus grandes avenidas, puentes, plazas y paseos, donde el hombre se ha complacido buscando las más variadas formas de luz y de color. En torno a esas arterias, se alzan majestuosos bloques de edificios, monumentos y joyas arquitectónicas.'
44. 'que distinguen e imprimen carácter a una gran ciudad'.
45. 'pero bien examinadas, siguen pareciéndose demasiado entre sí, son casi idénticas las celdas de ladrillo de sus pisos, iguales los problemas que plantean a sus moradores'.
46. 'y lo que más importa'.
47. 'sea al norte, sea al sur, todas las ciudades tienen su barrio feo'.
48. 'un barrio con callejas estrechas y malolientes, a las que apenas llega la luz del sol, un barrio de viviendas miserables, con el aire imprescindible para no ahogarse, poblado por gentes humildes obligadas a convivir con la delincuencia y la inmoralidad'.
49. 'que hacen su vida en la calle, la mejor escuela del vicio, niños abandonados a sus propios impulsos, sin la vigilancia de unos padres que los mandan al arroyo, sin darse cuenta de que el arroyo se los puede devolver convertidos en maleantes; niños viejos, aburridos y decepcionados, sin otra ilusión que embrutecerse más. Son las primeras víctimas del barrio, de ese barrio triste sin un solo detalle que nos sugiera algo hermoso, como si le faltara el consuelo de una sonrisa de Dios.'
50. 'la cuna del vicio'.

REFERENCES

Gorostiza, Jorge (2006), 'Una ciudad cualquiera en cualquier provincia de cualquier país', in R. Cueto (ed.), *Calle Mayor… 50 años después*, Valencia: IVAC La Filmoteca, pp. 109–64.

Gorostiza, Jorge (2016), *Panorámicas urbanas: 50 películas básicas sobre la ciudad*, Barcelona: Editorial UOC.

Zunzunegui, Santos (1996), *La mirada cercana*, Barcelona: Paidós.

FILMOGRAPHY

Albacete, Alfonso (2015), *Solo química*, Spain: Rodar y Rodar Cine y Televisión, Canal +, TV3 and TVE.

Almodóvar, Pedro (1983), *Entre tinieblas*, Spain: Tesauro, S.A.

Amadori, Luis C. (1965), *Más bonita que ninguna*, Spain: Cámara, P.C., S.A.

Amadori, Luis C. (1966), *Acompáñame*, Spain: Cámara, P.C., S.A.

Amadori, Luis C. (1967), *Buenos días, condesita*, Spain: Cámara, P.C., S.A.

Amo, Antonio del (1951), *Día tras día*, Spain: Altamira.

Armendáriz, Montxo (1986), *27 horas*, Spain and France: Elías Querejeta, P.C., S.L. – EITB.

Armiñán, Jaime de (1982), *En septiembre*, Spain: Punto Producciones, S.A.

Bardem, Juan A. (1956), *Calle Mayor*, Spain and France: Cesáreo González, P.C. – Ibéria Films – Guión P.C.

Bodegas, Roberto (1974), *Los nuevos españoles*, Spain: Ágata Films, S.A.

Bosch, Juan (1959), *A sangre fría*, Spain: Este Films – Urania Film.

Burló Moreno, Manuel (2016), *Rumbos*, Spain: Arcadia Motion Pictures.

Cadena, Jordi (1981), *Barcelona Sur*, Spain and Mexico: Fígaro Films, S.A.

Camus, Mario (1975), *La joven casada*, Spain and Argentina: Impala, S.A.

Comas, Ramón (1958), *Historias de Madrid*, Spain: Unión Cinematográfica Española, S.L.

Delgado, Fernando (1928), *¡Viva Madrid que es mi pueblo!*, Spain: Exclusivas Orozco.

Elorieta, José M. (1958), *El hincha*, Spain: Ansara Films.

Fernán Gómez, Fernando (1964), *Los palomos*, Spain: Estela Films, S.L.

Fernán Gómez, Fernando (1970), *Crimen imperfecto*, Spain: Pedro Masó, P.C. – Filmayer Producción.

Fernández Ardavín, Eusebio (1937), *La reina mora*, Spain: Campa, P.C.

Fernánez Ardavín, César (1962), *Cerca de las estrellas*, Spain: Aro Films, S.L.

Garci, José L. (1978), *Solos en la madrugada*, Spain: José Luis Tafur, P.C., S.A.

García Sánchez, José L. (1989), *El vuelo de la paloma*, Spain: Lolafilms – Ames Films – Ion Films – TVE.

García Sánchez, José L. (2000), *Adiós con el corazón*, Spain: Alta Films – Gaila – Antena 3 TV – Canal + – Galiardo, P.C.

Gil, Rafael (1959), *El Litri y su sombra*, Spain: Coral, P.C.

Giménez-Rico, Antonio (1986), *El disputado voto del señor Cayo*, Spain: Penélope, P.C.

Hernández, Antonio (1980), *F. E. N*, Spain: Micra Film.

Iglesia, Eloy de la (1983), *El pico*, Spain: Ópalo Films, S.A.

Iglesia, Eloy de la (1973), *Una gota de sangre para morir amando*, Spain: José Frade, P.C., S.A.

Iglesia, Eloy de la (1982), *Colegas*, Spain: Ópalo Films, S.A.

Lazaga, Pedro (1957), *Las muchachas de azul*, Spain: Ágata Films, S.A.

Lazaga, Pedro (1960), *Trío de damas*, Spain: Ágata Films, S.A.

Lazaga, Pedro (1961), *Trampa para Carolina*, Spain: Época Films, S.A.

Lazaga, Pedro (1966), *La ciudad no es para mí*, Spain: Pedro Masó, P.C.

Lazaga, Pedro (1976), *El alegre divorciado*, Spain and Mexico: Filmayer Producción, S.A. – Producciones Orfeo.

Leblanc, Tony (1961), *El pobre García*, Spain: Síntes Films, S.A. – San Pablo Films

Marquina, Luis (1953), *Así es Madrid*, Spain: Cinesol, S.A. – Asociación de Técnicos y Artistas (ATA).

Merino, Fernando (1969), *La que arman las mujeres*, Spain: Arco Films, S.A.

Neville, Edgar (1960), *Mi calle*, Spain: Carabela Films, S.A.

Neville, Edgar and Lefranc, Guy (1957), *La ironía del dinero – Bonjour la chance*, Spain and France: Los Films del Buho, S.L. – Les grands films français.

Noriega, Manuel (1923), *Alma de Dios*, Spain: Atlántida Films.

Nunes, José M. (1957), *Mañana*, Spain: Este Films.

Orduña, Juan de (1942), *El frente de los suspiros*, Spain: Compañía Industrial Film Español, S.A. (CIFESA).

Ozores, Mariano (1985), *¡Qué tía la CIA!*, Spain: Ízaro Films, S.A.

Ozores, Mariano (1988), *Hacienda somos casi todos*, Spain: Carlos Cascales Producciones y Distribuciones Cinematográficas.

Pérez Lugín, Alejandro (1924), *La casa de la Troya*, Spain: Troya Film.

Pérez Lugín, Alejandro (1926), *Currito de la Cruz*, Spain: Troya Film.

Perojo, Benito (1926), *Malvaloca*, Spain: Goya, P.C.

Perojo, Benito (1927), *El negro que tenía el alma blanca – Le danseur de jazz*, Spain and France: Goya, P.C. – Production Francaise Cinematographique.

Quadreny, Ramón (1943), *La chica del gato*, Spain: Campa, P.C.

Ramírez, Pedro L. (1957), *El tigre de Chamberí*, Spain: Aspa, P.C., S.A.

Regueiro, Francisco (1975), *Duerme, duerme, mi amor*, Spain: Serafín García Trueba, P.C.

Rey, Florián (1924), *La revoltosa*, Spain: Goya, P.C., S.A.

Rey, Florián (1935), *Nobleza baturra*, Spain: Compañía Industrial Film Español, S.A. (CIFESA).

Romero Marchent, Joaquín L. (1959), *Fulano y mengano*, Spain: Unión Industrial Cinematográfica, S.L. (UNINCI).

Rovira Beleta, Francisco (1953), *Hay un camino a la derecha*, Spain: Titan Films.

Salvador, Julio (1955), *Sin la sonrisa de Dios – Senza sorriso*, Spain and Italy: Laurus Films – Titanus.

Salvia, Rafael J. (1956), *Pasaje a Venezuela*, Spain: IFI Producciones, S.A.

Salvia, Rafael J. (1958), *Las chicas de la Cruz Roja*, Spain: Asturias Films.

Saura, Carlos (2004), *Taxi*, Spain: Filmart, P.C.

PART 2

MOBILITY

3

The Rhythm of the Modern City: Traffic and Mobility in Spanish Film, 1896–1939

Nuria Rodríguez-Martín, Complutense University of Madrid

In May of 1896, Madrid was the site of the first film screening in Spain. This was the year that Alexandre Promio, a cameraman for the Lumière Brothers, traveled from Paris in order to record and display some of the first urban film images ever made.[1] Since then, the Spanish capital has been both the protagonist and the stage for a wide and varied catalogue of feature films and documentaries which have given shape to numerous visions of the city, its inhabitants and urban space in constant transformation. This chapter focuses on the image of modern Madrid through film, centering on two of the elements most associated with metropolitan modernity during the first third of the twentieth century: traffic and mobility. Both phenomena go hand in hand with the development and proliferation of urban modes of transportation, the designation of space for parking and increased pedestrian traffic, all of which resulted from the demographic growth taking place during this time. These changes, coupled with the way the city center was planned, resulted in the appearance of what was famously called in the early 1920s as 'the traffic circulation problem' (Rodríguez-Martín 2017a).

In the most visual and expressive of ways, early Spanish film documents how traffic became an urban issue of great concern to both local authorities and the general population. Apprehensions about circulation problems in Madrid were not simply limited to issues of road congestion in specific areas of the city during different times of day. Generally speaking, traffic was understood to be at the heart of every modern, cosmopolitan city and as a result, it had a strong temporal element that touched on fears surrounding the disappearance of what was considered by some to be the traditional city of the past. The advent of electric urban streetcars and modern urban traffic management after 1900 further added to the impact of automobiles in ways that caused Madrid to increasingly look more like other large western cities, resulting in a great number of debates over whether or not Madrid was growing into a bright future or losing its identity.

A number of short films made in Madrid between 1896 and 1936 documented the transformation of the nineteenth-century city (which had been widely accessible to a predominantly pedestrian population) into a frenetic modern metropolis organized over an extensive network that relied on a massive supply of public transportation vehicles. Cinema provides us with an opportunity to get a closer look at the evolution of both street and pedestrian traffic in the city against the backdrop of an urban transformation that was psychological as well as material. The mechanization of transport and the increased use of the combustion engine were key components of the expansion of Madrid during this period. With strong and steady urban growth, the capital repeatedly surpassed its physical limits, absorbing bordering municipalities like Chamartín de la Rosa, Vallecas and Fuencarral, which by the 1930s would be considered neighborhoods within the city's boundaries (Ayuntamiento de Madrid 1929: 28–35; Otero Carvajal 2016: 260–62; Otero Carvajal and Rodríguez-Martín 2019: 22–23). These changes demanded a radically altered perception of time and space for the inhabitants of Madrid.

Madrid, 1896

The footage Alexandre Promio shot in June 1896 included 172 meters of film (barely six minutes in duration) that captured a variety of moving images including a daytime view of the Puerta del Sol, the heart of Madrid. These unique and exceptional images revealed to early film spectators the various aspects of everyday life in the most important plaza of the city on any given day. Madrid at that time boasted of nearly half a million inhabitants (Fernández García 1989: 34), and the urban space recorded by Promio includes elements of the nineteenth-century city that hint at the incipient transformation of Madrid in later years.

Some of the visual elements in this first footage of Madrid are static, such as the large three-armed gas streetlights and the billboard used to advertise theatrical shows that enjoyed a broad appeal. The moving elements are what truly capture the attention of the spectator, however, such as the rush of vehicles and pedestrians crossing in and out the shot in all directions for the duration of the footage. These vehicles are animal-drawn, since the combustion engine had not yet made its appearance in Madrid. Horse-drawn carriages and streetcars pulled by mules predominate in this most central of urban spaces. Particularly striking are the animal-powered vehicles of mass transportation, which were put in place in 1871 to connect the center of the city with the newly constructed neighborhoods

FIGURE 3.1: Alexandre Promio, *Scenes of Spain*, 1896. Black and white frame. Courtesy of the Filmoteca Española (Spanish Film Archive).

resulting from the city's 1860 Urban Expansion Plan. The larger scale of the city[2] created the need for the introduction of a means of transportation that already existed in other large cities and western capitals, sparking the first revolution in urban mobility. The carriages and streetcars that we see crossing the Puerta del Sol in the 1896 Lumière Studio film not only served to connect the urban center with the newly created neighborhoods to the north and east of the city, but also made the future expansion of Madrid possible. These first forms of public transportation capture the beginning of the end of the era of the '*walking city*', a metropolitan area that could be crossed by the majority of its inhabitants on foot.

These mule-powered trams are not the only vehicles in circulation shown in the scene captured by Promio, however. There is a great variety of types of cars and carriages that are also drawn by other animals, with men on horseback intermingling with dozens of pedestrians navigating the plaza. This cinematic evidence of everyday traffic in Madrid prior to the automobile age is also notable in that it indicates an absence of a rigid division between streets and sidewalks.

Pedestrians cross the Puerta del Sol in all directions and at any point in the road, since Madrid's streets at the time had no traffic signals to indicate where pedestrian, animal and vehicular crossings were supposed to take place.

Madrid, 1914

Cinematic footage from the streets of Madrid in the first years of the 1910s[3] shows that some late nineteenth-century road and pedestrian traffic characteristics persisted into the first years of the twentieth century. Existing film footage (of approximately 4 feet and 9 inches in length) takes us to some of the most important plazas and streets making up the urban center, starting with the emblematic Carrera de San Jerónimo, where the Congreso de los Diputados (House of Representatives) is located, and ending with several daytime scenes of the Puerta del Sol. The changes that occurred in Madrid's iconic urban spaces since 1896 is dramatic. If one compares footage shot between 1910 and 1914 with the images filmed by Promio mentioned in the previous section, the Puerta del Sol in particular is radically transformed. In the first place, the iconic public space is much more crowded than in 1896. Pedestrian traffic is substantial and the streetcars that now cross through are no longer pulled by animals, but powered by electricity.

These later images vividly demonstrate how the substitution of animal-powered vehicles for combustion and electric engines had a significant impact on Madrid's urban landscape. The columns and cables necessary to power these modern vehicles began to fill the streets and plazas. These new vehicles were also larger than their earlier animal-driven counterparts. The streetcar network had been extended by the end of the first decade of the twentieth-century, with 34 lines in operation that crossed the city in every direction, as well as connecting the center with several bordering municipalities. In 1910, the Compañía General de Tranvías de Madrid (General Trolley Company of Madrid) was the first trolley company in the capital, and claimed to transport approximately 80 million passengers annually (Burgaleta 1988: 81–83).

Another key element of modernity on display in the documentary film footage of the period is the prevalence of the advertisements affixed to these vehicles in the form of large billboards installed on top of the streetcars to promote a variety of businesses and market brands. This type of outdoor advertising experienced very strong and stable growth because it presented a steady source of income both for the transportation company and for the municipal government. The transportation company made money by selling advertising space and Madrid's City Council collected taxes on the display of advertisements on public roads (Rodríguez-Martín 2016). Outdoor advertisements also appeared on commercial signs, which were placed on the facades of the buildings surrounding the city's plazas. Some advertisements were expansive and captivating, drawing attention to the names of the stores. One very striking example in this footage simply reads: 'New York'. In the final seconds of the film, we observe that a car enters from the left of the shot. Although numerically speaking cars still made up a very small percentage of the traffic in Madrid,[4] the impact of automobiles on the population was enormous, largely due to the number of accidents that occurred every day. Large numbers of people were hit or run over. The figure was disproportionately high when one considers the relatively small number of automobiles in circulation in the capital at the time (Rodríguez-Martín 2017b: 168). A key factor contributing to this – even more than the rapid increase in the numbers of this new type of vehicle – was the lack of psychological adjustment to the new concept of speed limits, which was responsible for the majority of accidents recorded in Madrid. In 1910, city officials limited the speed of cars to 10 kilometers per hour, but by the end of 1927, the mayor had raised that limit to 30 kilometers per hour. In the early days of car culture in Spain, authorities responded with compassion and understanding to pedestrian complaints. They soon, however, began to blame pedestrians themselves for their reckless way of walking and navigating the streets. In 1908, the Mayor of Madrid (the Count of Peñalver, who was also a passionate motorist and president of the Real Automóvil Club de España [Royal Automobile Club of Spain]) put forth the following declaration:

> The automobile should not circulate through a town at excessive speeds, causing inconveniences and endangering neighborhoods; but at the same time, towns have no right to argue against the use of automobiles for pleasure through the streets and plazas of the city center, which motorists should be able to use with proper precautions. However, it is an intolerable attitude to pretend that these spaces are only suitable for social gatherings and recreation, as if citizens who travel by car should not deserve the same respect from pedestrians, that these pedestrians should inexcusably watch out for motorists.
>
> (El automóvil no debe circular por una población a velocidades excesivas, produciendo molestias y peligros al vecindario; pero éste, por su parte, no tiene tampoco derecho a disputar a los vehículos, la posesión y disfrute del centro de las calles y plazas, por el que podrá transitar de paso y con las precauciones debidas, cuando tenga que atravesarlas, pero siendo intolerable que pretenda convertirlo en lugar predilecto de tertulias y recreos, cual si los ciudadanos que van en coche no hubieran de merecer de los que van a pie el propio respeto que a éstos deben inexcusablemente guardar los primeros.)
>
> (Ayuntamiento de Madrid 1909: 24)

Responding to the growth in urban traffic, increasingly more restrictive traffic regulations were imposed on pedestrians in Madrid in an attempt to discipline and direct their movement through the streets of the city (Rodríguez-Martín 2017b). However, this short 1914 film makes clear that pedestrians often wandered through urban streets with seemingly no sense of order, even stopping in the middle of the street without showing any concern for the movement of vehicles around them. Another notable feature of this early urban footage is that when the pedestrians notice the presence of the camera and camera operators, some of the people in the scene stop and stare directly at the camera, with facial expressions ranging from curiosity to amusement. These reactions inevitably evoke a sympathetic smile from contemporary spectators, who likewise also find themselves curious and amused about their own subjectivity in light of their own set of new technologies of representation and how they create a sense of place.

Madrid, 1929: El Misterio de la Puerta del Sol

In 1929, film director Francisco Elías (b. 1890 [Huelva]; d. 1977 [Barcelona]), filmed the first Spanish movie with sound, *El misterio de la Puerta del Sol* (The Mystery of the Puerta del Sol).[5] The film is an oneiric comedy and a complex story about two young men who work for a newspaper printing press. They are obsessed with the Hollywood film industry and dream of becoming stars on the big screen. The film debuted in early 1930, but unfortunately used the Phonofilm system, a sound technology patented by American Lee de Forest[6] which was incompatible with the Spanish sound systems in use at the time. Consequently, the movie's success and reach were very limited, and it did not even play in Madrid (Faulkner 2017: 60–64).[7] The only existing print of the film was believed to have been lost for decades until a copy was recovered and restored in the mid-1990s by the Spanish Film Archive (Filmoteca Nacional de España) (Arce 2009; Sánchez Oliveira 2003; Del Amo 1996). *El misterio de la Puerta del Sol* was not only considered a pioneer for being the first full-length feature film recorded with sound in Spanish in history, but also because it contains the first aerial sequences of both Madrid and Barcelona captured from an airplane. It also serves as a valuable document to contrast the evolution of street traffic and mobility in the city in the late 1920s due to the inclusion of documentary scenes in the film. These scenes were shot in the Puerta del Sol and on the Gran Vía near Alcalá Street, which are the principal traffic hubs of the capital city. These locations formed the main commercial and leisure areas of the city and were characterized by a large number of stores, cinemas, cafés, bars, hotels, restaurants and theaters, in addition to being home to numerous offices and official headquarters (Baker 2009). This iconic center of modern consumption sustained an enormous influx of vehicles and pedestrians on a daily basis.

The Puerta del Sol in this 1929 film is unrecognizable when compared to the footage from 1896 and 1914. By the late 1920s, it is bustling with automobiles and electric streetcars, as well as groups of people waiting for vehicles to allow them to pass. Automobiles dominate the scene and are observed both driving and also parked in the middle of the road. The motorization of Madrid had become a reality. The city records indicate that more than 23,000 mechanical vehicles (private and official cars, taxis, motorcycles, trucks and vans) had permits to circulate in the city in 1929. This demonstrates a nearly 800 percent increase with respect to the number of permits registered in 1914. Nearly 14,000 additional vehicles, including streetcars, bicycles, horse-drawn carriages and cars contributed to the traffic in Madrid at the end of the 1920s. This was an extraordinary increase for a city whose central layout had just recently been modified, in which there were many streets that measured less than eight meters wide and were, therefore, incapable of absorbing the extent of the traffic.

> The number of people in the streets had also increased, since the population grew to exceed 800,000 residents. The first studies conducted on pedestrian traffic Madrid, completed in 1926, revealed that on average, more than 500,000 people concentrated in the Puerta del Sol and surrounding streets every day. This meant 48,000 pedestrians per hour were in the Puerta del Sol on average, and on the Gran Vía (Red de San Luis) an additional 26,000, according to the registered statistics.
>
> (Abarca 1926: 5)

This significant increase in road and pedestrian traffic in Madrid, within such a short time frame, posed a very real challenge for local authorities, especially when it came to the conflicts over public space that ensued (Rodríguez-Martín 2020). The constant reports in the press about traffic problems and accidents on public roads, together with the real need to impose order on the increasingly complicated tangle of traffic patterns, led City Hall to implement a series of measures which eventually resulted in the modern management of traffic in Madrid. Several of these measures were studied in other large European cities during multiple trips by Spanish technicians and municipal employees, which were then implemented in Madrid. Several sequences of *El misterio de la Puerta del Sol* document some of these measures to control traffic, which would eventually have a great a great impact on the city. One of the most important changes began in 1929, when the first police officers were trained to manage traffic (a measure that already had its equivalent in cities such as Paris, London and Berlin). Its members were distinguished by wearing a series of garments intended to be easily recognizable to drivers and pedestrians: a baton, and white helmets, gloves and belts. These officials soon became an ever-present and distinctive feature of Madrid's

FIGURE 3.2: Francisco Elías (dir.), *El misterio de la Puerta del Sol* (The Mystery of the Puerta del Sol), 1929. Black and white frame. Courtesy of the Filmoteca Española (Spanish Film Archive).

urban landscape. It should come as no surprise that they would clearly and visibly appear, hard at work, in the sequences of Elías's film shot in the Puerta del Sol and Gran Vía.

Other important changes in the traffic flow of Madrid can be seen in the sequences of *El misterio de la Puerta del Sol* that take place on the Gran Vía. The direction of the traffic pattern also changed, and vehicles no longer drove on the left, but on the right. When this change was implemented in April of 1924, the direction of traffic circulation was unified in all of Spain. Madrid was, before that time, the last city in the country that was still driving on the left. Also visible among the automobiles that appear in these scenes are taxi meters, identifiable by the large writing on the car windows stating the fare: 0.40 pesetas. The use of 'taxis', as the popular rental cars for individual transportation of passengers were called, took off quickly. In 1917, there were only nineteen automobiles in service to the public as 'taxis'. That number had reached nearly 100 at the start of the 1920s, but by the end of the decade there were more than 3,000. Taxis were seen as more than just a new form of transportation; they became a symbol of the modernization of Madrid. In the same year that *El misterio de la Puerta del Sol* was filmed, for example, the popular magazine *Estampa* reported that:

> the 'taxi' is already an essential element of the new panorama of Madrid, much like the mini-skirt, officers with batons, or skyscrapers on the Gran Vía. There are so many that we have run out of space in the streets and plazas for taxi stops [...] Taxis are egalitarian elements *par excellence*. It transports both the capitalist and the worker. They offer everyone the assurance of being able to arrive everywhere on time, quickly overcoming the ever-increasing distances to which Madrid is constantly extending.
>
> (el 'taxi' es ya un elemento esencial del nuevo panorama de Madrid, como la falda corta, los guardias de la porra o los rascacielos de la Gran Vía. Hay tantos que ya van siendo insuficientes calles y plazas para albergar sus puntos [...] Es elemento igualitario por excelencia. En su interior se alberga el capitalista lo mismo que el obrero. Dan a todo el mundo la seguridad de llegar con tiempo a todas partes, y de salvar rápidamente las distancias que Madrid alarga constantemente.)
>
> (E. R. 1929: n.pag.)

Just as this report highlights, the proliferation of taxis was a step toward the democratization of the use of cars. However, it also meant the end of the rented horse-drawn carriages, which were popularly known as *simones* (González-Ruano 1935: 6–7).[8] The disappearance of horses and of the long-standing profession of the coachman (now replaced by the *chauffeur*) is clear in the data provided by the Sociedad de Alquiladores de Carruajes (Society of Carriage Renters). Founded in 1897, this organization represented laborers who made their living providing animal-drawn transportation in the city of Madrid. In 1900, the society paid City Council taxes on 2,500 horses, and by December of 1935 only 29 horses and 11 members remained. In a letter addressed to the mayor of Madrid, the president of the society recognized,

> how obsolete they had become, since no one rents this type of carriage anymore [...], and of the few people who do use the service (almost all elderly), some no longer do so, preferring to enjoy more modern means of transportation. Others are discontinuing the use of the service for economic reasons.
>
> (el estado de agotamiento al que habían llegado, ya que nadie alquila un carruaje de esta clase [...], y por el contrario, las pocas personas que los utilizan (casi todas

> ancianas), unas lo abandonan para disfrutar otros elementos más modernos, y otras dejan el servicio por cuestión económica.)
>
> (San José 1932)

This transformation was widely noted in the press of the time through a variety of largely nostalgic and melancholy cartoons, articles and reports. The substitution of one more technologically advanced form of urban transportation for another was understood at a symbolic level as a swan song for the 'traditional' Madrid of yesteryear. The last horse-drawn carriages that managed to hang on into the 1920s and 1930s despite the overwhelming momentum of rubber tires and gasoline became the last remnants of a city that had already disappeared.

It is important to note that the growth and complexity of patterns of mobility in Madrid are not only evident in the images of Francisco Elías's film, but also in the sounds that accompany the scenes shot in the streets of the Spanish capital. Analyzing the sound content of *El misterio de la Puerta del Sol,* (Arce 2009: 643–44) highlights a number of points of interest. One hears the sounds of the street, noises from machines, as well as other sonic effects that are strange and even bothersome to modern-day spectators. In the scenes that take place in the Puerta del Sol and on the Gran Vía, the car horns particularly stand out in their intensity and persistence. In fact, the automobile horns captured in the film were one of the most singular, omnipresent and abhorred sounds of Madrid's traffic for the city's residents. The sound was so much of a bother that local authorities tried to implement all kinds of measures to suppress it, apparently with limited success. In 1924, the City Hall's director of urban traffic traveled to Paris in the hope of better understanding the flow of traffic in the French capital (Rodríguez-Martín 2019). The *memoire* from his trip recollects that he found it especially surprising that Parisian drivers did not tend to 'the overuse of car horns' (uso desordenado de la bocina) unlike in Madrid, 'where drivers are proud of disturbing pedestrians with their unbridled use' (los conductores tienen a gala aturdir al peatón con el uso desenfrenado del Claxon) (Abarca 1924: 6).

The constant use of car horns, particularly by taxi drivers, had turned the city into what a journalist for *La Época* described as *un infierno* ('hell') (Mascarilla 1934: 5). It is important to keep in mind that beginning in 1924, crosswalks in the streets were marked with white stripes. In 1926, Madrid started to install traffic lights, and this measure in theory should have made it less necessary to use horns to warn pedestrians of the presence of cars. If we take a look at the sounds recorded in *El misterio de la Puerta del Sol,* we can see that the recommendations made by City Hall to help create a more orderly use of horns did not seem to have much of an impact (Ayuntamiento de Madrid, 1926: 129–30). In fact, in the 1930s, the city undertook even more drastic action, which resulted in conflicts with the growing community of motorists. In 1934, for example, Mayor Pedro Rico's decision to silence taxi whistles at night instigated an angry backlash by the *taxistas*, who organized a strike in protest. To avoid further conflicts, it was decided to call a meeting of all interested parties. In July 1935, the Municipal Conference against Noise was held, modeled on similar initiatives in cities like London and New York.

As previously mentioned, the end of *El misterio de la Puerta del Sol* includes a number of extended aerial shots, which allow the spectator to appreciate the urban forms of both Madrid and Barcelona from a bird's eye view. These images are exceptional, both for their novelty and for the traces of modernity that they reveal from a privileged place high above Madrid's early twentieth-century development. The aerial images were of enormous interest to the public at the time. The same year *El misterio de la Puerta del Sol* was filmed, the popular graphic magazine *Nuevo Mundo* published two extensive photographic reports under the title 'Perpectivas modernas. El Álbum "Aéreo" de Madrid' (Modern perspectives. Aerial 'album' of Madrid) that promised readers 'a view of the Court [a nickname for Madrid] from a few meters of elevation allows us to get to know the city in a new and different way' (la contemplación de la Corte desde unos metros de elevación nos hace conocer a la ciudad de un modo nuevo y distinto). In the texts that accompanied the photographs, the journalist insists that the images display the contrast between the old, traditional city and the new, modern city, which he calls *Madrid Cosmópolis* (Ferragut 1929). This contrast is also evident in the moving aerial images of Elías's film. The sequence, which tells the story of two characters who travel by plane from Barcelona to Madrid in a frantic journey to save the life of a third character (an innocent man about to be executed for a crime he did not commit) is nothing more than a flimsy premise in the plot to introduce a series of aerial shots of both cities.

In the case of the images of Madrid, the recording takes us from the outskirts of the capital to the city center, and in doing so, documents the *Ensanche* (Urban Expansion Plan) of 1929. The *Ensanche* plan had been approved over 70 years ago, but from the air it can be clearly seen that there are many unoccupied and unfinished stretches of space. The appearance of easily recognizable majestic buildings such as the Ventas bull ring and the Hospital de Jornaleros de San Francisco de Paula (also known as the Hospital de Maudes) (Workers' Hospital of St. Francis of Paul) serve as reference points to establish that the footage captures the east and north portions of the city expansion. The camera then transports the viewers from the new portion of the city still under construction to the more compact historic city center. The colorful and jumbled urban patchwork of the old city center of Madrid contrasts with the initial scenes, which show alternating sequences of constructed buildings and empty spaces, with many streets and avenues scarcely developed.

FIGURE 3.3: Francisco Elías (dir.), *El misterio de la Puerta del Sol* (The Mystery of the Puerta del Sol), 1929. Black and white frame. Courtesy of the Filmoteca Española (Spanish Film Archive).

The images of the Gran Vía are striking because of the height of the buildings that run down both sides, particularly that of the National Telephone Company of Spain (CTNE). This building, the first skyscraper in the city and one of the first to be built in all of Europe, was inaugurated toward the end of 1929. Its height and overall aesthetic, inspired by American skyscrapers, fascinated many of Madrid's citizens and the press, making it the symbol of the modern and cosmopolitan capital that had emerged in the 1920s and 1930s. The rapid transformation and modernization of Madrid during this period (notably the motorization of the city and the construction of the first skyscrapers) are captured in *El misterio de la Puerta del Sol,* but Madrid's leap into urban modernity also caught the attention of the press outside of Spain (Anon. 1929: 11, 16, 1933a: 15–16, 18, 1933b). A 1926 article titled 'Spain bids for her place in the sun', published by the *The New York Times*, portrayed Madrid as a modern city in the following terms:

> A stroll round Madrid shows that the capital has gained confidence. Old Madrid, guitars, balconies, moonlight, beggars, dim churches, austere *hidalgos* and cloistered *señoritas* – it is all going, going, gone! In modern Madrid there are subways, automatic telephones, one-way streets, traffic towers, skyscrapers and bobbed hair. (Adam 1926: 11)

Foreign publications also reported the contrasts and apparent contradictions of modernity in Madrid, for example in the article 'Past and future rub elbows in Madrid', published in *The New York Times Magazine* in 1928. Efforts were made to try to explain the complexity of the Spanish capital to North Americans by using images of donkey-drawn carriages alongside Rolls Royce cars, skyscrapers juxtaposed with centuries-old churches. This journalist sought to confirm the rush of economic, social and cultural urban transformation in Madrid (Adams 1928). These transformations would only accelerate in the early 1930s, following the 14 April 1931 proclamation of the Second Spanish Republic.

Epilogue. Madrid, 1936–39: The Destruction of the Modern City

The outbreak of the Spanish Civil War, following the failed coup d'état on 18 July 1936, put an end to the process of modernization in Madrid. The capture of Madrid was a prime objective of the military coup, given its status both as the capital and as a major European metropolis. Due to the failed initial coup and to the repeated attempts by the rebel army to conquer the city, Madrid suffered more than two and a half years under siege, resulting in enormous suffering on the part of the general population. During the summer of 1936, the aerial and artillery bombings began in Madrid. These attacks were targeted at civilians, preceding the systematic bombings of many other cities during the Second World War. Madrid became a symbol of the struggle against fascism in interwar Europe as well as of the destruction of cities by new modern war technologies. The slogans of Republican propaganda traveled around the world, publicizing the brave fight within the capital city as well as the terrible human tragedy that ensued. Despite the thousands of victims, the injured and the many people forced to flee, Madrid's message was clear: '¡No pasarán!' 'Madrid será la tumba del fascismo' (They shall not pass! Madrid will be the tomb of fascism). A very important element of the war was propaganda, waged on both sides, and aimed largely at getting international support through the mobilization of public opinion. Cinematic propaganda played

FIGURE 3.4: *Madrid 1936–1937*, 1938. Black and white frame. Courtesy of the Filmoteca Española (Spanish Film Archive).

a prominent role, and dozens of fiction and nonfiction films about the Spanish Civil War were made. Many of these films were about the defense of Madrid (Pizarroso Quintero 2005; *Catálogo general del cine de la Guerra Civil* 1996).[9] One of the most iconic, entitled *Madrid, 1936–1937*, depicts the effects of the bombings during the first years of the siege. Each of its images conveys the devastation of the city to spectators: historic and public buildings destroyed, homes demolished, devastated infrastructure and groups of people shifting through the rubble on the streets.

Several shots feature the Puerta del Sol and Gran Vía, popularly known as the 'Avenue of Bombs' due to the sheer number of explosives detonated there. Locations which had until that time been the center of vibrant urban life were now desolate spaces, completely blocked, with no trace of mass transportation or cars. Absent was the intense traffic that, in the years leading up to the outbreak of the Civil War, had been one of the most visible signs of modernity in the capital city of Spain. What remained were gaping holes in the pavement among piles of debris, produced by the impact of explosives.[10] At dawn on 28 March 1939, the first Francoist military units entered Madrid. It was the last city to be occupied by the

FIGURE 3.5: *Madrid 1936–1937*, 1938. Black and white frame. Courtesy of the Filmoteca Española (Spanish Film Archive).

rebel army. However, the end of the war did not give way to the era of peace and reconstruction that Madrid's population yearned for after three years of violence, hunger and rationing. Rather, it marked the beginning of a very difficult postwar period, and a bloody dictatorship.

Translated by Maya Edwards.

NOTES

1. On the figure of Alexandre Promio and his work for the Lumière studio, see Seguin (1998).
2. The perimeter of Madrid before the *Ensanche* (Urban Expansion Plan) drafted by engineer Carlos María de Castro encompassed a surface of 777 hectares. After the approval of the expansion project, the city tripled in size, surpassing 2,294 hectares (Bonet Correa 1978).

3. The National Film Archives of Spain stores this footage under two titles, 'Madrid hacia 1910' and 'Madrid 1914', making it impossible to determine the exact date the filming took place.
4. In 1914, Madrid's City Hall issued 2,325 circulation permits to private vehicles. According to the records of the Municipal Traffic Office, in 1915 the number of moving vehicles (automobiles, trucks, motorcycles) had reached 2,592 in Madrid (Abarca 1926: 8).
5. The film can be watched in its entirety, free of charge on Radio Televisión Española's (RTVE) website ([http://www.rtve.es/filmoteca/peliculas/).
6. Patented by Lee de Forest in 1919. Compared with other sound systems that worked with disks, the *Phonofilm* recorded sound on the celluloid itself. See Arce (2009) and Fernández Colorado (1995).
7. *El misterio de la Puerta del Sol* debuted in Burgos in January of 1929. It was only shown in small provincial capitals like Zamora and in some villages before completing its run with promotional screening for the press in Madrid in late 1930 (*El Sol,* 8 December). Some of Madrid's newspapers wrote about the film, particularly in the sections that gave information about national cinematographic production. *Heraldo de Madrid* (20 November 1929); *La Libertad* (23 November 1929); *El Imparcial* (21 December 1929); *Atlántico* (5 January 1930). In 1935, the magazine *Cinegramas* published an interview with the film director, Francisco Elías, in which he talked about his career. He also explained that with his movie he had broken a financial record, given that it was recorded in a ramshackle house in Ciudad Lineal with a poor-quality sound machine, and had a budget of only 18,000 pesetas (*Cinegramas*, 59 [27 October 1935]). See also Elías's memoirs, published by José María Caparrós Lera (1992).
8. Simón was the name of the businessman who obtained the first license in 1835 for the use of horse- and mule-drawn vehicles and therefore became the origin of the colloquial term.
9. To commemorate the 70th anniversary of the beginning of the Spanish Civil War, RTVE screened *La guerra filmada* (The War on Film), an eight-episode documentary series featuring the accounts of a variety of political parties and labor unions, war correspondents and international news agencies housed in the archives of Spain's National Film Archives. *La guerra filmada* can be viewed at: http://www.rtve.es/alacarta/videos/la-guerra-filmada/.
10. On everyday life in Madrid during the war and postwar, see Gómez Bravo and Campos Posada (2016) and Pérez Olivares (2017).

REFERENCES

Abarca, Emilio (1924), *Memoria sobre la circulación de carruajes. Impresiones de mi viaje a París*, Madrid: Imprenta Municipal.

Abarca, Emilio (1926), *Exposición que acompaño al Reglamento del Tráfico*, Madrid: Imprenta Municipal.

Adam, George (1926), 'Spain bids for her place in the sun', *The New York Times*, 31 October, n. pag.

Adams, Mildred (1928), 'Past and future rub elbows in Madrid', *The New York Times Magazine*, 20 May, pp. 10–11.

Amor, Medardo (1996), 'El misterio de la Puerta del Sol. Una recuperación finalizada', *Archivos de la Filmoteca*, 22, pp. 54–57.

Anon. (1929), 'The new Madrid: A modern European capital', *The Times*, 18 January, pp. 11, 16.

Anon. (1933a), 'New Madrid; The capital of a dream', *The Times*, 1 March, pp. 15–16, 18.

Anon. (1933b), 'Skyscrapers for Madrid', *The New York Times*, 19 March 19, p. 6.

Arce, Julio (2009), 'Del *Kinetófono* a *El misterio de la Puerta del Sol*. Los comienzos del cine sonoro en España', *Revista de Musicología*, 32:2, pp. 625–45.

Ayuntamiento de Madrid (City Hall of Madrid) (1909), *Disposiciones relativas a automóviles. 1902 a 1908*, Madrid: Imprenta Municipal.

Ayuntamiento de Madrid (City Hall of Madrid) (1926), *Reglamento del Tráfico*, Madrid: Imprenta Municipal.

Ayuntamiento de Madrid (City Hall of Madrid) (1929), *Información sobre la ciudad. Año 1929. Memoria*, Madrid: Imprenta y Litografía Municipal-Instituto Geográfico y Catastral.

Baker, Edward (2009), *Madrid Cosmopolita. La Gran Vía, 1910–1936*, Madrid: Marcial Pons.

Bonet Correa, Antonio (ed.) (1978), *Plan Castro*, Madrid: COAM.

Burgaleta, Agustín (1988), *Madrid. 101 años de tranvías*, Madrid: Empresa Municipal de Transportes de Madrid.

Caparrós Lera, J. M.ª (1992), *Memorias de dos pioneros. Fructuós Gelabert. Francisco Elías*, Barcelona: Centro de Investigaciones Literarias Españolas e Hispanoamericanas.

Catálogo general del cine de la Guerra Civil (1996), Edición a cargo de Alfonso del Amo García, con la colaboración de María Luis Ibáñez Ferradas, Madrid: Cátedra.

Del Amo García, Alfonso (1996), 'Tiempos de cambio: restauración de la primera película sonora española', *Archivos de la Filmoteca*, 22, pp. 58–65.

E. R. (1929), 'Life seen from the back of a *taxi*', *Estampa*, 30 April, n.pag.

Faulkner, Sally (2017), *Una historia del cine español: cine y sociedad, 1900-2010*, Madrid: Iberoamericana.

Fernández Colorado, Luis (1995), 'El Phonofilm: un sistema ambulante de cine sonoro', in Asociación Española de Historiadores del Cine (ed.), *De Dalí a Hitchcock. Los caminos en el cine. Actas del V Congreso de la AEHC*. A Coruña: Centro Galego de Artes da Imaxe-Xunta de Galicia/A.E.H.C., pp. 107–15.

Fernández García, Antonio (1989), 'La población madrileña entre 1876 y 1931'. El cambio de modelo demográfico', in A. Bahamonde and L. E. Otero Carvajal (eds), *La sociedad madrileña durante la Restauracion 1876–1931*, Madrid: Comunidad de Madrid, pp. 29–76.

Ferragut, Juan (1929), 'Perspectivas modernas. El "Álbum" Aéreo de Madrid', *Nuevo Mundo*, 22 February and 19 April.

Gómez Bravo, Gutmaro and Campos Posada, Ainhoa (2016), 'Nuevas tendencias en el estudio de la Guerra Civil. La violencia y los estudios urbanos: el caso específico de Madrid', *Cuadernos de Historia Contemporánea*, 38: special issue, pp. 107–26.

González-Ruano, César (1935), 'Conmovedor centenario de los "simones"', *ABC*, 26 February, pp. 6–7.

Mascarilla (Pseudonym) (1934), 'La ciudad de los ruidos', *La Época*, 12 September, p. 5.

Otero Carvajal, Luis Enrique (2016), 'La sociedad urbana y la irrupción de la Modernidad en España, 1900–1936', *Cuadernos de Historia Contemporánea*, 38, special issue, pp. 255–83, DOI: 10.5209/CHCO.53678.

Otero Carvajal, Luis Enrique and Rodríguez-Martín, Nuria (2019), 'Infraestructuras urbanas y Modernidad. Nuevas necesidades y nuevos servicios de una España urbana moderna, 1900–1936', *Historia Contemporánea*, 59, pp. 21–57, DOI: 10.1387/hc.18522.

Pérez-Olivares García, Alejandro (2017), 'La victoria bajo control: ocupación, orden público y orden social del Madrid franquista (1936–1948)', Ph.D. thesis, Madrid: Universidad Complutense de Madrid.

Pizarroso Quintero, Alejandro (2005), 'La Guerra Civil española, un hito en la historia de la propaganda', *El Argonauta español*, 2, http://journals.openedition.org/argonauta/1195. Accessed 28 July 2018.

Rodríguez-Martín, Nuria (2015), *La capital de un sueño. Madrid en el primer tercio del siglo XX*, Madrid: Centro de Estudios Políticos y Constitucionales.

Rodríguez-Martín, Nuria (2016), 'La invasión de los bárbaros del anuncio. Una historia de la publicidad exterior en Madrid, 1900–1936', *Revista Internacional de Historia de la Comunicación*, 1:7, pp. 42–66, http://institucionales.us.es/revistarihc/documentos/rihc-07-articulo-03-publicidad-exterior.pdf. Accessed 30 September 2018.

Rodríguez-Martín, Nuria (2017a), 'La aparición del 'problema de la circulación' y los orígenes de la gestión del tráfico urbano en España, 1900–1936', *Historia Contemporánea*, 2:55, pp. 483–516, DOI: 10.1387/hc.17824.

Rodríguez-Martín, Nuria (2017b), 'En una población moderna hay que saber andar. Debates en torno a la regulación del tráfico peatonal en Madrid, 1900–1936', *Registros. Revista de investigación histórica*, 13:1, pp. 166–79, https://revistasfaud.mdp.edu.ar/registros/article/view/109. Accessed 30 September 2018.

Rodríguez-Martín, Nuria (2019a), 'Los viajes de estudio de los técnicos del Ayuntamiento de Madrid en el primer tercio del siglo XX: su impacto en los servicios públicos municipales', in J. M. Matés-Barco and A. Torres-Rodríguez (eds), *Los servicios públicos en México y España*, Madrid: Silex, pp. 209–29.

Rodríguez-Martín, Nuria (2020), 'La motorización de Madrid y las transformaciones en los usos de la calle, 1898–1936', in D. Sátyro Maia, M. B. de Barros Lima e Moura Filha and P. Dieb Martins (eds), *A Rua e a Cidade. Múltiplos olhares*, João Pessoa-PB: Editora da Universidade Federal da Paraíba, pp. 91–109.

Sánchez Oliveira, Enrique (2003), *Aproximación histórica al cineasta Francisco Elías Riquelme (1890–1977)*, Sevilla: Universidad de Sevilla.

San José, Alejandro (1932), 'Request to the local government', 8 August, Archive of Villa de Madrid (A.V.M). Secretary. Record 12-391-58.

Seguin, Jean-Claude (1998), 'Alexandre Promio y las películas españolas Lumière', *Cuadernos de la Academia*, special issue, *Tras el sueño. Actas del Centenario. VI Congreso de la Asociación Española de Historiadores del Cine*, 2, pp. 11–33.

4

Childhood Spectacle, Modernity and Madrid as a Dystopic City: Luis Lucia's *Cerca de la ciudad* (1952)

David Foshee, Texas Tech University

Think of the children. Most are hard headed. Children make good soil that is worth sowing. Think of the children.[1]

Don Felipe, *Cerca de la ciudad*

Ostensibly a simple religious comedy about a priest's efforts to rescue a group of orphaned boys living in Madrid's slums, Luis Lucia's *Cerca de la ciudad* (Close to the City) (1952) underscores, on a deeper level, the theme of money and the city: who has it and who does not. In the eight-minute neorealist prologue, Madrid is portrayed as a city of extremes. Shots of well-known monuments and modern skyscrapers are countered by those of the lesser known shacks and caves that surrounded the parish church of San Juan Bautista located near Canillas,[2] which lies along the present-day M-30 freeway corridor. Considered by most Spanish film historians belonging to the rather lightweight, popular *cine religioso* genre,[3] *Cerca* nevertheless engaged in a certain degree of social criticism, much like other Spanish films of the time that contained neorealist elements such as *Surcos* (Furrows) (Nieves Conde 1951) and *Muerte de un ciclista* (Death of a Cyclist) (Bardem 1955) by prominently featuring a series of shots of the capital's outlying neighborhoods (Heredero 1993: 197). Both in the urban center as well as in its surrounding suburbs, Madrid is portrayed as a heartless space structured by predatory capital.

The tension that is created during the dystopic portrayal of the city in the film's introductory segment disappears, however, making way for the child-centered narrative that follows. While taking into consideration existing scholarship dedicated to the study of the child in Spanish cinema,[4] this chapter looks at *Cerca*'s depiction of the interaction between childhood representation,[5] the portrayal of urban space and the tensions associated with modernity. Key to this argument is the use of a definition from cultural geography of childhood spectacle (Crain 1999; Katz 2008, 2011) along with David Harvey's theory of the urbanization of consciousness (1989). *Cerca* attempts to manipulate the viewer through the creation of three emotionally charged and powerful forms of childhood spectacle including the child as accumulation strategy, ornamentation and waste (Katz 2008: 9). Childhood spectacle, a product of modern culture, is utilized in the formation of a specific, idealized and ideological image of what the family and the city itself should look like. As such, *Cerca's* children in turn mirror the distinct urban spaces portrayed in the film. The poor orphans embody the neglected *chabolas* (slums) where they live while the child protagonists are transformed through the apparent miracle of money into an almost too perfect portrayal of the middle-class child. This idealized image bears a striking similarity to the prologue's picture-postcard view of Madrid's skyscrapers and busy upscale shopping district.

The Urbanization of Consciousness

Cities are giant, constantly evolving and devolving centers of capital. The construction of new high rises, shopping complexes and housing communities is paralleled only by the abandonment and destruction of many of its prior creations. This process is motivated by middle-class consumer demand for modern commodities.

> 'All that is solid' – from the clothes on our backs to the looms and mills that weave them [...] all these are made to be broken tomorrow, smashed or shredded or pulverized or dissolved, so they can be recycled or replaced next week, and the whole process can go on again and again, hopefully forever, in ever more profitable forms.
> (Berman 1982: 99)

This urban 'creative destruction' is a part of capitalism's ongoing process of accumulation and dispossession of wealth (Schumpeter 1942; Berman 1982; Harvey 1989). *Cerca*'s 1952 release occurred at a time when Spain experienced dramatic political and economic shifts that ushered in a more aggressive form of consumerism that was especially evident in the nation's largest cities. Urban Spain's postwar accelerated economic growth, well-documented by Tortella and Hout (2000: 146), can also be noted in the change in urban geography which exacerbated an already uneven urban economic development. Madrid's central districts housed the administrative seat of Francoism and was home to its urban elite. The poorest of the city's residents generally lived in slums that encircled that nucleus, essentially cut off from the center for at least three reasons. The 'Plan Bigador'

(1946), the Francoist project that meant to address Madrid's housing shortage after the war, simply had no measurable effect with the city lacking as many as 680,000 dwellings in 1950 (Sambricio 1999: 15; Cazorla Sánchez 2010: 118). In addition, large-scale construction companies and real-estate firms demanded exorbitant prices for ownership or rental of residential property in the center of Madrid (Juliá et al. 1994: 534). Finally, as Winkel has demonstrated, Franco had no desire for the urban poor and migrants to access the city center and used legal channels, urban planning and even propaganda to 'discipline space'[6] to ensure that they remained in the outskirts (Winkel 2014: 4). In essence, two Madrids emerged, both clearly visible in *terca*'s prologue, thus fanning the flames of economic and social class tensions.

At the same time, this external, physical conflict is paralleled by internal, institutional tensions that underlie the nature of modernity itself. In *The Urban Experience*, David Harvey stresses that as urban capitalism seeks to create an ever more productive space, a concurrent tension exists between it and the basic institutions of state, class, community, family and individual (Harvey 1989: 229–55). Of those five institutions, *Cerca* centers most on the family and the struggle to maintain its traditional identity in this (re)emerging capitalist/consumerist Madrid. 'Though the family may persist as a vital institution, its meanings and functions shift in relation to changing currents within the urbanization of capital' (Harvey 1989: 237). It is the middle class in particular that struggles to reconcile itself to changes wrought by capitalism's creative destruction, leaving the familial institution laid bare to its possible transformation. 'How to square the values and virtues of family life with the destructive force of money and capital is ever an interesting conundrum for bourgeoise ideology' (Harvey 1989: 238). *Cerca* depicts Madrid as a dystopic space in which modernity threatens the existence of the traditional middle-class family. At the same time, it utilizes the representation of childhood as a means of resolving that crisis while permitting the forces of capitalism (both constructive and destructive) to run their course. Specifically, a group of orphans is portrayed as first lacking family then later being incorporated into the orphanage as a form of nontraditional family thanks to the bourgeoisie's generosity. However, it is the child actors themselves, through cinematic spectacle, that permit the film's resolution and feel-good ending by attempting to put to rest any of those serious questions raised about the consequences of modernity and urbanization.

The Child as Spectacle

As Guy Debord wrote, 'when the real world is transformed into mere images, mere images become real beings – figments that provide the direct motivations for a hypnotic behavior' (Debord 1967: 6). Film creates and manipulates those images, in the process becoming a prime source of spectacle. Everything real becomes a representation and society confounds the image with the real. In the making of the spectacle, the child may well be the perfect subject for portrayal. Adults look to childhood as the future while recalling nostalgically their own. Children have been used throughout the history of filmmaking in virtually every role from a simple comic diversion to such serious subjects as the defense and construction of the nation state (Donald et al. 2017: 2). Childhood itself is a social construct that changes meaning through time and among cultures. Katz's theory of childhood spectacle is predicated on a shift in the perception of the child that occurred in the industrialized west after the Second World War.

> Children went from economic asset to liability in the global north as production was located increasingly outside the home, infant and child mortality decreased, and reproducing a differentiated labor force became attenuated. At the same time children became ever more psychic investments, [...] their 'value' especially as the likelihood of their survival was more secure, was increasingly psychological and emotional.
>
> (Katz 2008: 9)

In other words, a new perception of childhood emerged at roughly the same time *Cerca* was released. Childhood, viewed from a middle-class perspective, was a liability that required an emotional investment by parents and family for the future. Likewise, Caldwell explains that 'the twentieth century, especially the post-1945 period, saw increased external attention to the care and control of children' (Caldwell 2002: 5). These terms – 'care' (nourishing) and 'control' (discipline) – imply a dramatic shift in thinking about the purpose of childhood. Children were no longer viewed as assets (breadwinners) particularly in urban middle-class settings. It is precisely within this shifting context that childhood spectacle emerges as a key element in 1950s popular Spanish film.

Katz has succinctly delineated three forms of childhood spectacle: accumulation strategy, waste and ornament (Katz 2008: 9). Accumulation strategy is equated to 'the child as commodity that is niche-marketed to secure success in the insecure future' (Katz 2008: 10). In film, child protagonists typically fulfill this role in the creation of an emotional relationship between themselves and the spectator while ultimately being transformed into a powerful symbol of capitalist hegemony. On the other hand, 'the child as waste is a specter that haunts the figure of the child as accumulation strategy' (Katz 2011: 51). Functioning as the inverse of the child as accumulation strategy, the child as waste is dispossessed because of excess capital accumulation (Katz 2011: 50–51). On the big screen, children as waste are typically portrayed as delinquents or social outcasts (like the orphans) stripped of capitalist value as a function of dispossession. They are redeemable if (re)assembled within the accumulation strategy. Finally, 'children as ornaments are a materialization of childhood as spectacle that enhances and brings greater value to their possessors' (Katz 2008: 13). The ornamental child adds to the already developing theme of the film. They have little or no speaking roles but are used in shots through the mise en scène to dress up or decorate the capitalist/consumerist argument.

Cerca, Capitalism and the Dystopic City

Cerca's neorealist prologue precedes the opening credits and paints a picture of two distinct Madrids, beginning in its prosperous and historic center and ending in a devastatingly poor and underdeveloped suburb. A narrator employing a playful voice-over explains that the film encompasses a metacinematic 'behind-the-scenes' look at the making of a documentary about Madrid. In the opening shot, the director, camera and crew are situated alongside the Calle de Alcalá trying to capture the first rays of morning light as they fall on the iconic La Cibeles Fountain. The subsequent three minutes is composed of numerous low-angle shots of the city's historic monuments and modern skyscrapers. The camera emphasizes the verticality of the city, creating a distance between the viewer and those seemingly unreachable and uninhabitable edifices.[7] Reminiscent of De Certeau's classic definition of the concept city, they form part of 'the creation of a universal and anonymous subject which is the city itself' (de Certeau 1984: 94). As the scene of the monumental and modern Madrid appears on screen, the narrator details the failure of the proposed documentary by explaining that '[w]e devoted ourselves to collecting well-known perspectives of Madrid from familiar points of view. We were filming, for the first time, the pure essence of an urban documentary in a series of frames that later seemed to us too much like a postcard.'[8] This idealized picture-postcard view of Madrid focuses strictly on the built environment while underscoring the capitalist promise of the ultramodern.[9]

Recognizing the film's limitations by centering solely on Madrid's *cascarón*, ('shell'), the narrator signals a shift in trajectory from *monumentos y casas* ('monuments and houses') to *gentes por las calles y ambientes* ('people in the streets and their environment'). While a mobile camera (hidden in the back of a truck) scans the street like a giant panoptic eye, the film-within-a-film's director suggests that he will look to the pedestrians for signs of a more human and heartwarming Madrid. Not unlike De Certeau's walker, with the camera functioning as a form of mechanical *flâneur*, the film attempts to discover city life through these pedestrians. 'The act of walking is to the urban system what the speech act is to language or to the statements uttered' (De Certeau 1984: 98). A tracking shot made from inside the moving truck captures real-life shoppers, businessmen and merchants coexisting along the busy upscale Gran Vía sidewalk. Ultimately it is in this scene where the camera fixes on a young priest (played by Adolfo Marsillach), suitcase in hand, who is clearly out of place in this crowd. His difference is enough to capture the attention of the camera. No less important, the sidewalk scene conveys the message that the heart and life of the city is not to be found amongst the busy middle-class consumers and merchants with their sole focus on the act of buying and selling.

The final segment of the prologue provides a striking contrast between the shots of the urban milieu that comfortably housed the middle class and those of the destitute *chabolas* that encircled the city, especially in the east. Adding to the symbols of consumer power encountered along the Gran Vía sidewalk and in the shots of the monuments and skyscrapers, the final scene of the prologue begins outside the iconic Plaza de Toros in Las Ventas. Hundreds of spectators are rushing into the bullring as the camera follows the priest heading in the opposite direction. Dusty roads dissolve into trails and the modern buildings are replaced by crumbling shacks. A crescendo of dramatic music accompanies the voice-over narrator's description of the first shots of the *chabolas*. 'The Cibeles and the bullring mattered to no one here. This was another film, another distinct life that we were filming. We could not have found a better title for this film than [...] Near the city.'[10] *Cerca*'s extensive, two-minute neorealist footage underscoring the misery of the Madrilenian slums is a rare moment in 1950s Spanish popular film. Even the neorealist masterpiece *Surcos* (1951) lacks this lengthy, detailed perspective of the city's *chabolas* (Heredero 1993: 197–98). The opulence of the city center portrayed at the beginning clashes markedly with the extreme desolation seen in these shots of the surrounding suburbs. Thus, the prologue attempted to produce a tension (especially for middle-class viewers) through its focus on this spatial disparity and its portrayal of the modern city as a cold, heartless entity. Paradoxically, the film uses orphaned children living in those *chabolas* as the vehicle by which it reconciles that tension. Child spectacle becomes a focal point for middle-class concerns over the role of family in the rapidly changing urban landscape.

Children as Ornamentation

The film narrative concentrates on a group of poor, orphaned boys living virtually homeless in the *chabola*s. The child actors create a spectacle through the construction of images on-screen that in turn develop into extraordinarily cogent manipulators of the viewer in the portrayal of what institutions (such as the family) should look like. As the priest is shown arriving at his destination, the camera pans right spotlighting a well-maintained church (the parish church of San Juan Bautista) seemingly out of place in a sea of slums. The subsequent shot reveals a group of shabbily dressed boys playing ball directly in front of the church entrance. A large sign painted on the wall reads 'Ball playing prohibited!'[11] As Father José approaches, the boys scatter in all directions only to return to their game the moment after the cleric enters the building.

Calling to mind Katz's interpretation of child ornament, these anonymous boys, film extras without speaking parts, contribute to an already developing theme as elements (or ornaments) of the mise en scène. They reinforce the focus on the dystopic city. The image of these children clashes with the earlier portrayal of the urban consumerist middle class busily shopping along the Gran Vía. Moreover, placing the boys in the same shot as the sign, though undoubtedly a comic trope, draws critical attention to the question of space. These orphans lack space even for play, a direct result of their economic and familial circumstances, and as residents of this other poverty-stricken Madrid. Like the lifeless monuments and skyscrapers from the prologue, a similar low-angle shot portrays the church as both distant and unattainable. Equal to the tenuous and poorly constructed shacks and caves of the neighborhoods of the *chabolas*, these poorly dressed orphans represent a reflection (a human mirror) of the *chabolas* themselves. During this brief scene, every detail of their clothing and action is designed to replicate their surroundings. Just as the viewer was encouraged to feel compassion during the shots of slums, that emotion would certainly have resurfaced in this use of child spectacle.

At the same time, *Cerca* creates a buffer between the middle-class spectator[12] and the children. Children from the lower social class thumbing their noses at authority while playing beneath a sign that forbids them to do so recalls the picaresque of Spanish literature. Portrayed as an animal-like horde, these children are significantly removed from their well-mannered and educated middle-class counterparts. The viewer is encouraged to pity these ruffians who exhibit behavior that is deemed socially unacceptable. In her analysis of *Cerca*'s orphans, Labanyi notes that 'the implication is that the urban migrants in Madrid's shantytowns need to be "settled" via domestic family values' (Labanyi 2001: 36). While the film bemoans the consequences of modernity and class division, money remained key in cultivating acceptable childhood behavior through education and a structured home life. Because the orphaned boys lacked both, the middle-class viewer was socially distanced from the child as ornament living homeless and destitute in Madrid's *chabolas*. Through the creation of this middle-class buffer that separates the viewer from the indigent child, *Cerca* actually reinforces both class and spatial inequalities (the two Madrids) that it worked so hard to delineate in the prologue.

A subsequent scene also makes use of the child as ornament. At one moment in the film, the local newspaper article has just detailed the heroic deed of the orphans in recovering a respected citizen's money from a local thief while at the same time highlighting the orphanage's own desperate fiscal circumstances. A montage of eleven shots reveals several of Madrid's middle-class families reading the article while suggesting they are emotionally moved to donate money to the orphans. Two of those shots consist of well-dressed and mannered children sitting in their living rooms reading the article while making their financial contribution to the waifs, mimicking the responses of their parents. They too form a part of the mise en scène through the representation of a typical middle-class urban household's domestic space. These brief shots infer that Madrid's middle-class children were sympathetic to the plight of those orphans. Yet, the disparity between these images and those of the homeless boys playing in front of the church is so great that it appears to enhance the distance between the two groups. Ultimately the actions of these middle-class children as ornaments serve to reassure the bourgeoisie citizenry that they are not to blame for the devastating poverty witnessed in those scenes in and around the suburbs of Canillas.

Immediately after this scene, Don Felipe, a fellow priest and mentor to Father José, visits the orphanage. A seven-shot montage discloses the orphans' transformation (both in dress and actions) as a direct result of those donations. Gone is the picaresque image in front of the church, replaced now by a spectacle of children engaged in diverse forms of productive activities including studying, cooking, cleaning, worshipping and working. In one such shot, the priest and Don Felipe witness five boys diligently at work learning to build, sand and plane furniture. Because of the placement of the two montage scenes back-to-back, a causative relationship is established between the middle-class children's donations and the transformation of the orphans. The orphanage owes its existence to the generosity of the middle-class family, thereby reinforcing that institution as fundamental to the functioning of society. The nontraditional family of the orphanage is placed in a subservient role to that of the bourgeoisie family. Equally, the orphans in the shot are now dressed like the bourgeoisie but are shown performing a working-class occupation. On one level, these children appear transformed into the image of the middle-class child. Nevertheless, they continue to be engaged in work (carpentry) associated with the working class. Thus, at every turn, rather than resolving them, the child as ornament actually reinforces the class and family tensions created at the beginning of the film. Likewise, the perceived distance between Madrid's moneyed center and its abandoned suburbs is increased rather than reduced.

The Child as Waste

As Katz states, the 'children of waste' represent the dispossessed who lack opportunities in all aspects of society, especially in education, and are met with discipline, policing and surveillance often ensuring that he or she will end up in prison rather than experiencing a bright future (Katz 2011: 51). Just as the suburban neighborhood is portrayed as lacking an infrastructure of roads, transportation and even basic services like running water and sewage, so the city's small orphaned residents are presented as weak and sickly. Soon after his arrival at his new parish, Father José learns that it is inundated with orphaned, homeless boys. On that first day, the sacristan takes him to the 'home' of five brothers living alone, three of them too young to fend for themselves, a fourth disabled, while the fifth, Luis, attempts to care for the entire group. As he enters, the youngest, Pepe, lies bedridden from a leg injury. The sacristan explains to Father José that in comparison to most of the children of the neighborhood, Pepe is healthy. After recovering from the shock of hearing this news, Father José is determined to champion these young children back to health and in so doing he will rescue the neighborhood itself from neglect and misery.

At the same time, the disposability of the children as waste is in part a myth because they are essential to capital accumulation since they have 'a value analogous to an industrial reserve army' (Katz 2011: 51). *Cerca* implies that these children exhibit some behavioral defect, and if they would just act differently their social misfortunes would be resolved. For example, the teenage Luis is cast early on as a juvenile delinquent. In his initial appearance inside the church, he is caught trying to steal a silver candelabra from the altar. Located hiding in the confessional by the priest, he is convinced to return it. Thus, from this very moment, Luis as a child of waste begins his conversion. Luis's complete transformation from delinquent to angelic figure is captured in a shot late in the film where he leads a youth choir practice in preparation for the Christmas mass. Shown as a model of teenage responsibility, the same silver candelabra that he unsuccessfully tried to steal is visible over his shoulder as evidence that his behavior was to blame for his circumstances. Ultimately, Luis's character reinforces capitalist hegemony by demonstrating that while being dispossessed he desired nothing more than to be assimilated within middle-class society. Not unlike Luis's transformation, the suburb portrayed in *Cerca* would undergo a similar metamorphosis less than a decade later. By 1959, the urban landscape of Canillas had changed radically as the *chabolas* were swept away to make room for large-scale middle-class housing projects. An advertisement by the firm Saconia promised 'homes on the Barajas freeway with sun, air, light and a large park for your children. For a small down payment and monthly payments for five years you will be a homeowner in El

Parque de San Juan Bautista!' (Márquez 2009: n.pag.). Like the children as waste, who slowly disappear as they are transformed into a spectacle of the middle class, the neighborhood that surrounded San Juan Bautista Church would soon be converted into a bourgeois suburban oasis.

The Child as Accumulation Strategy

In film, the child as accumulation strategy focuses on the emotional relationship between the audience and the image of the child protagonists. 'The individualized investments in children as accumulation strategies are realized socially through some inchoate sense or fantasy wish-dream that they will "save the world" or at least save us from ourselves and the consequences of our actions and inactions' (Katz 2008: 12). On the one hand, these protagonists help to resolve tension or dilemmas. In this instance, the rather straightforward presentation of the dangers of urban capital to the moral values of family is countered by the orphan 'stars' that seek to not only uphold those values but remind the society at large of their importance. On the other hand, child protagonists lead to the creation of the child star which is itself a manipulation of capital designed to portray on screen a particular image of childhood. Debord notes that 'in societies where modern conditions of production prevail, life is presented as an immense accumulation of spectacles. Everything that was directly lived has receded into a representation' (Debord 1967: 2). For the French Situationist, life in the modern world has become increasingly fragmented. 'The spectacle consists in reunification of separate aspects at the level of the image' (Jappe 1999: 6). In the end, the child as accumulation strategy is used to forward capitalist goals through the resolution of tensions created by capitalism itself and in the creation of a mirror image of the middle-class.

As strange as it may seem, it is not too far-fetched to consider the most important of these child protagonists to be Pepito the ventriloquist doll belonging to Father José. Upon his arrival, the priest introduces Pepito to the sacristan, as his son 'born not of a woman but of a man, in the guise of the ventriloquist's dummy inherited from his fairground artist father, which he manipulates effectively throughout the film to win the slum boys over' (Labanyi 2001: 37). He is the perfect son who even assists his father in catechizing the young orphaned charges. He is the model of child accumulation spectacle because he represents both the apparent conflict and then becomes the star in its very resolution. When Father José is unable to financially continue caring for the orphans, he is forced to sacrifice his own son as a commodity by selling him at a second-hand shop in Madrid. In an emotional goodbye, Father José pleads with the shopkeeper to remember to take good care of his son (Figure 4.1). This tearjerker moment is also a reminder of the heartless nature of consumerism. Pepito, a symbol of the real-life child, is bought and sold like any other commodity. The film makes clear[13] that this transaction occurs in the heart of Madrid's s upscale, central shopping district, maximizing the existing tension between the urban center and the periphery. At the film's end, Don Felipe (the priestly representative of the middle class and the urban center) buys back Pepito and returns him to his 'father' and to the orphans. In the process, Pepito becomes a true star and example of accumulation strategy. He is reintegrated into his family through the power of middle-class money that permits a feel-good ending through the apparent resolution of the spatial and social class tensions presented in the film.

At the same time, Luis and his younger brother Manuel fulfill the role of child protagonist and accumulation spectacle. Both are transformed from orphaned child delinquents into spectacles of idyllic, middle-class children. When a Madrid store owner is robbed by a local thief, Luis, Manuel and several other orphans manage to recover the money for the store owner. As a result, a local newspaper prints the story and the middle-class readers respond en masse to the orphanage's

FIGURE 4.1: Still from *Cerca de la ciudad*, Luis Lucia (dir.), 1952. Spain. © Goya Producciones. Courtesy of the Filmoteca Española (Spanish Film Archive).

needs through the heroic efforts of the boys. Nevertheless, as spectacle, the images of Luis and Manuel have already been transformed into the middle class. Distant shots are replaced by touching close-ups which play on the cute aesthetic.[14] No longer simply poor orphans, these two characters function as child stars. The closing images of the film ironically resemble the opening shots of the prologue. Luis and Manuel are portrayed as picture-postcard examples of middle-class children. Not unlike the skyscrapers and monuments from the prologue that simply seemed too perfect, *Cerca*'s ending devolves into the mawkishness that Wright has observed as characteristic of the *cine religioso* (Wright 2013: 24). Nevertheless, by focusing on childhood representation and the portrayal of urban space, the film exposed serious class and family tensions by underscoring the existence of two different and very real Madrids. Ironically, like Pepito's sale at the pawnshop, Luis and Manuel are suddenly transformed from lower-class, delinquent orphans and packaged for sale as middle-class model citizens. Despite the film's focus on the miserable living conditions that the suburban poor endured on a daily basis, the syrupy happy ending erased any discomfort that the middle-class viewer might have felt.

In the first pages of his monograph devoted to comedy and Spanish popular film during the Francoist dictatorship, Steven Marsh reminds us that there has been a tendency to look at films produced within the first two decades of the Franco regime as contributing directly to the reinforcement of fascist values. Yet, those same films were extraordinarily diverse with respect to genre, style, plot and even ideology (Marsh 2006: 2). It is equally easy to overlook the feel-good religious comedy of the 1950s as lacking content worthy of serious consideration. Through its neorealist prologue and child-centered narrative, *Cerca de la ciudad* delineated tensions by pointing out the disparity that existed between an opulent city center and a desperately impoverished suburb. When Father José learns that he has just inherited the poorest church in Madrid (both economically and spiritually), Don Felipe advises him that the best way to rejuvenate both his church and parishioners is through the children. 'The children are fertile ground for sowing seed. Think of the children!' That line, repeated several times by Father José throughout the film, can equally be applied to the function of child spectacle in the film. Initially portrayed as dispossessed child delinquents, the child actors are transformed into the spectacle of middle-class perfection, thus eliminating the troubling tensions seen in the portrayal of economic injustice in two very different Madrids.

NOTES

1. 'Piensa en los niños. Los mayores tienen la cabeza dura. Los niños son buena tierra para sembrar. Piensa en los niños.'

2. San Juan Bautista Church was built in 1933 situated near the community of Canillas and specifically located in the neighborhood of Cerro de la Cabaña. The latter is considered one of the 'lost' barrios of Madrid levelled during the new construction developments of the late 1950s.
3. Wright maintains that the *cine religioso* consisted of films of the 1950s, often featuring children, with Catholic religious themes and defined by its 'mawkish sentimentality' (Wright 2013: 24). In addition, Faulkner cites the *cine religioso* as marking a transition from 'military to missionary tendencies' (2013: 43).
4. At the beginning of this last decade, two separate dissertations focused on the subject of the child in Spanish cinema including Anna Proffit's 'Representing the Child in Spanish film from *El pequeño ruiseñor* to *El laberinto del fauno*' (2011) and Miowei Weng's 'Franco's children: Representations of Franco-era childhood in contemporary Spanish literature and cinema' (2012). Covering the period from 1950 to 2010, Sarah Wright's *The Child in Spanish Cinema* (2013) is the first monograph dedicated to the study of the child in Spanish film. More recently Erin K. Hogan's *Two cines con niño: Genre and the Child Protagonist in Fifty Years of Spanish Film* (2018) examines ventriloquial dialogism, genre and the child protagonist in Spanish cinema. Finally, Sarah Thomas's *Inhabiting the In-Between: Childhood and Cinema in Spain's Long Transition* (2018) looks at the cinematic child of the Spanish Transition as an ambiguous, liminal figure that mimics the political uncertainty of that time.
5. Recent works that survey the role of children in film in the global context include Wojcik-Andrews (2001), Wilson (2003), Lebeau (2008), Lury (2010 and Donald (2017).
6. Using Foucault's description of disciplinary power, Winkel demonstrates 'how the discourse created by the period's official and artistic texts worked to organize the capital's citizens into ordered subjects. The implied citizen that was conceived of through urban planning and architecture emerged as a model to be followed by established residents and recent arrivals alike' (Winkel 2014: 4).
7. Lefebvre's concept of the representations of space, involves 'conceptualized space, the space of scientists, planners, urbanists [...] all who identify what is lived and what is perceived with what is conceived' (Lefebvre 1991: 38).
8. 'después nos consagramos a coleccionar perspectivas famosas de Madrid en ángulos característicos. Estábamos estrenando la esencia pura de un documental urbano en una serie de encuadres que luego nos resultaron demasiada tarjeta postal'.
9. Alsayyad explores the relationship between the built environment of cites in both pre- and post-Second World War films as a way of expressing both modernity and postmodernity and the utopic and dystopic (Alsayyad 2000: 268–81).
10. 'Las Cibeles y los toros ya no les importaba nada. Era otra película, otra vida distinta la que estábamos haciendo y para ella no hubiéramos encontrado un título mejor que [...] Cerca de la ciudad.'
11. 'Se prohíbe jugar a pelota'.

12. Wright maintains that the audience for the *cine con niño* was largely made up of middle-class mothers and their children (Wright 2013: 23).
13. Before selling the doll, the priest is shown visiting his old mentor Don Felipe (a resident of the city center). Stepping next door from this apartment, the priest enters the second-hand shop where three well-dressed boys are buying candy while a woman dressed in a fur coat hurriedly passes through camera view.
14. Wright defines the cute aesthetic as one that reflects the image of the middle-class child through shots designed to play on viewer emotion (Wright 2013: 32). Merish comments that this cute child of film is 'pure spectacle, pure display' (Merish 1996: 188).

REFERENCES

Alsayyad, Nezar (2000), 'The cinematic city: Between modernist utopia and postmodernist dystopia', *Built Environment*, 26:4, pp. 268–81.

Berman, Marshall (1982), *All That Is Solid Melts into Air: The Experience of Modernity*, New York: Simon and Schuster.

Caldwell, Lesley (2002), *The Elusive Child*, New York: Routledge.

Cazorla Sánchez, Antonio (2010), *Fear and Progress: Ordinary Lives in Franco's Spain, 1939–1975*, New York: Wiley-Blackwell.

Certeau, Michel de (1984), *The Practice of Everyday Life* (trans. Steven Rendall), Berkeley: University of California Press.

Crain, Patricia, (1999), 'Childhood as spectacle', *American Literary History*, 11:3, pp. 545–53.

Debord, Guy (1967), *The Society of the Spectacle*, New York: Zone Books.

Donald, Stephanie, Wilson, Emma and Wright, Sarah (2017), *Childhood and Nation in Contemporary World Cinema*, New York: Bloomsbury.

Faulkner, Sally (2006), *A Cinema of Contradiction: Spanish Film in the 1960s*, Edinburgh: Edinburgh University Press.

Harvey, David (1989), *The Urban Experience*, Baltimore: The Johns Hopkins University Press.

Heredero, Carlos F. (1993), *Las huellas del tiempo: Cine español, 1951–1961*, Valencia: Filmoteca Valenciana.

Hogan, Erin K. (2018), *Two cines con niño: Genre and the Child Protagonist in Fifty Years of Spanish Film*, Edinburgh: Edinburgh University Press.

Jappe, Anselm (1999), *Guy Debord* (trans. Donald Nicholson-Smith), Berkeley: University of California Press.

Juliá, Santos, Ringrose, David and Segura, Cristina (1994), *Madrid: Historia de una capital.* Madrid: Alianza Editorial.

Katz, Cindi (2008), 'Childhood as spectacle: Relays of anxiety and the reconfiguration of the child', *Cultural Geographies*, 15:1, pp. 5–17.

Katz, Cindi (2011), 'Accumulation, excess, childhood: Toward a countertopography of risk and waste', *Documents d'Anàlisi Geogràfica*, 57:1, pp. 47–60.

Kinder, Marsha (1983), 'The children of Franco in the new Spanish cinema', *Quarterly Review of Film and Video*, 8:2, pp. 57–76.

Labanyi, Jo (2001), 'The reticent screen: Internalizations of empire; colonial ambivalence and the early Francoist missionary films', *Discourse: Journal for Theoretical Studies in Media and Culture*, 23:1, pp. 25–42.

Lebeau, Vicky (2008), *Childhood and Cinema*, London: Reaktion.

Lefebvre, Henri (1991), *The Production of Space* (trans. Donald Nicholson-Smith), Oxford: Blackwell.

Lucia, Luis (1952), *Cerca de la ciudad*, Spain: Goyas Producciones Cinematográficas.

Lury, Karen (2010), *The Child in Film: Tears, Fears and Fairy Tales*, London: I.B. Tauris.

Márquez, Ricardo (2009), 'El Cerro de la Cabaña: Barrio desaparecido de Madrid', Historias Matritenses: Investigación sobre barrios desaparecidos y actuales, de Madrid, http://historias-matritenses.blogspot.com/2009/11/el-cerro-de-la-cabana-barrio.html#ixzz5O5RuBJB0. Accessed 21 May 2018.

Marsh, Steven (2006), *Popular Spanish Film Under Franco: Comedy and the Weakening of the State*, Palgrave Macmillan.

Merish, Lori (1996), 'Cuteness and commodity aesthetics: Tom Thumb and Shirley Temple', in R. Garland Thompson (ed.), *Freakery: Cultural Spectacles of the Extraordinary Body*, New York: New York University Press, pp. 185–203.

Proffit, Anna (2011), 'Representing the Child in Spanish film from *El pequeño ruiseñor* to *El laberinto del fauno*', Ph.D. thesis, Chicago: University of Chicago.

Rocha, Carolina (2012), *Representing History, Class, and Gender in Spain and Latin America: Children and Adolescents in Film*, New York: Palgrave Macmillan.

Sambricio, Carlos (1999), *La vivienda en Madrid en la década de los 50: El plan de urgencia social*, Madrid: Electa España.

Schumpeter, Joseph (1942), *Capitalism, Socialism and Democracy*, New York: Harper and Row.

Thomas, Sarah (2018), *Inhabiting the In-Between: Childhood and Cinema in Spain's Long Transition*, Toronto: University of Toronto Press.

Tortella, Gabriel and Hout, Stephan (2000), 'From autarky to European Union: Nationalist economic policies in twentieth-century Spain', in A. Telchova, M. Herbert and J. Pátek (eds), *Economic Change and the National Question in Twentieth-Century Europe*, New York: Cambridge University Press.

Weng, Miowei (2012), 'Franco's children: Representations of Franco-era childhood in contemporary Spanish literature and cinema', Ph.D. thesis, St. Louis: Washington University.

Winkel, Adam (2014), 'Zones of influence: The production of Madrid in early Franco Spain', Ph.D. thesis, New York: Columbia University.

Wojcik-Andrews, Ian (2000), *Children's Films: History, Ideology, Pedagogy, Theory*, New York: Garland Publishers.

Wright, Sarah (2013), *The Child in Spanish Cinema*, Manchester: Manchester University Press.

5

Elevators and the Poetics of Vertical Mobility in Spanish Film

Tom Whittaker, University of Warwick

Spain has the highest concentration of elevators per population in the world. Their ubiquity owes itself to the fact that the majority of Spaniards live in multistory buildings. A total of 65 percent of the Spanish population in 2012 lived in apartments – a proportion that, as Matt Phillips shows, makes Spaniards 'some of the world's pre-eminent apartment dwellers' (Phillips 2014). Indeed, elevators are such an integral part of Spanish urban centers that they most frequently go unnoticed, and as such, their broader social and cultural significance has been vastly overlooked. Writing about American elevators, Nick Paumgarten has observed that 'while anthems have been written to jet travel, locomotives, and the lure of the open road, the poetry of vertical transportation is scant' (Paumgarten 2008). To this effect, Paumgarten asks what there is to say about the elevator, besides the fact that 'it goes up and down' (Paumgarten 2008)? The routine and everyday experience of elevator travel is an example of what Georges Perec has called the 'infraordinary' (Perec 1997: 204), a term he uses for the kinds of mundane spaces and objects which are too often taken for granted, yet are pervasive to the spatial materiality of everyday life. The constant hum and whir of the machinery, the swoosh of the doors as they open and close shut, the soothing click as the elevator carriage passes each floor: these sounds mark out the routine rhythms – or what Perec has called 'background noise' (Perec 1997: 204) – of Spanish urban life.

Given the centrality of elevators to Spanish daily life, it is not surprising that they have frequently occupied an important location in Spanish cinema, particularly from the 1950s onwards, as it increasingly depicted the social issues of a nation that was becoming urbanized. Elevators in Spanish film figure not so much as a passive backdrop to the everyday lives of its characters, as much as a significant and dynamic element within many a film's mise en scène and narrative. Constituting a transitional space between the street and the apartment, the public sphere and the domestic, the elevator carriage is marked by a spatial ambiguity and in-betweenness that provide the filmmaker with several possibilities. The transience of the elevator makes for a literal vehicle for narrative progression, one that brings diverse characters fleetingly together within a small and enclosed place. In transporting characters from one space to another, from the outside to the inside or vice versa, it is also able to seamlessly connect together different locations and scenes within a film. As this chapter shows, however, elevator travel becomes most meaningful in Spanish cinema in the moments when its smooth and regular passage is broken. Many Spanish films feature elevators that are faulty or unreliable, an element which disrupts or defers actions within their narratives. While usually a taken-for-granted and normalized part of urban domestic life, elevator travel becomes particularly visible and audible when it breaks down. It is during these particular moments of rupture or interruption, I argue, that the elevator becomes most entangled with social and political significance. If, as Stephen Graham has argued, 'elevator travel has long been a central component of cultural notions of urban modernity' (Graham 2018: 135), this chapter shows how its place in Spanish film has frequently alerted us to the uneven and contradictory processes of Spain's urban modernization.

Vertical Mobility and ascenso social

When an elevator is finally installed in the building in the long-running television program *Cuéntame cómo pasó* (Remember When) (2001–present), the elderly grandmother Herminia (María Galiana) can barely contain her excitement. While Herminia is initially fearful of the confined space of the lift carriage, she soon enough adapts to elevator travel with unabashed joy. Repeatedly taking the elevator up and down just for the visceral thrill of it, she enthuses to her grandson, Carlos, 'Es como subir en un taxi' (It's like getting in a taxi).[1] *Cuéntame* is based on the experiences of the fictional Alcántaras, a 'typical' Spanish family, who live through the economic and historical transformations brought about during the late years of Franco regime (1939–75) and the subsequent transition to democracy (1975–82). The geographical trajectory of the Alcántaras has mirrored much of Spanish population during the years of *desarrollismo*. Together with her daughter Mercedes Fernández (Ana Duato) and her son-in-law Antonio Alcántara (Imanol Arias), Herminia migrated to Madrid from a tiny village in Albacete, settling in the fictional working-class *barrio* of San Genaro,[2] Madrid in the 1960s. As the many seasons of the program have gone by, the social advancement of the family has been indicated through their acquisition of consumer objects such as the washing machine and television set, and most significantly through Antonio's fetish for purchasing new cars. Taking place at the beginning of the twentieth series (which is supposed to be set in 1989) the belated arrival of the elevator therefore forms part of a broader narrative of the Alcántara family's upward social mobility. As well as facilitating Herminia's ease of movement because she increasingly struggles to climb the stairs, Mercedes hopes that the elevator will add value to the property of the building. While there has been much valuable work in Spanish Cultural Studies on how issues of movement have been central to Spain's entry into capitalist modernity, this has mainly been considered through the exploration of *horizontal* rather than vertical mobilities.[3] This more broadly reflects the way in which, as Stephen Graham has recently noted, vertical transportation and its infrastructures have been largely ignored in the Humanities and Social Sciences (Graham 2018: 81–82). As the history of the Alcántaras – and, by extension, that of Spain – illustrates, the horizontal mobilities intrinsic to urban modernity, such as rural-to-urban migration and the rapid rise of automobility, should also be considered alongside the significance of vertical mobility, here thrown into relief through the arrival of the elevator and its subsequent transformation of the everyday rhythms of the Alcántara family.

That the elevator in Spain has emerged as an index of upward mobility is intriguingly reflected in the Spanish term for social mobility, *ascenso social*, here noteworthy for its morphological proximity to the word *ascensor* (the Spanish word for elevator). Indeed, elevators frequently illuminate the ways in which vertical spatiality has been tied up with questions of economic power and status in Spain. If, as the geographer Tim Cresswell writes, 'movement is rarely movement; it carries with it the burden of meaning' (Cresswell 2006: 7), the upwards transitionary motion of elevators has frequently signified economic progress and advancement. As María Isabel Gea Ortigas notes, before the turn of the twentieth century, apartments on the lower floors of buildings were normally reserved for the wealthy (Gea Ortigas 2014: 18–19). With the arrival of the first elevator in Madrid in 1874 and their increasing use in the 1890s, vertical segregation began to disappear, and people from a variety of social classes were able to live across the various levels of apartment blocks (Gea Ortigas 2014: 18–19). A burgeoning fear of pollution and noise, however, saw the reversal of this trend, something which in turn led to apartments on the higher floors being more highly valued – provided, of course, that the buildings were equipped with elevators (Gea Ortigas 2014: 18–19).[4] In his cultural history of elevators in Europe and the United States, Andreas Bernard similarly shows how elevators led to a general revaloration of upper-story hotel rooms and dwellings, spaces that had previously been associated with the lowliest sectors of society (Bernard 2014: 69, 76).

The relationship between verticality and social hierarchy was explored in much Spanish cinema of the 1950s and the early 1960s, a time when the housing sector emerged as a major area of growth in the Spanish economy. Embracing a cinematic realism that had rarely been seen in Spanish film, several directors addressed the increasingly urgent issue of housing – or rather, the scarcity thereof – for many Spaniards living in in the city.[5] This can be observed in Fernando Fernán Gómez's *La vida por delante* (Life Ahead) (1958), in which the young couple Antonio (played by the director) and Josefina (Analia Gadé) desperately seek to buy their first apartment and enter the ranks of the expanding urban middle class.[6] The film satirized Spain's emerging political economy of bourgeois home ownership and rampant property speculation, national priorities that were signaled through the famous proclamation of the first Minister of Housing José Luis de Arrese in 1957 that '[q]ueremos un país de propietarios, no de proletarios' (we want a country of homeowners, not proletarians) (cited in Anon. 2014). The couple is enticed into buying an apartment off-plan on the third floor – sufficiently high enough, the salesman assures them, so as to avoid the noise of the street and the gypsies from below. Early shots of the location of a yet-to-be-built apartment block, its optimistic promise of verticality emphasized by the low-angle tracking of clouds in the sky, are soon enough juxtaposed with the material reality of their apartment, whose dimensions are so cramped that they will complain of being trapped *en una ratonera* (in a mouse trap). On their moving in, they discover that the elevator has broken down, thus forcing them to lug all of their belongings up the stairs. The apartment is as poorly maintained as the elevator: the door handle breaks off in his hand, the walls are as thin as paper and water fails to flow from the taps. The fragile materiality of the apartment, emphasized through claustrophobic mise en scène and shallow depth of field, takes its toll on their relationship, leading Josefina to break down in tears and say 'nuestro matrimonio se irá deshaciendo poco a poco como esta casa' (our marriage will fall apart bit by bit like this house). Fernán Gómez similarly embodied the role of a Spanish everyman looking for an apartment in his performance as the hapless Evaristo in *El inquilino* (The Tenant) (José Antonio Nieves Conde 1957), a film that was highly critical of Francoist housing policy. As a salesman (played by José Luis López Vázquez) shows Evaristo around a newly constructed apartment block, the tiny elevator becomes trapped between two floors, forcing them to clamber out onto the hallway. In both films, the promise of vertical social mobility, symbolized by the costly and modern apartment blocks, is presented as forever beyond the grasp of its protagonists.

Elevators in Spanish cinema not only dramatize the ways in which wealth is vertically distributed, but their presence and absence serve to underline social and geographical inequalities between characters.[7] The spectacle of the turn-of-the century elevator, with its wrought-iron surround and ornate metalwork, often signified wealth and economic means in Spanish film. In Fernando Fernán Gómez's *El mundo sigue* (Life Goes On) (1963, though not released until 1965), Faustino (again, played by Fernán Gómez) is so desperate to raise his socioeconomic status that he steals money from the bar where he works as a waiter. Unlike the cramped tenement block where his wife Luisita's family lives in Maravillas[8] – where his elderly mother-in-law (Milagros Leal), at the beginning of the film, is forced to carry her burdensome shopping up five flights of stairs – the bar is situated within a building whose relative wealth is indicated through the presence of the elevator. Fleeing from the bar with the money he has robbed, Faustino attempts to hide by running up the stairs, only to find that a smartly dressed couple has entered the elevator carriage some seconds later. Appearing to chase him up the stairs, the mechanized motion of the elevator swiftly outpaces Faustino, leaving him out of breath. Conveyed through a succession of quick cuts, the elevator here provides the audience with the rush and thrill of speed that is both mechanical and cinematic, pleasures that can also be found in chase-the-elevator scenes in other Spanish films, such as *Matador* (Pedro Almodóvar 1986), *Ópera prima* (First Work) (Fernando Trueba 1980) and *Séptimo* (7th Floor) (Patxi Amezcua 2013).

The elevator which appears in Carlos Saura's *Los golfos* (The Hooligans) (1960) presents itself not only as an indicator of wealth, but also an opportunity for crime. Filmed on location in the shanty towns of Legazpi, Madrid, the film centers on a group of delinquents who rob money in order to pay for their friend Paco's dream (played by Ramón Rubio) of becoming a bullfighter. Travelling to a more affluent neighborhood of the city, two delinquents follow a besuited man into an elevator with an elaborately decorated iron grille. The man stands next to the mirrored wall of the elevator, in whose reflection the two delinquents can be seen, who unbeknownst to him, prepare to assault him. The confined mise en scène of the elevator offers little possibility for camera movement or reframing, an effect that adds to the sense of foreboding entrapment. The boys quickly exit the elevator and slam its doors shut, leaving behind the unconscious victim within the carriage, hidden from view. They dispatch the lift back down for a few seconds before abruptly forcing it to stop, so that the carriage is suspended halfway between two floors, before fleeing with his money. Trapped in the liminal space between two floors, the ambiguous location of the elevator in this scene here demonstrates the extent to which the invention of the 'elevator created not only new visibilities but new invisibilities' within buildings (Bernard 2014: 57).

Broken Elevators and Uneven Modernization

The kinds of shanty towns in which the delinquents live in *Los golfos* would gradually be replaced by a proliferation of high-rise tower blocks, particularly in the suburbs and outer edges of the cities, where elevators were not so much a luxury but an absolute necessity. An iconic example of this was the housing complex of Concepción, in Madrid, constructed in the late 1950s so as to rehouse the shanty town population of La Ventilla. Nicknamed 'Las Colmenas' (the beehives) because of its unique cell-like panels, the distinctive buildings have been featured as key locations in *Colegas* (Pals) (Eloy de la Iglesia 1982), *Torremolinos 73* (Pablo Berger 2003) and most famously in *¿Qué he hecho yo para merecer esto!* (What Have I Done to Deserve This?) (Pedro Almodóvar 1984). Overseen by the property developer and mogul José Banus (whose company which he established with his brother Juan was also responsible for the construction of the Valle de los Caídos), the buildings became synonymous with *chabolismo vertical* (vertical shanty towns), a term used to describe the multistory housing projects that were hastily constructed in an attempt to mitigate the growing housing crisis at this time. Martin Wynn shows how in light of initiatives such as Social Urgency Plans (1957–58) and the National Housing Plan (1961), where the government offered attractive incentives to the private housing sector, dwellings became not only larger but substantially higher in terms of numbers of floors per block (Wynn 1984: 136). An emphasis on dense and compact urbanization was frequently favored, moreover, so as not to encroach on the surrounding agricultural land (cited in Phillips 2014). However, the modernist promise of vertical space and light soon enough gave way to what Amanda Cuesta describes as 'urbanismo de pésima calidad' (urbanism of terrible quality), with poorly served buildings lacking the most basic services such as streetlights, sewage, green spaces, schools, walk in clinics, security and street cleaning (Cuesta 2009: 185). *¿Qué he hecho yo para merecer esto!* shows how the toll of the failing infrastructure of Franco-era housing projects such as Las Colmenas weighed particularly heavily on women, something that is dramatized in the film through the recurring presence of the broken elevator in the film.[9]

In an echo of the opening sequence of *El mundo sigue,* the protagonist Gloria (played by Carmen Maura) walks past the broken elevator and prepares to climb the five flights of stairs, leaving some of the bags at the bottom of the stairwell before her ascent. As she enters the apartment, she wipes her brow and rests against the kitchen cupboards to gather her breath, as her mother-in-law (Chus Lampreave) complains 'Como no arreglen pronto el ascensor no voy a poder salir de casa. Me siento como una presa' (If they don't fix the elevator soon I won't be able to leave this house. I feel like a prisoner). Here, the broken elevator compounds the overriding sense of isolation that vertical urbanism has too often brought in Spain, a dynamic that is conveyed elsewhere in the framing of the buildings throughout the film. Frequent establishing shots of the tower blocks, photographed under a wet and wintry sky, emphasize verticality not so much as an indicator of linear progress but as an architecture of alienation. The final establishing shots of the film depict the tower blocks of Concepción straddling the edge of the

M-30 motorway, visually and symbolically separating the *barrio* from the center of the city. Almodóvar commented that 'El barrio de la Concepción es un personaje más. Supone la idea que el señor Banus y Franco tenían del confort, un confort solo digno del proletariado' (The Concepción neighborhood is another character. It implies the ideas that Señor Banus and Franco had about comfort, a comfort only that was only worthy of the proletariat) (Almodóvar 1984). Indeed, despite Spain's dramatically rising consumer power, it continued to be one of the most unequal societies in Europe from the 1960s to the end of the century (Radcliff 2017: 237). This was acutely felt on the urban peripheries, where the economic 'miracle' was barely felt by the majority of unskilled laborers and service sector workers who, like Gloria's family, struggled to make ends meet (Radcliff 2017: 238). Within the working-class suburbs such as Concepción, the broken elevator emerges as a failure of Franco-era housing policy, whereby the contract between property developers such as Banus and the state too often privileged speculation over the social provision of the population. In spite of this, the reliance on the stairwell nevertheless has the advantage of bringing Gloria into regular contact with her neighbors, enabling her to find rare moments of solace and solidarity with Cristal (Verónica Forqué) who lives one story above her, and the young girl Vanessa (Sonia Hohmann), whose supernatural telekinetic powers are able to suddenly halt the elevator midway in its ascent in an early scene.

The presence of broken elevators as an indication of an urban infrastructure that was frequently unfit for its population was similarly a theme in the Spanish comic strip *13, Rue del Percebe* (13, Barnacle Street) created by Francisco Ibáñez. Regularly appearing on the pages of *Tío Vivo* magazine in the 1960s, *13, Rue del Percebe* depicted the lives of several residents in a five-story apartment block. Ibáñez sought to represent the entire country within a page, whereby a cross-section of the building served also as a cross-section of the Spanish population, whose apartments were inhabited by characters such as a grocer, negligent vet and an elderly woman. Significantly, the cartoon revealed not only the interconnected lives of the residents, but the material infrastructures on which their lives depended, from its (usually semi-open) pothole at street level, to the plumbing and the chimney pots on the roof. This was particularly borne out through the running joke of the communal elevator, which emerged as a character in its own right. The elevator was either dangerously malfunctioning, with the carriage plummeting vertiginously to the ground, or frequently missing, thereby leaving unsuspecting users to fall into the elevator shaft below, which is covered in cobwebs.

As Geoffrey Bowker and Susan Leigh Star write, 'good usable [infrastructure] systems disappear almost by definition. The easier they are to use the harder they are to see' (cited in Graham 2010: 7). The failing infrastructure of the building was explicitly laid bare through the design of the page, exposing the inner workings of

FIGURE 5.1: Francisco Ibáñez Talavera, *13, Rue del Percebe*, 1963. Spain. © Editorial Bruguera.

FIGURE 5.2: Álex de la Iglesia (dir.), *La comunidad*, 2000. Spain. © Manga Films.

the elevator (the pulley, the hoist mechanism, the shaftway that is covered in cobwebs, for instance) that are usually invisible to the eye. The influence of *13, Rue de Percebe* has since been felt in the Spanish television comedy series *Aquí no hay quien viva* (No One Could Live Here) (2003–06), which similarly centers on the interconnected lives of inhabitants in a fictional apartment block, and the film *La comunidad* (Common Wealth) (Álex de la Iglesia 2000), a black comedy in which the residents of an apartment building fight over the stash of money that has been left behind by an elderly neighbor.[10] When Julia García (Carmen Maura), an estate agent who has discovered the money, tries to leave the building via the elevator with the money hidden in a suitcase, Domínguez (Enrique Villén) follows her in with a knife. Domínguez stops the elevator so that it is perilously suspended half way between two floors. Situated in the center of the stairwell, the elevator lacks internal security doors (a legal requirement in Spain since 1980 [Anon. 1988: 50]), a failing that swiftly turns out to have fatal consequences. While Julia manages to clamber out onto the landing successfully, Domínguez fails to do so, as the outdated suspension mechanism – whose rusty and cobweb-covered machinery are emphasized through close-up shots – begins to buckle under the weight. The elevator carriage then plummets to the ground, guillotining Domínguez's body in half.

Elevators, Fear and Social Change

If elevators have been associated with social mobility and modernization in Spanish film, they have also been harnessed for their cinematic potential to generate moments of tension and suspense. This can be seen in thrillers such as *Los atracadores* (The Robbers) (Francisco Rovira Beleta 1962) and *Toro* (Kike Maíllo 2016), where the elevator becomes the location of exciting shoot-outs, *Crimen de doble filo* (Double-Edged Crime) (José Luis Borau 1965), where a mysterious murder suspect repeatedly appears in an elevator and *Nadie oyó gritar* (No One Heard the Scream) (Eloy de la Iglesia 1973), where a body is dropped into a narrow elevator shaft. In its ability to elicit feelings of intense anxiety, the elevator here functions both as a setting and as a dramatic strategy, an effect that draws on the long-standing association that elevator travel has with claustrophobia. Stephen Graham has noted that 'the experience of being crammed in a box with strangers moving rapidly upward, pulled by a suite of hidden motors and cables, can induce powerful, almost primeval anxieties' and that psychologists subsequently recognize the fear of elevators as a serious and widespread phobia (Graham 2016: 135). The phobia of elevator travel grew substantially when automated elevators were introduced – a process that began as early as 1892 in the United States, when elevator attendants were phased out and replaced with carriages with push-button control (Hall 2003: 5), with the invention later arriving in Spain in the 1920s (Anon. 1988: 24). The shift from staffed elevators to automated ones, Stephen Graham observes, added 'the sense of desocialized vulnerability' of elevator travel (Graham 2016: 135).

This vulnerability is vividly conveyed in film, in particular, when people find themselves trapped within elevators. Indeed, this is the central conceit in the little-seen short film *El ascensor* (The Elevator) (Tomás Muñoz 1978), in which a disparate group of strangers find themselves helplessly trapped in an elevator carriage.[11] Despite their attempts at operating the button interface of the elevator, the strangers fail to take control of the stalled elevator carriage, their frustration and helplessness a reminder of our own obsolescence in the face of automated technology. Their patience is tested as they begin to panic and fight with one another, with one man taking books out of another man's bag and throwing them out of the elevator carriage onto the adjacent stairwell. The exaggerated physicality of the actors' performances echoes that of silent film acting, where the expansive and gestural style of acting would appear to overcompensate for the lack of words. Their anxiety is compounded by their intimate distance to one another, emphasized through the series of tight and constricting close-up shots of their faces. The relationship between confined space and bodily performance in the scene vividly illustrate the extent to which, as the American engineer and urban planner John J. Fruin has written, 'elevators represent a special circumstance in which pedestrians are willing to submit to closer spacing than they would usually accept' and that the 'involuntary confrontation and contact' at the typically small distance between people in an elevator 'is psychologically disturbing for many reasons' (cited in Paumgarten 2008).

In Eloy de la Iglesia's comedy *Miedo a salir de noche* (Fear of Going Out at Night) (1980), the fear of elevators emerges as a symptom of the broader social anxieties around crime that were felt during Spain's transition to democracy (1975–82). Set in an anonymous middle-class suburb of Madrid, de la Iglesia's film satirizes the ways in which the sensationalist right-wing press generated a moral panic around delinquency through their constant fixation with public insecurity and spiraling crime rates. As Paco, a mild-mannered banker (played by José Sacristán), and his colleague Loli (Tina Sáinz) take the elevator which transports them from the carpark to their office, Loli tells Paco that she was scared to leave her home on the weekend, before anxiously recounting the latest rape case she has heard in the news. As she describes the four suspects as bearded and wearing jackets, the scene cuts briefly to a flashback focalized from Paco's point of view, as he remembers seeing an intimidating group of men who fitted similar description in his local bar. The flashback is accompanied by the nondiegetic sound of a song by Los Chichos, a *rumba* group who were strongly associated with marginality and delinquency during these years. Paco's memory is suddenly disrupted by the sudden grinding of the elevator to a halt. Seeing that the carriage is left suspended between the third and fourth floors, Loli begins to panic and asks if they will soon run out of oxygen. Loli's irrational fear of crime is similarly shared by Paco's wife Begoña (Claudia Gravy), who arranges to have aluminum security doors attached to their apartment – only soon to discover that they are so strong that she becomes trapped inside.

This was an exaggeratedly comic reflection of the extent to which home security had become big business during these years: the sale of antitheft systems in Spain soared considerably between 1975 and 1979 (Hernando Sanz 2001: 266), while insurance companies capitalized on the public fear of crime, running a number of advertising campaigns urging people to secure their property (Huertas et al. 1978: 88). Begoña's fear of the invasion of her apartment extends as far as having a security device fixed in the communal elevator in their building, so that it can only be operated with a special key. Like the security doors, however, the device turns out to be ineffective; Paco is thus seen rushing up the stairs when attempting to rescue his wife from the apartment, as it takes too long to control the elevator. The significance placed on security systems and surveillance in Eloy de la Iglesia's film points to how the cultural imagination of the home, in the face of rapid social and political change, was reshaped by feelings of uncertainty. Yet if home security increasingly demarcates and territorializes the home as a fortress, the persistent noises of sirens, alarms and explosions that can be heard from the streets below constantly disturb the sanctity of the apartment, thereby troubling the boundaries between private and public space in the film. Constituting a threshold between these two spaces, the elevator emerges as a site which, in the words of Susan

Garfinkel, is 'enclosing yet permeable, separate from but integral to the architectural spaces' that surrounds it (2003) – one in which the spatial and social anxieties surrounding public disorder and social change are vividly played out.

As well as considering the elevator as a threshold between two different places, Garfinkel points to how this threshold can also illuminate the temporal dimension of elevator travel, in so far as it draws our attention to the moment of crossing from one state of being to another (Garfinkel 2003: 187). To this effect, she writes that 'we can think of the elevator as a sort of movable threshold that – because of the necessities of gravity – stretches out that crossing point in a suspended moment of time as well as space' (Garfinkel 2003: 187). This can be particularly felt in the film *Alicia en la España de las maravillas* (Alice in the Spain of Wonderland) (Jorge Feliu 1979), a darkly comic and surreal retelling of *Alice's Adventures in Wonderland* in which the protagonist travels back in time to experience the violent repression of the Franco regime. In its fluid exploration of space and time, the narrative appears to follow the jumbled logic of a dream. This is set in motion in an early scene in which the titular Alicia (played here by Mireia Ros) finds herself near a stream, where she sees a naked woman wearing rabbit ears.[12] The woman chases Alicia around the riverbank until she falls down a rabbit hole; yet quite unlike Lewis Carroll's story, the hole leads to an elevator. Alicia is gripped by fear as the elevator begins to make its rapid descent, as a low-angle shot shows the illuminated floor display panel above her head. Hearing the sounds of artillery and bombardments, she looks out of the elevator carriage window. To her surprise, she does not see the elevator's descent into the darkened shaft, but battle scenes from the Spanish Civil War, whose images are represented through excerpts of newsreel footage that have been edited into the sequence. In the film, which was made just after the Amnesty Law of 1977 and the Spanish Constitution one year later, the noise of conflict provides a subversive counterpoint to the *pacto de silencio* (the pact of silence), in which both sides of the historical political divide, Republicans and Nationalists, were granted an amnesty of sorts. Paumgarten has observed that an elevator ride can feel like teleportation, writing that 'you go in here and come out there, and you hardly consider you have raced up or down a vertiginous, pitch-black shaft', without thinking about the fact 'what lurks behind the outer doors is emptiness', which he describes as 'the void' (Paumgarten 2008). In Alicia's teleportation to the period of the Civil War, the void of the shaft – whose darkness is here, as we have seen, replaced with images and sounds of the conflict – assumes a particularly subversive meaning. As a temporal threshold, the location of the elevator therefore becomes central to the political critique of historical memory of Feliu's film.

Through pinpointing how elevators have occupied key moments in the mise en scène and narratives of several Spanish films, I have also sought to show how elevators can further our understanding of the development Spanish architecture and urbanism. If, as we have seen, Spanish cities became increasingly densely populated since the 1950s, access to vertical mobility correspondingly became the central to the lifeblood of Spanish urban life. The analysis of elevator travel can enrich our understanding of the contradictory processes of social mobility and modernization, as well as illuminating the cultural anxieties that Spain has encountered in the face of social and political change. In thinking about elevators conjuncturally, this chapter has shown that elevators do not just move up and down. Indeed, they have transformed the structures and spaces of Spanish cities and urban life, while at the time vividly reminding us of the unevenness and asymmetries that have been integral to these transformations.

Acknowledgments

I would like to thank Sally Faulkner and Alejandro Melero for their helpful suggestions during the initial stages of writing this chapter

NOTES

1. See also Borja Terán (2019), who observes the narrative and symbolic importance of the installation of the elevator in the series.
2. The fictional location of San Genaro was inspired by the *barrio* of Valdezarza in the district of Moncloa, Madrid. See Lázaro (2016).
3. Three groundbreaking monographs on this subject are Tatjana Pavlović's study on automobility, tourism and consumerism *España cambia de piel: The Mobile Nation* (2010), Jorge Pérez's study of the cultural representation of the road in Spanish film and literature and its relationship to national mobility, *Cultural Roundabouts: Spanish Film and Novel on the Road* (2011) and Sally Faulkner's study of social mobility in Spanish cinema *A History of Spanish Film and Society 1910–2010* (2013).
4. In *La torre de los siete jorobados* (The Tower of Seven Hunchbacks) (Edgar Neville) (1944), which is set in late-nineteenth-century Madrid, a song is performed by the vedette known in the film as 'La "Bella Medusa"', whose lyrics suggest the desirable status associated with apartments with elevators within the well-heeled district of Chamberí: 'Mano-la, Mano-la, toca por favor, Te van a poner un piso en Chamberí con ascensor y piano' (Mano-la, Mano-la, please play. They are going to give you an apartment in Chamberí with an elevator and a piano).
5. As Juan Antonio Ríos Carratalá shows, this was particularly the case in the neorealist-inflected *sainete* comedies set in Madrid of Marco Ferreri, Luis García Berlanga and Fernando Fernán Gómez, and the dramas of the José Antonio Nieves Conde, where housing is 'siempre capaz de condicionar de manera determinante la trayectoria de los protaganistas

enfrentados a las carencias, ilusiones y frustraciones derivadas de la problemática posesión de un lugar donde vivir' (always capable of shaping the trajectory of the protagonists who are faced with the economic hardship, dreams and frustrations arising from the problematic possession of a place to live) (Carratalá 1997: 83). As is well known, Nieves Conde's *Surcos* (Furrows) (1951) was the first significant film of this trend.

6. The success of *La vida por delante* swiftly led to its sequel, *La vida alrededor* (The Life Around Us) (Fernando Fernán Gómez, 1959).
7. The elevator is markedly absent in a number of films with choral structures about working-class lives in Madrid in the 1950s, with much of the social interaction between neighbors taking place on the stairwell – and often the courtyard – instead. Examples include *Historia de una escalera* (Story of a Stairway) (Ignacio F. Iquino, 1950), *El batallón de las sombras* (The Battalion in the Shadows) (Manuel Mur Oti, 1957) and *Historias de Madrid* (Stories from Madrid) (Ramón Comas, 1958).
8. The former *barrio* of Maravillas has since been subsumed into the neighborhood of Chueca.
9. Much of the location shooting of the entrance, hallway, stairwells and elevator that appears in the film took place in 4, Avenida de Donostiarra in Concepción, Madrid. The current-day porter of the building told me that the elevator that appeared in the film was replaced in the 1990s, after it had broken down in real life.
10. In Cecilia García's review of the film (2000), where she terms it a 'una película de acción doméstica' (an action film set in domestic space), she compares the block of flats in *La comunidad* to that of *13, Rue del Percebe*.
11. Along with the Spanish films *Las truchas* (The Trouts) (José Luis García Sánchez 1978) and *Las palabras de Max* (Max's Words) (Emilio Martínez-Lázaro 1978), *El ascensor* won the Golden Bear in the Berlin International Film Festival that year. *El ascensor* was shown in cinemas before the screenings of *Las truchas*.
12. Alicia is in fact played by four different actors throughout the course of the film: Mireia Ros, Silvia Aguilar, Montserrat Móstoles and Conxita Bardem.

REFERENCES

Almodóvar, Pedro (1984), press notes for *¿Qué he hecho yo para merecer esto!*.

Anon. (1988), *Ascensores y seguridad: El medio de transporte más utilizado*, Madrid: Euha.

Anon. (2014), 'España, líder mundial en ascensores', *El Mundo*, 13 October, https://www.elmundo.es/economia/2014/10/13/543bc293ca4741b2338b4587.html. Accessed 1 May 2019.

Bernard, Andreas (2014), *Lifted: A Cultural History of the Elevator*, New York: New York University Press.

Cresswell, Tim (2006), *On the Move: Mobility in the Modern Western World*, New York: Routledge.

Cuesta, Amanda (2009), 'Quinquis del barrio', in A. Cuesta (ed.), *Quinquis del 80. Cinema, Premsa I Carrer*, Barcelona: Centre de Cultura Contemporània de Barcelona, pp. 185–95.

Faulkner, Sally (2013), *A History of Spanish Film and Society 1910–2010*, New York: Bloomsbury Academic.

García, Cecilia (2000), 'Alex de la Iglesia: Después de cinco películas ya no creo que pueda asombrar a nadie', *La Razón*, 9 February.

Garfinkel, Susan (2003), 'Elevator stories: Vertical imagination and the space of possibility', in A. Goetz (ed.), *Up Down Across: Elevators, Escalators, and Moving Sidewalks*, London and New York: Merrell Publishers Limited.

Gea Ortigas, María Isabel (2014), *Diccionario breve de Madrid*, Madrid: Ediciones La Libreria.

Graham, Stephen (2010), *Disrupted Cities: When Infrastructure Fails*, London and New York: Routledge.

Graham, Stephen (2016), *Vertical: The City from Satellites to Bunkers*, London: Verso.

Graham, Stephen (2018), 'Vertical mobilities: Confronting the politics of elevators in tall buildings and ultra-deep mining', in M. Freudendal-Pedersen and S. Kesselring (eds), *Exploring Networked Urban Mobilities: Theories, Concepts, Ideas*, London: Routledge, pp. 80–107.

Hall, Peter (2003), 'Designing non-space: The evolution of the elevator interior', in A. Goetz (ed.), *Up Down Across: Elevators, Escalators, and Moving Sidewalks*, London and New York: Merrell Publishers Limited, pp. 59–78.

Hernando Sanz, Felipe Javier (2001), *Espacio y delincuencia*, Madrid: Consejo Económico y Social.

Huertas, J., Caballero Gil, Joan J. and Pascual Miralles, Remei de (1978), *Los hijos de la calle*, Barcelona: Bruguera.

Lázaro, Margarita (2016), 'Dónde está San Genaro, el barrio donde viven los protagonistas de 'Cuéntame' desde hace 15 años', *Huffpost, Tendencias*, 13 September, https://www.huffingtonpost.es/2016/09/13/san-genaro-cuentame_n_10751548.html. Accessed 1 June 2019.

Paumgarten, Nick (2008), 'Up and then down: The lives of elevators', *The New Yorker*, 21 April, https://www.newyorker.com/magazine/2008/04/21/up-and-then-down. Accessed 1 June 2019.

Pavlović, Tatjana (2010), *España cambia de piel: The Mobile Nation*, Bristol: Intellect.

Perec, George (1997), *Species of Spaces and Other Pieces* (trans. and ed. J. Sturrock), London: Penguin Books.

Pérez, Jorge (2011), *Cultural Roundabouts: Spanish Film and Novel on the Road*, Lewisburg: Bucknell University Press.

Phillips, Matt (2014), 'How Spain's bloody history gave it the world's highest concentration of elevators', *Quartz*, 9 October, https://qz.com/273214/how-spains-bloody-history-gave-it-the-worlds-highest-concentration-of-elevators/. Accessed 1 June 2019.

Radcliff, Pamela Beth (2017), *Modern Spain: 1808 to the Present*, Hoboken: Wiley Blackwell.

Ríos Carratalá, Juan Antonio (1997), *Lo sainetesco en el cine español*, Alicante: Universidad de Alicante.

Terán, Borja (2019), 'La felicidad de Herminia dentro de un ascensor y el trasfondo decisivo que simboliza de "Cuéntame"', *La Información*, 22 March, https://www.lainformacion.com/opinion/borja-teran/la-felicidad-de-herminia-dentro-de-un-ascensor-y-el-detalle-decisivo-que-simboliza-de-cuentame/6495490/. Accessed 1 June 2019.

Wynn, Martin (1984), 'Spain', in M. Wynn (ed.), *Housing in Europe*, New York: St Martin's Press, pp. 121–54.

PART 3

SURFACE TENSIONS

6

An Archi-Texture of Pleasure: The *Verbena*, the *Modistilla* and the *Mantón de Manila* in *Rosa de Madrid* (1927)

Juli Highfill, University of Michigan

During the first decades of the twentieth century, a new industry of pleasure transformed the traditional street fairs of Madrid, the *verbenas*, which had originated as festive events in honor of patron saints. Mechanical structures with ornate facades rose high above the neighborhoods, offering dizzying, body-tossing rides and an array of entertainments. At night the fairground became a multicolored 'electric landscape' that announced the new and exciting possibilities of modernity (Bruno 2014: 59).[1] The Machine Age offered new technologies for producing sensory experiences, available to thrill-seekers of all social classes. For brief suspended periods each spring and summer, workers, professionals, merchants, men and women freely mixed – all equal in their pursuit of bodily pleasures.

This new electrified fairground melded easily with age-old festive traditions, adapting to the tastes, fashions, customs and practices of each locale and retaining traces of the carnivalesque. In the modernized *verbenas* of Madrid, the spectacular 'feast for the eyes' was matched by a gastronomic feast of local foods. Fairgoers were immersed in the smells and tastes of local foods – *churros*, *rosquillas*, *tortillas* and *chorizos*, along with wine freely flowing from *botas* and *botijos* ('wineskins' and 'jugs') – as the sounds of *organillos* ('hurdy-gurdies') filled the air, churning out *chotis* in streets transformed into dance-floors.[2] Women strolled through the fairgrounds wearing the embroidered and fringed *mantones de Manila* ('shawls') and carrying painted *abanicos* ('fans'). Taken as a whole, these objects of tradition summoned powerful affective responses from fairgoers, creating a strong sense of cultural belonging. In particular, the decorative *mantones*, draped on women's shoulders and hanging above the fairways, signaled the interweaving of the traditional and industrial in a new archi-texture of pleasure.

Scenes of *verbenas* with their myriad diversions and traditional motifs figure prominently in Spanish cinema of the 1920s and 1930s. In films such as *La revoltosa* (1924), *La condesa María* (1928), *Gigantes y cabezudos* (1926), *La hija de Juan Simón* (1935) and *La verbena de la Paloma* (1935) the street fair, with its sensuous and licentious atmosphere, provided an ideal *locus amoenus* for romance and seduction.[3] It bears noting that cinema evolved in close kinship with the street fair as a spectacle featured in tents and nickelodeons and sharing the same vocation. Both the fairground and cinema sponsor new forms of 'publicness'; in Justus Nieland's words: they are spaces dedicated to 'the contagious, mechanical production of feeling' (Nieland 2008: 23). The architecture of pleasure that moved bodies through space found its analog in motion pictures that likewise 'moved' their spectators, providing the thrills and chills of on-screen adventure and romance.

To be sure, the fairground topos was only one among the various popular entertainments that early cinema drew upon when it was developing its techniques and mobilizing its audience. Miriam Hansen has noted that in the American context, the early film industry relied for its subject matter and representational strategies on a vast repertoire of commercial amusements: 'Wild West, minstrel and magic shows, the burlesque, the playlet, the dance number, pornographic displays, acrobatics, animal acts – all supplied the cinema with subject matter, performance conventions, and viewer expectations' (Hansen 1991: 29). In Spain, early filmmakers drew from similar entertainments, but above all, they looked to the *zarzuela* ('operetta') and *sainete* ('lyric theater') – genres that already enjoyed a mass audience.[4] Typically set in working-class neighborhoods, the *zarzuelas* fondly featured local customs and character types, thus partaking in the *costumbrista* tradition. Not surprisingly, they often included festive scenes of *verbenas*, particularly in their climatic moments. An ongoing cross-fertilization took place among different modes of popular performance, as the fairground festivities were transposed onto the stage in *zarzuelas* and *sainetes*, which in turn were projected onto the screen.

The film *Rosa de Madrid* (1927) displays this melding of popular cultural forms – among them, music, dance, theater and film. The original stage version (1925), written in verse by the *zarzuela* librettist Luis Fernández Ardavín, presented the story of an emblematic working-class *madrileña* who perseveres after being raped and dishonored. Early the following year, Luis Barta, a composer and member of a *zarzuela* family, wrote a catchy *chotis* with lyrics by José Soriano, based on the action in the play. The *chotis* (from *schottische*) is a two-step, slow-spinning dance, typically played by hurdy-gurdies in outdoor fiestas and *verbenas*, and embraced by the popular classes of Madrid since the mid-nineteenth century. To this day, 'Rosa de Madrid' remains one of the best-known songs of the genre, although its lyrics, sung by 'Rosa' in first person, were altered during the Franco era to remove all references to her rape and pregnancy.[5] In 1927, following the success of both the *chotis* and the play, Eusebio Fernández Ardavín, the playwright's brother, directed a film version that rejected the traditional, moralistic message of the play, thus affirming the relative freedom of the 'new woman' of the 1920s.

Early in *Rosa de Madrid*, the fairground becomes the site where the protagonists – the seamstress, Rosa, and the medical student, Enrique – meet and begin their romance. A series of parallel scenes have already introduced two groups of characters with plans to attend the Verbena de San Antonio that evening. While a group of medical students, all men, exit their *facultad* and convene in a billiard hall, another group of young *modistillas* ('dressmakers'), sporting bobbed hair and short skirts, leave the Madame Modes workshop after a day's work. In an abrupt shift, the fairground scene opens with a panoramic view of mechanical rides in motion – swinging gondolas in the foreground and a spinning carousel behind – followed by mini-cars whirling across the screen. Suddenly, the different shots overlap and converge, creating a dizzying montage of revolving rides packed with thrill-seekers. The segment culminates with a cardboard doll, wrapped in a *mantón de Manila* imprinted with roses (see Figure 6.1). Her eyes moving side to

FIGURE 6.1: Eusebio Fernández Ardavín (dir.), *Rosa de Madrid*, 1928. Spain. © Producciones Ardavín. Courtesy of the Filmoteca Española (Spanish National Film Archive).

FIGURE 6.2: Eusebio Fernández Ardavín (dir.), *Rosa de Madrid*, 1928. Spain. © Producciones Ardavín. Courtesy of the Filmoteca Española (Spanish National Film Archive).

side, the doll appears superimposed over a kettle of *churros* – a synesthetic scene that draws us, the spectators, into the swirl of multiple, heightened sensations of the street fair.

Immediately afterwards, the medical students appear at a booth that offers views of the firmament. While gazing through the telescope, they *descubre un nuevo lucero* ('discover a new star') in this otherworldly site of the fair. We too share the view through the circular lens, which moves upwards – first focusing on a woman's legs, sheathed in silk stockings, then on the fringe of the embroidered *mantón* and finally on Rosa herself, seated side-saddle on a carousel horse, mutely speaking the flirtatious language of the hand fan (Figure 6.2). As the carousel spins, a large crowd of male voyeurs (the medical students among them) jostle for a better view of Rosa and the other *modistillas*, their eyes avidly following the 'moving picture' before them. When the students themselves get on board, symptoms of vertigo ensue.

Writing of carnival scenes in *The Cabinet of Dr. Caligari*, Siegfried Kracauer described the fair as 'an enclave of anarchy in a sphere of entertainment [which] accounts for its eternal attractiveness. People of all classes and ages enjoy losing themselves in a wilderness of glaring colors and shrill sounds' which abounds 'in bodily sensations – from violent shocks to tastes of incredible sweetness' (Kracauer 1974: 73). The fairground sequence in *Rosa de Madrid*, while calling for a similar sensorial response from the audience, goes further by prompting a reflexive commentary on the film apparatus itself. Like the other mechanical rides, the merry-go-ground, with its blur of mounted figures, replicates the spinning film reel and the rush of photograms passing before the lamp. This metacommentary is even further extended via a direct gesture toward the audience. In a pair of reverse shots, the camera first provides a frontal view of the crowd of voyeurs, as if mirroring *us*, the crowd seated before the screen. Then it switches position, offering a view from within the on-screen crowd, so that 'we see what they see' and thus partake in the voyeuristic gaze. We are thereby drawn into the *populus*, into *popular* culture – that plane 'of belonging and identification' where 'affective relationships are articulated' (Nieland 2008: 20). It is no coincidence, then, that over the heads of the carnival crowd, we see a paradigmatic emblem of the popular, the *mantón de Manila*, hanging from a line, its fringe swaying in the breeze.

From the mid-nineteenth century onward, the *mantón de Manila* appears repeatedly – in *zarzuelas*, *sainetes* and later in film – as a powerful signifier for traditional popular culture. Metonymically, it stands for the woman of the people and bespeaks the language of coquetry. The colorful silk shawl was worn on festive occasions throughout the nineteenth and early twentieth centuries by women of all classes: by *majas* and *chulapas*, *cupletistas* and flamenco dancers, as well as by working-class women dancing the *chotis* in the *verbenas* of Madrid. Galdós in his novel *Fortunata y Jacinta* (1887) eloquently paid homage to the *mantón de Manila*: 'Envolverse en él es como vestirse con un cuadro. La industria moderna no inventará nada que iguale a la ingenua poesía del mantón salpicado de flores, flexible, pegadizo y mate, con aquel fleco que tiene algo de los enredos del sueño' (To wrap oneself in such a shawl is to be dressed in a painting. Modern industry has never invented anything equal to the guileless poetry of the shawl, strewn with flowers, supple, clinging, and smooth, with that fringe that suggests the entanglements of a dream) (Pérez Galdós 2015: 26). However, as Galdós wryly observes, a central irony inheres in this emblem of Spanish *casticismo*: 'esta prenda, esta nacional obra de arte, tan nuestra como las panderetas o los toros, no es nuestra en realidad más que por el uso' (this garment, this national work of art, as much ours as are tambourines and bullfights, in reality it is ours only by usage). For indeed, the *mantón* is entirely of foreign origin; an export from China, brought to Spain by Philippine middlemen during the Age of Empire. When inserted into cultural works – in films such as *La revoltosa*, *La verbena de la Paloma* and *Rosa de Madrid* – the *mantón* unfolds as 'memory fabric', as history worn, to borrow Giuliana Bruno's phraseology (Bruno 2014: 44). Such intimate objects of material culture serve as 'sensitive mnemonic fabrications'; they immediately elicit associative chains – recollections of empire, of collective gaiety, of sensual and aesthetic pleasure, feelings of belonging, thus creating a 'public intimacy of lived space' (Bruno 2014: 32). Nieland reminds us of a certain conservatism embedded in these cultural metaphors; with their soothing contact, they can elicit involuntary sympathies, 'contagious mimicry and hypnotic political identifications', which come to exert a kind of discipline (Nieland 2008: 23). In its tactile and sensuous address, the *mantón* figuratively dresses spectators, envelops them, acting as a *habit* (as both custom and garment) while drawing us into the *habitus* – that ensemble of social practices, attitudes, tastes and dispositions characteristic of a given culture.[6]

As a material metaphor, the *mantón de Manila* in *Rosa de Madrid* undoubtedly produces that soothing effect of cultural identification – that sense of belonging to the habitus, of being one among *el pueblo* of Madrid. But the ultimate effect in this film, I would argue, is not so much cultural discipline (in Nieland's sense), but rather an attempt to interweave popular traditions with the new possibilities of modern life, particularly for young working women. In a key scene, Rosa, on her Saint's Day, delights in a magnificent *mantón*, brought by a friend to brighten the setting for the party soon to take place. Alone in her workshop, Rosa lifts and caresses the shawl; then with a flourish, she wraps it around her body (Figure 6.3).

Arms akimbo, she sashays across the room, turning and admiring herself in the mirror. The shawl's surface, embroidered with roses, undulates with the movements of her body, as the long fringe swings back and forth. In an intertitle, lines from the stage play appear on screen: '¡Mantoncito de Manila! / ¡Rico pañuelo chinés! / Que se ciñe y se perfila / De los hombros a los pies' (Sweet shawl of Manila! / Rich Chinese silk! / that encircles and shapes the body / from shoulders to feet) (L. Fernández Ardavín 1954: 69). Enrique enters and observes from the doorway, exclaiming, '¡Vaya, estampa bonita!' (What a pretty picture!) (L. Fernández Ardavín 1954: 24). Although now engaged to another, Enrique goes on to declare his enduring love for Rosa. Since their first meeting long ago on the carousel, through her long disappearance, and after finding her abandoned and near death in the charity hospital where she gave birth, Enrique has remained 'entangled by the fringes of the *mantón*' – as he confesses in the play (L. Fernández Ardavín 1954: 24). However, Rosa's sense of honor compels her to reject his entreaties; she responds by asking, '¿Olvidas que para amante soy honrada y para esposa no lo fui? [...] La fatalidad hace imposible nuestro amor' (Do you forget that as a lover I am virtuous, while as a wife I was not? [...] Fate has made our love impossible) (E. Fernández Ardavín 1927: intertitle). Enrique, soon to be married, is a well-established doctor; Rosa is a single mother, a worker struggling to support herself and her child. Thus, within the narrative and thematic logic, the

FIGURE 6.3: Eusebio Fernández Ardavín (dir.), *Rosa de Madrid*, 1928. Spain. © Producciones Ardavín. Courtesy of the Filmoteca Española (Spanish National Film Archive).

mantón marks the barriers of class and gender, as well as the fluid but frustrated desire that would render the fabric malleable and permeable.

But the rigidity of those normative barriers becomes fully evident in subsequent scenes. First, Enrique's fiancée enters, observes him together with Rosa and reclaims her rights. Then during Rosa's Saint's Day banquet, the military officer responsible for her fate unexpectedly arrives. As they stand in the hall, removed from the guests, Miguel expresses his remorse for having violated and abandoned her. A few years before, while Enrique was away, Rosa had gone with her fellow *modistillas* to a *fiesta* in La Bombilla Park on the outskirts of Madrid. Amid the festivities, Enrique's friend, Miguel, gained Rosa's trust while enticing her with a bottomless glass of wine, as an *organillo* cranked out a *chotis*. Once she became inebriated, Miguel led her into the woods and took advantage. Rosa thus became a victim of date-rape, a common motif in Spanish cinema of the 1920s and 1930s.[7] Now, in response to Miguel's belated desire to 'pay his debts' and recognize his daughter, she emphatically rejects his offer: '¿Tu hija? ¿Quién es tu hija? ¿La que yo sola y desamparada traje a este mundo? ¿La que primero fue mi vergüenza y ahora es mi orgullo y mi esperanza? ¡Esa es hija mía! De ti. ¡No es nada!' (Your daughter? She whom I brought into this world, while destitute and all alone? She who was once my shame and is now my pride and hope? She is my daughter! To you [...] she is nothing!) (E. Fernández Ardavín 1927: intertitles). In this dramatic confrontation, the film underscores its critique of the double standard, a critique that would be reiterated in films from the late twenties through the years of the Second Republic – among them, *La condesa María* (1928), *La bodega* (1930), *La hija de Juan Simón* (1935), *Nobleza baturra* (1935), *¿Quién me quiere a mí?* (1936), *¡Centinela, alerta!* (1937) – at a time when the religious and social strictures on women's lives were losing their hold.[8] Not coincidently, in *Rosa de Madrid*, this tense encounter between Rosa and her rapist takes place before the altar to the Virgen de la Paloma, draped with the same *mantón de Manila* that Rosa had worn shortly before. Here the shawl works figuratively to mark the quandary faced by Rosa and other independent women in this time of transition – caught between the pressure to adhere to tradition and their desire to form part of the texture of modern life.

But beyond the thematic function of the *mantón*, this malleable, multivalent emblem also operates as metacommentary, making implicit reference to a film screen and by extension the sentient skin of the spectator. The scene when Rosa walks across the room while wrapped in the *mantón* – its embroidered roses rippling, its fringe swaying – echoes the fairground montage with the blur of bodies rushing by; for in both sequences the audience is asked to contemplate a 'motion picture within the motion picture'. More specifically, the *mantón*-in-motion calls for a haptic response from the audience, summoning an intimate, tactile relation with the screen – an 'ocular touching' in the words of Fernando Vela. In his influential essay of 1925, 'Desde la ribera oscura' (From the Dark Side of the River), Vela asserts that 'el cine nos enseña a ver, y con su gran lupa y su reflector nos lleva los ojos como de la mano y nos obliga a palpar ocularmente el controno de las cosas, a fijarnos en los mil movimientos' (Cinema teaches us to see, and with its great magnifying glass and reflector it summons not only our eyes but also our hands, and it obliges us to ocularly touch the surface of things, to attend to a thousand subtle movements) (Vela 1925: 209). In early cinema at large, the ubiquity of haptic gestures also reveals the medium's self-awareness of its disembodiment, its detachment from the audience, as if it might compensate for its own ephemerality. Hence, the frequent close-ups of silken skin, the backgrounds with rich fabrics, and the vertiginous fairground montages – all designed to invoke tactile vision, Vela's 'ocular touch'.[9]

Interspersed throughout *Rosa de Madrid* are occasional interruptions in the narrative thread that solicit an embodied, sensuous gaze, and which hearken back to the early 'cinema of attractions' – even though, by the 1920s, narrative film held sway. Tom Gunning, in his seminal essay, reminds us of how, during the first two decades of cinema (1890–1910), the audience encountered the new art primarily at the fairground, where it was one attraction among many (Gunning 1986: 65). When Sergei Eisenstein first conceived of a 'montage of attractions', he took his cues from the fairground rides, with the aim of subjecting the spectator to a 'sensorial and psychological impact' akin to a ride on a roller-coaster (Eisenstein, qtd. in Gunning 1986: 66). That impact could also be achieved through direct address, as when a vaudeville entertainer or carnival barker interacts with members of audience. Toward that end, the cinema of attractions flaunted its visibility; it sought to show what it could show, thus rupturing the fictional illusion as it engaged the audience. Even after the advent of continuity editing, Gunning notes, elements of the cinema of attractions – occasional exhibitions of visibility – continued to appear in narrative films such as *Rosa de Madrid*. We might recall the cardboard doll in that early fairground scene, a stand-in for Rosa herself. The figure is wrapped in a *mantón*; her eyes turn to each side and then look directly at the audience, thereby 'returning the gaze', asking us to attend to the surface of the screen, thus inviting a reflexive reading of cinematic experience (Kracauer, qtd. in Hansen 2012: 270).

But after each such interruption in the storyline, the magic of continuity editing works to reestablish the storyline and to draw us back into the fictional world, ensuring that we respond to the charm and sheer goodness of this emblematic working-class *madrileña*. We watch as Rosa, unlike the doomed fallen women in nineteenth-century literature, redeems herself through her virtue and hard work. It is significant that she is a *modistilla*, one among the thousands of seamstresses at work in Madrid at a time when *prêt-à-porter* was not yet widely available, and most middle- and upper-class women relied upon small workshops that produced fashionable *confecciones* suited to their tastes.[10] The popular term *modistilla*, the diminutive of *modista*, reflected a social prejudice against women who worked outside the home. According to historian Adela Nuñez Orgáz, the *modistillas*, like the *cigarreras* ('cigar rollers'), were considered women of questionable virtue: 'frecuentadoras de bailes y verbenas, con tendencias a prostituirse, [y] aficionadas a bebida' (habitués of dances and street fairs, with a tendency to become prostitutes, [and] a fondness for drink) (Nuñez Orgáz 1989: 436). Yet, as was the case with the nineteenth-century *cigarreras*, a cultural mystique developed around the *modistillas*. Their relative economic independence, their presence in public spaces, their presumed availability – all served to foster a widespread, erotically tinged fascination with young dressmakers. And although of limited means, the *modistillas*' skill with the needle enabled them to dress with flair.

The cultural fascination with these workers was reflected in popular performance, as the *modistilla* became a key character-type in *zarzuelas* and *sainetes* – among them, *El barberillo de Lavapiés* (Francisco Asenjo Barbieri 1874), *Las modistillas* (Sinesio Delgado 1885), *El año pasado por agua* (Federico Chueca and Joaquín Valverde 1889), *Me llaman la presumida* (Anselmo C. Carreño and Francisco Ramos de Castro 1935) – and in popular songs such as 'Batallón de modistas', 'Las alegres modistillas' and the *chotis* 'Rosa de Madrid'. The depictions of the *modistilla* in these works served to consolidate their *costumbrista* image as vivacious, flirtatious *pícaras* who sought out young *señoritos*, particularly students, to escort them to *verbenas* and outdoor cafes. Their appeal arose simultaneously from their boldness in deviating from the traditional feminine role and their adherence to the archetype of the saucy *madrileña*. As Angel del Río López notes in his study of the 'old professions' of Madrid: 'Se ha dicho que la modistilla es la que mejor ha representado siempre el espíritu y la personalidad de la mujer de Madrid' (It is said that it is the dressmaker who has always best represented the spirit and personality of the woman of Madrid) (del Río López 1993: 133). By the time the film *Rosa de Madrid* appeared in 1927, the archetype of the *modistilla* was already well established in popular performance and deeply rooted in the popular imagination.[11]

In contrast with the iconic image of the *modistillas*, their social reality was often harsh. Starting in adolescence as unpaid apprentices, the women worked closely together in small, poorly ventilated rooms at low wages for long hours, although gradually, over time, legislation limited their working day.[12] Yet despite these hardships, the evidence shows that the *modistillas* themselves took pride in their craft, savored their relative freedom and placed a high value on the comradeship they enjoyed at work and in their leisure time. Pilar Díaz Sánchez cites an interview with a seamstress, Petra Cuevas, who in the 1920s sewed in a large workshop: 'Había chicas de quince, dieciséis, hasta veinte años, todo lo más eran chicas de veinte años [...]; el ambiente era estupendo con tantas chicas jóvenes' (There were young girls from ages fifteen or sixteen up to twenty, the majority being girls in their twenties [...]; the atmosphere was fantastic with so many young girls) (Díaz Sánchez 1999: 281). She describes their outings in large groups composed of tailors and dressmakers, as they strolled along the Calle Alcalá: 'allí te salían novios [...], ¡la edad! [...], nosotras éramos bastante gamberras [...], nos reíamos mucho de todo el mundo' (you would find boyfriends there [...], we were at that age! [...], we were happy-go-lucky [...], we laughed a lot at everything) (Díaz Sánchez 1999: 281). Cuevas would go on to become a founder and leader of her local union, the Sindicato de la Aguja, and she recalls how, during the years of the Republic, the union established a library in her workshop. But even before the seamstresses began organizing in the 1930s, they participated in events and festivals that honored their profession – in *concursos* ('competitive fashion shows') and in celebrations that paid homage to the patron saint of their profession.[13] The dressmakers increasingly gained visibility, and their activities were often featured in the press. As Maite Barragán has observed in her study of visual culture and class in Madrid, the *modistillas* played a significant role in 'modeling a modern Madrid' (Barragán 2017: 28).[14] Over time, this traditional icon of the woman of the people converged with the image of the 'new woman', as the *modistillas* became integrated into the fabric of modern urban life.

The film *Rosa de Madrid* participates in this modernization of the archetype by resituating the *modistilla* in the vibrant commercial culture of the 1920s. Rosa becomes upwardly mobile, establishing a modest workshop and employing her former fellow workers. Scenes of camaraderie abound in the film, showing mischievous young seamstresses at work – gossiping, teasing, and laughing together – with Rosa, now the *maestra*, presiding benevolently over the group. Thanks to her talent and industriousness, the workshop prospers, and after a few years ascends to the level of high *couture*, designing and producing garments for the upper-class women of Madrid. A *desfile de modas* ('fashion show') – held in an elegant hall filled with well-dressed women and their husbands – marks her triumph. The models descend from a stage wearing embroidered, fur-trimmed coats, which, when removed, reveal the shimmering, short dresses that reflect the straight silhouette of the 1920s (see Figure 6.4). Long shots of the *desfile*, taken from a stationary camera at the rear of the room, alternate with reaction shots, showing the young women awed, the older women scandalized and their husbands titillated by the revealing new fashions. Among the most dramatic dresses is a silvery chemise with a dropped waist, its skirt covered with scalloped fringe that swings with the model's gait, echoing the movement of fringed *mantón*.

From the *mantón de Manila* to the spangled flapper dress, the *chulapa madrileña* is refashioned and refabricated as the 'new woman'. The film thus attempts to seamlessly meld popular, traditional culture with modernity. And ultimately, through an unlikely and maudlin 'happy ending' (facilitated by the suicide of Enrique's wife), Rosa and Enrique are united in marital bliss. The storyline harmoniously blends cyclical and linear time, starting from the revolving carousel and then unspooling as Rosa follows a downward then upward path. While occurring over a period of years, the action turns in accord with clearly marked 'seasons' – the spring of romance, the summer of dishonor, the fall of hardship and winter of despair, followed by another spring of redemption. The hyper-romanticized final shot, showing Rosa and Enrique in a flower-filled garden, is preceded by an image of a revolving earth – reiterating the merry-go-round – with the intertitle: 'La vida sigue su giro eternamente' (Life continues to turn, eternally) (E. Fernández Ardavín 1927: intertitle).

FIGURE 6.4: Eusebio Fernández Ardavín (dir.), *Rosa de Madrid*, 1928. Spain. © Producciones Ardavín. Courtesy of the Filmoteca Española (Spanish National Film Archive).

In redeeming the fallen woman, the film reflects the new freedoms and relaxed gender norms of the 1920s, and in so doing, makes a substantial departure from the play, written and staged just two years before (1925). The play offers a strong defense of traditionalism, summed up in an *intermedio* that mourns the death of Old Madrid: '¡Madrid, el viejo, se está muriendo! / ¡Nos abandona! ¡No volverá! [...] Vendió su alma por lo aparente de una mundana modernidad (The old Madrid is dying! / It is abandoning us and will never return! [...] it sold its soul for the semblance / of a mundane modernity) (L. Fernández Ardavín: 1954: 103–04). The eulogist goes on to decry the new Madrid's 'Parisian air', its 'taste for whiskey and make-up', its enthusiasm for football and boxing. Now the city has become 'an image from a magazine', wearing an expression that is 'very twentieth-century, very "Gran Hotel" ' (L. Fernández Ardavín 1954: 103–04).

This *intermedio* appears at the end of act two, after a funeral procession has passed under the balcony of Rosa's workshop. Madrid is mourning the death of

Tomás Bretón, the composer of the *zarzuela* titled *La verbena de la Paloma* (1894). Echoes of Bretón's work have already resounded through the play, given that at the end of each act, an accordion plays a song from the same *zarzuela*, '¿Dónde vas con mantón de Manila?' (Where are you going in your *mantón de Manila*?). As metaphor and motif, the *mantón* is omnipresent in the play, making an affective appeal that enwraps the audience in a soothing sense of nostalgia. Modernity, meanwhile, represents a menace: Rosa's rapist, an army pilot, is called a 'bird of prey'; the fashion show is deemed scandalous; and Rosa's dishonor is irrevocable. Compelled by social norms to refuse Enrique, she exclaims: 'Esa mancha que no se quita! / ¡La que siempre se lleva sobre la frente! / ¡La mancha vergonzosa negra y maldita! / ¡La que ha de separarnos para siempre!' (That stain that cannot be washed away / That one always wears on the forehead / the shameful stain, black and cursed / that must separate us forever) (L. Fernández Ardavín 1954: 73). On this point, the film presents a striking contrast by challenging the cultural norms that have long stigmatized all women deemed dishonored – in effect, showing that the 'shameful stain' is not indelible. And while in the film the *mantón* is equally present as a dominant trope, its affective appeal reflects a new desire – widespread among the public by this time – the desire to be modern, to embrace the new technologies, possibilities and freedoms of the era. The garment is capacious enough to envelop the motifs of modern urban life: the flapper dresses and bobbed hair, the newly purchased radio, Enrique's gleaming automobile, the electrified fairground and, above all, the free and easy interactions among the young *modistillas* and students. Moreover, the translation from the theater to the new medium of cinema in itself marks an embrace of modernity, further reinforced by the kinship established between the *mantón* and the film screen.

Despite its contrived and sentimental plot (we are, after all, in the domain of melodrama), I would submit that on both the narrative and formal registers, the film engages in what Nieland calls 'public pedagogy' (Nieland 2008: 3). He contends that cinema of the 1920s served as a 'training ground' that enabled 'the public to adapt playfully to new possibilities' (Nieland 2008: 3). On this point, Nieland cites Miriam Hansen who has argued that commercial film to a significant degree provided 'a matrix for modernity's liberatory impulses – its moments of abundance, play, and radical possibility, its glimpses of collectivity and gender equality' (Hansen 1999: 69). For Hansen, the 'mass-produced and mass-consumed phenomena of fashion, design, advertising, architecture and urban environment, of photography, radio, and cinema' – as well as the electrified street fairs, I might add – all comprised a 'vernacular modernism' that altered the 'fabric of everyday life, sociability, and leisure' (Hansen 1999: 59, 65). Hansen argues that 'cinema was capable of a reflexive relation with modernity and modernization', and furthermore, 'modernization inevitably provokes the need for reflexivity' (Hansen 1999: 69–70). As we have seen, *Rosa de Madrid* contains such instances of reflexive meta-commentary – notably, in the scenes with the spinning fairground rides and the rippling *mantón*; but more broadly, we also find a reflection on the profound changes that modernization had wrought upon social life at large. Thus, although a commercial melodrama, and while not engaging politics in an overt sense, the film cautiously nudges its audience toward a new sexual politics – a secular sexuality that challenges traditional Catholic morality. On the narrative register, it reflects the rapid modernization of the 1920s and anticipates the new freedoms of the second Republic. On the meta-register, the figures of the fairground and the *mantón* invite the public to read reflexively, to ponder that changing 'fabric of everyday life' as well as to reflect on mass mediation and sensory experience in a new society of spectacle. In so doing, the film solicits a haptic response – an *affective effect* at once involuntary and contemplative, while gesturing toward politics in the broad sense of the term. As Brian Massumi suggests: 'Affect is proto-political. It concerns the first stirrings of the political, flush with the felt intensities of life' (Massumi 2015: ix). 'To affect and be affected is to be open to the world, to be active in it', to be embedded in 'a larger field of life', a 'field of belonging' (Massumi 2015: ix, 6, 18). This openness, Massumi argues, is potentially 'the cutting edge of change' (Massumi 2015: ix).

During a time of vertiginous social change, *Rosa de Madrid* marshalled the affective power of cinema – its unique capacity to manufacture feeling – and invited its viewers to belong to this new archi-texture of urban life and to embrace its liberatory possibilities. A few years hence, the new sexual politics sponsored by the film, including the new freedoms for women, would be extended and legitimized by the Second Republic. For viewers today, however, it is unsettling to look back at a film that so exuberantly reflects this period of promise, while recalling how 36 years of dictatorship, under the auspices of National Catholicism, reversed those advances. Yet there is something to honor and knowledge to glean from these vivid cultural expressions of a moment in time when citizens so avidly desired and seized upon the new potentialities of modern life.

NOTES

1. Bruno refers here to Coney Island. I was unable to find historical or cultural studies dealing with the Spanish context. Scholarly work thus far has focused on American and British amusement parks and fairs. However, these studies can be extrapolated to Spain, given the similar development of the industrialized urban fairground throughout the western world: see Bennet (1986), Kane (2013, 2017), Rabinovitz (2012), Toulmin (2003) and Wood (2017).

2. The *chotis* (from *schottische*), although called the 'Scottish dance', originated in Germany; it is a partnered dance with a slow polka rhythm.
3. *La Revoltosa* (1924) was directed by Florián Rey; *La condesa María* (1928) by Benito Perojo; *Gigantes y cabezudos* (1925) by Florián Rey; *La hija de Juan Simón* (1935) by Nemesio M. Sobrevila and José Luis Sáenz de Heredia; *La verbena de la Paloma* (1935) by Benito Perojo.
4. Cánovas Belchi adds to his article a 'Catálogo de películas de zarzuela' that cites 81 films produced in Spain between 1896 and 1937 (the list continues up to 1985). Note that these '*zarzuela* films' are broadly defined, including short segments with songs and *sainetes*, and a number of popular *zarzuelas* underwent several film adaptations (Belchi 2011: 82–85).
5. Sara Montiel famously sang the sanitized version of 'Rosa de Madrid', beside a *pianola* in *La violetera* (1958).
6. As conceived by the sociologist Pierre Bourdieu, *habitus* is simultaneously cognitive and embodied, internal and external; it is 'not only a structuring structure, which organizes practices and the perception of practices, but also a structured structure', a positioning within a social field of power relations and an outcome of a historical process (Bourdieu 2010: 166).
7. I have found no scholarly work on rape in Spanish film in the 1920s and 1930s, despite its prevalence as a plot motif. However, scholars have addressed rape as represented in film from the Franco and post-Franco eras. See Gil Gascón (2010) and Martin-Márquez (1999).
8. *La condesa María* (1928) and *La bodega* (1930) were directed by Benito Perojo; *Nobleza baturra* (1935) by Florián Rey; *La Hija de Juan Simón* (1935) and *¿Quién me quiere a mí?* (1936) by José Luis Sáenz de Heredia (with Luis Buñuel as non-credited co-director); *¡Centinela, alerta!* (1937) by Jean Grémillon (also with Luis Buñuel as uncredited co-director).
9. For discussions of hapticity in film see the essays by Burch (1990), Lant (1995) and Marks (1998).
10. In her historical study, Nuñez Orgáz observes the difficulty in determining the number of *modistas* working in Madrid in the first decades of the century, given that labor statistics at that time did not differentiate according to gender. Utilizing available data for the year 1905, she was able to make an estimate, based on a list of specific jobs typically performed by women; she infers that of the 23,959 workers in the needle trades, the majority would have been women (Nuñez Orgáz 1989: 437). For other studies on the *modistas*, refer to Barragán (2017), del Río López (1993), Díaz Sánchez (1999) and Mendoza Gurrea and García de la Noceda (1999).
11. Fernández Colorado notes that another film (long lost), *Estudiantes y modistillas* (Juan Antonio Cabero), premiered a few months before *Rosa de Madrid*; the former film overshadowed the latter and significantly undermined its success (Fernández Colorado 1997: 66). The original play by Antonio Casero, *Estudiantes y modistillas: Comedia asainetada y peliculesca en tres actos*, features a dishonored *modistilla*, who bears a child, and is ultimately redeemed and reunited with her repentant seducer. Like *Rosa de Madrid*, this play condemns the injustice of the double standard, notably in a young woman's

lines: 'yo no sé con qué derecho nos tratan como a un pitillo cualquiera, que se fuma, y la colilla, al arroyo' (I don't know by what right they treat us like a cigarette that after they smoke it, they throw the butt to the gutter) (Casero 1929: 57).

12. According to Nuñez Orgáz, the *modistillas*' working hours, often fourteen hours during the nineteenth century, was reduced to eleven hours in 1900, to ten in 1907 and eight in 1919, with Sunday as a day of leisure (Nuñez Orgáz 1989: 441–42).
13. *Modistillas en imágenes*, edited by Mendoza Gurrea and García de la Noceda, contains photographs of the *modistillas* of Barcelona and Valencia, who celebrated Saint's Day of Santa Lucía. For the *modistillas* of Madrid, San Antonio de Padua was their patron saint. They celebrated on 13 June by visiting the Ermita de San Antonio de la Florida and by attending the Verbena de San Antonio – the same fair that Rosa attends in the film.
14. I am indebted to Maite Barragán for calling my attention to the cultural significance of the *modistilla*. See her chapter, 'The fabric of the city: Magazines, modistillas, and the Gran Vía', which includes a discussion of a stunning photograph from *Estampa* (21 February 1928). The image shows a crowd of stylish *modistillas* holding open copies of the same magazine as they advance abreast along the Gran Vía, the city's most modern avenue. '[A]t once readers and features of the magazine', they 'perform for the camera as literate, urbane, and apparently independent characters and embody the 1920s ideal of womanhood' (Barragán 2017: 33).

REFERENCES

Anon. (1999), *El mantón de Manila*, exhibition catalog, Museo Municipal de Madrid, Madrid, Fundación Loewe.

Bakhtin, Mikhail (1984), *Rabelais and His World* (trans. Hélens Iswolsky), Bloomington: Indiana University Press.

Barragán, Maite (2017), 'Mediating modernity: Visual culture and class in Madrid, 1926–1935', Ph.D. thesis, Philadelphia: Temple University.

Bennet, Tony (1986), 'Hegemony, ideology, pleasure: Blackpool', in T. Bennet and C. Mercer and J. Woollacott (eds), *Popular Culture and Social Relations*, Milton Keynes, UK: Open University Press, pp. 135–54.

Bourdieu, Pierre (2010), *Distinction: A Social Critique of the Judgement of Taste* (trans. Robert Nice), London: Routledge.

Braithwaite, David (1968), *Fairground Architecture: The World of Amusement Parks, Carnivals, and Fairs*, New York: Frederick A. Praiger.

Bruno, Giuliana (2014), *Surfaces: Matters of Aesthetics, Materiality, and Media*, Chicago: University of Chicago Press.

Burch, Noël (1990), *Life to Those Shadows* (trans. Ben Brewster), Berkeley: University of California Press.

Cánovas Belchi, Joaquín (2011), 'Identidad nacional y cine español: El género chico en el cine mudo español, a propósito de la adaptación cinematográfica de *La verbena de la paloma* de José Buchs, 1921', *Quintana*, 10, pp. 65–87.

Casero, Antonio (1929), *Estudiantes y modistillas: Comedia asainetada y peliculesca en tres actos*, Madrid: La Farsa.

Díaz Sánchez, Pilar (1999), 'Del taller de costura a la fábrica: El trabajo de las mujeres en la confección-textil madrileña', *Cuadernos de Historia Contemporánea*, 21, pp. 279–93.

Fernández Ardavín, Eusebio (1927), *Rosa de Madrid,* Spain, Producciones Ardavín.

Fernández Ardavín, Luis (1954), *Rosa de Madrid, Comedia popular en tres actos y en verso*, Colección Teatro 102, Madrid: Ediciones Alfil.

Fernández Colorado, Luis (1997), '*Rosa de Madrid* 1927', in J. Pérez Perucha (ed.), *Antología crítica del cine español, 1906–1995*, Madrid: Cátedra/Filmoteca, pp. 65–67.

Gil Gascón, Fátima (2010), 'Rape and sexual harassment in Spanish cinema during the early years of the Francoist regime', *International Journal of Iberian Studies*, 23:3, pp. 179–95.

Gunning, Tom (1986), 'The cinema of attraction: Early film, its spectator and the avant-garde', *Wide Angle*, 8:3–4, pp. 63–70.

Hansen, Miriam (1991), *Babel and Babylon: Spectatorship in American Silent Film*, Cambridge: Harvard University Press.

Hansen, Miriam (1999), 'The mass production of the senses: Classical cinema as vernacular modernism', *Modernism/Modernity*, 6:2, pp. 59–77.

Hansen, Miriam (2012), *Cinema and Experience: Siegfried Kracauer, Walter Benjamin, and Theodor Adorno*, Berkeley: University of California Press.

Kane, Josephine (2013), *The Architecture of Pleasure: British Amusement Parks, 1900–1939*, Ashgate Studies in Architecture, Farnham: Ashgate.

Kane, Josephine (2017), 'Mechanical pleasures: The appeal of the British amusement parks, 1910–1914', in J. Wood (ed.), *The Amusement Park: History, Culture and the Heritage of Pleasure*, London: Routledge, pp. 31–56.

Kracauer, Siegfried (1974), *From Caligari to Hitler: A Psychological History of the German Film*, Princeton: Princeton University Press.

Lant, Antonia (1995), 'Haptical Cinema', *October*, 74, pp. 45–73.

Marks, Laura U. (1998), 'Video haptics and erotics', *Screen*, 39:4, pp. 331–48.

Martin-Márquez, Susan (1999), *Feminist Discourse and Spanish Cinema: Sight Unseen*, Oxford: Oxford University Press.

Massumi, Brian (2015), *Politics of Affect*, Cambridge, UK: Polity.

Mendoza Gurrea, Iñaki and García de la Noceda, Nuria (2013), *Modistillas en imágenes: Pioneras en la integración laboral de la mujer (1929–1936)*, Madrid: Creaciones Vicent Gabrielle.

Nieland, Justus (2008), *Feeling Modern: The Eccentricities of Public Life*, Urbana: University of Illinois Press.

Nuñez Orgáz, Adela (1989), '"Las modistillas" de Madrid, tradición y realidad', in J. Anadón and A. Bahamonde Magro and L. E. Otero Carvajal (eds), *La sociedad madrileña durante la Restauración, 1876–1931*, Madrid: Consejería de Cultura de la Comunidad de Madrid, pp. 435–50.

Pérez Galdós, Benito (2015), *Fortunata y Jacinta: Dos historias de casadas*, Madrid: Paradimage Soluciones, https://books.google.com.gi/books?id=PHxJCgAAQBAJ&printsec=frontcover&hl=es&source=gbs_vpt_read#v=onepage&q&f=false. Accessed 4 September 2018.

Rabinovitz, Lauren (2012), *Electric Dreamland: Amusement Parks, Movies, and American Modernity*, New York: Columbia University Press.

Río López, Angel del (1993), *Viejos oficios de Madrid*, Madrid: La Librería.

Toulmin, Vanessa (2003), *Pleasurelands: All the Fun of the Fair*, Sheffield: National Fairgrounds Archive and University of Sheffield Library.

Vela, Fernando (1925), 'Desde la ribera oscura (Sobre una estética del cine)', *Revista de Occidente*, 23, pp. 202–27.

Wood, Jason (ed.) (2017), *The Amusement Park: History, Culture and the Heritage of Pleasure*, London: Routledge.

7

Surface Tension and Utopian Underworlds: Orpheus and the Executioner in Luis García Berlanga's *El verdugo* (1963)

Patricia Keller, Cornell University

> *That this book is a history of a shadow that is a shadow of.*
>
> Susan Howe, *That This*

> *Surface tension can turn both façade and framed picture into something resembling a screen. This contemporary screen [...] far from representing any perspectival ideal, is no longer containable within optical framings, and cannot be likened to a window or a mirror, but is to be reconfigured as a different surface.*
>
> Giuliana Bruno, *Surface*

Introduction: An Elsewhere, a Beyond

Cinema: an art caught between the 'here' and an always shifting 'elsewhere'. John Berger, in his essay 'Ev'ry time we say goodbye' refers to the cinema as a mode of transport that carries the audience away from where they are, and brings them toward the unknown. In this action, the screen is 'no longer a surface but a space' (Berger 2001: 475). And in this space, the spectator experiences movement, not because things are actually moving, Berger notes, but 'because a film is a shuttle service between different places and times' (Berger 2001: 476). The movement takes place elsewhere, in a space at once recognizable and unnamable. In cinema, when the story is too clean and 'tailor-made', or when a film becomes 'null and void' simply because there is nothing but story, then 'there are no real surfaces to cling to' (Berger 2001: 478). But a cinema that reflects ordinary life and presents its spectator with familiar events by constructing and inhabiting space offers itself as a 'spatial practice of cognition' (Bruno 2007: 26). Understood in this way, cinema becomes an inhabitable space, a mode of dwelling, and a kind of 'living architexture', in the words of Giuliana Bruno. In this gesture, which is also an *offering*, there exists the possibility of rediscovery and revelation (Bruno 2007: 25–26). We rediscover the world we already inhabit after 'an absence elsewhere' that films afford us. Berger writes: 'No other narrative art can get as close as the cinema to the variety, the texture, the skin of daily life. But its unfolding, its coming into being, its marriage with the Elsewhere, reminds us of a longing, or a prayer' (Berger 2001: 478).

Texture, skin, daily life. Being here, traveling elsewhere. These are our coordinates and our points of departure. Like Berger, Giuliana Bruno, in 'Motion and emotion: Film and the urban fabric' (2007), discusses the *transito* at the heart of cinema. She analyzes the cinematic as a particular itinerancy that takes place through cultural forms of transmission, which involves not only physical motion (movement) but also takes into account a specific 'epistemology', including 'circulation, migration, passage, traversals, transitions, transitory states, spatial erotics, and [...] affects' (Bruno 2007: 26). Such transmission occurs through 'the act of joining cinema and architecture, not optically but haptically' (Bruno 2007: 25). In combining these two experiential modes of viewing, navigating, building and inhabiting, one begins to 'corrode [the] oppositions' of 'mobility/immobility, inside/outside, private/public, dwelling/travel' (Bruno 2007: 25). Bruno has in mind a certain kind of remapping wherein we approach both media – cinema and architecture – as 'permeable intersubjective spaces' (Bruno 2007: 25). In this reconfiguration, the merging of spatial and affective practices, at the intersection of movement and habitation, lies knowledge – the 'rediscovery' toward which Berger turns (along with Víctor Erice and Maurice Blanchot, as we will see later). At this point, in the time-space of *transito*, we are 'forced to rethink cultural expression itself as a site of interior/exterior travel and dwelling', what Bruno poignantly calls a 'porous geo-psychic in-between' (Bruno 2007: 25).

This chapter aims to draw on Berger's and Bruno's ideas in order to explore how the diverse spaces that comprise Luis García Berlanga's 1963 film *El verdugo* (The Executioner) – the prison, the apartment, the dream home, the construction site, the bedroom, the church, the city hall, the airport and the island – form an intricate network of social, political, cultural, countercultural, sexual, affective, architectural and cinematic economies.[1] Economies in constant flux. Ones that, like cinema itself, oscillate between light and darkness, clear vision and shadowed sight, vitality and mortality, the forward impulse of life and the unbearable burden of death, and between surface and depth. Between façades and 'debths' (after Susan Howe). Ones not unlike what Bruno identifies as the 'fabric of film experience which involves an intimate spatial binding – an experience always [itself] in flux' (Bruno 2007: 18).

Unique to the context of Berlanga's *El verdugo*, filmed and produced at the beginning of Spain's period of economic liberalization under the Franco dictatorship – a period of intense growth under what I would call the cloak of a 'dark aperture' – these spaces reflect and critique modernization efforts that were taking place not only in urban centers but also on the periphery, from the politics of new public housing projects to the cultural cachet of tourism.[2] Equally, in every corner of Berlanga's geo-psychic-temporal-spatial-social-cultural-political cartography, the failures of Francoist modernization and the legacy of death and violence passed down from generation to generation are unsettlingly revealed. Reflection and critique perhaps best exemplified in two lines spoken with equal conviction by the frail, ageing state executioner of the narrative, Amadeo. At the beginning of the film, Amadeo proclaims to the two undertakers who give him a ride home from the prison where he has just performed an execution, 'los tiempos han cambiado' (the times have changed), a statement, in part, referencing the traffic and public transit commuter congestion that Amadeo would otherwise have had to navigate on his return home. Yet to the contrary, the laws governing this world have not changed at all. A few scenes later, at home, speaking about the ethics and 'humanity' of his profession, Amadeo asserts: 'pero si existe la pena alguien tiene que aplicarla' (if the death penalty exists, someone has to execute it).[3] His political position will be reaffirmed, several scenes later, when in need of a signature for the official form required for his son-in-law's application for the title of *verdugo,* Amadeo shows up at Madrid's *Feria del Libro* to request the 'John Hancock' of his favorite academic author, Corcuera, who agrees to give Amadeo a signature while nonchalantly professing 'society needs an executor of justice'.

The law, we will see, is always double. It is both the law of the state and the law of the father, which will have to be handed down from father to son, or in this case from Amadeo to his future son-in-law and heir to the family's professional legacy, José Luis, a simple undertaker and bachelor who works at a local mortuary but dreams of going to Germany to become a mechanic.[4] That the law, in this twin sense, should be framed as the intangible yet palpably contentious and uncoveted inheritance of the future generation of a Spain on the cusp of change yet deeply rooted in tradition reveals the burden at the heart of everything the figure of the *verdugo* represents. That this burden of inheritance – marked here specifically by the relay between father and future son-in-law – should be inextricably tied to questions of family, domesticity, propriety and most of all the problem of 'home' is an ingeniously subversive gesture on Berlanga's part. In fact, Berlanga takes such subversion one step further by establishing an explicit correlation between the official title of 'executioner' and the ultimately empty promise of new housing. In this way, *El verdugo* stages the complexity of how the past persists in and permeates the present by linking the question of futurity to the problem of legacy.

But the fact that the film also achieves this link between future and past by staging these tensions through a web of urban spaces in the present – some crowded and claustrophobic, others vacant, hollow and obscure – is crucial to understanding the crisis at the heart of Berlanga's critique. When assembled together into a map, these spaces become surfaces, containers, archives, passages and passageways, the textures of which are intricate and layered. The film moves seamlessly from the congested fabric of the urban (the cramped living quarters of the protagonists, the heavy traffic and the oasis of an afternoon picnic in the *campo* are stages for territorial competition, even the church is 'overbooked' with events), to the vast vacancies of the still unpopulated city outskirts where, we are told, the mountains are visible though never actually seen. Where the film eventually lands, so to speak, is on the island, a utopian geography where vacation destination, the spectacle of international tourism and the perilous underworld of one's duty to the state all converge. The film's end, in many ways, can be read as the demise of Spain's future. Its forward movement unmasked as nothing other than a momentous impasse. In the movement across these spaces, the film sheds light on the dark social reality of 1960s Spain erected on an irreconcilable geometry of desires and a contradictory pattern, repeatable as it is foreseeable, of fear. The spaces in *El verdugo*, from the mainland to the island, from the prison to the beach, and from the bedroom to the boat, all reveal anxious landscapes – ones riddled with modern anachronisms and paradoxically plagued by what we might call 'nostalgia for the future'. Andreas Huyssen, in 'Nostalgia for Ruins', traces the link between nostalgic desire and the figure of the ruin. He writes:

> [P]redominantly negative coding of nostalgia within modernity is easily explained: nostalgia counteracts, even undermines linear notions of progress, whether they are framed dialectically as philosophy of history or sociologically and economically as modernization. But nostalgic longing for a past is always also a longing for another place. Nostalgia can be a utopia in reverse. Temporality and spatiality are necessarily linked in nostalgic desire.
>
> (Huyssen 2006: 7)

This is precisely why, according to Huyssen, the architectural ruin is a figure that triggers nostalgia since it stands as 'an indissoluble combination of spatial and temporal desires' (Huyssen 2006: 7). What is intriguing about the way nostalgia works in Berlanga's film is that the 'ruin' is equated with the present moment. The figure that combines temporal and spatial desires into a projected future is not, in fact, historical ruins, but the construction site – the 'ruins in reverse', as we shall see – that promise a new horizon of modern experience, of wealth, prosperity and happiness. In the ruin, the past is present but no longer accessible, if we follow

Huyssen's analysis. But in Berlanga's film, the future fantasy of a better life, the 'dreamworld' of new housing that will offer views of breathtaking landscapes and with them the guarantee of clearer vision, is precisely that imaginary place that fuses spatiotemporal desires (a longing not to return to the past but to break free from it). The past lives on through familial repetition and legacy despite any attempts to erase or 'build over' it. This new view brings with it a future death, summed up neatly in an exchange between José Luis and Carmen, when dancing together in the countryside he gently asks her: 'Carmen, ¿te gusta? Bonito paisaje. ¿A ti dónde te gustaría morir?' (Carmen, do you like the view? It is a beautiful landscape [...] Carmen, where would you like to die?)

All of this brings us back to the idea with which we began: transport, transition, *transito*. Movement in, across and between urban and nonurban sites, private as well as public domains, familial and state obligations (and crises) are all problematized through the particular spatial logic – the cinematic cartography – of the film's crisscross shuttling between modernization, visualized as a new horizon of experience, and the present conditions of social life inseparable from a pervasive culture of death and terror. James Donald, writing about how new forms of media shaped the metropolis in early cinema, locates modernity at the crossroads between 'the utopian will to visibility' and the 'irredeemable opacity of the social' (Donald 1999: 86). As we will see in the pages that follow, Berlanga's cinematic vision (and revision) of Spanish modernization during the economic boom known as the *apertura* (liberalization, democratization, internationalization) and the open door policies that created opportunity for foreign investment, exportation and the so-called worlding of Spain emerge from the tension between the dystopian will to legacy in the name of progress and the relentless, dominant force of death that blindingly eclipses any possibility of a peaceful future.

> *The (im)mobile film spectator moves across an imaginary path, traversing multiple sites and times. Her fictional navigation connects distant moments and far-apart places. Film inherits the possibility of a such a spectatorial voyage from the architectural field, for the person who wanders through a building or a site also absorbs and connects visual spaces.*
>
> Giuliana Bruno, 'Motion and emotion: Film and the urban fabric'

The Future's Dark Horizon

The characters in Berlanga's films are often plagued by investing too much in the future. They hopelessly look toward the promise of salvation, redemption or just the chance of upward mobility that tomorrow never brings.[5] *El verdugo* is no exception to this. Amadeo, the father and bearer (literally the 'executor') of the law, eagerly awaits his imminent retirement, the day when he can 'pass the *garrote*' off to some new functionary of the state. Carmen, his daughter, waits to get married, start a family and move into a new home. José Luis, the undertaker-cum-*verdugo* of the film's title, looks forward to the day when he has enough money to leave Spain, go abroad and study to become a car mechanic. Future time is pregnant with possibility and full of dreams – retirement, marriage, family, travel, job security, affordable housing. But these possibilities are all codified in a cycle of violence perpetuated in the name of progress, procreation, modernization and even leisure. As such, the future becomes overinvested and burdensome insofar as it belongs to the past, steeped in and dictated by a weighted, fraught repetition of history. These repetitions, predictable and uncanny, forecast the future as a dark horizon, one that is attainable but ultimately hopeless, doomed to failure in being so deeply entrenched in the past. At the same time, these repetitions shroud the present in a sinister social trap – a kind of cultural claustrophobia, producing not so much a state of paralysis (due to lack of mobility) as the perpetuation of a circuitous, dead end loop. The present moment becomes a kind of living ruin that inscribes and monumentalizes the past, and at the same time mortifies the future. Indeed, futurity is confined to the demands – the legacy – of the past. As such, inhabiting the future (through family, housing, work) thus becomes a one-way street, permissible only by erecting a vision of that future tethered to the irreparable monument of the past.

When Amadeo returns home one day to announce the good news to his only daughter, Carmen, that they have been awarded municipal housing, he envisions something of a dream – the house will be spacious, with a view, three bedrooms and heat.[6] Much like the promise of new housing in which Amadeo, Carmen and José Luis all eventually invest, the future holds the promise of new vistas and horizons and provides the possibility of expansion, visibility, fresh perspectives and new landscapes. As the counterpart to the 'living ruin' of the present moment's underdeveloped, overpopulated and uninhabitable economic reality, laden with constricted hallways and cramped rooms governed by the gaze of the past (a point to which I will return later), the construction sites operate as pure fantasy – an escape from the throngs of modern urban life. That is to say, construction of the future becomes the answer to the crowded shape of the present. And thus, the construction site proper figures as a 'ruin in reverse'.[7]

> *Thus one lives a film as one lives the space that one inhabits – in haptic intimacy. In this psycho-physical domain of intimacy, one absorbs, and is absorbed by, moving images and their tales of inhabitation.*
>
> Giuliana Bruno, 'Motion and emotion: Film and the urban fabric'

Carceral Space, Domestic Space

But the present, understood as a time that is ominous and ensnared in darkness, begins tellingly not in the space of the home (future or present), nor the city streets, but in the prison. Visually, the prison scenes (in Madrid, at the beginning of the film, and in Palma de Mallorca, at the end) look like inversions – negatives – of the 'positive' view of the new housing projects. Dim lights, with multiple gates, bars and nontransparent windows, the visual elements of the prison mise en scène contrast sharply but also foreshadow acutely the natural light, open doorways and overall spaciousness of the new homes under construction, introduced to us through a number of upward pan shots featuring the towering cranes, scaffolding and other building equipment used in their fabrication. Whereas the prison is enclosed unto itself, with a visual grammar of grids, dark interiors, multiple locked doors and guarded thresholds, the new housing site appears expansive and vast, its walls porous and still undefined, with open access to the exterior world and a clear view of the horizon in the distance. As one passes through this latter space, one enters into a dream world, an invitation to imagine a better living arrangement and thus a better quality of life. By contrast, as one crosses the thresholds of the prison, in the narrative world of the film, one is enlisted in a series of ethical compromises that go hand-in-hand with working for the state. The difference is notable, yet the affinities are what interest me here. The housing projects are partitioned *by* the state; the prison space is organized by duty *to* the state. As if two sides of the same coin, this correspondence between prison and home, between carceral and domestic space, only intensifies as the film progresses. Both spaces are organized rectilinearly, with clean vertical lines, 'the skyline subdivided by girders', in David Cairn's words (2016: 2); the angular, negative space in one is visually mirrored by the contrasting angles and positive space of the other. The interplay of light/darkness, open/closed doors, empty/full rooms, in each establishes a certain degree of visual continuity and complementarity (Figure 7.1).

Even the sound of the mailing address that José Luis will give to the group of German tourists who stop and ask him to take their picture in Palma (a scene which will be read in detail later on for its strange, compelling recourse to photography) echoes the geometric design and architectural layout of a prison: 'Polígono sur, Grupo 4, Bloque 17, Madrid' (Polygon South, Group 4, Block 17, Madrid). Earlier, when the housing project is still under construction, the family of three visits what will become their future home: 'tercera derecha' [third floor on the right], a four story walk-up with all the amenities one needs – 'cocina, cuarto de aseo, comedor con terraza, un dormitorio, otro dormitorio, y otro dormitorio' (kitchen, bathroom, dining room with balcony, bedroom, another bedroom, and another bedroom) in the distance several high rises in progress are visible, all symbols of the modernization vision that would come to transform the Spanish landscape. In this

FIGURE 7.1: Prison cell darkroom. Luis García Berlanga (dir.), *El verdugo*, 1963. Spain. Used with permission of Egeda and Mercury Films.

scene, there are already overtones of illicit behavior and delinquency that reinforce the connection between the illusion of future freedom and the inescapability of the past. The light, the visibility of the horizon – '¡Qué luz! ¡Vaya vistas!' (What great light and views!), exclaims José Luis; 'Si se ve hasta Guadalajara' (You can see all the way to Guadalajara), Carmen responds – initially opens the door to their creative (soon to turn competitive) imaginings. The fantasy of place, ownership and a clean, ordered space is abruptly interrupted when a scandalized José Luis peers out the window as he goes to discard a piece of trash only to notice a man (presumably homeless) defecating within plain sight on a grassy knoll nearby.[8]

With regard to the film's narrative structure, the space of the prison and the new housing site complete one another. What we come to see is that the new home – a legal right that the *verdugo* has, being a state employee – can be retained only through continuance of the profession in the family. In a sense, the housing solution can only happen through a marriage between family and state. Upon Amadeo's retirement, the home would be lost by the 'divorce' that would inevitably incur, the breach of allegiance between family and state, caused by his stepping down. Thus, the plot twist in which José Luis, in a double bind, must abandon his dreams of leaving Spain, in order to marry Carmen (because she is pregnant) and assume the official title of executioner (following in Amadeo's footsteps in order to secure their family right to municipal housing). Prison is the space of confinement, discipline and death, a space tethered to professional duties and routine, but not without an air of the familiar and the everyday. Home, as it turns out, is a prison too. A fact further underscored several scenes later, in a flash forward, when a mattress is delivered to the new apartment. The camera, positioned squarely in the middle of the house, functions as the all-seeing eye that transforms the spaciousness previously envisioned into what David Cairns calls an 'infuriating obstacle course' – here, the dream house 'becomes another trap, a compartmentalized panopticon, a prison devoid of privacy' (Cairns 2016: 3).

Crossing the Threshold

The prison. The penitentiary. The jail. This is the space within which *El verdugo* begins. The space where Berlanga positions his camera carefully. And lingers. Where he situates and holds us. It is a simple, uncrowded space with multiple doors, and thus multiple thresholds that will be crossed. It is a guarded space – protected and locked from the outside world. And it is a space shrouded in death. But before we see the first signs of what will mark this place as one linked to and governed by a certain economy of death, we are introduced to the space of the prison through the everyday – the common and quotidian. Here is the opening shot: the camera frames two hands as they tear a piece of bread into smaller pieces, before stirring them in a large cup of coffee. A man eats breakfast while reading the newspaper. It is an ordinary scene, a familiar one. Morning rituals and routine habits. The man wears dark glasses and a white blanket over his shoulders. There is a knock at the door. As the man discards the blanket to grab his cap and set of keys, we understand that he is an officer.

The two men at the door are undertakers who have come to retrieve a body. They cross the threshold, and upon entering the scene, one of them carries a plain wooden coffin horizontally on his shoulder, which obscures his face. It is the first time the audience sees José Luis. We will soon learn that he is the protagonist, and the future heir to the uncoveted role of 'executioner' referenced in the film's title. He walks toward the camera and sets the coffin down upright, now vertically positioned exactly in front of his own body. The guard tells him to put the coffin against the wall. The two undertakers sit down on a bench beside the coffin and smoke a cigarette, waiting. Reverse shot: through a second door, opposite the first, a group of 'officials', men who 'were all present', enter the scene. The event has taken place. Moments before the undertakers are called to walk through the second door, the executioner exits. A small, elderly man with a raspy voice who, upon arriving on the scene, misplaces his bag (*el maletín*). The undertakers retrieve the body of the executed prisoner, load the truck and, after offering a ride to the *verdugo*, exit the prison slowly through the main gates. The camera remains inside the prison courtyard until their truck is out of sight and the gates have closed. Cut to inside the truck where Amadeo, the ageing, frail yet fiery *verdugo*, laments that 'los tiempos han cambiado' (times have changed). It is a striking opening sequence – one that I detail here in order to highlight the fact that the entire film is effectively staged in the limited but suggestive action of the first few minutes.

Doors, doorways, gates. As the opening scene foreshadows, the characters in *El verdugo* are constantly crossing through, over, and under various thresholds. These thresholds lead into other worlds, new worlds that are also unmistakably underworlds. Dystopian visions masked as investments in a future born from the crisis of the present moment. With each traversal, José Luis seems to step into a different zone of the underworld, as if each space constituted a distinct level of the 'inferno' that is modern urban life and the current conditions of 'home'. The most dramatic threshold being, of course, an entirely invisible but socially and politically constructed one: the threshold into the family/state dynamic – a marriage of social and political orders that determines the protagonist's fate by forcing him to inherit 'the family profession'. This invisible threshold is carefully anticipated by a number of scenes in which José Luis actually crosses the threshold – the liminal space between present and future, between underworld and utopia, between reality and death – beginning, at the outset, with his initial entrance into the prison. Berlanga's prison naturally restages an official though not overtly legible space of incarceration, where exits and entrances alike lead to an atmosphere of death – something that will fortify the link between José Luis as future executioner and the figure of Orpheus. The question of atmosphere meets the process of inscription into death, which I will suggest has to do with a particular photographic logic governing the film's visual and narrative frame.

> *It is because each photograph always contains this imperious sign of my future death that each one, however attached it seems to be to the excited world of the living, challenges each of us, one by one.*
>
> Roland Barthes, *Camera Lucida*

> *Subjects of photography, seized by the camera, we are mortified – that is, objectified, 'thingified', imaged.*
>
> Eduardo Cadava, *Words of Light*

Photographic Frames and the Logic of Mortification

From the jail to the city streets, and from the streets to the executioner's humble abode, another more grave, less savory threshold is crossed when José Luis, upon returning the forgotten *maletín* to Amadeo, is invited in and immediately presented to Carmen, Amadeo's unmarried daughter. Here we see a different kind of underworld replicated in the intimate, private space of the family quarters – a purgatory, located between the paradise promised by the new apartment and the inferno of the workplace, respectively the prison and the morgue, each literally entrenched in the labor of death. José Luis is already a proto-Orpheus figure upon his descent into the underground tunnels of the city, tracking Amadeo with his suitcase in hand. Curiously, in this scene, his Orphean descent is not initiated by a desire to retrieve something or someone (Eurydice in the original myth) but rather to return the undesired bag to its rightful owner – the *maletín* containing the *verdugo*'s instruments of death. Like something out of a dark fairytale, José Luis enters the family house only to find himself trapped, in part by the laws of hospitality, as he is invited to coffee, a small gesture of gratitude for his valiant efforts to restore some kind of order. José Luis takes a seat at the table and as Amadeo begins to unpack the bag, casually taking out his *garrote* and placing it on the kitchen table, he introduces Carmen, whom he wishes to marry off, as 'muy limpia' (very clean). Thus begins a series of other transversals – the crossing from bachelor to boyfriend, boyfriend to husband, husband to father and father to eventual bearer of the family 'fortune', by inheritance of the executioner 'trade'. The crossing from one status to the next carries with it an implied transition from sin to redemption, from impoverishment to wealth, and from lack to fulfillment, all of which will involve elaborate plot points and farcical interpretations in order to 'bend the law' in their collective favor.

Already inscribed within the logic of return and inscription, this family living room scene is a pinnacle moment of intersectionality internal to the film – a crossroads between familial desire, political indoctrination, the future/past temporality of image archives and the laws that govern each. Indeed, photography plays a key though often understated role in *El verdugo*, a role that begins in this very scene where the ominous gaze of ancestral eyes extends beyond the frame to keep watch. In the confined space of the living room, the presence of family photographs is notable, even dominant. Indeed, the multiple temporal references embedded within these photographs is highlighted in a quick exchange between José Luis and Amadeo – the former asks Carmen '¿es su prometido?' (is this your fiancé?), referring to a framed picture on the wall, to which Amadeo quips '¡No! Es ese del reloj' (No! He is the one who gave me the watch). Lineage 'gifts' time (marked here by the watch that Amadeo proudly wears), but interestingly this gift, and the temporal order it references, is established through the medium of photography (marked here by the photographic object, the framed family portrait proudly displayed). The future is determined by the gaze of the past. José Luis turns to the photographs in an innocent attempt to ask about the prospects of Carmen's future, but the answer he, in turn, receives from her father suggests that they are *already* looking at the past. An uncanny moment, to be sure, the future, with all of its still unknown dark horizons, is already the past. There are no less than eleven different portraits framed on the walls in this scene, and as a startled José Luis sweeps the room with his eyes, Amadeo reassures him that all are 'parientes' (family relatives). The authority of the photographic frame will extend throughout the film, in subtle but significant ways, just as the photographic object – the image itself – will conjure associations with *memento mori*, through connections either to the family archive or to the idea of celebrity.

Barajas. A pilot and flight attendant, stylish and modern in appearance, descend the stairs of an IBERIA plane. This is the first shot in the short but memorable airport sequence, where José Luis and his colleague arrive on scene to transport a body to the cemetery. Before they unload the plane's cargo, they have their picture taken in front of the plane, where José Luis, concerned about the details of the picture, asks the cameraman to make sure the plane is in view. The souvenir snapshot is taken and, moments later, when the customs officers insist that the coffin be opened for inspection before the family is allowed to exit, the bereaved widow compares the corpse to a photograph she is holding, hysterically exclaiming: '¡no es él!' (it is not him!). The photograph that José Luis holds in his hand finds a peculiar parallel with the photograph that the widow holds in hers, in a state of disbelief as she holds the image up to the face of the body in the coffin. Photography functions as a portal into estrangement, a mode of conjuring otherness that, while only hinted at in this brief scene, will be elaborated much more fully as the film progresses. Here, the specific link between the photographed subject and the corpse is noteworthy. Roland Barthes in *Camera Lucida*, his seminal study of photography's relationship to death and desire, writes,

> [I]f the photograph then becomes horrible, it is because it certifies, so to speak, that the corpse is alive, as corpse: it is the living image of a dead thing. For the photograph's immobility is somehow the result of a perverse confusion between two concepts: the Real and the Live.
>
> (Barthes 1981: 78–79)

This connection between image and corpse, between photography and 'being-toward-death', is precisely what Eduardo Cadava, drawing on Maurice Blanchot's work, theorizes in the following passage:

> There can be no image that is not also an image of death. Nevertheless, this image-corpse, *a kind of tomb in which subject and object are encrypted*, at the same time points to what cannot be reduced to the photograph – the photograph itself. As

> its own grave, the photograph is what exceeds the photograph within the photograph. It is what remains of what passes into history. It turns in on itself in order to survive, in order to withdraw into a space in which it might defer its decay, into an interior – the closed-off space of writing itself. *In order for a photograph to be a photograph, it must become the tomb that writes, that harbors its own death. If the photograph is the allegory of our modernity, it is because, like allegory, it is defined by its relation to the corpse.*
>
> (Cadava 1997: 10–11, emphasis added)

Photography, the art of capturing and reproducing stillness, the tomb that produces and encrypts death, is doubly reconfigured in Berlanga's airport, a space emblematic of mobility, freedom and flight. The photographic object (the souvenir portrait) will be a surprise gift for Carmen, but it also represents a confrontation with death that is alienating and unspeakable. The gift is here also a gift of death; the photograph is, in Cadava's words, a tomb that recalls past and future deaths, a 'paper graveyard'.

Moments later, José Luis steps aside to make a phone call to the cemetery but in reality, he calls Carmen to tell her of the surprise gift now fictionalized as a celebrity encounter – a signed picture of Charleton Heston, the star of *Ben Hur*, who was supposedly at the airport earlier that day. The undertaker, the corpse and the actor are here entangled and triangulated by photography, the evidentiary force of which is called into question twice – first because the dead body being transported does not match the image in hand, and second because the celebrity was not at the airport on the day his photograph was allegedly taken. The airport itself is a zone of transport, transportation, *tránsito*, to return to the ideas with which this essay began, but it is recognized here doubly as a place of internationalization and cinematic culture, on the one hand, and the unrecognizability and estrangement of death, on the other. From the airport we move back to the space of the family home. The scene cuts to a frame of a wall featuring a dozen photographs in collage; a hand suddenly removes one picture of a cyclist, framed in close-up. The camera is now situated in Carmen's bedroom, where it is implied that the two lovers have just spent the afternoon together. José Luis inquires about the cyclist (presumably a former boyfriend) and Carmen shrugs off an answer with indifference: 'he won a lot of races, you know?, but then he left like all the others.' When José Luis asks if he can tear up the picture (presumably to replace it with his own portrait, recently gifted to her) – 'Carmen, ¿lo rompo?' (Carmen, should I tear it up?)[9] – it is the decisive moment that precedes Amadeo's return home with the announcement of the new apartment, 'ya tenemos piso, ya estoy en la lista' (we already have an apartment, I am already on the list). Destruction of the photograph (and the past life it indexes) precipitates the family's future 'pact', its very constitution.

FIGURE 7.2: Double thresholds, the family house. Luis García Berlanga (dir.), *El verdugo*, 1963. Spain. Used with permission of Egeda and Mercury Films.

In this moment, Carmen and José Luis are 'caught in the act' and Amadeo, shocked at the discovery and devastated by the fact that their illicit affair will now compromise any chance of obtaining their dream home, dramatically laments the lost view from the windows of their would-be-future house: '¡Qué pena! Con aquellas vistas se veía la sierra' (What a pity! With those views you could see the mountains). Carmen proposes that José Luis assuage Amadeo's anxiety about their 'sinful' relations by asking her father for her hand in marriage. Visually the scene is impressive – the compact space of the two bedrooms, adjacent but dissected within the frame, will directly mirror the two opposite bedrooms of the new apartment layout, some scenes later (Figure 7.2).

In the background, the walls are lined with photographs and newspaper clippings, a heap of images; in the foreground, that heap is reproduced with a few key details of the mise en scène that allude to the ominous shadow cast over their future domestic life: the stacks of dishes on the credenza alongside a small clock and a framed portrait of the father's father, underneath the chandelier (the room's only light source) which is cut off from view. The family photographs on the archway between Carmen's and Amadeo's bedrooms, now seem to take on a more palpable significance as sites located between past and present, the surfaces of which establish history's confluence with the present moment. The eyes of the father's father lodged between and peering over the two generations.

As surfaces, the family photographs in this scene, ineffably, intractably reflect 'the catastrophe', which in Roland Barthes's theorization constitutes every photographic image. To observe 'an anterior future of which death is the stake' and to come into knowledge, through the photograph's presence, of a future death, are precisely the elements that make the observer shudder in horror (a horror evoked, in the aforementioned link between the image and the corpse). 'Whether or not the subject is already dead, every photograph is *this catastrophe*', Barthes writes – the disaster 'which has already occurred' and yet, in the space of the image, the very one that has not yet come to pass (Barthes 1981: 96, emphasis added). The tension that underwrites the future anterior is, accordingly, performed in every photograph – a temporal antagonism between the 'once was' and the 'will be' that Barthes locates at the very heart of the photograph's future-past temporality: 'this will have been'. In these dueling temporalities, the pastness of the event captured on film implicates future interpretability and significance. Death and the referent are one and the same. Thus, the paradox at the heart of the medium: the fact that while its 'record' offers proof of some 'unique event', the photograph's index always points toward something outside the frame – the 'once was' which always also certifies an eventual 'will be' and thus retains within it the potential to return again. At this junction of divergent temporal modes of existence and legibility, '[e]ach photograph is read as the private appearance of its referent: the age of Photography corresponds precisely to the explosion of the private into the public, or rather into the creation of a new social value, which is the publicity of the private' (Barthes 1981: 98).

These first scenes, which pivot on photography, are bookended by family affairs and domestic interiors, but the next scene related to photography, and specifically to questions of public/private, interior/exterior, will take place on the island of Palma de Mallorca. The island, remote but still worldly (upon the family's arrival, where we find signs for an international beauty contest, 'El Festival Mundial de Elegancia y Belleza – Elección de Miss Naciones Unidas'), offers a dreamworld, the utopian counterpart to the dystopian reality of urban life. José Luis has been summoned to Mallorca to perform his first 'job' as the new official state *verdugo*, and it is here, off shore from mainland Spain, where death's warrant will seal his fate. The family – Amadeo, Carmen and newborn son – accompanies José Luis, for moral support and besides, they never really had a honeymoon, and the fresh ocean air will be good for the baby, and Amadeo has never been there before. The mounting list of reasons make the trip to Palma de Mallorca, dreaded by the now totally angst-ridden and inconsolable José Luis, a vacation destination for the others, a point Berlanga will exploit throughout the island scenes, showing us a land of beauty pageants and cheap souvenirs, blonde-haired tourists from neighboring northern countries and sunny beaches.

Upon arrival, the family exits the boat and two Guardia Civil are waiting to escort the young executioner to the prison. Taking Amadeo's advice, a very reluctant José Luis goes to his post in the hope that at the last minute an 'indulto' (pardon) will spare him this dreaded executioner's task. Cut to a sunny terrace scene, where an ecstatic José Luis returns not having executed the prisoner and delighted in relief, since due to the prisoner's sudden illness the execution had to be postponed. Overcome with joy at the news of not having to carry out his duties, he tells the family that they must remain on the island to await further instruction. In celebration, José Luis grabs his son and holds him up in the sky, against the backdrop of a dramatic seascape. The shot frames a perfect family picture, from left to right: Amadeo, Carmen, José Luis and baby all stand together on the terrace, content; the line of inheritance can be traced in their movement and ascension, ending with the son (and future heir) suspended in the air. Cut again to a kiosk where souvenirs are sold. A group of German tourists ask José Luis if he will take their photo, a snapshot of their sunny Spanish beach holiday. Three women pose in stereotypical Spanish flair – the first holds *castanets*, the second sports a comically oversized *sombrero*, and the third sings '*olé, olé*' as he snaps the picture. José Luis, *verdugo*-turned-vacationer, fumbles with the camera in his momentary role as photographer. At first he does not know where the viewfinder is or how to work the shutter, a direct parallel to his lack of knowledge about how to perform an execution and his lack of experience regarding how to operate the *garrote* – a joke that gets recycled on several different occasions.

We could say that, as camera operator, José Luis participates in a particular process of mortification. By 'embalming' the image of the tourists whom he 'captures', they are frozen in a future anterior time, a state of preservation whereby, once developed and inscribed in the photographic surface, they will become the 'catastrophe' underwriting their very image – the possibility of their inevitable and repeated death in the future. But, an equally if not perhaps more curious moment of mortification occurs when José Luis asks for his own photograph (with Carmen) to be taken in return. Once captured on film his fate is sealed as he becomes the petrified, mortified object; the image that says '[h]e is already dead and he is going to die' (Barthes 1981: 95).[10] We do not see the resulting photographic image since it is still in the tourist's camera, and thus will need to be developed abroad (in Germany, noncoincidentally) before being sent to him by mail. But the absence of the picture only seems to reinforce the fact that, in this moment, José Luis is inscribed in death. It is, indeed, a moment of double inscription since he is enlisted as both photographer and photographed subject, executioner and corpse. Eduardo Cadava, writing about 'mortification' in relation to photography, suggests that inscription in death is at stake in every photographic act:

> [W]e need only know that we are mortal – the photograph tells us we will die, one day we will no longer be here, or rather, we will only be here the way we have always been here, *as* images. It announces the death of the photographed.
>
> (Cadava 1997: 8, emphasis in original)

This announcement, an utterance that Cadava will suggest is death spoken through the image, perfectly summarizes the souvenir photograph scene:

> *The photograph, like the souvenir, is the corpse of experience.* A photograph therefore speaks *as* death, as the trace of what passes into history. *I*, the photograph, the spaced out limit between life and death, *am death*. Yet, speaking as death, the photograph can be neither death nor itself. At once dead and alive, it opens the possibility of our *being in time*.
>
> (Cadava 1997: 128, emphasis added)

If we follow this logic, then the performative trajectory for the protagonist is thus: he undertakes death, he executes death and finally he becomes an image of death. The executioner, by the film's end, is captured by death, and thus becomes what his title very beginning: a figure of death itself.

> *Cinema authorizes Orpheus to look back without letting Eurydice die.*
>
> Víctor Erice, 'Writing cinema, thinking Cinema'

Orpheus Revisited

Cast as a figure of death itself, José Luis at the film's close must confront death through death. His metaphorical descent into the underworld, which began once he crossed the threshold of the prison and continued when he entered into the family structure, becomes actualized in a tourist spectacle, simulating Hades, that takes place in the darkened, stalactite caves of the island. Taking their seats among the crowded bleachers of foreign tourists, José Luis and Carmen sit down to watch the show, despite the fact that they cannot understand a word (the announcer speaks in German, highlighting that they are the real foreigners in this scene). As the lights go dim, the main attraction turns out to be the arrival of the Guardia Civil, now looking for José Luis. In a slow-paced rowboat, floating down the imitation 'River Styx', the officer, megaphone in hand, repeatedly calls out his name: 'Don José Luis Rodríguez, si se encuentra entre los presentes, tenga la bondad de bajar al embarcadero' (if you are present, please be so kind as to come down to the dock) (Figure 7.3).

FIGURE 7.3: The Guardia Civil looking for José Luis in the island underworld. Luis García Berlanga (dir.), *El verdugo*, 1963. Spain. Used with permission of Egeda and Mercury Films.

He willfully ignores their summons, until the *guardia* enters the space of the crowd and inquires directly '¿es Ud. don José Luis Rodríguez?' (are you Mr. José Luis Rodríguez?) to which the protagonist awkwardly responds 'esta es mi mujer' (this is my wife). José Luis accompanies the officers and boards the rowboat, leaving one spectacle for another, and importantly leaving Carmen behind. Now, literally transported toward death, is it not Orpheus and Eurydice whose gazes fatally meet, but Orpheus and the executioner.

In the original myth, Orpheus descends to Tartarus to restore his beloved Eurydice to the upper world. His music 'soothes the savage heart of Hades', god of the underworld, who allows him to bring her back to the light of day upon one condition: that he not look back at Eurydice until they have safely passed through the darkness. They make their way through the dark passage and 'it was only when he reached the sunlight again that he turned to see whether she was still behind him, and so lost her for ever' (Graves 1993: 112). Orpheus, often accused of letting Eurydice die a second time, fails to save her because he chooses to look back. In Berlanga's inverted revision of the myth, José Luis as the stand-in for Orpheus does not gaze back at Carmen, even as she offers to go with him, but instead he looks straight ahead. Terrified, even paralyzed with fear, the protagonist looks at death straight on, and in this gesture – which is to say, in not letting Eurydice die a second time with his backward glance – he effectively ushers her into death all the same.

I began this essay with John Berger's discussion of the transport inherent to cinematic experience – the way films bring us to an 'elsewhere', a space at once perceived and yet unknown; at once familiar and yet to be discovered. The shuttle between different places and times, between the 'here and now' and the 'then and there', is an action – a crucial movement in time and space – that links cinema to a twin gaze. It looks forward and backward simultaneously. Toward the future and the past, tomorrow and yesterday. For Spanish film auteur and theorist Víctor Erice, cinematic invention – the medium's future, but also its dual-drive toward mystery and revelation – is uniquely linked to the condition of contemplating the future *through* the past. In his short but extraordinary essay 'Writing cinema, thinking cinema', he contends that '[a]mong other things cinema today exists to make what we had already seen return, for better or worse. Its future, in this sense, is its past, but on the condition of contemplating it with undeceiving eyes, without fear' (Erice 2000: 269). Erice concludes the essay by drawing on the immortalized words, concrete and enigmatic, of fellow filmmaker Jean-Luc Godard, who affirmed that 'cinema authorizes Orpheus to look back without letting Eurydice die' (Erice 2000: 269).

For Erice, cinema figures as the machinery of reanimating the past, bringing it back to light, as it were. It is the device, the place, that makes ghosts visible; it is the mechanism for projecting them back into what will have been some future time; it is the discovery that what we had already seen returns with cinema – the space of the screen that invites us 'to contemplate with undeceiving eyes' (Erice 2001: 269). The backward glance permitted in cinema, indeed constitutive of cinema's flow and multidirectional movement through time, back/forth, in Erice's writing, is directly linked to the Orpheus myth. Just as Orpheus's gaze translates into a kind of curse in the myth, the same backward glance, in cinema, can rescue Eurydice from, rather than banish her eternally to, the darkness. The action of the gaze so forbidden in the myth is thus the same one that allows its object the possibility of rematerializing in the world. The original myth asks us to think what it means not to look back; to keep the gaze forward, away from the darkness and toward the light. But Erice's rereading of the tale, not entirely unlike Berlanga's project, asks us to consider a different question: What does it mean to look back and not lose sight? To look back into the shadows without fear of letting someone or something perish forever?

I have made a case throughout this essay of Berlanga's critique of the forward-oriented, blindly progressive and modernly anachronistic investment in the future that bypasses consideration of the actual conditions of the present, the same mindset that would rewrite the past rather than examine how it persists in the present; how, in its very inscription it *cannot* be rewritten. Like Berger and Bruno, for Erice, the power of cinema, through its textures, frames, edges and luminous shadows, lies in its instruction – how it invites *us* to look back, teaching us *how* to look backward by taking up the retrospective gaze as a contemplative gesture rather than a nostalgic one. It may be that the key to understanding Berlanga's executioner lies in this very gesture.

Coda: Stranger Shores

The last images of *El verdugo* show us not the anchor of the family home – the homestead, the prize, the dream realized at long last – but the boat that will transport the family, crossing back again from the island to the mainland. Perhaps even more notable, Berlanga leaves the audience with one final shot of a second boat, that Amadeo with grandson in arms, gazes out upon as he waves 'goodbye'. The camera stays here. Aboard the second boat, a small group of people, wearing formal attire, dance wildly to lively pop music. It is a party boat, though what they are celebrating remains unclear. Off screen (and now positioned directly behind the camera) everything and nothing have changed for the newly branded executioner and his family. Yet, the very last image tells us that the times, indeed, have changed. And there is a new geography in view, one with unknown inhabitants, unseen horizons and small vessels setting sail for stranger shores.

NOTES

1. The eighth feature film written and directed by Luis García Berlanga, and winner of the FIPRESCI (International Federation of Film Critics) prize at the Venice Film Festival. The title is translated as 'The Executioner', but also has appeared as 'Not on Your Life' in some English translations.
2. Scholarship on *El verdugo* is as extensive as it is significant for understanding the ever-shifting political landscape of Spanish cinema, especially during the early and middle years under dictatorship. This essay, I hope, adds to the long list of compelling interpretations of Berlanga's masterpiece by bringing the aspects of myth, photography and architecture into the wider discussion. Although my readings here focus on the little-discussed visual interplay of surfaces, domestic spaces and transitional architectural structures, I also have relied on many sources which reach beyond this scope in order to gain a deeper comprehension of the cultural and literary context within which *El verdugo* emerges. For reasons of space, I have limited a small handful of these sources to this note, for those wishing to investigate further. For a solid, concise overview of the historical context and the film's subjection to censorship, please see D'Lugo (1997), Schwartz (1986) and Marsh (2012), the latter of whom discusses Berlanga's cinema in terms of a critical political force that consistently and acutely critiques power structures through the language of 'absurdity' while at the same

time maintaining a strong commitment to 'the popular'. For readings that dissect the film's dark comedic elements and the political nature of its satirical slant, see Marsh (2003) and Sánchez-Biosca (1997); for a discussion of comedic conventionalism as it intersects with theatricality, see Ríos-Carrtalá (2007). For a similar discussion but in the context of the film script's relation to other Spanish literary works, see Zunzunegui (2012). For an interpretation of *El verdugo* that is both historical and humanist, see Mira (2005), who argues that given Berlanga's own political position being much more difficult to pinpoint, his film really offers a meditation on ethics through the kafkaesque lens of frustrated social integration.

3. 'But if the law imposes a sentence, someone has to carry it out' is the English translation in the subtitles of the remastered edition of the film by Criterion Collection (2016).
4. Family and State will enter into a 'marriage' along with the Church, thus forming the perfect triangle that would uphold Francoist ideals for the nation: State, Family, Church (replicated in the national slogan 'Una, Grande, Católica'). We see this played out later on when José Luis and Carmen get married in the church, a space which Berlanga satirizes through a visual contrast of light/darkness, where eventually total darkness 'overshadows' the 'light' of their union. The church, while not explicitly represented in the first half of the film, is subtly suggested in Amadeo's name, which means 'one who loves God'.
5. This is perhaps most explicitly seen in Berlanga's classic film *Bienvenido Mr. Marshall* (1953), where the entire town of Villar del Río, under the leadership of their mayor, Don Pablo (who like the character of Amadeo, is also played by Spanish actor José Isbert), disguises itself as a 'typically Spanish' (i.e. Andalusian) village in the hopes of impressing a group of American diplomats who will be traveling Spain's countryside to evaluate those areas most in need of assistance under the Marshall Plan, the US economic recovery package for assistance to Western European nations in the wake of the Second World War. Of course, being in disguise, the plan backfires and the diplomats never actually stop in the town to see the elaborate masquerade that the villagers have undertaken to transform their surroundings into a performance of 'Spanishness', nor do they witness the impoverished reality lurking underneath this performative façade. Another example of the failures ascribed to overinvestment in the future and specifically related to the problem of housing is Marco Ferreri and Raphael Azcona's dark satire, *El pisito* (1958).
6. Amadeo gratifyingly reads the announcement of their future dream home: 'tres habitaciones, calefacción' (three bedrooms, heat).
7. This phrase is taken from the American land art and conceptual artist Robert Smithson.
8. The scene in its entirety is remarkable for many reasons, not least of which has to do with its careful positioning in a triangulated sequence, couched between the hasty marriage of Carmen and José Luis in the church (a comedy of errors as they begin the ceremony the lights gradually go out) and the subsequent scene in city hall, the seat of government regulation and authority, where José Luis must 'enlist' himself as official *funcionario* so that they do not lose their place in line for state housing.

9. It is difficult not to make an immediate association with Juan Antonio Bardem's 1955 classic melodrama *Muerte de un ciclista* (Death of a Cyclist) when José Luis asks to throw out the cyclist: (JL: '¿Lo rompo [...]?' / C: '¿Qué?' / JL: 'el ciclista'). In Bardem's film, the cyclist represents sin, deceit and an ill-fated attempt to cover-up a crime. The cyclist (or rather, his untimely, accidental death) becomes the scapegoat for why the two lovers, Juan and María José, cannot be together. Insofar as the cyclist in Berlanga's film is a reference to Bardem's cyclist, it is interesting to note that in this context, the cyclist's image has survived his (former cinematic) death, and here meets death once again.
10. Worth noting here is the direct correlation between three distinct scenes, a line that visually and conceptually triangulates beginning, middle and end through the coffin/corpse/photograph metaphor: the first scene where José Luis carries the coffin into the prison and sets it down in a position that mirrors and also covers his entire body; the airport scene where José Luis metaphorically mirrors the corpse in the coffin through a bizarre, parallel photographic action; finally, this third scene featuring his momentous capture, and thus his mortification.

REFERENCES

Barthes, Roland (1981), *Camera Lucida: Reflections on Photography* (trans. R. Howard), New York: Hill and Wang.

Berger, John (2001), 'Ev'ry time we say goodbye', in Geoff Dyer (ed), *Selected Essays*, New York: Pantheon Books, 2001, pp. 474–82.

Berlanga, Luis García (2016), *El verdugo*, 1963, USA: Video Mercury Films, 1991, Criterion Collection.

Bruno, Giuliana (2007), 'Motion and emotion: Film and the urban fabric', in A. Webber and E. Wilson (eds), *Cities in Transition: The Moving Image and the Modern Metropolis*, London: Wallflower Press, pp. 14–28.

Bruno, Giuliana (2016), *Surface: Matters of Aesthetics, Materiality and Media*, Chicago: University of Chicago Press.

Cadava, Eduardo (1997), *Words of Light: Theses on the Photography of History*, Princeton: University of Princeton Press.

Cairns, David (2016), 'By the neck', in *El verdugo*, Criterion Collection Edition booklet, n.pag.

D'Lugo, Marvin (1997), *Guide to the Cinema of Spain*, Westport, CN: Greenwood Press.

Donald, James (1999), 'Light in dark spaces', *Imagining the Modern City*, Minneapolis: University of Minnesota Press, pp. 63–92.

Erice, Víctor (2000), 'Writing cinema, thinking cinema' (trans. Guy Wood and Julie Croy), in Linda C. Ehrlich (ed.), *The Cinema of Víctor Erice: An Open Window*, Lanham, MD: Scarecrow Press, pp. 267–69.

Graves, Robert (1993), *The Greek Myths: Complete Edition*, New York: Penguin Books.

Howe, Susan (2017), *Debths*, New York: New Directions.

Huyssen, Andreas (2006), 'Nostalgia for ruins', *Grey Room*, 23: Spring, pp. 6–21.

Marsh, Steven (2003), 'Luis García Berlanga', in *Senses of Cinema*, 25, March, http://sensesofcinema.com/2003/great-directors/berlanga/. Accessed 29 July 2019.

Marsh, Steven (2012), 'Comedy and musicals', in J. Labanyi and T. Pavlovic (eds), *A Companion to Spanish Cinema*, Malden, MA: Wiley-Blackwell, pp. 193–99.

Mira, Alberto (2005), '*El verdugo / The Executioner*', in *The Cinema of Spain and Portugal*, London: Wallflower Press, pp. 109–17.

Ríos Carratalá, Juan A. (2007), '*El verdugo* y la tragedia grotesca', *ALEUA: Anales de Literatura Española*, 19, pp. 219–35.

Sánchez-Biosca, Vicente (1997), 'Un realismo a la española: *El verdugo* entre humor negro y modernidad', in A. Bussière-Perrin and V. Sánchez-Biosca (eds), '*El verdugo' – 'Le Bourreau' de Luis García Berlanga: En homage à Ricardo Muñoz Suay*, *Co- textes*, 36, pp. 79–89.

Schwartz, Ronald (1986), *Spanish Film Directors (1950–1985): 21 Profiles*, Metuchen: Scarecrow Press.

Zunzunegui, Santos (2012), 'Strategic Auteurism', in J. Labanyi and T. Pavlovic (eds), *A Companion to Spanish Cinema*, Malden, MA: Wiley-Blackwell, pp. 160–71.

PART 4

THE EVERYDAY

8

Mediating Everyday Life: Domestic Architecture in Spanish Film

Josefina González Cubero, University of Valladolid – Centro de Estudos Arnaldo Araújo

Alba Zarza-Arribas, University of Valladolid – Centro de Estudos Arnaldo Araújo

Architecture has been a part of cinema since the advent of the seventh art in two different ways. In general, the real city was featured in films with a documentary bent that reflected their own historical time. In contrast, cinematic architectural interiors in feature films were somewhat different in that they stemmed from the tradition of theater with sets constructed *ex profeso* for the emerging cinematographic entertainment industry. This parallel exterior/interior tension in the history of urban film meant that the celebration of the metropolis in the so-called City Symphony Films during the first two decades of the twentieth century barely paid attention to the interior spaces of actually existing buildings. At the same time, feature films made during this time period almost exclusively avoided exhibiting or recreating the exterior facades of the interior spaces constructed on film sets. Faithfully showing both the inside and outside of the same architectural structures (real, fictitious or a hybrid of the two) was not typically the goal of early cinema, where the environment that framed a film's dramatic action was often merely suggested.

Aside from a few scattered bits of information on the dates and authorship of the first moving images filmed in Spain, urban spaces appeared for the first time in the footage of Madrid and Barcelona captured in 1896 by one of the camera operators of the Lumière brothers, Alexandre Promio.[1] This so-called living or animated photography was warmly received in Spain, a country with endemic economic and social challenges but where there was a growing demand for the new 'attraction films' among the viewing public in the largest Spanish cities. Barcelona was the primary center of film production at the beginning of the twentieth century and Spanish cinema produced works of the highest technical quality. Most notable was the work of the Aragonese Segundo de Chomón, who was interested in two very distinct types of cinematographic expression: picturesque scenes of Barcelona, Burgos, Gerona and Toledo as well as intensely innovative narrative 'attraction' films.

Filmmaking technology evolved during the second and third decades of the century and Madrid eventually replaced Barcelona as the center of film production, consolidating the industry. This was when fictional feature film gained ground, to the detriment of the other traditional popular urban amusements such as the *folletín* ('serialized melodramatic stories'), historic adventures, one-act dramatic farces, the *zarzuela*, melodrama and moralizing drama. The influence of these genres was waning, but they nevertheless continued to strongly influence the themes of the films made during this period. These films of the 1910s and 1920s in Spain were usually made with sets constructed of cardboard and reflected urban and domestic *costumbrista*[2] stereotypes, but the capital city made only fleeting and sporadic appearances. The same occurred in Barcelona's filmic output, even in Catalan *film noir*.

Serving as an allegory of the shift of the film industry to Madrid from Barcelona, the first sound feature film, *El misterio de la Puerta del Sol* (The Mystery of the Puerta del Sol 1929) by Francisco Elías Riquelme, captured not only the increasing urban dynamism of both cities but also a significant change in how cities are portrayed, both from the ground and from the air. On the pretext of the airplane trip of the protagonists Mr Carawa (Jack Castello) and Lia de Golfi (Nita Moreno) to save the unfortunate Pompeyo Pimpollo (Juan de Orduña) from being executed by *garotte*, Elías Riquelme inserted lengthy aerial views of Barcelona and Madrid. The first ones emphasize the grid of the blocks of the 1859 Plan de Reforma y Ensanche (Expansion and Reform Plan) of Ildefonso Cerdá. The footage of the second series of shots shows Madrid's Gran Vía under construction, following the 1899 project of the municipal architects José López Sallaberry and Francisco Andrés Octavio Palacios. The images of the flight over the capital captured the Gran Vía's most iconic buildings, but they also exhibited the imposing party walls of the city's new great artery, contrasted with blocks from the so-called Madrid of the Austrians (the section of the city planned in the sixteenth century during the reign of the Hapsburgs). This contrast between the modern and premodern exposes the open wounds in what constituted, at the time of filming, the most recent transformation of the city. In addition, local and *avant-garde* cinema also embraced architecture. Ernesto Giménez Caballero, concurrent with the 'magical realism' of the artists of the Generation of 27, tried his hand in 1930 at creating a *costumbrista* documentary cinema in *Esencia de verbena* (The Essence of the Fair). Taking a cue from the visual experimentation of 'pure' avant-garde cinema, the film utilized the architecture of Madrid's *verbena* festivals.[3] In terms of editing and composition, however, Giménez Caballero's film pales in comparison to the plastic and poetic qualities of José Val de Omar, who would later feature architecture in the experimental, atavistic and mystic portraits of the country in his *Tríptico elemental de España* (Elementary Triptych of Spain): *Aguaespejo granadino* (Water-Mirror of Granada 1952–55), *Fuego en Castilla* (Fire in Castile 1958–60) and *Acariño galaico* (Galician Caress 1962–82).

The vocation of artistic modernity coexisted during the first decades of the twentieth century with debates over national identity that took form in both film and architecture. This was a period when Spanish directors and actors looked for work in Hollywood as well as architects who, as foreigners, pontificated on the hallmarks of Spanish architectural identity. From Argentina, Martín Noel considered the meaning of Andalusian identity, while Alfredo Baeschlin, a Swiss resident living in Spain, explained that it was necessary to capture the diversity and idiosyncrasies of all regions of the Peninsula, a stance that added to internal cultural discussions concerning the construction of what it meant to be Spanish and about how to successfully create a truly national cinema and architecture. The 1929 Ibero-American Exposition of Seville and International Exposition of Barcelona would go a long way toward establishing a series of stereotypes of vernacular and historicist architecture that would paradoxically mask the consensual plundering of the heritage they defended.

Against this backdrop, the concept of the 'modern' entered into the professional world of architecture through publications and the visits of European architects who were the protagonists of the Congrès International d'Architecture Moderne (International Congress of Modern Architecture, or CIAM). Such advocates viewed modern architecture as a redemption from the ills that afflicted society through the study of minimum housing, subdivisions and modern urbanism in the four CIAM congresses celebrated in different cities across Europe.[4] They defended proposals in which only a few Spanish architects participated. The systematic disconnect, for example, between the projects presented to the Spanish Concurso Nacional de Vivienda Mínima (National Minimum Housing Competition) organized by Fernando García Mercadal in preparation for the second CIAM in Frankfurt in 1929[5] with the international proposals was proof of Spain's own distinctive set of interests. The avant-garde architecture of these professional groups rarely crossed the border into Spain. When it did, it arrived late. International art cinema and architecture documentary films had even less of an impact during this period.

Filmmaking continued during the Spanish Civil War (1936–39) for propagandistic purposes on both sides and recorded the impact the battles had on the country's cities, as well as creating highly politicized feature films to satisfy a variety of ideologically motivated populations. At the same time, in terms of architecture, the magnitude of the housing shortage got worse due to the military conflict and forced the government, imposed by General Francisco Franco's *coup d'état*, to enact the Ley del Régimen de Protección a la Vivienda de Renta Reducida (Government Law of Reduced Rent and Housing Protection) on 19 April 1939. With barely any mention of the overall social purpose of the law, this legislation recognized the housing problem and created a means to solve it: the Instituto Nacional de Vivienda (National Institute of Housing, or INV) that would remain in place from 1939 to 1977. Soon after, in 1939, the INV enacted its own Norms and Ordinances for state-subventioned housing, which established legal requirements, architectural forms and project organization, making this an important document in that it demanded mandatory compliance for all architectural projects. These laws paved the way for the normalization of state housing policies that was solidified with the Planes Nacionales de la Vivienda (National Housing Plans) for 1944–54, 1956–60 and 1961–76 that determined all of the residential housing construction for a wide variety of social groups, including the ideologically adept middle class which was granted access to relatively large, state-subventioned housing built with public funds.

The film industry backed by the Franco dictatorship was largely unaffiliated with this social panorama, and concentrated its efforts on producing films that celebrated the politics of the regime.[6] The historical feature films and folkloric *costumbrismo* genre were designed to reinforce the values of the victors and to help spectators to forget the war. New debates about national cinema and architecture, aimed to support the new regime, took place under a set of new ideological assumptions that were radically different than what had come before, and both film and architecture were seen as useful and closely related instruments for the indoctrination and social control of the masses. Reconstruction was put in the hands of the Dirección General de Regiones Devastadas y Reparaciones (General Direction of Devastated Regions and Repairs, or DGRDR) between 1938 and 1957. The DGRDR was tasked to 'restore' the morale of the population (Cárdenas Rodríguez 1941: 153) by replacing everything from real-estate properties and monuments as well as the promotion of rural space as important ways to secure and strengthen the social stability of the autarkic agricultural base. The harsh postwar years accentuated the problems of lack of access to housing, overcrowding and lack of urban hygiene that plagued large Spanish cities. To alleviate these problems, Madrid was placed front and center with Pedro Bidagor's ambitious 1941 Plan General de Ordenación (General Ordinance Plan), which was eventually approved and developed in 1946, after having to navigate through some resistance from the most powerful Francoist political families (López Díaz

2003). Bidagor was inspired by the previous Zuazo-Jansen project of 1929 that tackled the urban phenomena of the large-scale metropolis and relied on a growth model based on the planned decentralization of the urban population. The city was to be surrounded by a green belt that took advantage of existing streams and riverbeds, concentrically pushing the satellite cities outward by scattering the workers among suburbs as a response to the uncontrollable urban growth that blocked the bourgeois extension of the city.[7]

The realist pragmatism of Bidagor's Plan that took into account what was happening in the suburbs is evident in the tone of the film *El último caballo* (The Last Horse) (Neville 1950), but not in its values. This film is considered to be the first Spanish neorealist comedy and was directed by Neville after his varied experiences in United States. The film is a declaration of individual resistance to the inexorable advance of modernity in Madrid. It features the great daytime footage of the cosmopolitan center as well as the sets of the Gran Vía at night, both captured by Siegfried Burmann (Sigfrido Burman) with the special effects of Pierre Schildknecht (Pedro Schild).[8] The protagonist Fernando (Fernando Fernán Gómez) moves through the streets with his horse Bucéfalo. Like a modern Quixote, he searches the city for lodging for his animal companion despite the fact that motorized transport had long taken over the city. Both rider and horse wind up in the outskirts of Madrid, in a place where a farmer refuses to sell his land to real-estate investors. In real life, unlike in the film that celebrates the rural, change was inexorable. The economic misery of the country and the acceleration of urban industrialization contributed to the massive migratory movements of the rural population to the big cities, which offered better work prospects in industry, construction and other services while promising an increase in quality of life.

Despite the existence of a boom in historical films[9] promoted by the Valencian production company Cifesa (1932–65) that was supported by sectors of the Falange, the 1950s was truly the period of Spanish realist cinema (Deltell Escolar 2006). These types of films place social problems at the forefront, pushing aside past historical accomplishments and unleashing the misery and the majesty of the capital. This cinema often converts the city into a synecdoche of the nation. Madrid was the perfect site to shoot films, in part because it housed the headquarters of the major production companies. Initially, Francoist cinema was made with the Spanish spectator in mind, although as Spain's political isolation began to soften, Spanish film began to cross national borders. A great number of titles were released and quite a few of them focused on the most widespread problem afflicting the urban population: the lack of adequate housing. Due to the overarching desire of Spaniards for better housing, film during this period often featured residential architecture that became an emblem and backbone of the fundamental filmography in this and successive decades. Most of the many films that fall into this category demonstrate the contrast in housing quality for Spain's different social classes and exploited these differences in order to drive filmic narrative. These inequalities are found through representations of the housing of the bourgeoisie built in the nineteenth century, through the depiction of different types of mass housing (from the modest housing of the middle-class to the sublet and to the substandard housing of the *corralas*), until arriving at the self-constructed slums and the *chabolas* ('shacks') that were the result of massive migration to the cities.[10]

Housing is the vital epicenter that represents the family, and film is the means to present those families within the housing that characterizes them. The residences of the aristocratic class introduce the viewer to the mansions of long-established proprietors, whose luxurious interiors were captured by the camera in *Segundo López, aventurero urbano* (Segundo López, Urban Adventurer) (Mariscal 1952), for example. More commonly portrayed were the houses of the upper bourgeoisie or the high-ranking bureaucrats who lived on the floors of shared, collective apartment buildings in the central historic districts and in the *Ensanche*, as captured in *El último caballo* mentioned above.

FIGURE 8.1: Edgar Neville (dir.), *El último caballo*, 1950. Spain. © Edgar Neville.

Their interiors are similar to those of the elderly mother of the protagonist Alberto Closas in the emblematic *Muerte de un ciclista* (Death of a Cyclist) (Bardem 1955), whose sets were designed by Enrique Alarcón,[11] trained as an interior designer. The spacious living room and dining room are the heart of the home and are tied together in *enfilade*[12] and parallel to the illuminated principal façade, enabling the image to capture the depth of the spatial arrangement of this kind of nineteenth-century housing. The sets for the principal rooms were decoratively overdone, with coffered ceilings and large furniture that had been inherited over the course of multiple generations, accompanied by the thick curtains that create a heavy and dark environment that seem to match the age of the home's occupant.

These kinds of domestic spaces were necessary for the kind of representation of social class that can also be found in *Plácido* (García Berlanga 1961), a film where Christmas Eve dinner (Figure 8.2) is contrasted to great effect with an aristocratic space and with the protagonist's home on the outskirts of Manresa (Barcelona) on a hillside slope.

FIGURE 8.2: Luis García Berlanga (dir.), *Plácido*, 1961. Spain. © Jet Films.

FIGURE 8.3: Ramón Comas (dir.), *Historias de Madrid*, 1957. Spain. © UCE Films.

This domestic space is an 'all-in-one' kitchen-dining-living room with a bedroom and is similar to the home of Pepe (José Luis López Vázquez) and Consuelo (Julia Gutiérrez Caba) in the Madrid suburb in *Un millón en la basura* (A Million in the Dustbin) (Forqué 1967) and that of Amadeo (José Isbert) in *El verdugo* (The Executioner) (García Berlanga 1963), both of which have two bedrooms. All are either situated on the ground floor, which is where workers and low-level public servants often lived in apartment buildings during this time period, if not in basements and attics.

Due to the declining housing market, still suffering the after-effects of the war and attempting to dodge the speculative intentions of real-estate owners, the tenants are almost invariably on the verge of homelessness. The farcical comedy *Historias de Madrid* (Stories from Madrid) (Comas 1957) depicts a *comunidad de vecinos* ('tenant's association') that intends to hold on to the homes they inhabit by resisting the unfair efforts of the building's owner, the lawyers, firefighters and even employees of the city government to remove them (Figure 8.3).

In the same way, *El inquilino* (The Tenant) (Nieves Conde 1957) (considered along with *El pisito* [The Little Apartment] [Ferreri and Martínez Ferry 1958] and *El cochecito* [The Little Coach] [Ferreri 1960] to be three of the very best examples of Spanish neorealism) presents the vicissitudes of a married couple as they find housing for their family after receiving an eviction order while workers continue

FIGURE 8.4: José Antonio Nieves Conde (dir.), *El inquilino*, 1957. Spain. © Films Españoles Cooperativa.

demolishing their building in the neighborhood of Lavapiés, currently named Palacio. The deep focus shots of the domestic space (Figure 8.4) capture all three rooms of the apartment in order to stress the bareness of the central space of the living-dining room and the two lateral bedrooms of the parents and children, of distinct ages and sexes, that together with the interior adjoining kitchen and the entrance constitute the entirety of the house, whose arrangement in *enfilade* and parallel to the façade refers to the upper-class domestic spaces.

The everyday, real-world experience of attempting to maintain a roof over one's head was a recurring theme in film during this time period. The housing crisis unleashed real estate speculation in the apartments of the bourgeoisie with the subletting of bedrooms and shared access to kitchens. This collective housing experience is depicted by Juan (Fernando Fernán Gómez) and Carmen (Elvira Quintillá) in *Esa pareja feliz* (That Happy Couple) (García Berlanga and Bardem 1951), when they find in the rooftop terrace of the building a place of escape from

FIGURE 8.5: Marco Ferreri and Isidoro Martínez Ferry (dir.), *El pisito*, 1958. Spain. © Documento Films.

their stark apartment and the ruckus of the building's common patio area. The film includes an interesting critique of concrete as a new construction material that confronts more traditional types of masonry. Very similar is the bedroom of Rodolfo (José Luis López Vázquez), the protagonist of *El pisito*, which is sublet to Doña Martina (Concha López Silva) and equipped with very few pieces of worn furniture, and which is really the dining room of the apartment. The home of the old woman, whom Rodolfo needs to marry in order to inherit the subsidized rent contract when she dies, reconstructs a centrally located Madrid bourgeois apartment in detail (Figure 8.5).

Paradoxically, in the film this apartment is located in a *corrala*, a densely populated building surrounding a patio with open corridors framed by wood. In reality, such a relationship is impossible because the rooms of the *corralas*, like the ones in which Petrita (Mari Carrillo) lives with her sister and her family, are very small. This common typology of the collective residential building, generally with a narrow front and street access through a large door, is one of the most

FIGURE 8.6: José Antonio Nieves Conde (dir.), *Surcos*, 1951. Spain. © Atenea Films.

commonly represented forms of housing in Spanish film of this period. These small homes lacked adequate hygiene and had communal toilets located off of the corridors that surround the open space at the center of the *corrala*, a central space that was the lifeblood of the building and where the daily interaction with neighbors took place.

Entirely consistent with the Falangist ideological line on housing requirements and policy,[13] Nieves Conde's film *Surcos* (Furrows) (1951) (Deltell Escolar 2006: 105), characterized by its dark critical realism (Figure 8.6), depicts the arrival of a rural family to Madrid and the rapid urbanization of the working-class neighborhoods in which it takes place.

The neighborhoods of Lavapiés and Embajadores make up the built environment of the film, as well as the *corrala* where the family lives. The set of the domestic space was created by architect Antonio Labrada, who was part of Regiones Devastadas and whose expertise the director acknowledged in an interview, saying that 'in *Surcos* one can't speak of a set designer but rather a film architect' (Cobos 1997: 124). The dwellings making up these *corralas* consist of kitchen-dining-living spaces where the inhabitants live without private bedrooms,

FIGURE 8.7: Luis Marquina (dir.), *Así es Madrid*, 1953. Spain. © Cifesa and Cinesol, A.T.A.

sleeping separated only by curtains, or one or two bedrooms in the different apartments as seen in *Así es Madrid* (Such Is Madrid) (Marquina 1953) (Figure 8.7) in the sets created by Luis Pérez Espinosa and Gil Parrondo.

The most economically disadvantaged sector of the city's population that bordered on extreme poverty was concentrated in the squalor of the *chabolas* that were located in the peripheral rings of the city and built by the marginalized squatters themselves. These self-constructed slums, largely lacking in infrastructure and minimal living standards, were occupied by a great variety of people: rural immigrants in *Cerca de la ciudad* (Near the City) (Lucia 1952), social outcasts like Jacinto (Antonio Vico) and Pepote (Pablito Calvo) in *Mi tío Jacinto* (Uncle Hyacinth) (Vajda 1956) who live in a shack scarcely capable of holding two rickety beds and a table (Figure 8.8) and gypsies in *Tiempo de amor* (Time of Love) (Diamante 1964).

The film *Un ángel tuvo la culpa* (An Angel's Fault) (Lucia 1960) reflects this side-by-side coexistence and the contrast between this low-quality housing that is destined to disappear with the new, more modern buildings that are encroaching on these parts of the city (Figure 8.9).

FIGURE 8.8: Ladislao Vajda (dir.), *Mi tío Jacinto*, 1956. Spain. © Chamartín, Falco Film and Enic.

FIGURE 8.9: Luis Lucia (dir.), *Un ángel tuvo la culpa*, 1960. Spain. © Exclusivas Floralva Producción and Santos Alcocer P.C.

FIGURE 8.10: Fernando Fernán Gómez (dir.), *La vida por delante*, 1958. Spain. © Estela Films.

These cinematographic images are powerful and convincing. The threatening, looming housing blocks are for the wealthy and are not meant for the inhabitants of the *chabolas* who lack the means to buy them.

Private housing initiatives received a great boost from the 1954 Ley sobre Protección de Viviendas de Renta Limitada (Law of Reduced Rent and Housing Protection) and the II Plan Nacional de la Vivienda (Second National Housing Plan) of 1956–60, both of which shared the objective of constructing a high number of state-planned homes. This legislation created housing categories that allowed for even smaller living spaces than the ones proposed by previous legislation. At the same time, separate legislation in the form of the Ley de Arrendamientos Urbanos (Urban Leasing Laws) in 1946, 1955 and 1964 eliminated the prewar renting regulations. The interior spaces of these new homes are expertly ridiculed in the mise en scène of the film *La vida por delante* (Life Ahead) (Fernán Gómez 1958). The constrained movements of Antonio (Fernando Fernán Gómez) and Josefina (Analía Gadé), the lack of intimacy as a result of the open interior patio (Figure 8.10) and, above all, the negligible quality of the construction are the main sources of the film's humor.

FIGURE 8.11: Luis García Berlanga (dir.), *El verdugo*, 1963. Spain. © Naga Films and Zabra Films.

A similar critique is found in *El verdugo* when the lack of space in the new home of José Luis (Nino Manfredi) is evident even before the building is finished (Figure 8.11) and, once construction is complete, these constraints are accentuated since the living room is connected to every other room in the house.

In terms of film style, the combination of grotesque realism with *costumbrista* and neorealist elements allowed for a cinema of dissent that was often capable of eluding censorship. Deeply rooted in the dual traditions of theater, picaresque literature and Madrilenian farce, the urban films of this time period were not to the liking of the Franco regime. Some censors also looked down on this form of popular cinema, a sentiment expressed by one critic who wrote that 'olía a cocido' (smelled like stew).[14]

During Spain's march to the consumption-driven drum of *desarrollismo* (late Francoist modern economic development), commercial comedies made up the most popular film genre. In these films, social issues either disappear entirely or are transformed into a light, nonthreatening dialogue between tradition and modernity. These popular comedies often dealt with both the old and emerging bourgeois families that increasingly inhabited the new buildings constructed in the privileged zones of the elegant suburbs. In the house of the father of María José (Mabel Karr) in *El día de los enamorados* (Valentine's Day) (Palacios 1959) situated on the Paseo Pintor Rosales from the Cornisa of Madrid, for example, the wide terraces flow toward the Casa de Campo (Figure 8.12) while those of the

FIGURE 8.12: Fernando Palacios (dir.), *El día de los enamorados*, 1959. Spain. © Asturias Films and AS Films.

flat of Agustín Valverde (Eduardo Fajardo) of *La ciudad no es para mí* (The City Is Not for Me) (Lazaga 1966), situated in the Parque de las Naciones (the work of architect Eleuterio Población Knappe), form the prominently featured façade of the building looking toward Guzmán el Bueno Street (Figure 8.13).

The interiors are made up of large rooms with several areas centered around the fireplace that combine elements of design with traditional furnishings and service areas where domestic maids work in large, well-equipped kitchens. This luxurious form of living is characterized by an abundance of space, tasteful modern décor and panoramic views of large parks.

The Franco regime's decision to open up to the outside world along with the creation of centers of industrial development in different cities in Spain with the three Planes de Desarrollo (Development Plans) between 1964 and 1975 resulted in the rapid growth of many cities, which subsequently transformed the landscape and the consumer habits of middle-class Spaniards, who began to focus more on home ownership as the goal or dream that would usher them into the upper class. Just as these plans were being realized, however, another concern materialized. The sugary sweet film *La gran familia* (The Great Family) (Palacios 1962) and its three sequels reflect the stereotypes prevalent during the Franco regime concerning the

FIGURE 8.13: Pedro Lazaga (dir.), *La ciudad no es para mí*, 1966. Spain. © Pedro Masó Producciones Cinematográficas.

ideal family, featured in this film by the marriage of Carlos (Alberto Closas) and Mercedes (Amparo Soler) together with their fifteen children and grandfather. The large apartment where they live in central Madrid, with relatively modern amenities (two bathrooms and central heating), is that of a comfortably well-off family headed by a father who is a professional. One of the father's principal worries is how to afford a vacation for his large family. This concern would become more common in the films of the time, which progressively dealt with the phenomenon of coastal tourism that was increasingly located in nonmetropolitan residential areas.

With a clear understanding of the capacity of cinema to be used as propaganda and a means of indoctrination of the masses, the regime produced official state films which were coetaneous with the fictional films of the larger film industry in order to spread its ideals and accomplishments. The newsreels known as NO-DO (short for Noticiarios y Documentales Cinematográficos [Newsreels and Cinematographic Documentaries]) were produced between 1943 and 1981[15] and for decades established the form and tone of the audiovisual news reports of the Franco regime. NO-DO, as the only and obligatory newsreels, spread a particular Spanish reality whose main characteristic was what Rafael Tranche and Vicente Sánchez-Biosca have called 'banalidad como sistema' (banality as a system) (2006: 514). NO-DO formed a propagandistic cinema that rarely focused on the individual and only

FIGURE 8.14: NO-DO Nº 764A (1957). Courtesy of the Filmoteca Española (Spanish Film Archive).

showed sporadic images of everyday actions such as the demolition of shacks and images, as seen in Figure 8.14, that depict the arrival of the displaced with their belongings to their new homes in the heralded San Fermín neighborhood of Madrid, as seen in the 1957 NO-DO Nº 764A.

In addition to the newsreel, NO-DO produced the weekly magazine *Imágenes* (Images) and documentary films that reused sequences from the newsreels to document and summarize the nature of the urban evolution undertaken by the INV and the Ministry of Housing (1957–77). Through reports concerning the activities of the Planes Nacionales de la Vivienda (National Housing Plans) and the Planes de Urgencia Social (Emergency Social Plans) of various cities (Madrid in 1957, Barcelona in 1958 and Bilbao in 1959), NO-DO captured on many different levels the urban and construction policies of the regime.

Going from a modest to a grander scale, the 1959 documentary *Sesenta mil viviendas. Plan de Urgencia Social de Madrid* (Sixty Thousand Homes. The Social Emergency Plan of Madrid) and issue 1034 of the 1964 magazine *Imágenes*, titled *25 años de paz: España edifica* (25 Years of Peace: Spain Builds, Domínguez)

FIGURE 8.15: Manuel Domínguez (dir.), *25 años de paz: España edifica*, NO-DO *Imágenes* Nº 1034, 1964. Courtesy of the Filmoteca Española (Spanish Film Archive).

showed the reconstruction work, the destruction of the shacks[16] and the establishment of new residential areas, including footage paying particularly close attention to the interiors of the new but modest homes (Figure 8.15).

In contrast, the use of aerial views and panoramas to create the cinematographic image of the new growth of Spanish cities was used in this documentary, with the camera acting as a witness to the magnitude of both the modern urban interventions and deficiencies, as highlighted in *La vivienda en España* (Housing in Spain) (Marrero 1972). Filmed eight years after the commemorative short film of the 25 years of official housing policies and Franco's dictatorship, this film continued to take note of the great vacant spaces between the newly constructed neighborhoods (Figure 8.16).
However, the treatment of public spaces in the street, plazas and neighborhood has improved considerably with pavements, the creation of parks and gardens, and even the incorporation of public art.

The final years of Francoism and the beginning of the political transition to democracy were marked by a rather uneven film production when it comes to

FIGURE 8.16: Juan Antonio Marrero (dir.), *La vivienda en España*, 1972. Instituto Nacional de la Vivienda and NO-DO. Courtesy of the Filmoteca Española (Spanish Film Archive).

architecture as a cinematic theme. This was a time when Spanish film was divided between work that prioritized political commitment to social issues on the one hand and more popular film celebrating the frivolity of the *destape*[17] that resulted from Spain's desire for freedom after four decades of dictatorship. However, four films shot in Madrid serve to skip over this period and to maintain the central thread of the role underscored by the city and housing following the creation and evolution of the development of the Ampliación del Barrio de la Concepción, as exemplified in the film *Día de los muertos* (Day of the Dead) (1960), the first documentary film short of Julián Marcos and Joaquim Jordà, *Tiempo de amor*, *Colegas* (Pals) (Iglesia 1982) and *¿Qué he hecho yo para merecer esto!* (What Have I Done to Deserve This?!) (Almodóvar 1984).

Bidagor's Plan for Madrid recognized, as mentioned earlier in this essay, an urban reality what was already in place. The future residential suburbs for workers were meant to create the exterior ring of his imagined city. These suburbs had their antecedent in the agricultural or workers' neighborhoods that had sprung up under the protection of a succession of Leyes de Casas Baratas (Affordable

Housing Laws) in 1911, 1921, 1922 and 1925. Their seminal nuclei arose at the end of the nineteenth century in the small towns that bordered the capital. The neighborhood of Concepción, situated in the municipality of Canillas, was the seed from which the new suburb of the same name was built (1947–53)[18] after the annexation of the neighboring towns to the larger city center in 1949. The 3,000 homes and public spaces of the neighborhood were superior in quality to those of the subsequent expansion, announced in 1958 and named the Ampliación del Barrio de la Concepción (the Extension of the Barrio de la Concepción).[19] This project initially consisted of ten superblocks containing 5,000 homes, nine of which were constructed parallel to each other and perpendicular to what would eventually become the M-30 freeway.

These peripheral neighborhoods emerged everywhere under Francoist urban legislation. They were far from the historic city center and poorly connected through transportation infrastructures. These areas were not always self-sufficient and often lacked high-quality social services. For decades they have been ringed by horizontal lines of barren lands and never benefitted from the completion of Bidagor's aforementioned urban plan for introducing green spaces between them. The enormous scale of the Ampliación del Barrio de la Concepción remained isolated like phantasmagorical blocks of funeral niches looming in the background of visitors that come to the Almudena Cemetery in the film *Día de los muertos* (Day of the Dead) (1960). The cinematic treatment of these spaces differs from the evasive lateral appearance of the ends of these blocks in the final scene of the film *Tiempo de amor*, toward which the young couple walk on the still under construction unpaved surface of the M-30 freeway, after having helped a gypsy woman give birth in a shack in the neighborhood formerly known as San Pascual or La Bomba.[20]

Moving into the 1980s, the Ampliación del Barrio de la Concepción became densely populated and its location was often used to explore certain common urban themes. *Colegas*, a film closely associated with Spain's *cine quinqui*,[21] explores social marginalization and delinquency, while *¿Qué he hecho yo para merecer esto!* in a more comic tone delves into the stifling everyday life and work of Gloria (Carmen Maura), a cleaning lady and housewife. The superblocks in which the families live are formed by independent units constructed in the form of an H, a characteristic design for the new urban developments that featured an interior neighborhood patio divided by stairs, which by default become the only space of contact between neighbors. Each stairwell encapsulates a microcosm of distinct ways of life. Even though everyone living in these structures is struggling economically, the exchanges that take place in the stairwells reveal a variety of social differences.

FIGURE 8.17: Pedro Almodóvar (dir.), *¿Qué he hecho yo para merecer esto!*, 1984. Spain. © Tesauro.

A typical home in the Ampliación del Barrio de la Concepción, recreated in the studio for the Almodóvar film *¿Qué he hecho yo para merecer esto!* but based on a real-life model, was around 60 square meters large and consisted of a living room, three bedrooms, a kitchen, a bath and hallway. In the two films mentioned above, the common factor is overcrowding, more severe in *Colegas* than in *¿Qué he hecho yo para merecer esto!* where the kitsch embellishment brings humor to the negative aspects of domestic life in the most long-standing tradition of *costumbrista* farce. The rigid repetition of the wall of balconies from which Gloria appears, gradually incorporated into the interior of the houses, means that the inhabitants face endless replicas of themselves in this form of postmodern vertical *chabolismo* (Figure 8.17).

The realistic depiction of the neighborhood in both films was not so much a criticism of the modern city (which was more an aspiration for social transformation by thinkers and architects than a constructed reality) as much as a critique of its perverse qualities. Thus, these films criticize how the modern city was used to justify the fierce private speculation that Madrid suffered with the consent of the dictatorship. The arrays of buildings, rising from the earth and populating a vast wasteland, speak through powerful and eloquent images in these films. In *Colegas*, the social life of adolescents takes place on the heaps of rubble left behind after the construction process while toward the end of *¿Qué he hecho yo para merecer esto!* the image of the lizard (tellingly named Dinero [Money]) resting on a broken brick that the grandmother (Chus Lampreave) lovingly collects captures an isolation that has completely disappeared now that the neighborhood has been so thoroughly sutured into Madrid's surrounding neighborhoods.

When access to housing once again became a less pressing issue in the 1980s, cinema returned to romanticize the urban center, especially the different categories of bourgeois housing from the nineteenth century. Bohemians, intellectuals and professionals from different economic classes come together during the cultural optimism of the *movida* that extended from Madrid to other cities in the rest of Spain portrayed as taking place in housing that permitted new types of alternative and liberating forms of social life. This way of living prevails until interrupted in the high-end modern loft of Pepa (Carmen Maura) in *Mujeres al borde de un ataque de nervios* (Women on the Verge of a Nervous Breakdown) (Almodóvar 1988), a studio recreation by art director Félix Murcia (Murcia 2002: 140) that is entirely inconsistent with the eclectic buildings used in the background in the film's street scenes.[22] The 220 square meter apartment serves as a base for the protagonist's trysts and consists of a large two level living room with the kitchen and bedroom on each side, all of them with views through the big windows to a large terrace with a privileged vantage point of the skyline of an embellished Madrid painted in the background. But what truly characterizes this modern home is how it creates an urban simulation of nature. In the two films of Almodóvar mentioned in this essay, it is only through the views from the terraces to the exterior urban panorama seen through the eyes of the protagonists that we come to ascertain their social status as well as the kinds of tastes found of the interiors of their homes (Figure 8.18).

During the growth of the modern 'welfare society' and the accompanying boom in urban construction, the middle class aspired to improve their social status by acquiring property in low-density urban areas on the urban periphery (Simón Ruiz 2015). This push initially started with the new settlements at the beginning of the twentieth century and adapted a more advanced form in the Poblados Dirigidos de Renta Limitada (Directed Rent-Controlled Settlements) of the 1950s, which were designed by an entire generation of young architects who mixed together different types of housing and turned into what came to be known as the popular and successful 'Spanish urban sprawl' since the 1980s. Unlike earlier housing, a new type of two-story, single-family row house made up the monolithic suburbs of these social climbers, the so-called *adosados* after which the film *Adosados* (Suburbs) (Camus 1995) took its name. This film explores how the well-ordered life of the family of Andrés (Antonio Valero), a successful accountant, is torn apart by a little white lie he tells his wife (Ana Duato). The film takes place in the perfect house of the perfect couple, a spacious and comfortable architectural set design created by Rafael Palmero, where behind the home's domestic nature hides the

FIGURE 8.18: Pedro Almodóvar (dir.), *Mujeres al borde de un ataque de nervios*, 1988. Spain. © El Deseo and Lauren Film.

fragile consistency of their lives and the isolation and loneliness of the building's inhabitants (Figure 8.19).

Diametrically opposed to this experience is the unclassifiable documentary *En construcción* (Work in Progress) (Guerín 2001), a work that does not interest itself in housing as a finished product as much as the process of urban transformation and its social impact. Resembling *cinema-verité*, the film converts the spectator into a *flâneur* who contemplates the construction of a new building inside the Barrio Chino of Barcelona (Figure 8.20), condensing the real duration of the long construction process in layers of time. The film describes the urban process instead of emphasizing the goal of the material fact of the completion of the building in a way that pieces together the fragments of the lives that happen inside and near it.

In 1998, the conservative government promulgated the Ley de Suelo (Land Use Law), declaring all ground to be 'urbanizable' unless expressly prohibited. The uncontrolled explosion of construction throughout all of Spain as a result of said law created the illusion of the idea of progress that sustained the country's economic growth. Like a fallen angel, this boom ended at the beginning of the twenty-first century with a collapse that resulted in a dire financial crisis that was hardly linked to plunging home values. This scenario left sectors of the population defenseless before the evictions of people unable to pay off the easy mortgages they had previously acquired for their homes. This experience is reflected in a series of contemporary documentary and narrative films such as *Techo y comida* (Food and Shelter) (Castillo 2015), *Cerca de tu casa* (Near Your House) (Cortés 2016) and *La granja del Pas* (The Paso Farm) (Munt 2015), just to name a few.

FIGURE 8.19: Mario Camus (dir.), *Adosados*, 1995. Spain. © Enrique Cerezo P.C.

FIGURE 8.20: José Luis Guerín (dir.), *En construcción*, 2001. Spain. © Ovideo.

This filmography has had an impact thanks to its social commitment to addressing these controversial themes. If the second half of the twentieth century promoted the idea in Spain that it was a great achievement to own a home and learn to live within its architectural form, the beginning of our current century has begun with a sense of despair over the fact that housing continues to be the great challenge on which the survival of urban dwellers depends.

The life of residential buildings and everyday homes,[23] both real and invented, is recorded through film with great emotional impact. Cinematic architectural forms and spaces are unfailingly tied to the feelings of their inhabitants, the common men and women who make up Spanish cities. As film spectators, the sentimental involvement with the diegesis of the screen drives us to architecture, because fictional lives and the spaces they inhabit speak to our own memories and experiences. At the same time, this cinematographic baggage is what mediates our perception of the real buildings in which we live.

Acknowledgments

This work was funded by national funds through FCT – Fundação para a Ciência e a Tecnologia, I.P., through project UIDB/04041/2020.

A. Zarza-Arribas gratefully acknowledges financial support from Fundação para a Ciência e Tecnologia (FCT, Portugal) through grant SFRH/BD/141720/2018.

Translated by David Foshee.

NOTES

1. These 1896 films include *Place du port à Barcelone* (Port square in Barcelona) (Promio 1896a), *Puerta del Sol* (Promio 1896b) and *Porte de Tolède* (Gate of Toledo) (Promio 1896c).
2. Translator's Note: *Costumbrismo* is a term used in the Hispanic world for the literary and pictorial interpretation of everyday life, mannerisms and customs in the nineteenth century. *Costumbrismo* can be satiric, moralizing or can romanticize quaint folkloric detail.
3. Translator's Note: A cross between an amusement park and dance party, *verbenas* in Spanish cities usually take place after dark in the summer. Madrid's most famous *verbena* takes place on 14 August, which is the *Noche de la Virgen de la Paloma* (Night of the Virgin of the Dove) in the Plaza de la Paja, Calle Toledo and up to the Plaza de las Vistillas. This celebration has been made into a series of popular operettas and films.

4. The International Congresses of Modern Architecture took place before the Second World War in La Sarraz Castle, Switzerland, 1928; Frankfurt, 1929; Brussels, 1930 and Athens, 1933.
5. To better appreciate the differences between the Spanish proposals and those of the Second International Congresses of Modern Architecture, see 'Concurso de la vivienda mínima' (1929) and *L'habitation minimum* (1997).
6. *Frente de Madrid* (*Carmen fra i rossi*, Madrid Front) (Neville 1939); *Sin novedad en el Alcázar* (*L'assedio dell'Alcazar*, The Siege of the Alcazar) (Genina 1940); and the Spanish productions *¡A mí la legión!* (Follow the Legion!) (Orduña 1942); *Rojo y negro* (Red and Black) (Arévalo 1942) and *Raza* (Race) (Sáenz de Heredia 1941), among others.
7. Sambricio (2003a: 13–14) detects in the architecture of the Francoist regime a certain continuity with pre-Civil War architectural sensibility, while he argues that Franco-era urbanism undergoes a radical break by looking toward new solutions.
8. Until recently, set directors in Spanish films appeared as 'decorators' due to a lack of definition and recognition for the profession of set design in general. For an in-depth study of set designers in Spain, see Gorostiza (1997).
9. These historical films take place during Spain's imperial period after the marriage of the Catholic Kings and the War of Independence against the French. The most well-known titles include Juan de Orduña's *Locura de amor* (Madness for Love) (1948); *Agustina de Aragón* (Agustina of Aragon) (1950); *La leona de Castilla* (The Lioness of Castile) (1951) and *Alba de América* (Dawn of America) (1951) as well as *Lola la Piconera* (Lola the Coal Girl) (Lucia 1951) and *Amaya* (Marquina 1952).
10. For further information on housing issues in Madrid during and after the Spanish Civil War, see Sambricio (2014: 63–105).
11. Among other things, Enrique Alarcón is primarily responsible for the cinematic architecture of films such as *La calle sin sol* (The Sunless Street) (Gil 1948); *Muerte de un ciclista* (Death of a Cyclist) (Bardem 1955); *Calle Mayor* (Main Street) (Bardem 1956); *Los jueves, milagro* (Miracles of Thursday) (Berlanga 1957); *El inquilino* (The Tenant) (Nieves Conde 1957) and *Las chicas de la Cruz Roja* (Red Cross Girls) (Salvia 1958), *Los golfos* (The Delinquents) (Saura 1959); *El día de los enamorados* (Valentine's Day) (Palacios 1959) and *El cochecito* (The Little Coach) (Ferreri 1960).
12. Translator's Note: An *enfilade* is a suite of rooms formally aligned with each other and a common feature in the grand European architecture since the Baroque period.
13. Minimal hygienic requirements were met in terms of ventilation, natural light and water supply, in accordance with the different characteristics of each region. The stated requirements were that 'each living unit must be organized according to the following principles: the separation of the bedrooms of the parents and the children by gender; to give the housing unit a room that "symbolizes the idea of a home" ' (*Servicios Técnicos de FET y de las JONS* [1939: 29], cited in López Díaz [2003: 29]).

14. This is the reproach of Wenceslao Fernández Flórez, a member of the Board of Censors, to Fernando Fernán Gómez (Fernán Gómez 1990: 70).
15. The Spanish NO-DO newsreel, first created in 1942, was screened before the beginning of all feature films and was obligatory in all of the movie theaters in Spain and its colonies until 1975. NO-DO served as the propaganda tool par excellence of the regime and were aimed at the mass movie-going general public until production stopped in 1981. In addition to the newsreels, the NO-DO production company created the magazine *Imágenes* and 570 films, mostly documentaries in black and white as well in color. For more on the history and social function of the NO-DO, see Tranche and Sánchez-Biosca (2006).
16. The efforts of the dictatorship to eradicate the *chabolas* is the topic of the documentary *Ocharcoaga* (Grau 1961) produced by the Ministry of Housing but destined only to be seen by Franco himself. The purpose of the film was to prove that the marginal type of housing in the neighborhood of Bilbao represented in the film had been eradicated.
17. Translator's Note: Film of the *destape* period in Spain (a popular term meaning a period of 'uncovering or opening up') is defined by its high erotic content featuring gratuitous female nudity. These films made up a significant portion of all Spanish film production in the years after the easing of censorship laws after the death of Francisco Franco in 1975.
18. For the history and evolution of the Barrio de la Concepción, see Roldán Calzado (2013).
19. For specific information on the Extension of the Barrio de La Concepción and its cinematic representation, see Andrés Moncayo (2014).
20. The *La Bomba,* or 'Without permission' neighborhood consists of a group of self-made housing structures constructed in large part by rural migrants from Extremadura and Andalucía to the capital city. The building process took place at night in order to avoid police patrols.
21. Translator's Note: 'Cine quinqui' in Spain was an enormously popular genre of crime and delinquent films made during the transition to democracy in the late 1970s and 1980s. In addition to the films mentioned here, other notable examples include *Yo, el Vaquilla* (Me, the Heifer) (Loma 1985); *Los placeres ocultos* (Hidden Pleasures) (Iglesia 1977) and *Juventud drogada* (Drugged Youth) (Truchado 1977), where socially marginalized criminals (themselves known as *quinquis*) played theatrical versions of themselves.
22. The film presumably takes place in the attic of the Casa Marqués de Morella on 7 Montalbán Street, a 1906 building of architect Felipe Mario López Blanco in a wealthy zone of Madrid between the Paseo del Prado and Retiro Park, similar to the family home of his lover Iván (Fernando Guillén) in building 38 on Almagro Street, a work of the architect Augusto Martínez de Abaria, constructed from 1912 to 1914.
23. According to Rafael Moneo, the life of the building far from the architect who conceives of it is the inexorable destiny of architecture, which only qualifies as architecture when it abandons the drawing and becomes a constructed reality: 'Me gusta ver cómo el edificio asume su propia condición, vive su propia vida' (I like to see how the building takes on its own condition, lives its own life') (Rafael Moneo 2004: 614).

REFERENCES

Almodóvar, Pedro (1984), *¿Qué he hecho yo para merecer esto!* (What Have I Done to Deserve This?!), Spain: Tesauro (Sets: Román Arango and Pin Morales).

Almodóvar, Pedro (1988), *Mujeres al borde de un ataque de nervios* (Women on the Verge of a Nervous Breakdown), Spain: El Deseo S.A. and Lauren Film S.A. (Art Director: Félix Murcia).

Andrés Moncayo, José Manuel de (2014), 'La arquitectura de los contenedores sociales en el cine: La Ampliación del Barrio de la Concepción de José Banús', *Square and Circle. Crítica, Ciudad y Arquitectura*, 21 November, https://squareandcircle.wordpress.com/tag/cine/. Accessed 30 July 2018.

Arévalo, Carlos (1942), *Rojo y negro* (Red and Black), Spain: Compañía Española de Propaganda, Industria y Cinematografía S.A. (CEPICSA) (Sets: Antonio Simont).

Bardem, Juan Antonio (1955), *Muerte de un ciclista* (Death of a Cyclist), Spain and Italy: Trionfalcine and Guión Producciones Cinematográficas (Sets: Enrique Alarcón).

Bardem, Juan Antonio (1956), *Calle Mayor* (Main Street), Spain and France: Suevia Films, Play Art and Iberia Films (Sets: Enrique Alarcón).

Camus, Mario (1995), *Adosados* (Suburbs), Spain: Enrique Cerezo P.C. (Art Director: Rafael Palmero).

Cárdenas Rodríguez, Gonzalo (1941), 'La reconstrucción nacional vista desde la Dirección General de Regiones Devastadas', *II Asamblea Nacional de Arquitectos*, Madrid, 25 June 1940, pp. 145–55.

Casares Rodicio, Emilio (ed. and coord.) (2011), *Diccionario del cine iberoamericano. España, Portugal y América*, vol. 3, Madrid: SGAE.

Castillo, Juan Miguel del (2015), *Techo y comida* (Food and Shelter), Spain: Diversa Audiovisual (Art Directors: Amanda Román and Paco Cárdenas).

Claver Esteban, José María (2012), *Luces y rejas: estereotipos andaluces en el cine costumbrista español (1896–1939)*, Sevilla: Centro de Estudios Andaluces.

Cobos, Juan (1997), 'Entrevista con Nieves Conde', *Nickel Odeon: revista trimestral de cine*, 7, pp. 120-129.

Comas, Ramón (1957), *Historias de Madrid* (Stories from Madrid), Spain: UCE Films (Sets: Tadeo Villalba).

'Concurso de la vivienda mínima' (1929), *Arquitectura*, 123, pp. 286–299.

Cortés, Eduard (2016), *Cerca de tu casa* (Near Your House), Spain: Bausan Films, Televisió de Catalunya (TV3) and Televisión Española (TVE).

Deltell Escolar, Luis (2006), *Madrid en el cine de la década de los cincuenta*, Madrid: Ayuntamiento de Madrid.

Diamante, Julio (1964), *Tiempo de amor* (Time of Love), Spain: Época Films (Sets: Ramiro Gómez).

Domínguez, Manuel (1964), *25 años de paz: España edifica* (25 Years of Peace: Spain Builds), Spain: NO-DO.

Elías Riquelme, Francisco (1929), *El misterio de la puerta del Sol* (The Mystery of the Puerta del Sol), Spain: Hispano de Forest Fonofilms (Sets: Paulino Méndez).

Fernán Gómez, Fernando (1958), *La vida por delante* (Life Ahead), Spain: Estela Films (Sets: Eduardo Torre de la Fuente).

Fernán Gómez, Fernando (1990), *El tiempo amarillo. Memorias (1943–1987)*, Madrid: Debate, vol. 2.

Ferreri, Marco (1960), *El cochecito* (The Little Coach), Spain: Films 59 (Sets: Enrique Alarcón).

Ferreri, Marco and Martínez Ferry, Isidoro (1958), *El pisito* (The Little Apartment), Spain: Documento Films (Sets: José Aldudo).

Forqué, José María (1967), *Un millón en la basura* (A Million in the Dustbin), Spain: Pedro Masó P.C. and CB Films (Sets: Antonio Simont.).

García Berlanga, Luis (1957), *Los jueves, milagro* (Miracles of Thursday), Spain and Italy: Ariel, S.A. and Continental Produzione Domiziana Internazionale Cinematografica (Sets: Enrique Alarcón).

García Berlanga, Luis (1961), *Plácido*, Spain: Jet Films (Sets: Andrés Vallvé).

García Berlanga, Luis (1963), *El verdugo* (The Executioner), Spain and Italy: Naga Films and Zabra Films (Sets: José Antonio de la Guerra).

García Berlanga, Luis and Bardem, Juan Antonio (1951), *Esa pareja feliz* (That Happy Couple), Spain: Films Españoles Cooperativa (Sets: Bernardo Ballester).

Genina, Augusto (1940), *Sin novedad en el Alcázar* (*L'assedio dell'Alcazar*) (The Siege of the Alcazar), Italy and Spain: Film Bassoli and Ulargui Films (Sets: Gastone Medin).

Gil, Rafael (1948), *La calle sin sol* (The Sunless Street), Spain: Suevia Films (Sets: Enrique Alarcón).

Giménez Caballero, Ernesto (1930), *Esencia de verbena* (The Essence of the Fair), Spain.

Gorostiza, Jorge (1997), *Directores artísticos del cine español*, Madrid: Filmoteca Española, Ediciones Cátedra.

Gorostiza, Jorge (2016), *Panorámicas urbanas. 50 películas esenciales sobre la ciudad*, Barcelona: Editorial UOC.

Grau, Jorge (1961), *Ocharcoaga*, Spain: PROCUSA, Ministerio de la Vivienda.

Gubern, Román et al. (2000), *Historia del cine español*, Madrid: Ediciones Cátedra.

Guerín, José Luis (2001), *En construcción* (Work in Progress), Spain: Ovideo.

Historical Archive of NO-DO (2018), http://www.rtve.es/filmoteca/no-do/. Accessed 10 July 2018.

Iglesia, Eloy de la (1977), *Los placeres ocultos* (Hidden Pleasures), Spain: Alborada P.C. (Sets: Justo Pastor).

Iglesia, Eloy de la (1982), *Colegas* (Pals), Spain: Ópalo Films (Sets: Juan Puerto).

L'habitation minimum (1997), Facsimile of Julius Hoffmanns publication from 1933, Zaragoza: Delegación de Zaragoza del Colegio de Arquitectos de Aragón.

Lazaga, Pedro (1966), *La ciudad no es para mí* (The City Is Not for Me), Spain: Pedro Masó Producciones Cinematográficas (Sets: Antonio Simont).

Loma, José Antonio de la; Loma Jr., José Antonio de la (1985), *Yo, el Vaquilla* (Me, the Heifer), Spain: Golden Sun, Jet Films and In-Cine Compañía Industrial Cinematográfica. (Set Decoration: Joaquín de Miguel).

López Díaz, Jesús (2003), 'Vivienda social y Falange: ideario y construcciones en la década de los 40', *Scripta Nova. Revista electrónica de Geografía y Ciencias Sociales*, 7:146 (024), http://www.ub.edu/geocrit/sn/sn-146(024).htm. Accessed 23 July 2018.

Lucia, Luis (1951), *Lola la Piconera* (Lola the Coal Girl), Spain: Cifesa (Sets: Siegfried Burmann).

Lucia, Luis (1952), *Cerca de la ciudad* (Near the City), Spain: Goya Films P.C. and Exclusivas Floralva Producción S.A. (Sets: Eduardo Torre de la Fuente and Bernardo Ballester).

Lucia, Luis (1960), *Un ángel tuvo la culpa* (An Angel's Fault), Spain: Exclusivas Floralva Producción and Santos Alcocer P.C. (Sets: Siegfried Burmann).

Marcos, Julián and Jordà, Joaquim (1960), *Día de los muertos* (Day of the Dead), Spain: Uninci SA.

Mariscal, Ana (1952), *Segundo López, aventurero urbano* (Segundo López, Urban Adventurer), Spain: Bosco Films.

Márquez, Ricardo (2011), 'El barrio de la Concepción – Madrid', *Historias matritenses. Investigación sobre barrios desaparecidos y actuales de Madrid. Viejos estudios cinematográficos de Madrid. Historias con encanto del Madrid antiguo. Viejos tranvías madrileños*, 13 March, http://historias-matritenses.blogspot.com/2011/03/el-barrio-de-la-concepcion-madrid.html#ixzz5HFVLOI1u. Accessed 23 July 2018.

Marquina, Luis (1952), *Amaya*, Spain: Cifesa (Sets: Luis P. Espinosa).

Marquina, Luis (1953), *Así es Madrid* (Such Is Madrid), Spain: Cifesa and Cinesol, A.T.A. (Sets: Luis Pérez Espinosa and Gil Parrondo).

Marrero, Juan Antonio (1972), *La Vivienda en España* (Housing in Spain), Spain: Instituto Nacional de la Vivienda and NO-DO.

Moneo, Rafael (2004), 'La soledad de los edificios/The Solitude of Buildings', in *El Croquis*, Madrid: El Croquis, pp. 608–15.

Munt, Silvia (2015), *La granja del Pas* (The Paso Farm), Spain: Intent Produccions and Televisió de Catalunya (TV3).

Murcia, Félix (2002), *La escenografía en el cine. El arte de la apariencia*, Madrid: Fundación Autor.

Neville, Edgar (1939), *Frente de Madrid* (*Carmen fra i rossi*, Madrid Front), Italy: Film Bassoli.

Neville, Edgar (1950), *El último caballo* (The Last Horse), Spain: Edgar Neville (Sets: Siegfried Burmann. Special Effects: Pierre Schildknecht).

Nieves Conde, José Antonio (1951), *Surcos* (Furrows), Spain: Atenea Films (Sets: Antonio Labrada).

Nieves Conde, José Antonio (1957), *El inquilino* (The Tenant), Spain: Films Españoles Cooperativa (Sets: Enrique Alarcón).

NO-DO Nº 764A (1957), Spain: NO-DO.

Orduña, Juan de (1942), *¡A mí la legión!* (Follow the Legion!), Spain: Cifesa (Sets: Emilio Ferrer).

Orduña, Juan de (1948), *Locura de amor* (Madness for Love), Spain: Cifesa (Sets: Siegfried Burmann).

Orduña, Juan de (1950), *Agustina de Aragón* (Agustina of Aragon), Spain: Cifesa (Sets: Siegfried Burmann).

Orduña, Juan de (1951a), *Alba de América* (Dawn of America), Spain: Cifesa (Sets: Siegfried Burmann).

Orduña, Juan de (1951b), *La leona de Castilla* (The Lioness of Castile), Spain: Cifesa (Sets: Siegfried Burmann).

Palacios, Fernando (1959), *El día de los enamorados* (Valentine's Day), Spain: Asturias Films and AS Films (Sets: Enrique Alarcón).

Palacios, Fernando (1962), *La gran familia* (The Great Family), Spain: Pedro Masó Producciones Cinematográficas (Sets: Antonio Simont).

Promio, Alexandre (1896a), *Place du port à Barcelone* (Port Square in Barcelona), France and Spain: Société Antoine Lumière et ses Fils.

Promio, Alexandre (1896b), *Puerta del Sol*, France and Spain: Société Antoine Lumière et ses Fils.

Promio, Alexandre (1896c), *Madrid, Porte de Tolède* (Gate of Toledo), France and Spain: Société Antoine Lumière et ses Fils.

Rodríguez Merchán, Eduardo (2011), 'Historia del cine español', Pantalla Caci, http://pantallacaci.com/ibermedia-digital/contexto-historico/historia-del-cine-espanol/. Accessed 18 July 2018.

Roldán Calzado, Juan Luis (2013), *La Concepción y San Pascual*, Madrid: Temporae.

Sáenz de Heredia, José Luis (1941), *Raza* (Race), Spain: Cancillería del Consejo de la Hispanidad (Sets: Luis Martínez Feduchi and Siegfried Burmann).

Salvia, Rafael J. (1958), *Las chicas de la Cruz Roja* (Red Cross Girls), Spain: Asturias Films (Sets: Enrique Alarcón).

Sambricio, Carlos (ed.) (2003a), *Plan Bidagor 1941–1946: Plan General de Ordenación de Madrid*, Madrid: Comunidad de Madrid, Nerea.

Sambricio, Carlos (ed.) (2003b), *Un siglo de vivienda social: 1903–2003*, Madrid: Nerea.

Sambricio, Carlos (2014), 'Un siglo de vivienda social en España', in *I Congreso Nacional sobre Vivienda Social* (El verdadero problema de la vivienda 'No tenerla'), 14 and 15 March, Seville: Real Fundación Patronato de la Vivienda de Sevilla, pp. 63–105.

Sambricio, Carlos and Sánchez Lampreave, Ricardo (eds.) (1997), *La vivienda protegida: historia de una necesidad*, Madrid: Ministerio de Vivienda.

Saura, Carlos (1959), *Los golfos* (The Delinquents), Spain: Films 59 (Sets: Enrique Alarcón).

Simón Ruiz, Alfonso (2015), 'El chalé adosado, sueño de la clase media', *CincoDías*, 2 October, https://cincodias.elpais.com/cincodias/2015/10/02/sentidos/1443811010_551662.html. Accessed 20 July 2018.

Tranche, Rafael R. and Sánchez-Biosca, Vicente (2006), *NO-DO. El tiempo y la memoria*, Madrid: Cátedra.

Truchado, José (1977), *Juventud drogada* (Drugged Youth), Spain: Amanecer Films (Sets: José Antonio de la Guerra).

Vajda, Ladislao (1956), *Mi tío Jacinto* (Uncle Hyacinth), Spain and Italy: Chamartín, Falco Film and Enic (Sets: Antonio Simont).

Val del Omar, José (1952–82), *Tríptico elemental de España* (Elementary Triptych of Spain): *Aguaespejo granadino* (Water-Mirror of Granada), *Fuego en Castilla* (Fire in Castile) and *Acariño galaico* (Galician Caress), Spain.

9

Through the Looking Glass: Images of the Ordinary World in Oscar-Nominated Spanish Cinema

Emeterio Diez Puertas, Camilo José Cela University

María de Arana Aroca, CEU – San Pablo University

Spanish cinema enjoys a variety of forms and structures, but it usually adheres to the model provided by classical drama, where the elements of storytelling include *climax, incident, conflict, archetype* and, as we will see in this chapter, concepts such as *verisimilitude, identification* and *suspension of disbelief*. It is through these latter techniques in particular that the viewer is invited into the world on the screen. These narrative mechanisms allow us, just as in Lewis Carroll's *Alice Through the Looking-Glass*, to cross through the mirror and enter into fictional worlds (Eco 1984: 217–24).

Those worlds are often imagined through narrative strategies that create the location of the story through what Bakhtin called a *chronotope* (Bakhtin 1981: 84–258), which he defines as a particular space-time. Sometimes *chronotopes* create the everyday, sometimes the fantastic, on occasion the oneiric and, in the case of science fiction, the marvelous. Oftentimes the scenario in which a story takes place is established in the first few words of a novel, in the first scene of a play or in the first minutes of a movie. It is at these points where the reader or the viewer plunges into the ordinary world in which the story is going to take place (Vogler 2007: 83–97). For example, see the first sentence of *Don Quixote*: 'In a village in La Mancha, the name of which I have no desire to recall [*topos*], there lived not so long ago [*cronos*], one of those gentlemen who always have a lance in the rack, an ancient buckler, a skinny nag, and a greyhound for the chase [*character*]' (Cervantes 1998: 25). The content and form of these first words fix the *chronotope* of the *story*, the *protagonist*, the *actantial object*[1] and the *genre*, and as a result the reader's imagination creates the world in which the story takes place. Naturally, every possible world stems from and contains a concrete ethical or ideological conceptualization, which means that every work has its own vision or worldview (Dilthey 1976: 133–54; Diez Puertas 2014: 248).

What is relevant here to the study of filmic architectural and urban spaces is that the filmmaker can only create *chronotopes* resorting to ephemeral architecture such as sets, or filming in indoor or outdoor locations where one can find architecture or landscaped nature. This means that a film's set designer has to create an architectural world in a variety of ways in order to build a new reality shown on a screen to the viewer, a 'looking-glass reality'. This fictional scenery has to enable the transformation of the screen into a soft like gauze and then a sort of a mist so the audience can 'go through the looking glass' and discover an active world. The idea developed in this chapter is that in order to go 'through the looking glass' in the first minutes of the story, a film must provide the viewer with an architectural code of recognition, transformation and spatial construction.

The initial dramatic situation is of vital importance in screenplays that, with every scene, provide a framework that creates the story's location and time. For example, in *Mi querida señorita* (My Dearest Señorita) (1972), the first line of the screenplay says: 'Adela's House (Bedroom). Int. Day'.[2] We have the *cronos* (day) the *topos* (interior of a bedroom in the house) and the *character* (Adela). It is true that the script is not the movie. *El nido* (The Nest) (1980) begins with a frame that says 'Pine forest. Exterior. Day',[3] but the first frame of the film is the second of the script: 'don Alejandro Matesanz's house. Exterior. Day'.[4] Nevertheless, the *chronotope* is always clearly defined.

The point being made here is that in the first few minutes of a film, the initial dramatic situation includes the photography of the territory where the action will take place. The sets with which the film begins are more than a mere spatiotemporal framework and often have greater value than the subsequent sets seen throughout the film. It is important to note as well that often in feature film, the sets of the last scenes echo those that appear in the beginning, which means that films will often end with a slight variation on the ordinary world presented in the initial shots. If in every film there is a process of *semiosis* of the production of signs to be interpreted, the initial dramatic situation becomes a privileged place for analysis, to ask questions about the meaning and, as is explored in this volume, to study the relationship between architecture and worldview within the Spanish context. Given the characteristics of this volume, we have chosen to analyze a sample of films that are as international as possible, by focusing on the nineteen Spanish films chosen by Hollywood to compete in the Oscars in the 'Best Foreign Language Film' category, presenting five particular cases in detail. What this approach reveals has a dual nature: the ordinary world that Spain wants to project in Hollywood and, at the same time, the architectural image through which the members of the Academy have, over the years, crossed, going 'through the looking glass' and entering the Spanish spatial imaginary.

To analyze the architectural codes established by these images, we will follow the guidelines for urban perception outlined by Kevin Lynch in his book *The Image of the City* (1990). He looks at the city from the point of view of the urban planner/architect and wonders which qualities a city should have. According to his thesis, the city's scenery is something that we share with the rest of its inhabitants, becoming ourselves a part of this very same scene. Through surveys, he studies how people perceive and describe different cities. Their answers allow him to list the distinguishing elements that make it possible to recognize the image of the city and to make it understandable, since the construction of a mental image of a space is only possible if it is 'clear' or 'legible'. Lynch concludes that people understand the city as a series of *nodes, districts, landmarks, edges* and *paths*. Our perception of the city is fragmentary and partial, Lynch concludes, and it is only by integrating these isolated perceptions that we create its image in our minds. This integrative life experience is echoed by every film spectator during the process of watching a film. For these reasons, Lynch's ideas about the mental construction of urban space can also be used to discover the defining spatial elements that construct a filmic narrative image. In other words, the elements of an urban image come through when the image of a cinematic *chronotope* is created by a filmmaker.

La venganza *(Vengeance) (1958): The Path of Reconciliation*

Lynch points out that paths are the routes that observers follow and as such they must be identifiable and continuous. In the city, these paths are the streets, the alleys, the avenues or the boulevards. In the countryside, they are the roads that lead to a town and the trails that lead to a place where there is a fountain, a meadow or a mill. As Lynch explains, the need for a sense of direction is satisfied by the organization of the physical world. All paths are differentiated by the number of lanes, their width or the geometry of their design, and they can be understood in relation to other elements such as landmarks or edges (Lynch 1990: 49–62). How this functions can be seen in *La venganza* (Juan Antonio Bardem 1958), a film whose ordinary world begins with a path. The first moments show a rural road, which is an element that transforms nature into an ordered space. *La venganza* consists of a long road trip, which also works on a metaphorical level to create the film's meaning. The script of *La venganza* places the beginning of the story in 1931 and opens with the phrase: 'This is how Juan came to town.'[5] The film starts with a panoramic view of the fields, which are carefully cultivated, immense and create a sense of loneliness. The camera pans the landscape until it pauses on the small village of Sabiote, in the province of Jaén. This is the protagonist's initial destination and the camera focuses on the path that leads Juan Díaz there. Many stories start when characters arrive or leave, or when they set out on a path. Lynch suggests that these routes tend to be designed with origin and end points. If the routes are clear, they give the observer a sense of location within any place, at any time. They allow one to understand the scale and grasp the distance travelled or yet to be travelled, because the perception of space is always related to the sequence of events. The same happens in a story. The return or departure of the hero takes place in order to achieve a goal or a cure such as love, money or justice, for example. In *La venganza,* the protagonist arrives on a road and meets two *guardias civiles* ('military policemen'). The bodies of the policemen form the two jambs of the space of a physical door that becomes a threshold. It is the gate of the law that can be crossed only when the protagonist shows his identification papers (Figure 9.1).

Soon after, Juan's purpose is clear. He has been in prison for ten years for a crime he did not commit and returns to the village with the intention of killing Luis (also known as 'the Crooked One'[6]) whom he believes is guilty of his false

FIGURE 9.1: Juan Antonio Bardem (dir.), *La venganza*, 1958. Spain. © Metro Goldwyn Mayer.

accusation. But circumstances force him and his sister to join his enemy's team of workers harvesting wheat, which puts off their revenge. Together they travel through the landscapes of Andalucía, Castilla-La Mancha and Madrid, mowing the grain fields where their personal histories evolve. The cinematography of Mario Pacheco transforms the countryside into landscape. Critics of this film have always commented on the great beauty of the natural settings chosen by the film's artistic director Enrique Alarcón. The roads are the only lines that are drawn on the cultivated surface of the landscapes created in this film, underscoring the capacity of cinema to use the expressive peculiarities of paths as an element of meaning. The urban film spectator enjoys being exposed to unknown places, however. As the director himself said in an interview, these places are 'a few meters from the great national highways'.[7]

La venganza is also a road movie because it can be understood as the journey along a long path pointing toward change perceived both geographically and metaphorically. The film advances through three regions of Castile while the hero suffers a series of trials that causes him and his fellow travelers to be transformed until the conclusion, when both the protagonist and his sister decide not to proceed with their planned act of revenge. This realistic, seemingly possible world within the film created by Bardem clearly contains a political worldview. The paths are a metaphor for the roads that Spain could have taken in 1958, a country still very much divided by the Civil War of 1936. The action of the film takes place in 1931, but this was a strategy to avoid any possible imposition on the part of the censors. What Bardem proposes, then, is to take the path of national reconciliation: to find a path to peace between both sides, Republicans and Francoists, much as the Communist party of Spain proposed in 1956.[8] This idea is expressed in the scene where the workers doing the harvesting (the people) meet a writer (the intellectual), a character who stands in for the director's voice. He tells them that

> the important thing is to talk to everyone and see what they think and what hurts each one of them or what they are happy about or what their hopes are. Often people are enemies simply because they occupy separate spaces and don't talk to each other.[9]

Plácido *(1961): Nodes and Simulacra*

For Lynch, nodes imply strategic points, centers or nuclei in the city. They can be the confluence of paths or the central spaces of districts, a crossroads, a corner where people gather, a park or a square. They can be places from which one leaves or toward which one walks. The observer can enter into the nodes and, even though they are conceptually modest, they can be almost dimensionless, or they can even be expansive areas in cities. City dwellers decide which direction to take in the nodes, and the urban elements that surround them are perceived with more attention and clarity (Lynch 1990: 72–78). Many nodes, like paths, are named by the signs that hang from the walls of the city, such as 'Times Square' or 'Washington Square'. These signs are also recognized in the credits of *Plácido*, the 1961 film directed by Luis García Berlanga. The very beginning of the film presents the plot in a caricatured way, while the credits gradually appear on posters that recall the signage of the streets and squares, anticipating how the city will make up the scenery that gives continuity to the story.

Plácido opens by presenting the spectator with a node. The screenplay states that the first scene consists of the following: '1 – Streets and square with evacuation kiosk – (Ext. – Day)'.[10] This particular node is Manresa Square on Christmas Eve, 1961 (Figure 9.2), but it exemplifies what any Spanish provincial town square is like. Only the most attentive observer will realize that it is Manresa if she looks, for example, at the advertising that later appears in the train

FIGURE 9.2: Luis García Berlanga (dir.), *Plácido*, 1961. Spain. © In-Cine.

station. It was only for production reasons that the film was shot in Barcelona and in Manresa (García Berlanga 1994: 1). The storyline called for any anonymous town. In the square, a delivery vehicle crowned with a Christmas star enters the scene from a distance and then circles the place. This vehicle drives the plot of the film, because Plácido, the owner, must pay his monthly car payment so the bank does not repossess the property on which his livelihood depends. The film hinges on the adventures of Plácido and his family over the period of one day and takes place between the aforementioned urban node and his family's home on the outskirts of town.

The square is not only a public place where people come together but also one of gossip, status-making and pretense. This is why city councils usually place benches for people to sit on in public squares, along with newspaper or music kiosks, in addition to trash bins and public toilets because this is a space where leisure and public services converge. It is in the square where the action of *Plácido* begins. To be precise, the action begins in the public urinals, tucked away in a semi-underground space. These were, in their day, one of the most important urban solutions to prevent cities from being centers of disease, although working there was one of the least desirable occupations one could have. The public urinal is the place where we meet perhaps not the most destitute citizens of the city (within the film, these are the senior citizens in the asylum), but certainly the poorest of the city's workers: Plácido's family. His wife works and practically lives in this underground space, simultaneously attending to the public and to her family with the same sense of familiarity. She is first seen at work with her baby in her arms, yelling at her brother who is shaving in the public sink as if he were at home.

This space anticipates the choral nature of the film, which consists of a great number of characters who come and go. This combination of Christmas and public bathrooms, the spiritual and the fecal, is entirely consistent with the type of everyday worlds created by García Berlanga. García Berlanga was known for his peculiar humor that came from a sense of the chaos, meaninglessness and absurdity of collective daily life and this is why his films are so conducive to satires of Spanish behavior. Best captured in the title that García Berlanga initially proposed for the film (subsequently banned by the censors) *Siente un pobre a su mesa* (Seat a Poor Man at Your Table), the film satirizes the practice of Catholic charity prevalent at that time in Spain. *Plácido* portrays charity as annoying and cumbersome and the poor as something that gets in the way. There are two superimposed spaces in the film: the festive bourgeois world represented by the Christmas star and the world of the resigned poor, who are invisible except when they satisfy the vanity of the former. In fact, Christmas dinner is a mockery: the bourgeois welcome the poor as in a performance. That is why the carol at the end of the film, when Plácido's family arrives at his home empty-handed and with no desire to celebrate, makes an ironic statement:

> Mom, there is a little boy at the door shivering from the cold…Tell him to come in and warm up. Because in this world there is no longer any such thing as charity, nor has there ever been or ever will be.[11]

Los Tarantos *(1963): Opposing Districts*

Districts, says Lynch, are homogenous sections of the city that have certain characteristics that distinguish them from surrounding areas. You can enter them, but you can also see them from outside or from their edges. The physical characteristics that define them such as textures, symbols, types of construction, their uses and the activities that take place in them are continuously present, and they can often be distinguished by certain types of inhabitants or characteristic sounds (Lynch 1990: 66–72). One of the Spanish films that best demonstrates how districts shape the ordinary worlds of protagonists is *Los Tarantos*. Filmed with a realistic aesthetic, the action takes place in Barcelona in the early 1960s and attempts to recreate gypsy traditions in an almost ethnographic way. The film's style is somewhat surprising because it takes flamenco out of the folkloric world typical of Spanish musical cinema and places it within the context of everyday life with a near-documentary naturalness.

The theme is not new and is based on a play by Alfredo Mañas entitled *Historia de los Tarantos* (The Story of the Tarantos), a drama that, in turn, is inspired by Shakespeare's *Romeo and Juliet*. As such, it is a love story between two young people who belong to dueling families and has a predictable fatal outcome. Here, the story presents the opposition between two gypsy families, the Tarantos and the Zorongos. The old disputes are kept alive through continuous confrontation and the drama flares up again when two young people from these families fall in love. If *West Side Story* (Robert Wise and Jerome Robbins 1961) shows the confrontation between two ethnic groups, between those who considered themselves to be the 'natives' pitted against the 'immigrants', in *Los Tarantos* the conflict is between rival families of the same ethnic group, but with different ways of relating to the territory where they live. In fact, the duality and the conflict between pairs permeates the entire film, and the ordinary world of each of the two protagonists is shown to be clearly differentiated.

The film begins with the fixed image of an urban neighborhood next to the market onto which the credits are projected. One hears, synchronous with the image, the rhythmic tapping of the flamenco music. This is fundamental because it completes the characterization of the spatial context. The rhythm adds a layer onto the image that makes the space more specific by selecting for the viewer which group of people within this diverse city space will serve as the protagonist. It is the territory in which the Tarantos move, a district with an urban structure of paved streets and alleyways, markets and bars. The city is made recognizable through the presentation of urban landmarks such as the Mercado del Born, with which the film opens, the bullring Las Arenas and the municipal slaughterhouse – elements that serve to distinguish and define this neighborhood.

After a fight between members of the two families that exemplifies an enmity reaching far back into the past, the Zorongos flee, crossing the edge of the city delineated by the train tracks, eventually reaching the slums of Montjuic and Somorrostro (Figure 9.3). This ordinary world is located in a high place from which can be seen the industrial areas of the city and, far beyond, open fields. This is the margin of the city and reaches the sea – that ultimate limit to the mainland. Here we meet the confrontation of the two worlds. The sedentary lifestyle that had made the Tarantos economically prosperous was portrayed by an urban neighborhood, a static and solidly built environment. Meanwhile, the Zorongos' neighborhood is shown to be full of motion and creates a sense of weightlessness. In fact, the first image of this space presented is in full motion, with a dance, in contrast to the initial fixed photo. The streets here do not have cobblestones. Instead, they are made of earth and improvised dance floors are created with cardboard.

FIGURE 9.3: Francisco Rovira-Beleta (dir.), *Los Tarantos*, 1963. Spain. © Sigma III.

The building structures on the beach, where it is always windy, are fragmentary, sometimes because they are in ruins, but also because that is how they were originally constructed.

In short, the first image of the film serves to construct the ordinary world of the characters while also serving as the key to understanding the main theme of the film, which is the significance of territory. The romantic storyline and the confrontation between families overlap with the underlying theme of the opposition between a sedentary lifestyle and nomadism. Thus, the neighborhoods of the protagonists, which make up two territories with very different qualities, reflect the inherent conflict within this gypsy ethnic group. Ever since the arrival of gypsies to the peninsula in the fifteenth century, their history has been shaped by mistrust, on the part of nongypsies, of nomadism. Through the years, this lifestyle has been associated with idleness and delinquency and frequently considered to be something to be resisted.

Tristana *(1970): The Edge as Enclosure*

Edges are linear elements that one cannot always walk along. They are not considered paths, although they can coincide with them. According to Lynch, they are limits between two different states; border elements such as walls, fences, valleys or rivers that act as parallel references. The strongest of them are not necessarily the most prominent but those that offer greater continuity and, also, greater impenetrability, such as walls and moats. The edge allows us to perceive the entirety of a district or a city, and to discover its character and recognize it (Lynch 1990: 62–66).

One salient example of the presentation of the ordinary world as an edge is *Tristana*, directed by Luis Buñuel. *Tristana* is based on a novel by Benito Pérez Galdós (1843–1920) whose action takes place in the district of Chamberí in Madrid, around the year 1891. Buñuel, however, moves the action to Toledo in 1923 and makes the city a fundamental element of the film. Although the script only mentions a 'provincial city',[12] Buñuel always thought about filming parts of Toledo as his co-scriptwriter, Julio Alejandro, recalls: 'we had very clear locations in mind. Those places are not casual references, but the heart and soul of the script. The city marks the script in such a way that it would be very, very hard to set it anywhere else'. Shifting the time period of the story and preserving the location in Madrid would have demanded a great number of changes from the original text related to social customs. But the city of Toledo makes the story of Don Lope more plausible, since he is a gentleman who presumes to be liberal but has all the characteristics and quirks of a Spanish *hidalgo*. Proof of this is his relationship

FIGURE 9.4: Luis Buñuel (dir.), *Tristana*, 1970. Spain. © Mercurio Films.

with Tristana, a young orphan whom he welcomes when her parents die and who eventually becomes his protégé, his lover and his wife. Toledo in 1923 is the type of city that can, still, accommodate old-fashioned *hidalgos*. This is precisely the idea that is presented to us in the first shot of the film: a provincial city, small and isolated, shown from the south, rising to the border of the Tagus River, almost frozen in its physiognomy since the seventeenth century (Figure 9.4).

This shot that opens the movie and serves as a background to the credits is an image that recalls the Toledo paintings of El Greco and Ignacio Zuloaga. It presents an impenetrable edge along the river built as a continuous perimeter that makes the city recognizable. While El Greco, at the beginning of the seventeenth century, chose the most modern view of the city that included the Hospital de Tavera, the Puerta de Bisagra (the Bisagra City Gate of Toledo) or the Alcázar fortress, avoiding the presence of the medieval religious buildings, in *Tristana* these are precisely the buildings that are captured in the panning shot. Toledo is presented as a compact element, almost like a landmark in itself, with the cathedral, the Church of Santo Tomé, the seminary and, on the western boundary, San Juan de los Reyes, accompanied by the sound of the bells ringing, accentuating the city's religious nature. After this establishing shot, the action situates Tristana and her companion Saturna walking outside the walls, emphasizing the idea of a closed, isolated and medieval city.

Just as the trumpets of the priests demolished the walls of Jericho, in *Tristana* the sexual perversion of the characters and the violence of the workers against authority has the potential to break down the physical and psychological borders and edges of Don Lope and Tristana's world. Buñuel's surrealism, with its appeal to the oneiric, the incongruous, the symbolic, the erotic, the anarchic and the chaotic, was the way to overcome the traumas generated by a conservative and Catholic education. Something similar happens in *Tristana*. Buñuel introduces the perverse real and the oneiric hyperreal; kissing the recumbent statue of Cardinal Tavera and dreaming about the head of Don Lope in the form of the clapper of a bell. Because, as Pelosi says, 'Buñuel is not so interested in the subject of the subdued woman, but the internal process of degradation and perversion that Tristana suffers throughout the film'.[13]

In this sense, the film comes full circle. In the climactic scene, Don Lope is lying in bed, very sick and fearing some sort of revenge from Tristana. Tristana does, in fact, open the bedroom window when it is snowing so that the cold of the street will accelerate his death. She then remembers her previous life in a series of short scenes that lead to the moment that the film begins; that is, when she and Saturna were on the other side of the wall, on the edge. With this ending, we see them walking toward the interior of the city and the space of the enclosure. It is as if the narration began again, as if another Tristana was to meet Don Lope; as if still, in 1970, when the film was shot, there were similar stories. Buñuel always said: 'Yes, I am Don Lope. It's become my story. Very liberal, very anti-clerical at the beginning and then, in old age, sitting at a cozy table, drinking hot chocolate – and what chocolate! – with three priests. And outside, the snow keeps coming down' (Aub 2017: 104).

Volver a empezar *(Begin the Beguine) (1982) and the Landmarks of Nostalgia*

Landmarks, writes Lynch, are reference points observed from the outside. They can be either far away or local and, also, be inside or outside of the city. Uniqueness is key in these elements, as they need to be able to be unequivocally distinguished. For this reason, they are easier to identify if they have a well-defined shape, if they contrast with their background and if they are located in a prominent place. Lynch also says that the image of landmarks is strengthened if they are located at a place where decisions are made, or if they are linked to a story, a sign or some other form of meaning (Lynch 1990: 78–83).

In the first Spanish film to win an Oscar, *Volver a empezar* directed by José Luis Garci, the landmarks allow the filmgoer to recognize the city of Gijón. At the same time, because the landmarks are related to the history of the protagonist, the writer Antonio Miguel Albajara, these urban elements introduce us to his past. The action begins with his arrival in Gijón after a long exile in the United States due to the Spanish Civil War. He returns to Spain for a brief stay, shortly after democracy has been established and the dictatorship is over. This is his last farewell to his native land since he has been diagnosed with a fatal illness.

The first scenes of the film depict the arrival of a train to the city, which ever since the silent film era was a way for cinema to represent the railway station as the gateway to both the city and the ordinary world. Subsequent to these first images begins a tour of a number of landmarks. In this case, these are readily recognizable points in the city that range initially from the most general, universal or impersonal to the most intimate until the camera finally rests on the family home. First, the loading docks and cranes of the port and then the station's identifying place sign, which consists of the purely informative word 'Gijón', work together to define the city. This objectivity shifts, however, when the camera reaches the Robledo Cinema. This is the first landmark where the objective description of the city is overlapped with the subjectivity of the main character (Figure 9.5). The movie house can be widely recognized as a characteristic landmark of the city of Gijón, but Antonio's gaze secludes it in the sphere of intimacy, memory and nostalgia. It is an urban reference, but a personal one as well.

The way that the landmark is connected to the character is always through the gaze. No one can enter a landmark. It is a visual reference, a reference point,

FIGURE 9.5: José Luis Garci (dir.), *Volver a empezar*, 1982. Spain. © José Esteban Alenda.

clearly differentiated from the nodes, the paths or the neighborhoods in which the inhabitant or, in our case, the protagonist and, by extension, the viewer, can be located. Thus, we will see how Antonio Miguel Albajara does not enter any of the subsequent landmarks, but only looks for their surface image. One sees how the tour of the port, the beach or the old Mercado de la Pescadería (Fish Market) differs from a tourist's journey by the protagonist's expression when he observes the series of urban landmarks. Places that create a recognizable city are linked to nostalgia, as can be seen in the look of the protagonist, who is reliving his own personal history. The protagonist's gaze points out the landmarks that are being visited in the present and that will be recalled as scenery of the past throughout the film. Just as the appearance of landmarks in urban space facilitates the recognition and remembrance of a path walked, their sequence in the film is linked to the memory of a time lived: in this case, the 1930s. These are the years that are evoked in the opening credits with the instrumental version of the song that gives title to the film, *Begin the Beguine*. The 1930s were the key moment in the life of the characters, the years that defined their lives, those longed-for years when they were connected by love and friendship and separated by war and exile.

The final credits are presented as a double or mirrored image. A dedication – long and explicit – appears 'to the men and women who began to live their youth in the thirties'[14] and the musical version is no longer instrumental, but choral with verses such as '[i]t brings back a memory ever green'. The film, however, is not only about the specific life histories of the characters, or even the nostalgic and personal relationship between the present and the past. The film's worldview is inseparable from its historical moment: the transition to democracy. When the film was released, critics thought of the film as a tribute to the exiles of the Civil War and a lesson in democracy in the sense that Garci proposed a reunion and a solution for the Spanish people worried about the future of the country. As Garci notes, 'It's a film without anguish for distressed people'.[15] This is a film meant to overcome the anxiety of an uncertain historical moment. In other words, the nostalgia for the past must be overcome because the country has changed, as the protagonist realizes. Garci said that the film 'is the story of a people who have faith in life and have never been disenchanted. Perhaps today is time to start over again, because it's the only way to do things right'.[16]

The Efficient Image: Object, Structure and Meaning

Our hypothesis throughout these pages has been that the signs that allow us to understand the image of the built city are also those that allow us to understand the image of the cinematic city. Thus, the world of audiovisual fiction is constructed with paths, edges, districts, nodes and landmarks much like the cities of urban planners. It should be noted that the image of this specular city is also the superposition of the many different categories that are apprehended on an individual level. In order to make a systematic exposition, these pages have been devoted to exemplifying each of Lynch's distinctive city elements with a specific film. However, several of the films belonging to the sample could have served as examples and, above all, in ordinary worlds, as in our cities, the division into strict, clear categories is not always possible. These elements that have been described separately usually appear together or overlap with one another: there are paths that coincide with edges or landmarks located within nodes.

For example, Lynch's three elements (edge, path and landmark) characterize *Secretos del corazón* (Secrets of the Heart) (Montxo Armendáriz 1997). At the beginning of the film, two fatherless brothers have to cross a river (an edge) every morning on the way to school. The older brother, Juan, uses a shortcut to cross the river by stepping on stones. But Javi, who is eight years old, is afraid. He says that he prefers to go over the bridge because he needs a firm path. Juan responds: 'Only chickens cross the bridge! Coward!'[17] This situation helps the director to develop the idea of the crossing of the river as a metaphor for the child who has to cross another border: a border of secrets tied together with fears, silences and lies. In the film, the secrets are represented by a landmark, the abandoned mansion where a crime of passion took place. As the director makes clear in his discussion of his work, in this film the secrets of sex and death are the ones that the child discovers (Armendáriz 2000: 5).

Another example of overlapping demarcating spatial interrelationships can be found in *Mamá cumple 100 años* (Mama Turns 100 Years Old) (Carlos Saura 1979). The film opens by showing us the edge of Madrid while playing the pasodoble *Dos de mayo* (Second of May), composed in 1908 by Federico Chueca to commemorate the fight against the French. The camera moves, panning to the left and down to show us an area in the mountains where two landmarks are located: a grave and the house where the story takes place. This film is the continuation of *Ana y los lobos* (Ana and the Wolves) (Carlos Saura 1973), so the house is the same and the grave belongs to José, the authoritarian character and collector of military uniforms (Sánchez Vidal 1988). In this sequel, the building and the grounds are the objects of a family dispute. The children want to sell everything to let urban speculators into the neighborhood and even try to hasten the death of their own mother. In other words, the landmarks are the objects of speculation and their demolition is nothing more than the demolition of a Francoist society betrayed from within. The film can, therefore, be understood as another interpretation of the Spanish transition to democracy. The mother says, reviewing her life, that it is the history of the country: 'So much cruelty! So much stupidity! So much pettiness, my children! How much useless suffering! How much useless sacrifice!'[18]

In short, Lynch argues that an effective image requires the identification of an object; that is, a recognition that the object is an entity distinguishable from its environment. This is only possible if it has a structure and if it includes a spatial relationship with other objects as well as with the observer. What is more, it must have a certain meaning for the observer. Throughout this chapter we have seen that the urban elements enunciated by Lynch shape an image of the ordinary world in meaningful ways that are connected to the director's worldview. Thus, in our analysis of Spanish Oscar-nominated films, we have recognized the filmic morphology of the paths in the fields of Castile, of the nodes in the squares of provincial cities, of districts in the gypsy neighborhoods of Barcelona, of edges in the walls of imperial Toledo and, finally, discovered the landmarks in nostalgia-scattered Gijón.

Translated by Dania Al-Barghuthi.

NOTES

1. Translator's Note: In the structural semantics model developed in 1966 by semiotician Algirdas Julien Greimas, the actantial object is one of three roles typically performed in storytelling: (1) the hero or villain who opposes the hero; (2) the sender who initiatives the quest and (3) the object of the quest. Julia Kristeva, Vladimir Propp and more recently Bruno Latour have used the concept in their work on mediation and translation.
2. 'Casa de Adela (Dormitorio). Int. Día' (Armiñan 2003: 203).
3. 'Pinar. Exterior. Día' (Armiñan 2003: 327).
4. 'Casa de don Alejandro Matesanz. Exterior. Día' (Armiñán 2003: 329).
5. 'De cómo Juan llegó al pueblo.'
6. 'el Torcido'.
7. 'a escasos metros de las grandes carreteras nacionales' (Bardem 2002: 241).
8. Coinciding with the twentieth anniversary of the beginning of the Spanish Civil War, the Communist Party declared that it was prepared to end the division opened by war and work for national reconciliation. From that moment it renounced the violence and put an end to the guerrilla warfare that had been waged.
9. 'lo importante es hablar con todos y ver qué piensan y qué le duele a cada uno o de qué se alegra o cuál es su esperanza, que muchas veces los enemigos lo son por estar apartados y sin hablar y no por otra cosa.'
10. '1 – Calles y plaza con quiosco evacuatorio – (Ext. – Día)' (García Berlanga 1994: 1).
11. 'Madre, en la puerta hay un niño, tiritando está de frío... Dile que entre y se calentará. Porque en este mundo ya no hay Caridad ni nunca la ha habido ni nunca la habrá.'

12. 'ciudad de provincias'.
13. 'a Buñuel no le interesa tanto la temática de la mujer sometida, sino el proceso interno de degradación y perversión que sufre Tristana a lo largo del filme' (Pelosi 2011: 102).
14. 'a los hombres y a las mujeres que empezaron a vivir su juventud en los años treinta'.
15. 'Es una película sin angustias para la gente angustiada' (Garci 1982: 46).
16. 'es la historia de una gente que tiene fe en la vida y nunca ha estado desencantada. Quizás hoy es el momento de volver a empezar, porque es la única manera de hacer bien las cosas' (Garci 1982: 46).
17. '¡Por el puente solo cruzan los gallinas! ¡Cobarde!'.
18. '¡Cuánta crueldad! ¡Cuánta estupidez! ¡Cuánta mezquindad, hijos míos! ¡Cuánto sufrimiento inútil! ¡Cuánto sacrificio inútil!'.

REFERENCES

Armendáriz, Montxo (2000), *Secretos del corazón*, Madrid: Ocho y medio.

Armiñán, Jaime (2003), *Eva sin manzana. La señorita. Mi querida señorita. El nido*, Madrid: Cátedra.

Aub, Max (2017), *Conversations with Buñuel: Interviews with the Filmmaker, Family Members, Friends and Collaborators*, Jefferson, NC: McFarland & Company.

Bakhtin, Mijail (1981), 'Forms of time and of the chronotope in the novel', in Michael Holquist (ed.), *The Dialogic Imagination: Four Essays*, Austin: University of Texas Press, pp. 84–258.

Bardem, Juan Antonio (2002), *Y todavía sigue*, Barcelona: Ediciones B.

Buñuel, Luis (2013), *My Last Sigh: The Autobiography of Luis Buñuel*, New York: Vintage Books.

Cervantes, Miguel de (1998), *Don Quixote de la Mancha*, New York: Modern Library Edition.

Diez Puertas, Emeterio (2014), *Narrativa fílmica,* Madrid: Fundamentos.

Dilthey, Wilhem (1976), 'The types of world-view and their development in the metaphysical systems', in H. P. Rickman (ed.), *Selected Writings*, Cambridge, UK: Cambridge University Press, pp. 133–54.

Eco, Umberto (1984), '*Lector in fabula*: Pragmatic strategy in a metanarrative text', in *The Role of the Reader: Explorations in the Semiotics of Texts,* Bloomington, IN: Indiana University Press, pp. 200–60.

Garci, José Luis (1982), '*Volver a empezar*, nueva visión de Garci', *ABC*, 6 January, p. 46.

García Berlanga, Luis, Azcona, Rafael, Berlanga, Luis G., Colina, José Luis and Font, José Luis (1994), *Plácido*, Madrid: Alma Plot.

Lynch, Kevin (1990), *The Image of the City*, Cambridge: MA, The MIT Press.

Madrid Brito, Débora (2011), 'Por un antiguo agravio. *Los Tarantos* y su referente literario', *Revista Latente: Revista de Historia y Estética del Audiovisual*, 9, pp. 89–106.

Mañas, Alfredo (1963), 'La historia de los Tarantos', in Federico Carlos Sainz de Robles (ed.), *Teatro español, 1961–1962*, Madrid: Aguilar, pp. 350–411.

Pelossi, Claudia Teresa (2011), '*Tristana*, del caleidoscopio de Galdós al laberinto de Buñuel', *Gramma*, 22:48, pp. 89–107.

Sánchez Vidal, Agustín (1988), *El cine de Carlos Saura*, Zaragoza: CAI.

Vogler, Christopher (2007), *The Writer's Journey: Mythic Structure for Writers*, Studio City, CA: Michael Wiese Productions.

PART 5

MEMORY AND THE MONUMENTAL

10

Who and What Was José Antonio Nieves Conde Criticizing in the Film *El inquilino* (1957)?

Susan Larson, Texas Tech University

Carlos Sambricio, Polytechnic University of Madrid

In March of 1955, the production company FilmArte was commissioned to make a documentary film entitled *La Obra Sindical del Hogar* (Archivo General de la Administración. Cultura: sig.36/04757). The screenplay for the film was subsequently written by Alfredo Marquerie[1] in compliance with the instructions of the Delegación Nacional de Sindicatos, the organization charged with regulating and coordinating Spain's industrial workers in what were called the *Sindicatos Verticales* (Vertical Unions) during the Franco regime. Marquerie is frequently remembered as one of the contributors to the Germanophile and anti-Semitic anthology *Poemas de la Alemania eterna* (1940) and the screenplay for *La Obra Sindical del Hogar* was a coarse exercise in political propaganda in the same vein.

> A working-class married couple wanders the streets looking in vain for a house where they can live within their means, receiving the same response everywhere they go: either all of the rooms have already been rented and if there are any available, they are too expensive for their budgets. They are disappointed. When the husband is working in the factory a siren goes off announcing that it is time for lunch, and he tells his workmates about his situation. One of them tells him that he read that the Obra Sindical del Hogar has been told by the nationalist government to build 40,000 homes for industrial workers within the year. The husband responds by saying that 'I have a wife and two children and I still haven't been able to find anything. What you're telling me isn't true.' At this point the workshop steward, who is the representative of the union, says 'You have no right to doubt this [...]

> our State keeps its promises. What you are reading here will soon be a reality [...] Housing projects are undertaken out of love and concern.[2]

On the surface, Marquerie's proposed 1955 documentary is formulaic and underwhelming. The screenplay is primarily based on wide shots of suburban trolley stops; the married couple walking down the street; shots of the façades of buildings with balconies and windows; of the married couple expressing their disappointment; of the factory building; of the workers leaving the factory and eating in the lunchroom; close-ups of the title of the newspaper and the Official State Bulletin where the housing announcement appears: all of these complemented by images of building sites in Madrid, Toledo, Cuenca, Guadalajara, Segovia and Ávila. What is of interest in the screenplay, however, are shots 37, 45, 46 and 47. In shot 37, for example, there is mention of a white line dramatically being drawn, crossing through a diagram portraying details and measurements of a 'model home'. Shot 45 mentions a cardboard model of the home; shot 46 consists of a map of Spain featuring different locations where the number of housing units the government are displayed; and shot 47, a chart with detailed information about how much cement, how many bricks, how much land and how much iron will be required for construction.

It is clear these particular shots in Marquerie's screenplay were applauded by Juan de Esplandiu and Manuel Nolla, the Francoist censors, by the comments they wrote in their February 1955 report saying that 'the formidable idea' behind the film had merit, emphasizing that 'in Madrid and its surrounding regions it's important that the government's proposed housing plan be carried out as quickly as possible'.[3] The reference to the 'proposed housing plan' referred not just to the increase in the number of houses to be constructed, but also to a shift in the type of housing that they thought should be built after the end of the Civil War.

After the Civil War and well into the 1960s, the Franco regime was in desperate need of a positive public relations campaign when it came to housing. The number of homes built by the Spanish government during the first fifteen years after the Civil War was shockingly inadequate. Even the Obra Sindical itself recognized in the documents they presented in 1957 as part of the exhibit of the Pavilion of the Internationale Bauausstellung of Berlin[4] that between 1938 and 1942 not a single housing unit had been constructed by the Obra Sindical del Hogar's Servicio de Arquitectura (see Figures 10.1 and 10.2).

The vast majority of the buildings that were constructed during this time were the official government buildings housing the civil servants and military officials of the Franco regime. It is also important to remember the startling affirmation of the *Revista Sindical de Estadística* (Journal of Union Statistics) in 1958 that between 1939 and 1956 the Obra Sindical del Hogar had constructed only 113,625 housing

FIGURE 10.1: Triptych produced by the Obra Sindical del Hogar for the Internationale Bauausstellung in Berlin, 1957, first panel.

units (Hurtado 2002: 68–70). Considering the fact that this number covers a period of sixteen years and taking into account the fact that Spain at this time was made up of 50 provinces and much of its housing had been destroyed by the war, the mean was an average of a mere 87 housing units per province per year, and approximately 147 housing units per year in Madrid. To make matters worse, the significant problem of the almost complete lack of attention by the government to the construction of affordable housing after the war was furthered by the snail's pace of the construction that the Obra Sindical del Hogar was able to undertake. On many occasions, construction was stalled for extended periods of time until economic circumstances improved. One of the most notable examples of this can be found in the 600 housing units on Céa Bermúdez Street set aside for Parque Móvil employees waiting for homes that were promised to them in 1941 but were not finished until 1954.

In 1955, the number of *chabolas* (self-constructed, sub-standard housing units or 'shacks') and caves in which some of Madrid's inhabitants lived rose to above 18,000.

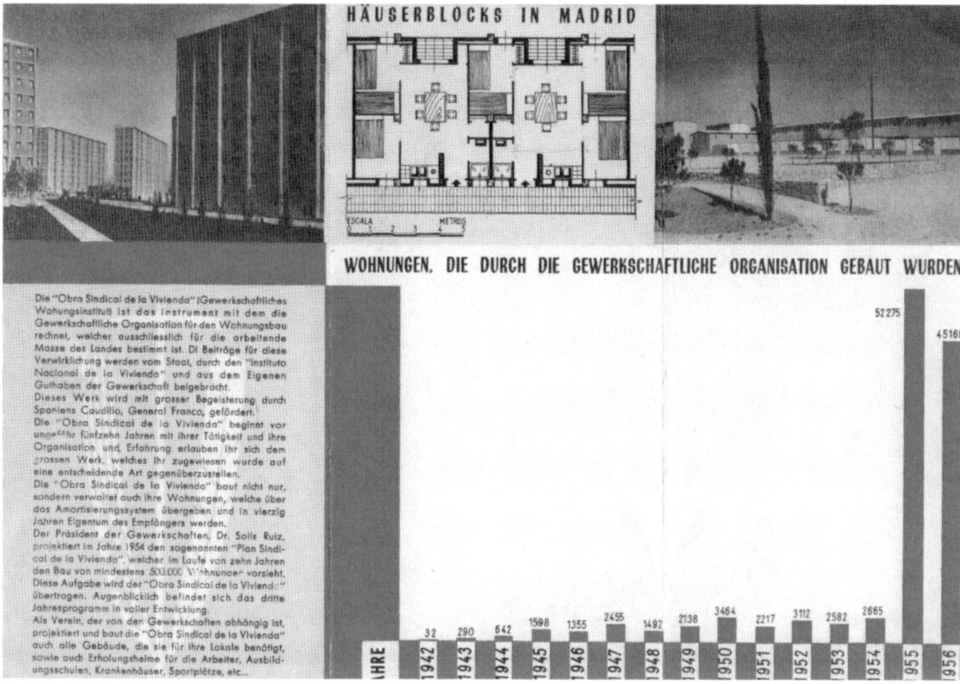

FIGURE 10.2: Triptych produced by the Obra Sindical del Hogar for the Internationale Bauausstellung in Berlin, 1957, second panel.

The number of families renting individual rooms in larger homes with access to a kitchen reached around 20,000; the number of families living on abandoned farm land, according to the municipal count, reached around 5,000; the number of families involved in eviction proceedings as a result of the changes brought about by the new Ley de Arrendamientos Urbanos reached an estimated 7,000; the families that had since 1936 been living in public buildings such as slaughterhouses, bathhouses and schools, for example, hovered around 1,000 and, it is estimated that around 10,000 families were living in short-term boarding houses, hostels and other types of emergency housing. If one takes these numbers into account, it is clear that some 60,000 housing units needed to be added to the city's offerings in order for life to return to normal. These numbers are considered to be a low estimate, however, because they do not begin to take into account the number of housing units required to accommodate the waves of migration from the countryside to the city after the Civil War (Sambricio 1999: 16–20).

Spanish authors wrote a number of outstanding and insightful novels and essays about housing issues and daily life in Madrid (both the city center and the peripheral districts) during this period. Some of the most notable include those of

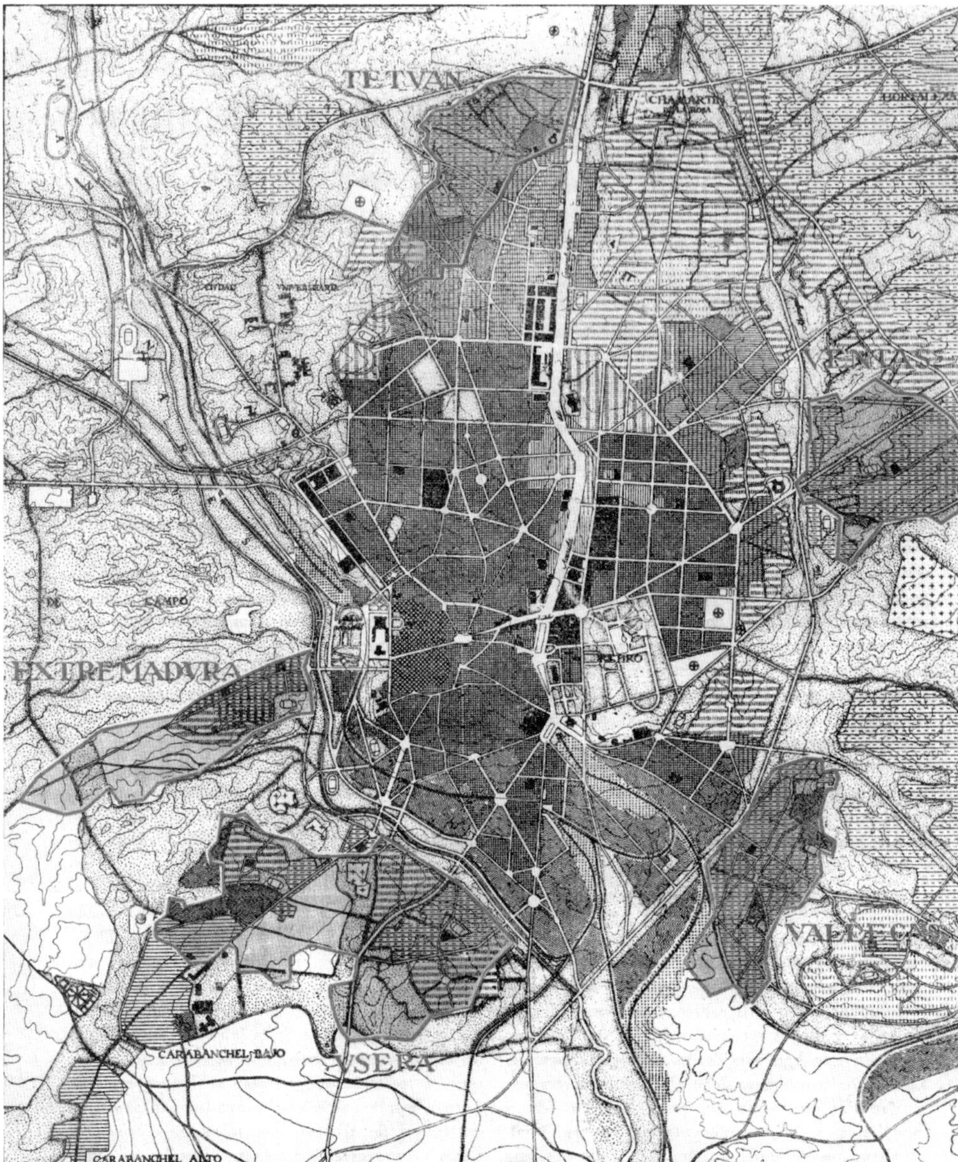

FIGURE 10.3: Locations of *chabolas* and caves used for domestic residences in 1940 in Madrid from the government publication *Reconstrucción*, 1:2 (1940).

Antonio Ferres (*La piquet*, 1959), Luis Martín-Santos (*Tiempo de silencio*, 1962), Carmen Martín Gaite (*Esperando el porvenir*, 1994), Ramón Nieto (*La patria y el pan*, 1962), Ignacio Aldecoa (*Al otro lado*, 1973) and Juan García Hortelano (*Nuevas amistades*, 1959). The filmic counterpart to this literary impulse can be found in the work of directors such as José Antonio Nieves Conde (*Surcos*, 1951), Luis Lucia (*Cerca de la ciudad*, 1952), Ana Mariscal (*Segundo López, aventurero urbano*, 1953) and Marco Ferreri (*El pisito*, codirected with Isidoro M. Ferry in 1959). These films represented the situation of people living in the city's slums or desperately looking for housing and served as a stark contrast to others of the time that perpetuated a decidedly uncritical resignation and celebration of working-class life, such as Luis Marquina's *Así es Madrid* (1953), Arturo Ruiz-Castillo's *El guardián del paraíso* (1954) and Ramón Comas's *Historias de Madrid* (1958).

Poverty, hunger and lack of housing were Spain's principal problems during the post-Civil War years. One of the film directors to best capture these social problems was Nieves Conde, who simultaneously captures both the official version of Spanish life trumpeted by official Francoist propaganda and the experience of everyday life. In his 1957 feature film *El inquilino*, the protagonist (the father of a large, soon-to-be homeless family played by iconic actor Fernando Fernán Gómez) reads the many posters plastered on the walls of the offices of Spain's Ministry of Housing that are radically and cruelly out of joint with his own lived experience: 'Man can only achieve his destiny if he has a home of his own'; 'lack of housing is the most pressing problem of our time' and 'housing speculation is a criminal act'.[5] The censors, conscious of the implicit criticism of the Spanish government's housing policies in these scenes, demanded that the following text be added to the film's opening titles:

> Public housing is the most universal of all contemporary social problems and our society shares the responsibility of facing it together. We should not place our trust exclusively in the State, which, we must recognize, puts all of its resources into resolving this grave problem. This film attempts to symbolically bring to light for the public some of the failings of modern society that have to do with this overwhelming situation that is of such great concern to the government and to all men of good faith.[6]

One of the concerns of the early Franco regime was to make a radical break with the culture of the Second Republic (the period between 1931 and 1936) when a series of democratically elected, liberal governments held the reins of power. When it came to proposing a new kind of city and housing, the propaganda slogans of the regime such as 'Ni un hogar sin lumbre, ni un español sin pan' (No home without light, no Spaniard without bread)[7] proved empty indeed. The immediate and utter failure of the government's agrarian policy (in a country whose industrial infrastructure had largely been destroyed by the war) resulted in the arrival of the peasantry *en masse* to Spain's major cities. For almost twenty years after the end of the Civil War, these migrants from the countryside to the cities sought to leave poverty behind in order to achieve the freedom to make new lives for themselves. From 1942 on, the topic of the lack of affordable housing became increasingly urgent and resulted in heated debates. The more practical, immediate problems of the lack of construction materials and the search for housing design solutions

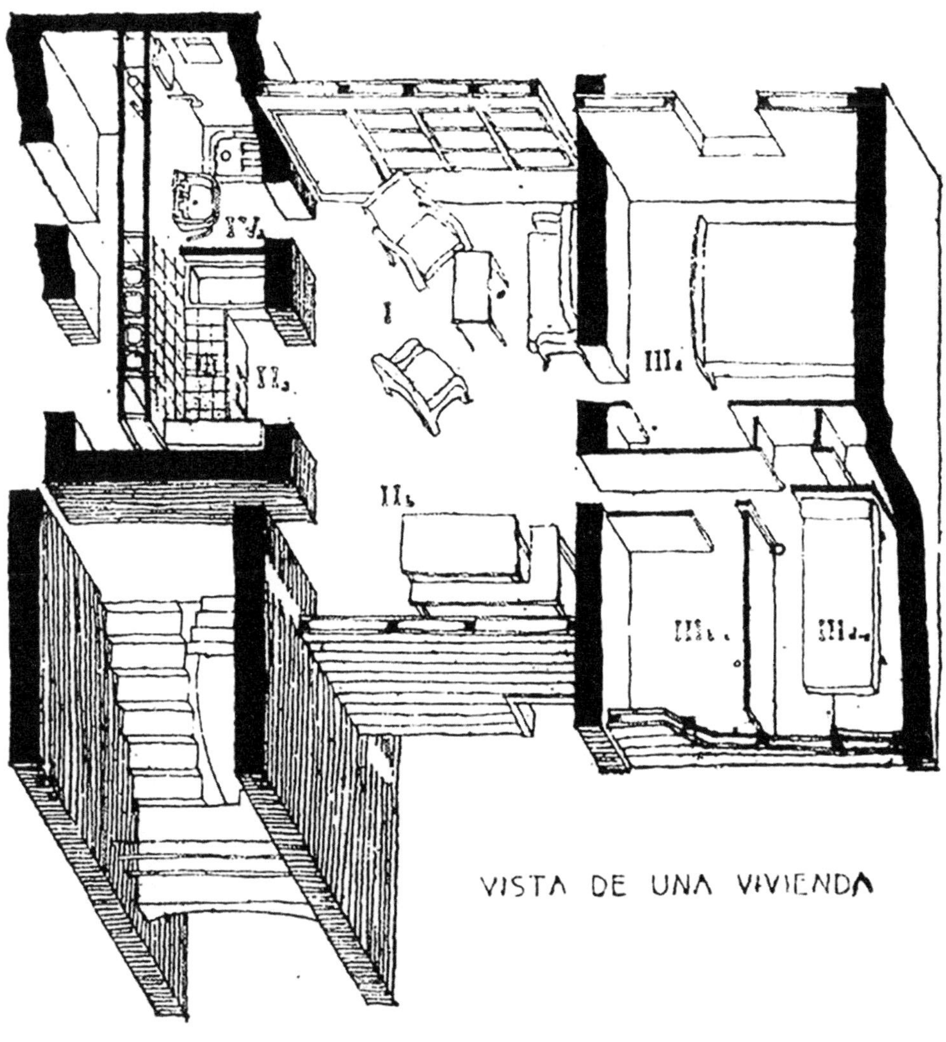

FIGURE 10.4: Miguel Fisac's axonometric drawing of a housing unit for the Architecture Competition of the Fifth National Architecture Assembly of 1949.

clashed with the grandiloquence of those who celebrated the handful of monuments built by the regime.

In 1948, architect and urban planner Miguel Fisac (1913–2006) began to challenge and confront almost every aspect of the housing situation – both the plans for housing reform and Francoist monumentality – by abandoning nostalgic references to the architecture of the past and working with a bold new concept. In his essay 'Las tendencias estéticas actuales' (Tendencies in Present-Day Aesthetics) he argues that just as Spanish composer Manuel de Falla had produced work that would eventually be considered universal, Spanish architecture had to accomplish the same, taking a cue from the affordable housing projects designed by Alvar Aalto in Sweden (Fisac 1948: 23–24). Fisac's contribution was more than just a formal alternative: for the first time, architects were proposing that real housing needs and new uses of interior space needed to respond to designs that had always been present in everyday architecture.

At the same time, another, more modern concept was introduced: the idea of 'comfort'. In a country such as Spain that was suffering from high levels of poverty and hunger, Fisac not only advocated for the use of modern Nordic furniture in the homes of working-class families, but he also pushed for the construction of *la casa que crece* ('the house that grows'), which was an important idea articulated in Weimar Germany by Martin Wagner in his influential 1932 publication *Das Waschende Haus.* This model relied on a fixed central nucleus (kitchen, living room and bathroom) that had a flexible number of bedrooms that could be added to satisfy the needs of family units that might numerically grow and shrink over time. While this project of Fisac's was underway, Francisco Javier Sáenz de Oiza (1918–2000), who had recently returned from a year-long stay in the United States, took things even further. While working for the Jesuit organization Hogar del Empleado, he took as a point of departure Le Corbusier's 1952 'Unité d' Habitation' in Marseille (see Hurtado 2002: 64–78) and adapted it into a low-cost alternative by using metal and formica furnishings instead of the Nordic designs proposed by Fisac. This low-cost alternative was necessary because there was often an absurd disconnect between the intended and actual uses of these housing units when the new occupants arrived and the traditional furniture they brought with them barely fit within these recently constructed, modern spaces.

Between 1953 and 1957, the debate over affordable housing brought about by the aforementioned migration from the countryside to the city forced government officials and architects to consider abandoning traditional ways of building in order to make way for more industrialized, modern forms of housing. Ideas from outside of Spain increasingly began to have an impact on what Spanish housing should look like. It is clear that there were contradictions: the image of the housewife so

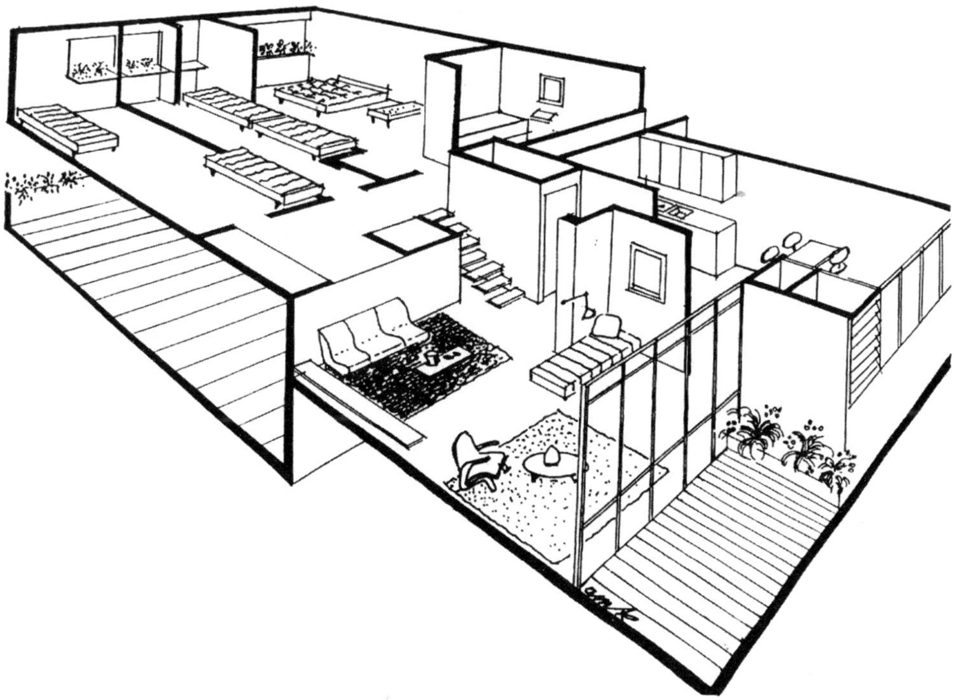

FIGURE 10.5: Francisco Javier Sáenz de Oiza's axonometric drawing of a housing unit for the architecture competition for the Río del Manzanares Project in Madrid, 1953.

common in the propaganda of the Sección Femenina[8] was based on a fourteen-part code of behavior laying out the 'servicio obligatorio para todas las mujeres' (obligatory service for all women) that included advice for them to meet their husbands returning home after a day of work to 'make him feel at ease. Let him recline in an armchair or in the bedroom. Make him feel like he is in heaven, have dinner ready, straighten the house and do not complain.'[9]

In July of 1954, the government passed the Plan Nacional de Vivienda (National Housing Plan) that laid the groundwork for the construction of 550,000 housing units in five years, and at the same time it also proposed its housing plan for Madrid. When in November of 1954 the Civil Government of Madrid announced the details of the new urban policy, 25,000 applications were immediately filed for only 2,000 units. This pattern was repeated again in August of 1955, when 35,000 applications were filed for a total of only 3,000 units (Anon. 1954: 11).

Against this backdrop, we can appreciate the political objective of the documentary film whose screenplay Marquerie wrote for the Obra Sindical del Hogar, which was to present the Plan Sindical that had been approved in May of 1954

FIGURE 10.6: Traditional middle-class Spanish home interior in 1942. Black and white photograph. Courtesy of the Archivo General de la Administración (General Administration Archive) of Madrid.

for the construction of 20,000 housing units a year across the country, with fifteen areas in Madrid alone targeted for 9,304 homes. On one hand, new legislation imposed a certain type of modern design for the buildings. These designs were for massive blocks with shared open spaces that, in an effort to cut costs, eliminated the traditional Spanish interior patios and prohibited balconies and other forms of decoration that also stemmed from traditional Spanish architecture. On the other hand, this new architecture had to accommodate two options. The first was to design units whose usable space totaled between 64 and 100 square meters distributed between the kitchen, dining room, living room and between two and five bedrooms and bathrooms with central heating, hot water, a shower-bath, toilet, ceramic sink, painted walls, a living area with a window, built-in electric sockets, floors with high-quality cement tiles and doors for all rooms and built-in closets. The second was for much more modest units of between 35 and 58 square meters, with a kitchen-dining area of more than 14 square meters with one to four bedrooms and a bathroom. This second type of housing made up 90 percent of all construction during the first year this legislation was in place and the larger units made up only 10 percent. Only one year later, however, the numbers shifted to 75 percent and 25 percent, respectively. It is precisely this shift in prioritizing larger rather than the smaller units that is captured in the aforementioned shot 37 of Marquerie's screenplay of the documentary where a white line crosses out the original dimensions of the 'model home' that epitomized the new type of housing being celebrated in the film.

This collective desire for larger, more modern housing lies behind the unforgettable dream sequence in Nieves Conde's feature film *El inquilino* when the protagonist dreams of the type of home he would like to find in the film's nonexistent 'Barrio de la Felicidad' (The Neighborhood of Happiness). The architectural, cinematic fantasy created here relies on humor that stems in part from the doubling up of this desire for home with the desire of the protagonist expressed upon the appearance of the scantily clad maids who cater to his every need, taking a cue from the Sección Femenina's instructions for housewives mentioned earlier in this chapter. The real interest here, however, lies in how the dream home is decorated. In contrast to the nineteenth-century furnishings and decorations witnessed in the scene in the beginning of the film when Evaristo's wife goes to the home of the owner of the building in which her family lives – the Marquis – to ask for help in the dream sequence the furniture is strikingly modern, marked by the appearance of the famous 'butterfly chair' designed in 1938 by the Spanish design team in exile made up of Antonio Bonet Castellana, Juan Kurchan and Jorge Ferrari (a chair also known as the BKF, using a complication of the first initials of their last names). Evaristo, the protagonist of the film, is a white-collar professional whom the spectator does not expect will be homeless. He belongs to that class of workers Siegfried Kracauer wrote about in his 1926 *Die Angestellten* (The Salaried Masses): a new class of worker who shares many of the same living conditions with the working class, but does not identify with them, differentiating themselves in terms of habits, ideology and aspirations. Evaristo exemplifies this modern, urban type who has a new way of working, dressing and engaging in leisure activities and who will subsequently demand a new type of housing.

This demand is evident in Marquerie's screenplay in the way it reflects how, after the Civil War, the concept of 'comfort' works its way into the Spanish cultural imaginary. Shots 45, 46, 47, 57 and 58 of the screenplay exemplify what José Luis Pardo means when he says that 'una vivienda es digna por haber sido erigida de acuerdo con una regla invisible que la hace deseable' (housing is dignified if it has been built according to an invisible rule that makes it desirable) (Pardo 2006: 65). The first shot describes a scale model of a housing unit and emphasizes the unfulfilled demand for housing in Spain during the years 1954–55; the second of the shots, with its map of Spain overlaid with statistics of existing housing units and those the regime planned to build, sets up expectations for the immediate future; and the third mentions the amount of cement, bricks and iron that will be used. The culmination of the characteristics of this new type of housing takes place in subsequent shots 57 and 58 that describe the interior space of the model home and how the spaces are used by their occupants, lingering over the details of the bathroom layout and fixtures in shot 61, the dining room in shot 62 and the kitchen, where the screenplay calls for close-up and medium shots of the woman of the house.

It is shot 67 that follows the gaze of the worker looking at his own home while a voice-over of the union representative on the shop floor echoes the words with which the documentary started: 'You have no right to question [...] the State keeps its promises. What you are reading here will soon be a reality [...] Housing projects are undertaken out of love and concern.' Housing projects were most certainly not undertaken out of love, however, as is evident in the overwhelming failure of the government's Plan Sindical.

Conceived as an ambitious solution to Spain's social housing problem, the Plan Sindical was not up to the task of coming up with the raw materials necessary for a boom in construction to take place. Nor did it account for a way to confront the inflation of land values of more than 300 percent in the many urban areas where new building should have taken place. In light of this failure, in 1957, Franco reshaped his government and created a new Ministry of Housing, placing José Luis Arrese at the helm.

The policies of the new ministry quickly exposed the administrative inefficiency of the Obra Sindical, despite the fact that the few buildings that were built were of generally high quality. Arrese quickly imposed a new set of housing policies and actually asked film director Nieves Conde to film *El inquilino* (whose plot strikes a remarkable resemblance to the plot of the documentary analyzed in this essay) to include the pious, moralizing statements of the Obra Sindical mentioned above that are put to such humorous use. The 1955 documentary was meant to serve the purpose of reinforcing the confidence of Spanish workers in the State and its official labor unions. In contrast, Nieves Condes's feature film is structured in a way that leaves the door open to undermining the ideology of the nationalist project. What Nieves Conde could not have known when he made the film, however, is that just a few months later, Arrese would transfer the capacity to satisfy the urgent demand for public housing almost entirely to the private sector.[10]

The shock resulting from this radical change in the construction and financing of Spanish housing on the part of the Ministry of Housing and many other members of the Cabinet is well documented (Sambricio 1999: 52–58). It is also well known and frequently commented upon in Spanish film history that Nieves Condes's film *El inquilino* has two endings: the original, pessimistic and more realistic ending and the happy ending that was imposed by the censors against the director's wishes. The 1955 documentary screenplay and the 1957 film can be better understood when viewed in tandem. Considered together, they bring to a close a period in the history of public Spanish housing legislation and policy that made way for a subsequent philosophy that would look almost entirely to the private sector for solutions.

It was certainly the end of an era, but the comments about modern 'comfort' in the screenplay of the documentary and the dream sequence of the film *El inquilino* – in particular when the children run with excitement to tell their father about the new fixtures in the bathroom or the wife's enthusiasm over the shiny, spotless tiles in the kitchen, everyone's surprise over the new refrigerator and washing machine – proves that the concept of 'comfort' was by that time unquestioned and that the idea of what acceptable public housing should look like and who should have access to it had dramatically changed.

NOTES

1. Alfredo Marquerie (1907–74) was an important poet, dramatist, drama critic and theater director who participated actively in Spain's twentieth-century cultural politics. A student of Antonio Machado during his childhood in Segovia, Marquerie was a member of the historical avant-garde and wrote for magazines such as *Alfar*, *Mediodía*, *Manantial* and *Parábola*. A Republican newspaper editor during the first years of the Second Republic, Marquerie's politics shifted in 1933, when he became a Falangist and frequented *tertulias* at La Ballena Alegre where the founders of the cultural arm of the extreme right such as Agustín de Foxá, Rafael Sánchez Mazas, Víctor de la Serna and Dionisio Ridruejo would meet on a regular basis. After the Civil War, Marquerie was the theater critic for the newspaper *ABC* from 1944 to 1960.

2. 'Un matrimonio obrero recorre en vano las calles a la busca de un piso donde poder albergarse con arreglo a sus disponibilidades económicas recibiendo, en todas partes, idéntica respuesta: bien no hay cuartos desalquilados, bien cuando los hay están fuera de sus recursos. Decepcionados, y ya el marido en la fábrica, cuando [...] suena la sirena que marca la hora del almuerzo y comenta en breve dialogo con sus compañeros la situación, uno de ellos dice haber leído que la Obra Sindical del Hogar ha sido encargada por el Estado para la realización de unas 40.000 viviendas para trabajadores, y ello en el plazo de un año. El trabajador escéptico le responde "tengo mujer y dos hijos y aún no he podido encontrar nada. Dudo de que eso que afirmas sea verdad". Y es entonces cuando el enlace sindical de la empresa contesta "No tienes derecho a dudar', Las promesas que hace nuestro Estado se cumplen." Leed ahí [...] Eso será pronto una realidad. Obras son amores.' The phrase 'obras son amores' is the first half of the Spanish popular saying 'obras son amores y no buenas razones'.
3. 'en Madrid y provincias se llevan a término a ritmo acelerado las obras que en el Plan propuesto harán posible la idea gubernamental'.
4. Interbau Berlin 1957. Spanien. Gewerkschaftliche Bauten.
5. 'Solo con vivienda propia puede el hombre cumplir su destino social'; 'El problema de la vivienda es el más acuciante problema de nuestro tiempo' and 'La especulación sobre la vivienda es un hecho criminal'.
6. 'El problema social de la vivienda es el más universal de los problemas de nuestro tiempo. La sociedad tiene el deber de sentirlo solidariamente, y no confiar exclusivamente en el Estado, quien, justo es reconocerlo, trata por todos los medios de resolver o aminorar tan grave problema. Esta película intenta sacar simbólicamente a la luz pública algunos de los fallos de la moderna sociedad en torno a ese ingente hecho que tanto preocupa a nuestro Estado y a todos los hombres de buena voluntad.'
7. These slogans were used by Francisco Franco in a political speech on 28 September 1936.
8. The 'Sección Femenina' was the women's branch of the Falangist political movement in Spain and an extension of women's domestic role to the public sphere, founded in 1934 and not disbanded until 1977.
9. 'Hazlo sentir a sus anchas. Deja que se recueste en un sillón o se recueste en la habitación, hazlo sentir en el paraíso, ten lista la cena, arregla tu casa y no te quejes.'
10. Larson likewise concludes that 'the censored version of the film [*El inquilino*] flounders, seemingly proving that no one is safe, that the right to housing on which Spanish families depend lies neither in the hands of the government nor in those of the hard-working individual, but rather is subject to the whims of the highly unstable market' (2012: 125).

REFERENCES

Aldecoa, Ignacio (1973), *Cuentos completos*, Madrid: Alianza Editorial.

Anon. (1954), *La Obra Sindical del Hogar y la Arquitectura. Plan Sindical de la Vivienda: Decretos-Ley de 14 y 29 de mayo de 1954. Normas para la confección de Proyectos de Grupos de viviendas 'tipo social' para el programa*, https://sede.fomento.gob.es/NR/rdonlyres/B957A32D-2019-4FC6-B90D- 8F44F8A7A843/104323/L_150755.pdf. Accessed 19 June 2019.

Ferres, Antonio (1959), *La piqueta*, Barcelona: Destino.

Fisac, Miguel (1948), 'Las tendencias estéticas actuales', *Boletín de la Dirección General de Arquitectura*, 9, pp. 21–25.

García Hortelano, Juan (1959), *Nuevas amistades*, Barcelona: Seix Barral.

Hurtado, Eva (2002), *Proyecto para la construcción de 600 viviendas en la urbanización del río Manzanares, 1953*, Madrid: Fundación COAM.

Kracauer, Siegfried (2008), *Los empleados: Un aspecto de la Alemania más reciente*, Barcelona: Gedisa.

Larson, Susan (2012), 'The spatial fix: Censorship, public housing and the altered meanings of Nieves Conde's *El inquilino*', in B. Fraser (ed.), *Capital Inscriptions: Essays on Literature, Film and Urban Space in Honor of Malcolm Alan Compitello*, Newark: Juan de la Cuesta Hispanic Monographs, pp. 123–36.

Marquerie, Alfredo (1940), 'Paracaidistas del Reich', in F. de Urrituia (ed.), *Poemas de la Alemania eterna*. Madrid: Imprenta de Ernesto Giménez, p. 26.

Marquerie, Alfredo. *La Obra Sindical del Hogar* (screenplay), Madrid, Archivo General de la Administración. Cultura: sig.36/04757.

Martín Gaite, Carmen (1994), *Esperando el porvenir*, Madrid: Siruela.

Martín-Santos, Luis (1962), *Tiempo de silencio*, Barcelona: Seix Barral.

Nieto, Ramón (1962), *La patria y el pan*, Barcelona: Seix Barral.

Pardo, José Luis (2006), 'Vivienda, intimidad y calidad', *Arquitectos*, 176:4–5, pp. 63–68.

Sambricio, Carlos (1999), *La vivienda en Madrid en la década de los años 50. El Plan de Urgencia Social*, Madrid: Ministerio de Fomento.

Wagner, Martin (1932), *Das Waschende Haus, Ein Bei trag zur Lósung der stadtischen Wohnungsfrage*, Berlin/Leipzig: Deutsches Verlagshaus Bong.

11

Madrid 1964: Icon of Modernity or City of Memory? A Look at the 'Details'

Vicente Sánchez-Biosca, University of Valencia

In 1964, the city of Madrid was decked out for the so-called '25 Years of Peace', a colossal propaganda campaign devised by the Minister of Information and Tourism Manuel Fraga Iribarne for the purpose of highlighting the achievements of the Francoist regime since the Nationalist victory of 1939. Instead of basing this vindication primarily on military triumph, it emphasized the work undertaken by the regime in recent decades. In other words, the purpose of this collective event was to legitimize the regime by controlling discourses of successful modernization and urbanization while at the same time avoiding the now-troublesome principles that had led to the military coup. The official Franco-era newsreels (Noticiarios y Documentales Cinematográficos or NO-DOs) played a crucial role in this campaign, depicting in their three weekly installments a celebratory image of the country grounded in industrial development, tourism, modernity and comfort. Spain's capital city figures prominently in this campaign, which was a mass-media effort whose components worked together to glorify the cosmopolitan image that associated Madrid (and by extension Spain) with other European cities with its accelerated urban rhythms and mobility, its vibrant traffic-filled avenues, emblematic new construction projects, museums and other spaces set aside for culture. At the same time, however, Madrid's ceremonial locations referenced in the so-called military crusade of the Civil War were etched on these same spaces of modernization and economic development through memorials, monuments to the fallen, triumphal arches and ceremonial rituals. It is worth noting that the annual 1 April military parade commemorating Victory Day was particularly spectacular in 1964.

This chapter analyzes the dialectic between modernization and the city of memory based on a number of images and words extracted from three films, all of them produced around this key year in the history of the Francoist regime, namely *Franco, ese hombre* (José Luis Sáenz de Heredia 1964), *¿Por qué morir en Madrid?* (Eduardo Manzanos 1965) and the comedy *La ciudad no es para mí* (Pedro Lazaga 1966). In all three cases, the films are read symptomatically; meaning they are analyzed in a way that relies less on the explicit theses of the films' narratives than on details expressed in the voice-overs and the initial shots of each film; elements that would easily go unnoticed in a study that took a strictly narratological or purely ideological approach.

This study is an analysis of 'details' as conceived by art historian Daniel Arasse in his discussion of painting: 'The detail manifested itself as an *écart* [gap] or a resistance in relation to the whole picture; it seemed to have the function of transmitting partial information, different from the overall message of the work or indifferent to it' (Arasse 2008: 9). This approach is, in a way, very close to what Siegfried Kracauer proposed in his seminal 1927 essay 'The Mass Ornament' where he points out that '[t]he position that an epoch occupies in the historical process can be determined more strikingly from an analysis of its inconspicuous surface-level expressions than from that epoch's judgments about itself' (Kracauer 1995: 75). The goal of this essay is to demonstrate that one can read seemingly superficial details during moments where a film either conceals or disguises them, for example during the opening and closing credits (to which few spectators pay much attention) or in the initial, establishing scenes at the beginning of feature-length films and documentaries. Deliberately or not, these details can tell us about the collective imaginary of an era, about that which is taken for granted and requires no explanation, making the film analyst's work akin to that of a discourse archeologist.

From Cosmogony to Symbolic Military Takeover

> An everyday miracle is taking place all over the city: the sun is rising. As on the first day of creation, it happens slowly and silently, as if humbly trying to keep his imposing greatness from being noticed. This city, like so many others of its kind, has known very tragic dawns, the distressing sound of vehicles coming to a sharp halt, drill-like doorbells, rifle shots heard just over the horizon and gunshots coming from the stairwells. Fortunately, all of this has been forgotten because many years have passed since all of that sadness took place: twenty-five, to be exact.
>
> Since then, all of the city's sunsets have been blissfully pleasant, but today's in particular bears a special sign of a remarkable memorial: the twenty-fifth anniversary of Peace is being commemorated by Spain's marching soldiers.
>
> It is still very early. With the awakening of the birds, the ringing of the bells, and the flapping of the flags comes the last-minute hanging of the banners. Naturally

> lazy fountains resume their graceful monologue in the early dawn and everything comes alive with the morning wake-up call that echoes the unforgettable presence of the children of those one-time junior officers [*alféreces provisionales*][1] of more than a quarter century ago.
>
> (Sánchez Silva and Sáenz de Heredia 1975: 9–11)

These are the words of the voice-over featured in very first moments of *Franco, ese hombre*, a propaganda film directed by José Luis Sáenz de Heredia, the same filmmaker who more than two decades before had made the famous 'crusade' film *Raza* (1941). The hagiographic ecstasy of Sáenz de Heredia's *Raza* is entirely consistent with the '25 Years of Peace' campaign in 1964. The Francoist regime a quarter of a century later was still trumpeting the legend of its birth on the occasion of the July 1936 military uprising and had mobilized new legitimizing tactics for the regime's accomplishments: economic development, the formation of a middle class, entering more fully into modernity with new media and technologies, increased access to comfort and leisure, and the transformation of the country into a tourist destination. Fraga in his role as Minister of Information and Tourism, with the support of the dictatorship's mass media outlets, relentlessly promoted this vision of a modern nation through the issuing of stamps and currency, literary contests, art exhibits, special editions of the NO-DO newsreels, its weekly series *Imágenes* and TV ads for the inauguration of the Prado del Rey studios.[2] Madrid was presented as the showcase par excellence at the heart of this modern transformation, effectively equating the capital city with Spain as a nation.

In the film's first few moments, the city is, in essence, the anthropomorphized protagonist who wakes up and welcomes her heroes like a generous hostess. The first shots of *Franco, ese hombre* reflect something very particular: an undefined outline that begins to appear in the dim light of dawn. The camera, filming from an elevated location, pivots on its axis to show a metropolis extending into the background. The reference in the voice-over to creation corresponds to a cosmogony that is poetically transmitted by the soft sunlight coming from the mountain range, bathing an inert Madrid with its first rays. An additional symbolic meaning is superimposed, moreover, when we hear the famous verses of the Falangist hymn *Cara al sol* (Face to the Sun): 'Onwards, squadrons, to victory, / a new day dawns in Spain!'

There is nothing surprising about this: the dawn motif was a visually recurring constant in Falangist culture. One prime example of this can be found in the visual poetics of the transfer of the mortal remains of the founder of the Falange, José Antonio Primo de Rivera, from Alicante–where he had been executed in November of 1936–to the monastery at El Escorial. The cadaver was carried on the shoulders of the old guard of the Falange during a ten-day journey that comprises much of the film *¡Presente! En el enterramiento de José Antonio Primo de Rivera* (Departamento

Nacional de Cinematografía, 1939) (Tranche and Sánchez-Biosca 2011: 360–78). Although the emphasis of *Franco, ese hombre* shifts its attention at one point away from this dawn motif, the regime's unconscious is inexorably revealed on the very day that the victory is to be celebrated twenty-five years later. Superimposed images allow the viewer to submerge himself in the streets of the capital, which are still practically empty and crossed only occasionally by an isolated vehicle with its headlights on. In the background is Nuevos Ministerios, an example of official state architecture of the 1950s that, with its distinctive arches, unmistakably references postwar urban reconstruction. The shots of Madrid that follow are highly emblematic: the Cibeles Fountain seen next to the Municipal Post Office followed by the Puerta de Alcalá. This sequence also features the starkly backlit equestrian statue of the Marqués del Duero located on the Paseo de la Castellana, with his outstretched arm pointing ahead, seems to be making a 'Roman salute' in the low-angle shot taken from a distance. The camera carries us next down the Paseo del Prado to the statue of Neptune. As the sun gains strength, the Nuevos Ministerios site reappears, this time with a very particular detail: to the right of the frame, a huge poster advertises the aforementioned campaign of the '25 Years of Peace'.

It is at this point that the dormant city begins to give rise to human activity and the shots that follow show the preparations for a parade. A small bonfire, tents and empty chairs are arranged in rows, and tanks and armored vehicles are washed early in the morning before they depart. An unmoving soldier stands guard, followed by a shot of *alféreces provisionales* getting in formation, followed by the inevitable *legionarios*. Meanwhile, political messages and slogans abound in the form of luxurious draperies and numerous flags waving from balconies. This combines to create the impression that on that particular day the city had surrendered to an occupying army. All this is nothing but a short, preliminary prologue to the arrival of the Head of State parading along the Paseo de la Castellana (or the Avenida del Generalísimo, as it was renamed in 1939). Franco is seemingly carried away by the masses in a modern convertible – an exceedingly common scene created by the political leaders of the time, especially the fascists – but with a decidedly premodern and colonial feel created by the presence of the *guardia mora* (mounted guard) on their horses.[3] Franco walks toward the grandstand, an ephemeral architectural form erected year after year for the parade. He greets his comrades in arms amidst the hustle and bustle of a variety of cameras surrounding him, all filming and photographing his ascent to the privileged place from which he speaks.

Let us pause for a moment to consider the meaning of this short sequence, which is a very particular iteration of an urban symphony with explicit, albeit fleeting allusions to *Berlin: Symphony of a Great City (Berlin, die Synfonie der Großstadt)* (Walter Ruttmann 1927), as well as to *A Man with a Movie Camera* (*Человек с киноаппаратом*) (Dziga Vertov 1929), seen from the point of view of

FIGURE 11.1 a–d: José Luis Sáenz de Heredia, *Franco ese, hombre*, 1964. Spain. © Lidisa.

FIGURE 11.1 a–d (continued)

the empty chairs viewing the show. The film progresses from the inert city to the dynamic city, but there is an important difference. The activity in this film is not the same as that of the modern city that used to be the rage in the cinema of the 1920s; it is an urban military takeover, but only for one day. The motion of the city does not stem from industry or everyday traffic. Instead, a sense of mobility is created from a city that is simultaneously proudly decorated for a celebration and transformed into a kind of warning. This is a city that is shedding its everyday appearance in order to accommodate the agents of the past who, on just such a day years ago, forced the city of Madrid (the emblem of Republican resistance) to submit. The city belongs here to the uniformed army, the grandstands and the undisputed leader, the 'Generalísimo' of the Armies of Land, Sea and Air. This is not, then, a city exhibiting its modern condition: on the contrary, its streets and its traditions, represented through precise photography and poetic light, are at the service of ritual. The beginning of the film leads us from the Falangist cosmogony (a palingenesist myth of destruction and reconstruction) to the city as a ceremonial stage on which the past regains its hold on the present.

The ephemeral architecture constructed on the Avenida del Generalísimo replaces the usual imagery that associated the main urban artery with the modern. The raised platforms for public speaking and the chairs demarcating the privileged places from which the parade will be contemplated replace the city's usual swarms of chaotic pedestrians that fill the city streets. The tanks and armored vehicles evoking the wars of yesteryear take over the usual positions of private and public transport vehicles resulting in the protocol of military order displacing the frantic movement of the great city for a limited period of time. The allusions to the urban symphonies of the 1920s seem to do nothing but emphasize how conscious the film's creators were about the great difference in what they were showing. What is missing here is precisely what was in abundance in the images of the official newsreels of the Franco regime, the aforementioned NO-DO, which reached their most prolific heights between 1960 and 1967. This was also clear in the weekly series *Imágenes*, which would set aside several audiovisual segments of about ten minutes each dedicated to promoting the advances of industry, entertainment, culture, art and agriculture among other things, always placing an unmistaken emphasis on modernity and development and always celebrating the cosmopolitanism of the urban center. The increasing influence of television, as well as popular cinema, would be no less emphatic in reveling in both tourism and hectic urban life.

Indeed, the military choreography and politicized decorations with which the city is adorned for these and other ritual events contrast with the everyday life of the modern developing city of which the Franco regime was so proud. Film may be the ideal means, even involuntarily to some extent, to get across this contradiction. As a means of communication capable of movement and sound that ever since the 1950s portrayed panoramas and brought vibrant color to whatever was being represented, film adds to these qualities the potential to create a mass spectacle that still exerted enormous power in 1964. For this reason, the abundance of modernity celebrated in the films of the mid-1960s is a dramatic contrast with the commanding exaltations of the heroic past and the military coup that founded the dictatorship.

Most significant, however, is that the film *Franco, ese hombre* never speaks explicitly about Madrid, only of Franco.[4] It is a hagiography in images of the life of the 'man sent from heaven' who had gone from being a military general in Africa to the 'Generalísimo' and who could boast, as was so common in the propaganda of the regime, of the prestige of having given the country a quarter century of 'peace'. To get beyond Spain's *años de hambre* ('years of hunger'), to push for progress, to create the middle class; all of this was attributed to a Franco who appeared in public more and more frequently dressed as a civilian instead of as an army general. That these parallel strategies coexisted with harsh political and social repression is not what is most relevant here. What is important to remember is the fact that in its collateral or even peripheral gestures, a film like this one expresses fundamental symptoms of two different everyday urban imaginaries in the mid-1960s. These brief shots, existing almost on the margins of the stated primary purpose of the film, speak loudly to those who know how to read the 'details'.

Reliving the Pain of the Capital

There is an inverse ideological tension inherent in other films about Franco that take place in Madrid. In 1963, the French filmmaker Frédéric Rossif screened his film *Mourir à Madrid*, which he had managed to shoot in Spain. He was given permission by the Spanish authorities to make a documentary about Spanish tradition, folklore and artistic beauty entitled *L'Espagne éternelle*. Back in Paris after collecting the footage, Rossif and his producer Nicole Stéphane confessed to having resorted to subterfuge in order to put together what was actually a radical invective against what they called the 'scandal of Spain', namely, the collusion that western democratic countries maintained in the early 1960s with the Franco regime, which had been a former ally of the fascist regimes defeated in 1945. Madrid was Spain for Rossif and the city was, quoting a famous verse by Paul Éluard, the 'capital of pain', that is, the purest expression of the last romantic war and the suffering of a bombarded civilian population.

As expected, the Franco regime was enraged, not so much by the overt political attack as by the denial of its modernization and the peace it boasted of having achieved for the country. The emblem, Madrid, was taken up as a gauntlet by the regime itself in response and, although they objected to the film's interpretation of the Civil War, the most stinging critique of the regime by virtue of its subtle and indirect nature was the film's questioning of Madrid's iconic modernity. *¿Por qué morir en Madrid?* (Eduardo Manzanos 1965) was one of the cinematic answers to this attack and, as Nancy Berthier (2005: 127) accurately points out, it means the first confrontation, both through its verbal and visual discourses, of two distinct memories of the Civil War. The symptomatic aspect important for us here is that, above and beyond the controversy over the course of the war itself, the film – a 1960s cinematographic narrative by two illustrious representatives of the France regime – advocates not for military victory, but for development, welfare and peace, with Madrid playing a central role. The diatribe against rural Spain depicted in *Mourir à Madrid* was the central issue of the new filmic response. However, before the cinematic response in *¿Por qué morir en Madrid?* is clearly articulated, some powerful symbolic shots – details that apparently go unnoticed because they accompany and at the same time are disguised by the credits – speak with a clear voice of a much more eloquent discourse. Let us take a magnifying glass and look closely at the first moments of the film in order to recognize the nature of this Francoist strategy.

While the credits scroll down the screen, a camera shows a panoramic view of the city contemplated from the watchtower of the Torre de Madrid, located on the Plaza de España. The view presented here is that of the old, historic city and points to the exact place where Franco's troops entered the capital on 28 March 1939. A panning shot gradually shows other iconic spaces, including the Plaza de España itself, specifically the ever-recognizable Edificio España, constructed between 1948 and 1952. The end of the Gran Vía makes a strategic location from which to extend subsequent shots of the Royal Palace in the background and the statue of Don Quixote and Sancho Panza. Another key moment is a high-angle shot of the Gran Vía where it joins with Alcalá, probably taken from the balcony of the headquarters of the Secretaría General del Movimiento[5] with the iconic Metrópolis building clearly visible in the background. What follows as the credits continue is a shot of the Prado-Recoletos axis and the Alcalá-Gran Vía junction once again, with the camera most likely located on top of a car and, later, a still shot of the Cibeles Fountain. This is followed by a tracking shot that attempts to capture the realism that was so fashionable in fiction films of the time for its evocation of the style of documentary reporting – this shot in particular depicting Emilio Castelar Square, with its homonymous statue. The Puerta de Alcalá seen from Calle de Alcalá and the Nuevos Ministerios building taken from the Plaza de San Juan de la Cruz close this brief transitory moment.

To reiterate something fundamental: these shots are diluted by the credits and they are almost imperceptible. However, these recognizable places, icons of

FIGURE 11.2: Eduardo Manzanos (dir.), *¿Por qué morir en Madrid?*, 1965. Spain. © Divisa.

Madrid, appear to be full of the banality of everyday life: the incessant traffic, the busy daytime shots capturing the daily routine. Even though no words have been spoken, everything works together here to plunge the viewer into a dynamic Madrid that combines modern and administrative state architecture with the asceticism that characterized Nuevos Ministerios. In other words, before the voice-over begins, before the first arguments are revealed and positions taken on the war, before we even know what the subject of this film about combats and battles is, what suddenly appears is the busy cosmopolitan modernity of the everyday: a bustling, productive peace embedded within the modern city and its icons. Only when the credits are finished does an intertitle explain the purpose of the film and the voice-over exposes its objectives as follows:

> Because the earth is round, everyone locates his navel wherever he wants. We are not the navel of the world, but there Spain is, in its place, a bridge between Europe, America and Africa, the center of the West. It is an open country, a modern country. Built upon an old site and full of historical and artistic grandeur. Each year millions

FIGURE 11.3: Eduardo Manzanos (dir.), *¿Por qué morir en Madrid?*, 1965. Spain. © Divisa.

> of tourists from all over the world cross into its borders. Gautier's Spain is as buried as Mr. Gautier himself. There are no bandits on our roads. Sometimes bandits come from outside, like that long-haired Englishman who came with bombs. Some people bring a simple movie camera and they say they want to make a documentary about bullfighting scenes, Holy Week processions and great paintings by Velázquez, El Greco or Ribera. This documentary will be entitled *L'Espagne éternelle* and will try to exhibit [...] 'the white walls of Spain as if they were still life paintings'.[6]

The shots that accompany this voice-over could not be more eloquent: the globe turning, followed by the map of Spain with superimposed arrows pointing to its center, which is not the center of the country but of the world, with Madrid as its capital. What follows is an accelerated collage of photos depicting the beauty of Spain as it appears in contemporary touristic brochures that lead one around Madrid: castles and plains, medieval buildings and groups of tourists, all highlighted by contrasting low- and then high-angle shots that culminate in a panoramic view of the El Escorial monastery. But this dynamism is unexpected. Coinciding with the voice that announces the flow of visitors, we observe the

FIGURE 11.4: Eduardo Manzanos (dir.), *¿Por qué morir en Madrid?*, 1965. Spain. © Divisa.

landing of airplanes, the caravans of cars that crowd the roads and, meanwhile, proudly displayed beaches full of sunbathers against a backdrop of modern buildings. Likewise, the static engravings of the Romantic era, of exotic and Orientalist Spain, are face to face with hectic roads. The subsequent film, then, is a response to Rossif's film that, due to production issues, the Francoist regime decided not to exhibit and that goes beyond our current argument here.[7]

In short, this response to the diatribes of war, this answer to the attacks of those who remind the regime of its fascist past, is achieved by looking at the present; that is, at the work that has been done. Madrid is the synecdoche, the *pars pro toto*, of Spain; the present, the metaphor of Franco's reason for being. Economic development and social welfare are the most incontestable arguments, although the Franco regime does not hesitate to appeal to its 'legitimate origin' when necessary. A micro-choreography of the big city, a slice of reality captured by the camera (compared to the urban symphonies evoked above) is a symptom. It is miniscule, but due to its apparent lack of direct functionality in the film, it very clearly reveals the discourse of the regime, which is simultaneously constructed by using both direct propaganda and misunderstanding. It is effective because it is subtle.

When Praising a Village Becomes a Tribute to the City

The symptomatic reading proposed here is all the more significant when it fills the *dead time* of a film; its waste, such as credit titles, or brief introductions before giving way to the fundamentals of narrative structure or the theme of a documentary. A very eloquent manifestation of this dynamic is nestled between the cracks of a film that became popular in the 1960s: *La ciudad no es para mí* (Pedro Lazaga 1966), starring the famous comedian Paco Martínez Soria. This actor embodied the figure of an old *paleto* ('a country bumpkin') or a recent arrival from the Aragonese countryside to cleanse the city of the corrupt behavior supposedly so common in the lives of urbanites and, in this particular case, the marriage of his son. The city to which the protagonist comes from the imaginary village of Calacierva, with his beret, his chickens under his arm, his wineskin and his *maño* accent, is Madrid. Before the story even begins, however, the fictional characters are introduced and the conflicts are announced. The film starts in a highly stylized and fictional mode by representing the capital of Spain in a comic tone. This sequence that precedes the story starts with the quiet and seemingly eternal image of the sky, the church and the fields of Calacierva. But the previous sequence, combining the credits with the voice-over and documentary tone resorting to collage is so detached from the film that it disappears as if by magic into the urban diurnal and nocturnal symphony into the style of a newsreel. Once again, this is a detail that aesthetically and formally challenges the film. It may seem that this initial sequence lacks significance, but the opposite is true.

It is clear that both the subject and plot of *La ciudad no es para mí* are primarily motivated by the city. The pace of the film is fast and the initial sequence extensive. While electric guitar music composed by Antón García Abril accompanies the credits, the camera laterally slides over a panoramic view of Madrid seen from the tree-lined area of the Casa de Campo, most likely from the viewpoint of what is known as Garabitas Hill. The camera pauses when the Tower of Madrid appears and a powerful zoom jumps in its direction, effectively penetrating the heart of the capital. A low-angle shot of a street lamp gives rise to a reverse zoom at the end of which the frame shows the entire Plaza de España. The unmistakable icons of the city follow, one by one: the Cibeles Fountain with its iconic Post Office, the Gran Vía from Callao and in the direction of the Plaza de España and, once the fragment has been connected to the surrounding neighborhood, it continues to lay on more and more details. The Gran Vía is the privileged location where both this daytime micro-scene and the nocturnal collage that follows will take place. The cinemas, the theaters with their luminous advertisements for future attractions, the traffic and the reflections of the nocturnal rain on the pavement are the objects that the film unfolds and assembles through a collage effect. This is not a

FIGURE 11.5: Pedro Lazaga (dir.), *La ciudad no es para mí*, 1966. Spain. Courtesy of Mercury Films.

metaphor: it is a direct association with the themes of the urban symphony. To be clear: it is an exultant Madrid, a city of which the technicians and the director seem to feel implicitly proud, even though the ironic voice-over and the film as a whole reflect a certain antiurban sentiment that results in a defense of the eternal values originating in the countryside.

What kind of statement is made by the voice-over that guides us through this 'detail'? It goes something like this:

> Madrid, capital of Spain. 2,647,253 inhabitants. Growth rate: 129 people every day. Transient population: 360,580 people; 472,527 vehicles. 110,853 potholes and sinkholes. One birth every 45 seconds, two and a half weddings per hour, and one death every minute and a half. And banks, lots of banks. Well, not this kind, there aren't many of these any longer.[8] And supermarkets, lots of supermarkets, and houses, houses under construction, mountains of houses under construction, and pharmacies, tons of pharmacies, and the parking lots, kilometers of restricted

FIGURE 11.6: Pedro Lazaga (dir.), *La ciudad no es para mí*, 1966. Spain. Courtesy of Mercury Films.

> parking, and fines, too many fines. This is a city where everything has to be done very quickly. As we were saying, in this city everything has to be done very quickly. [*acceleration of the image*][9]

Lighting gadgets, lenses and camera movements, editing techniques, fast-paced camera movements are all used at the service of an idea: the frenzy of the city, stressful no doubt, but visually very attractive. When, after four and a half minutes, the image places us, thanks to the narrator's voice, in an anodyne village where time seems to stand still, everything seems to have changed. The grammar of the editing will be different and the ways that the camera is used, with few exceptions, will have little to do with what has just been explained. The story becomes more theatrical. The technique that unfolds is, therefore, meant for the beginning, much as the so-called montages of Hollywood cinema were detached from the narrative sequences in whose structure they were embedded.

There is not the slightest doubt that this detail responds to a trend of the time, to an urban imaginary that was all the rage in mid-1960s Spanish cinema; so much so, that it equates cinema with modernity, cinematographic technique with representation of the city, rhythm with progress, hectic life and 'peace', in the Francoist sense of the word. Thus, Francoist *desarrollismo*[10] is legitimized between the lines, without having to renounce or threaten the memory of where it came from or its repression.

Conclusion

The city in Spanish cinema of the 1960s is both a stage for storytelling and an object of documentary. All of this is evident in its design and its narrative function for both the urban characters and those who arrive from the countryside. In subsequent decades, the outsiders would emigrate to Europe from other continents. Likewise, since the 1950s, other spaces in the metropolis contrast with the sleek city center: namely, suburban neighborhoods, areas of crime, poverty and marginalization. All of this, in its complexity, is made up of the explicit politics of authors, schools, tendencies or the Francoist regime as a whole through its documentary apparatus hegemonized by the NO-DO's documentaries and newsreels. But there is another space that has been interrogated here through three significant examples: an urban imaginary that, in the hands of the (not always homogeneous) architects of the regime, adheres to the city because it sees in it a sign of the present that seems to escape ideology and that converges with the discourse of *desarrollismo* postulating that progress is modernity and that the past is overcome through well-being brought about by consumerism. When these manifestations emerge from the explicit program (both narrative and conceptual), they have the virtue of providing something that could possibly be called an obliviousness to time, something that manifests itself apart from the basic structure of the script and the stylistic form of the film as a whole. When these details transversally invade feature films, documentaries or newscasts, the analyst must attend to their forms, as Kracauer said, convinced that they are more revealing than the more direct political assertions being made at the time. Perhaps it is not a matter of deciding between a dichotomy, but of merely vindicating the less visible to carry out, as Daniel Arasse laid out in his foundational text about the 'detail' in painting, a story that captures the urban imaginary as it obliquely manifests itself in a handful of cinematographic shots.

Acknowledgments

This text is especially indebted to Rafael Rodríguez Tranche for his exhaustive knowledge of the city of Madrid. I am also grateful to Olga García de Fez for her study of the films starring Paco Martínez Soria in her Ph.D. dissertation.

Translated by Consuelo del Val.

NOTES

1. Translator's Note: *Alféreces provisionales* were soldiers with little training who were allowed into the military ranks by the Francoist forces to quickly increase their numbers during the Spanish Civil War with the understanding that their duties would end as soon as the war had concluded.
2. Aguilar (1996: 164–83) accurately analyzes the campaign launched by the Cabinet and conducted by Fraga's Ministry of Information and Tourism.
3. Translator's Note: The *guardia mora* was a body of personal bodyguards from Morocco that accompanied Franco in all major commemorative events and reminded spectators of the dictator's North African colonial campaigns.
4. See Sánchez-Biosca (2006: 191–96) for signs of the Francoist regime's rhetorical shift in Spanish cinema. Berthier (1998: 136–42) has studied many aspects of the national premiere and the subsequent history of the film.
5. Translator's Note: Located on the Calle Alcalá 44, the 'Edificio CNS' proudly displayed the *yugo and flechas* ('the yoke and the arrows') – the iconic symbols of the Falangist movement used by the Franco regime – until April of 1977.
6. 'Como la tierra es redonda, cada uno le pone el ombligo donde quiere. Nosotros no somos el ombligo del mundo, pero ahí está España en su sitio, puente entre Europa, América y África, centro del Occidente. Es un país abierto, un país moderno. Levantado sobre un solar antiguo y lleno de grandezas históricas y artísticas. Cada año por sus fronteras entran más millones de turistas de todo el mundo. La España de Gautier está tan enterrada como el propio Sr. Gautier. En nuestros caminos ya no hay bandoleros. A veces los bandoleros vienen de fuera, como este melenudo inglés vino a ponernos bombas. Hay quien se trae una simple cámara cinematográfica y dice que desea hacer un documental sobre escenas taurinas, procesiones de semana santa y grandes pinturas de Velázquez, El Greco o Ribera. El documental se va a titular *L'Espagne éternelle* y trata de exhibir [...] los muros blancos de España a manera de naturalezas muertas.'
7. The setback that *Mourir à Madrid* meant for the regime resulted in a series of negotiations and the pressure of Spanish diplomats to prevent or delay its release to some sequences is documented in Liogier (2005) while Berthier (2005) notes the cuts that were made to the film that resulted in these pressures.
8. Translator's Note: The narrator employs the double meaning of the word *banco* in Spanish for both for 'bank' and 'bench'.
9. 'Madrid, capital de España dos millones seiscientos cuarenta y siete mil 253 habitantes. Crecimiento vegetativo: 129 personas cada día. Población flotante: 360580 personas; 472.527 vehículos. 110.853 baches y socavones. 1 nacimiento cada 45, dos bodas y media por hora, y una defunción cada minuto y medio. Y bancos, muchos bancos. Bueno, de estos no, de estos ya no quedan. Y supermercados, muchísimos supermercados, y casas, casas en construcción, montañas de casas en construcción, y farmacias, toneladas de farmacias, y zona azul, kilómetros de zona azul, y multas, demasiadas multas. Esta una ciudad donde

todo hay que hacerlo muy deprisa. Como íbamos diciendo, en esta ciudad todo hay que hacerlo muy deprisa.' [*aceleración de la imagen*].

10. Translator's Note: Francoist *desarrollismo* (often translated in the press and subsequent academic scholarship in English as the 'Spanish economic miracle') was initiated in 1959 by technocrats (most of whom belonged to the Opus Dei) who replaced the previous Falangist political guard. *Desarrollismo* resulted in the creation of a larger middle class marked by a high degree of depoliticization that historians and sociologists have termed *franquismo sociológico*. This period of rapid industrialization ended in approximately 1974, but only after Spain had experienced the second highest growth rate in the world, after that of Japan.

REFERENCES

Aguilar, Paloma (1996), *Memoria y olvido de la Guerra Civil española*, Madrid: Alianza.

Arasse, Daniel [1992] (2008), *Le détail. Pour une histoire rapprochée de la peinture*, Paris: Flammarion.

Berthier, Nancy (1998), *Le franquisme et son image. Cinéma et propagande*, Toulouse: Presses Universitaires du Mirail.

Berthier, Nancy (2005), '*Por qué morir en Madrid* contra *Mourir à Madrid*: las dos memorias enfrentadas', *Archivos de la Filmoteca*, 51, pp. 126–40.

Kracauer, Siegfried (1995), 'The Mass Ornament', in *The Mass Ornament. Weimar Essays* (trans. Thomas Y. Levin), Cambridge: Harvard University Press, pp. 75–86.

Lagaza, Pedro (1966), *La ciudad no es para mí*, Spain: Mercury Films.

Liogier, Hélène (2005), 'El escándalo de *Mourir à Madrid*. Una "Película ofensiva para España"', *Archivos de la Filmoteca*, 51, pp. 111–25.

Manzanos, Eduardo (1965), *¿Por qué morir en Madrid?* Spain: film never released.

Rossif, Frédéric (1962), *Mourir à Madrid*, France: Athos Films.

Sáenz de Heredia, José Luis (1964), *Franco, ese hombre*, Spain: Madrid Chápalo Film.

Sánchez-Biosca, Vicente (2006), *Cine y guerra civil española. Del mito a la memoria*, Madrid: Alianza.

Sánchez Silva, José María and Sáenz de Heredia, José Luis (1975), *Franco... ese hombre*, Madrid: Lidisa.

Tranche, Rafael R. and Sánchez-Biosca, Vicente (2011), *El pasado es el destino. Propaganda y cine del bando nacional en la guerra civil*, Madrid: Cátedra.

12

Making Madrid Plastic: Waste and Space in Pedro Almodóvar's Post-*Movida* Films

Samuel Amago, University of Virginia

The Spanish philosopher Marina Garcés argues that novelty is the privileged ideology of modernity (Garcés 2019: 204). The fetishization of the new leads us ever forward through an increasingly cluttered trash-filled present and into an ever-receding future. The relentless renewal upon which capitalist modernity has been built has stranded us in an empty wasteland of signifiers that point only to themselves: 'consumption turns novelty into the product of the season and chains us to a desire for a permanent change that transforms nothing' (Garcés 2019: 204). As a palliative, Garcés proposes a radical regeneration of politics and their accompanying discourses, the creation of a new language that would break those neoliberal forms of political representation and epistemological stagnation (Garcés 2019: 208). This chapter traces some of the roots and ramifications of Madrid's long-term investment in precisely this kind of neoliberal ideology of novelty, and how the city's most visible auteur visualized that novelty through a protracted aesthetic investment in plastic.

Throughout the 1980s, Madrid's regional authorities labored to forge a new regional identity that would distance the city from its historical association with the Franco dictatorship. This process was implemented through the convergence of three principal institutional factors: (1) the gradual diffusion of centralized, national control of the country; (2) the establishment of an independent municipal administration after the elections of 1979 and (3) the creation and consolidation of the autonomous Community of Madrid (Stapell 2010: 26–29). According to Hamilton Stapell, Madrid's particular historical experiment with regionalism functioned as a way to insulate the Spanish capital from its antidemocratic recent history, 'in part because of the need to "forget" the past and in part because of the direct association of Francoism with Spanish nationalism' (Stapell 2010: 26).

Creating a novel Madrilenian identity and infrastructure was not an unproblematic project, nor was it ever complete. As Teresa Vilarós outlines in her classic book on the topic, one of the foundational problems of Spain's transition to democracy was the fact that it was built upon a Francoist substrate, and thus the Transition itself amounted to a kind of *lavado de imagen* ('whitewashing') that did not go far enough to break with the authoritarian past. Although the *pacto de olvido* ('pact of forgetting') certainly functioned through the late 1970s and into the 1980s to allow for the manufacture of a provisional kind of political consensus, the problematic desire to turn the page on the country's violent past resulted in what would later be described as a *borradura histórica* ('historical erasure'), in Vilarós's words, that even today has important cultural and political repercussions.[1]

The principal aim of this chapter is to outline how Pedro Almodóvar's films of the 1980s respond to and reflect Madrid political elites' project of transforming the Spanish capital city's lived environment into an ahistorical place propitious for capital investment and urban modernization. It begins with an overview of the ideological and material processes that transformed Madrid's urban space, and asks what role the country's most internationally recognized auteur had in visualizing a new transitional culture populated by neurotic inhabitants obsessed with clearing their habitat of any traces of the past.

In an evocative essay analyzing what he calls the 'excremental politics' of post-dictatorship Spain, Germán Labrador Méndez has described how, after 1975, the country's political class redefined its linguistic and aesthetic boundaries in line with a more hygienic or antiseptic way of doing things (Labrador Méndez 2010: 234). This ostensibly 'clean' Transition Culture was designed, from the beginning, precisely not to ruffle feathers. It was always, in Isidro López's words, an 'aproblematic' culture:

> La Cultura de la Transición es, fundamentalmente, una cultura aproblemática, para la que meramente nombrar el conflicto social o político es un acto performativo de consecuencias terribles: el conflicto se vuelve real. Siendo así, la Cultura de la Transición se nutre, más que compite, con la ideología económica, el otro gran relato aproblemático acerca de cómo se ha producido la integración vertical de 'la sociedad' en los últimos treinta años.
>
> (Transition Culture is fundamentally an aproblematic culture in which the mere mention of political or social conflict signifies a performative act with terrible consequences: the conflict becomes real. Thus, Transition Culture feeds on – rather than competes with – economic ideology, which is the other aproblematic grand narrative of vertical integration that has taken place over the last thirty years.)
>
> (López 2012: 77)

Vilarós was one of the first cultural critics to describe in particular how the Transition was actually 'una voluntad de construcción de un pasado histórico, dedicado no sólo a no mostrar ninguna de sus lacras sino, más agresivamente, a reconformar este pasado' (a desire to construct a historical past dedicated not only to not showing any of its blemishes but also, more aggressively, to reshaping that past) (Vilarós 1998: 240). Merino and Song showed later how traces of contamination of Francoist ideology and discourse are still imbedded in the cultural present (Merino and Song 2005). And you do not have to dig very deep to find them.

What Vilarós calls a 'lavado de imagen' ran parallel to a coordinated effort to create a distinct Madrilenian identity focused wholly on the present and 'based specifically on the promotion of local – or regional – attachments' (Stapell 2010: 26). The Transition-era cleanup of Madrid was not only ideological, cultural, economic or discursive. It was also literal and material, requiring the employment of thousands of trashcans, the removal of abandoned vehicles from city streets, the separation of different classes of waste, the establishment of the city's first recycling program and glass collection in some parts of the city, the washing of building facades, remediation of air pollution, creation of green spaces and extension and reform of parks, waste water purification and tree-planting campaigns (Stapell 2010: 55–56).

These processes of urban refinement and sanitation were part of political elites' strategy to modernize the capital city. In the films directed and produced by the Almodóvar brothers through the 1980s, filmgoers could see this urban transformation taking place before their eyes. In Agustín Almodóvar's first appearance in *Mujeres al borde de un ataque de nervios*, for example, he plays a real estate broker. When Pepa enters his office, he can be seen tinkering with a scale model of Madrid apartment buildings, while a panoramic view of future construction sites appears on a massive poster behind him. The fact that El Deseo's executive producer should be depicted in the film as a man who plays with and profits from the commodification of urban space is fitting, since audiovisual culture has always played a crucial part in packaging and promoting space. Viewed more than 30 years later, the film also provides present-day viewers with a temporal-historical perspective on a modern Madrid in transition. That same Madrid was a place where the architects of Spanish democracy worked to create a clean, shiny mise en scène for the consolidation of the aspirationally ahistorical market-oriented society that we know today.

Every process of modernization, every project of refinement, creates residues. Madrid's urban and architectural development is a case in point. Dumpsters filled with construction waste were common enough on Madrid's streets throughout the 1980s and 1990s that they enjoy a visible presence in *¡Átame!* (1989), *Mujeres al borde de un ataque de nervios* and *Carne trémula* (1997). There was sufficient

FIGURE 12.1: Pedro Almodóvar (dir.), *Mujeres al borde*, 1988. Spain. © El Deseo.

building debris occupying Madrid's streets that public service announcements funded by the Ayuntamiento sought to inform Madrilenians of the importance of separating consumer waste from construction waste, and by the early 2000s the massive urban projects undertaken by Ruiz Gallardón's administration required a sustained – and much criticized – publicity campaign that recommended, rhetorically, that Madrilenians ask themselves '¿Qué pasaría si nunca pasase nada?' (What would happen if nothing were ever to happen?) (Bécares 2006).

Trash, waste disposal, and public service announcements played crucial roles in Tierno Galván's plans to forge a fresh new Madrid. As part of his regional government's efforts to restore faith in public institutions, an array of city bureaus was reformed or reorganized in the 1980s, including the restructuring of the Departamento de Saneamiento (Sanitation Department) (Stapell 2010: 65). The city began to systematize its garbage processing and disposal practices, and in so doing, the autonomous government sought to exercise administrative control over local authorities; this was part of the political project of consolidating the new autonomous political organization stipulated by the Constitution of 1978. In July of 1985, Eduardo Mangada, the Community of Madrid's *consejero* ('counselor') of the Ordenación del Territorio, Medio Ambiente y Vivienda (Bureau of Land, Environment and Housing) stated in a press conference that the Autonomous Community of Madrid had the 'moral and political authority' to demand that the region's Ayuntamientos respect their agreements with local authorities to create and maintain dumps for trash and industrial waste

(Anon. 1985b). A document authored in 1984 reported on the existence of more than 250 *vertederos incontrolados* ('unregulated dumps') in and around Madrid (Manzano 1984). As part of the amalgamation of diverse waste disposal operators in Madrid, a plan was put in place to create ten waste treatment facilities within the autonomous Community of Madrid that would supplant the numerous unregulated waste sites throughout the region. (One of these sites appears in *Mujeres al borde* when Candela [María Barranco] discards the suitcase her lover had left in her apartment.)

A report presented in Rome by the Unión de Regiones Capitales de la Comunidad Europea (European Community Union of Regional Capitals, or URCCE) in November of 1986 noted that the city was producing 1.5 million tons of solid waste, of which 64,000 tons were toxic or dangerous. A crucial goal of Madrid's autonomous government was to eliminate what were called *puntos negros* ('black spots'), or *vertederos incontrolados*, of which there were approximately 180, made up of 'urban waste' and 70 others composed of industrial waste. Alongside the closing of these unauthorized dumps scattered throughout the city, the government pursued the creation of a system of *estaciones de transferencia* ('transfer stations') and *reconversion de residuos* ('waste conversion') that would precede garbage transferal to regulated dumps controlled by the Community of Madrid. In the spring of 1986, there were eight independent dumps functioning in the municipalities located in the southern periphery of Madrid that were closed with the inauguration and the opening of a larger waste facility in Pinto. These smaller landfills were then sealed and reformed for subsequent urbanization (Anon. 1986b). Following a lengthy negotiation between local and autonomous Community of Madrid authorities, the Ayuntamiento de Pinto and the Comunidad de Madrid signed an agreement by which the Pinto solid waste facility would treat and eliminate the solid waste from those eight municipalities. The comments of Carlos Penit, the communist mayor of Pinto, offer a useful snapshot of how politics in Madrid were still being negotiated at the local and municipal levels through patronage and compromise:

> Se ha ganado una batalla en relación con la autonomía municipal y se ha sentado un precedente importante. La Comunidad ha cedido, y nosotros hemos aceptado algo que no nos gusta a cambio de prestaciones económicas importantes. En el momento de la firma recibimos 85 millones de pesetas, y la Comunidad se compromete también a realizar obras por valor de 200 millones.
>
> (A battle has been won for municipal autonomy and we have set an important precedent. The Community relented and we have accepted something that we do not like in exchange for important economic benefits. In signing the agreement, we

> received 85 million pesetas and the Community has promised to realize projects in the amount of 200 million pesetas.)
>
> (Anon. 1986a)

A year later, in April of 1987, the industrial waste dump in San Fernando de Henares would also open, once again in spite of strong local opposition. While the mayor of San Fernando refused to authorize construction of the facility, the Consejo de Gobierno Regional (the Regional Government Council) finally overturned his decision based on a controversial interpretation of the *ley del suelo* ('land law'). This process of centralization of solid waste treatment had begun as early as 1984 with the Plan del Tratamiento y Eliminación de Residuos Sólidos Urbanos (Plan for Treatment and Elimination of Urban Solid Waste), whose main purpose was to eliminate the more than 250 *vertederos incontrolados* ('unregulated dumps') that were in existence in the region, while accommodating the 12 million metric tons of *residuos urbanos e industriales y de escombros* ('urban and industrial residues and construction waste') of which it was estimated that 6 million were being dumped into natural areas. The plan also envisioned the construction, between 1985 and 1987, of nine new regional landfills with sanitary controls, two transfer stations and one recycling plant (Manzano 1984).

Alongside these tussles between regional and municipal interests, local authorities worked to build public awareness of sanitation and cleanliness. Madrid's Ayuntamiento initiated a series of public information campaigns, such as the *Lo natural es dejar limpio* ('The natural thing is to keep it clean') of 1987, whose object was to 'concienciar a los madrileños para que respeten el entorno y eviten su degradación no dejando abandonadas las basuras' (raise Madrilenians' awareness, promote respect for their surroundings, and avoid environmental degradation by not throwing their trash indiscriminately) (Anon. 1987b: n.pag.). Environmental education programs and public service campaigns aimed to 'elevar el nivel de eduación ciudadana' (elevate levels of citizen awareness) and to draw attention to domestic waste production and how that waste was causing problems locally (Anon. 1985a: n.pag.). These kinds of 'informal' educational projects were part of both the Community and Ayuntamiento of Madrid's ambition to foster greater citizen participation in the reformation and cleanup of the city and region. These campaigns continued through subsequent administrations.

Public service announcements promoting cleanliness and civic responsibility have always played a part of the state-sponsored externalization of economic costs of a growing capitalist consumer economy and the increased waste production that necessarily comes with it. A survey of Almodóvar's films of the era demonstrates that the director was clearly perceiving and filtering these new regimes of urban transformation on-screen: garbage trucks and sanitation workers trundle through the nocturnal streets of Madrid in *Mujeres*, Becky del Páramo steps in dog shit upon her arrival in Madrid after a long hiatus (*Tacones lejanos* 1991), a drunken, slumbering Ricky (Antonio Banderas) is awakened by a street cleaning truck in *¡Átame!*, and many of the parodic commercials appearing in Almodóvar's films tellingly promote cleaning products. Discourses of urban cleanliness functioned as a purposeful method of shifting Madrilenians' attention away from the past and onto the present. In the urban environment of Transition-era Madrid, news outlets reported on events such as the *gran barrida* ('cleanup') taking place in the Puerta del Sol, where 1,000 people were given brooms to sweep the sidewalks. The *gran barrida* coincided with a study by Cogesep, a sanitary contractor hired by the Ayuntamiento, which found that some 7,400 syringes and nearly 1.5 million cigarette butts were collected in one day in February of 1987 (Anon. 1987c).[2]

This is not to say that Madrid was not an empirically dirty place to live in the 1980s. Spain's right-leaning newspaper *ABC* corroborates the widely held view of Madrid as, by European standards, an extremely disordered and grimy locale. A two-page photographic spread published in the Sunday, 4 October 1987, paper shows piles of garbage on Madrid's streets, with a caption reading

> [l]as imágenes muestran el aspecto indecoroso que presentan las calles del centro de Madrid. Los montones de basura acumulada, las cajas y los desperdicios en medio de las calles confieren a la capital de España una imagen impropia de una ciudad desarrollada.[3]
>
> (These images display the indecorous appearance of the streets in the center of Madrid. The piles of accumulated trash, boxes and castoffs in the middle of the street convey an improper image of Spain's capital as a developed city.)
>
> (Anon. 1987a)

A letter to the editor signed by the Spanish ambassador José María Campoamor published a few months earlier, in *El País*, complained that even toward the end of the 1980s the city was still one of the dirtiest in Europe (28 February 1987). What is noteworthy about these editorial complaints about Madrilenian trash is how both *ABC* and *El País* corroborated a generalized idea that the appearance of trash on the street was seen as somehow antimodern or 'improper' for a developed nation with European aspirations. The political rhetoric of hygiene overlaps with Madrid's efforts to consolidate its authority and to 'cleanup' the city, yet always with an eye toward perceptions of the city abroad. One also has the sense that politicians saw the 'dejunking' of Madrid's streets as a way to free Spaniards from the perception of links to a dirtier authoritarian past, while also confirming, for their European neighbors, that Spain had left its grubby provincial history behind.

It is worth remembering that the interrelated procedures of literal garbage production, disposal and processing continued alongside the cultural and symbolic processes by which the entire country sought to sanitize its public spaces, removing many monuments to Franco and his followers. These measures were not carried out without opposition, and they continue to be controversial to the present day. Stapell attributes increasing civic confidence in Madrid, in part, to the removal of more than two dozen street and plaza names honoring Franco-era figures of political and cultural importance. The Paseo de la Castellana (formerly called the Avenida del Generalísimo) was one of the more noteworthy avenues to revert to a less politically unsavory title (Fuente Lafuente 1980). Tierno Galván remarked, in defense of that particular onomastic project, that 'we are ready for the Civil War to erase itself from [our] consciousness and have it remain only with the intelligentsia as a historical memory' (cited in Stapell 2013: 65). One of Almodóvar's most quoted comments of the era had to do with his rejection of Franco's memory (Vernon 1993: 28).

Viewed alongside the themes and forms of his 1980s films, Almodóvar would seem to share Tierno Galván's approach to history and memory. The exuberant early films especially reflect a cultural present wholeheartedly engaged in the project of reinventing itself. The past and its archaeological debris are pictured either as a wasteland or an archive ripe for reappropriation and recontextualization. Aguilar and Payne have outlined more recently how the Transition was, for a variety of reasons and with an array of consequences, always loathe to recognize or account for past violence. As is well known, the dominant critique of Spain's transition to democracy was the near absence of any kind of cultivation of 'contentious coexistence', especially in terms of any official acknowledgment of and reparations for the crimes committed during a brutal Francoist repression (Aguilar and Payne 2016).

There is perhaps no film that depicts more coherently the ongoing dynamics of Madrid's transformation from quaint center of Francoist society to late capitalist European capital than *Mujeres al borde de un ataque de nervios* (1988). The film was written and produced just after Tierno Galván's death, during a time when Madrid's experiment with regionalism was coming to an end. The elections of 1986 marked the moment when the PSOE's (the Socialist Party's) national leaders embraced wholeheartedly a 'tendency towards neoliberalism and European convergence' that favored 'centralization and stability over greater mobilization' (Stapell 2013: 7). As one of the Transition's foundational fictions, the film was the first to bring Almodóvar to mainstream global prominence as democratic Spain's most visible and colorful auteur. The movie demonstrates how the field of cultural production worked hand in hand with market capital and the Spanish political class in imagining a democratic state populated by emotionally damaged citizens obsessed with getting rid of any traces of the past.[4]

As the film begins, Pepa (Carmen Maura), like the other women referenced in the film's title, is disconnected, temporally and spatially unmoored during the dramatic two days and two nights that unfold in Madrid. All the film's women are 'out of time' or 'out of synch'. For them, the present is a time out of time. The idea of obsolescence that is suggested symbolically by these free floating characters is incarnated in the film through repeated visual instances of garbage, trash, debris, detritus and rubbish. Dumpsters appear throughout the mise en scène: Iván's suitcase is discarded by Pepa then reclaimed by his new girlfriend; Candela appears atop a mound of garbage at an unregulated dump at a graveyard on the outskirts of Madrid, where she discards the evidence that her terrorist lover has left in her apartment; Pepa's note to Iván is thrown away by his ex-wife, then recovered from the bin by Pepa, then found again by sanitation workers on the sidewalk. Garbage trucks lumber through Madrid as nocturnal witnesses to the dramas unfolding throughout the city. People are continually attempting to abandon things for which they no longer have any use.

When Pepa ejects the answering machine from her apartment, she also begins the process by which she will eventually reject the temporal, medial and spatial logics for which it stands. The machine's totemic value within her lived environment can be apprehended through its monolithic appearance within her mise en scène. In *Mujeres*, the medium really is the message, since telephones and answering machines do not function as intermediaries at all. The technologies of connection that appear so prominently in the film – the screen, the projector, the movie camera, the telephone, the answering machine, the microphone – are all devalued as modes of communication. These media do not communicate anything except their own frivolity; they are objects soon-to-be-obsolete.

Fittingly, *Mujeres* opens with an establishing shot of an unrealistic looking housing block, which purports to represent the protagonist Pepa's home in a fashionable part of the city. Gorostiza points out that 'the scene is that of a fake, upscale penthouse, which can be considered as a reproduction of Madrid [*sic*]' (Gorostiza 2008: 37). It is located, most likely, on Calle Alcalá, although characters mention the address Montalbán 7. The same mockup of the apartment building appears in a later scene, when Pepa visits her real estate agent to put her penthouse apartment on the market (Figure 12.2).

As noted earlier, the appearance of Almodóvar's brother Agustín – who also happens to be his executive producer and cofounder of El Deseo, their production company – in the role of real estate agent is a noteworthy detail. When he first appears on-screen, Agustín is placing a Captain America toy on a scale model of a new apartment building (see Figure 12.1). The image is particularly evocative because it is a reflexive moment in a film that is single-mindedly concerned with the aesthetics of urban and interior design. This picture of Almodóvar's executive producer playing with a miniature Madrid in transition (other establishing shots of the real city show construction cranes, and background images contain dumpsters

FIGURE 12.2: Pedro Almodóvar (dir.), *Tacones lejanos*, 1991. Spain. © El Deseo.

filled with building debris) acknowledges the close relationship between processes of transnational capital investment and the creation of urban space, and it signals the crucial role that cinema and TV have always played in promoting those political and economic activities.

The building mockup also gestures toward the manner in which design itself is an increasingly crucial component of Almodóvar's macro-melodramatic film world. As Marsha Kinder has illustrated across several important essays, 'Almodóvar's all-accommodating form of macro-melodrama led him to treat his films as part of the same super-text, as an unfolding narrative network of melodramatic tales in a wide range of tones whose boundaries frequently dissolve and re-congeal into new patterns' (Kinder 2013: 285). The Madrid reflected in those films, from *Pepi, Luci, Bom* (1980) to *Los amantes pasajeros* (2013), is another melodramatic super-text where we can see the evolving image of an urban space progressively transformed and stripped of its historical referents. Almodóvar's movies in turn have drawn from an array of cultural materials external to his film world, part of the authorial 'database' from which he draws images, sounds and people. In keeping with this chapter's focus on waste and Madrilenian architecture, I want to insist that the plasticity of Almodóvar's film world responds to and reflects the dominant political and economic commonplace that viewed – and continues to view – the Spanish capital city as utterly, fundamentally and permanently plastic. By 'plastic', I mean capable of being molded, shaped, twisted and formed into an image befitting the late capitalist modernity to which its contemporary politicians and financiers have always aspired.

Plastic is the dominant material metonym of 1980s Madrid. Its mutability, relative economy of production and consequent ubiquity in the consumer-driven Spanish society of the 1980s makes plastic an important material player in Madrid's *movida*. And plastic is what makes Almodóvar's world go around: from acrylic furniture to obsolete cassette tapes, and from vinyl discs to latex dildos, plastic is everywhere. Silicone, too.[5] Plastic, as 'the archetypal material of invention' (Gabrys et al. 2013: 28), also stands as the sign and symptom of mass consumption, ecological contamination and disposal. It has also become an increasingly large part of our diet, our ecologies and ourselves.[6]

If, in *¿Qué he hecho yo para merecer esto!*, from 1984, the main characters were constantly being hailed by consumer products to which they had limited access, by the time *Mujeres al borde* is produced, four years later, there is so much plastic stuff, junk, devices and things that Almodóvar's women now have to find methods of discarding of them. Lucía (Julieta Serrano) is the only character to hold onto things, but it is her inability to let stuff (and people) go that in some way code her as imbalanced or psychologically unstable. Girelli notes how 'Lucía's acquisition of subjectivity is heavily regulated by patriarchal manipulation' in the film, and how one of the manifestations of her psychosis is apparent in her 'maniacal identification with bygone fashion' (Girelli 2006: 256). Although Girelli suggests that the film allows for the possibility that Lucía's insanity may be a masquerade, there is nonetheless a link established in the film between the performance of emotional instability and an inability to relinquish her hold on the souvenirs she uses to remember the past. In this regard, she, like Pepa, is a quintessential denizen of 1980s Madrid. But this is not the only thing to be gleaned from the film. The reiterated returns of jettisoned materials throughout the narrative demonstrate repeatedly that permanent discarding is impossible. Throughout *Mujeres*, objects are constantly returned to their owners or picked up by others, demonstrating that there is never a 'simple periphery to which objects can be jettisoned' (Gabrys 2013: 78). Like a bad penny, plastic always comes back. Is there a more fitting material metonym for the project of post-dictatorship Spanish culture and urban space?

Design – urban, plastic, biological, personal – has always played a vital role in the formal structure of Almodóvar's filmworlds. But what I want to emphasize in the concluding pages of this chapter is how the logic of disposal – the throwing away or casting-off of things, usually plastic things – in the 1980s films functions to create new social relations. Images of electronic artifacts and plastic castoffs in *Mujeres* draw attention to the ways in which obsolescence functions to 'demarcate duration' (Gabrys 2013: 15), or to bracket time. As Jennifer Gabrys elaborates in an evocative essay on media in the dump, 'When we insert these failed objects into the archive, we encounter their impermanence in high relief' (Gabrys 2006: 162). Impermanence, though, does not mean disappearance. Relations between people and things remain fluid, always allowing for new possibilities, new uses, new roles and new relations. Disposal is but one phase of the extremely long life of consumer electronics and plastics. In Almodóvar's films, the notion of 'using up' and discarding are constitutive of social relations in the modern city. Plasticity characterizes the relations between men and women in *Mujeres* at the same time that the plastic souvenirs of which people wish to free themselves stand for a sentimental past that they would just as soon forget. The movie is all about getting rid of inconvenient traces of the past: a suitcase, a vinyl disc, a cassette tape, a synthetic-leather shoe. But these things always come back. What Almodóvar's films demonstrate is that things and people become entangled and attached. Things are not done with us even if we are done with them. Plastic in Almodóvar's world is imbued with an animistic power to return, to spring back into place.

In the ahistorical milieu of 1980s Madrid, people use plastics to maintain psychic and emotional attachments. The idiosyncratic curation of outmoded plastics is a way of creating meaning in Almodóvar's world. I noted above that Lucía is a collector of outdated fashion. In *Matador* (1986), María (Assumpta Serna) keeps a museum of Diego memorabilia. And, in *¡Átame!* Marina (Victoria Abril) and her neighbor both display dolls and action figures in their bedrooms. Action figures appear in Esteban's room toward the beginning of *Todo sobre mi madre* (1999). There are rows of collectible toys (cars, mostly) next to Alicia's (Leonor Watling) room, which we see when Benigno (Javier Cámara) roams through her house following his interview with her psychiatrist father in *Hable con ella* (2002). There are the *joyas* (jewels) ('es un plástico buenísimo' [it is a very high-quality plastic]) that Agustina curates as keepsakes from her disappeared mother in *Volver* (2006) and the *muñecas* that Soledad (Lola Dueñas) brings with her from her aunt's house, and that later Raimunda's (Penélope Cruz) daughter plays with while talking to Irene on the bed: '¿Te gustan las muñecas?' (Do you like dolls?).

If we hold these plastic toys in our mind and consider the architectural mockups appearing in Almodóvar's movies (Figures 12.1, 12.2 and 12.3), a series of interrelated hypotheses arise in response to the question I asked, in the opening pages of this essay, about what Almodóvar has to say about architecture and the urban in Madrid. Gorostiza describes the replicas appearing in Almodóvar's films mainly as icons of Madrid. In *Kika* (1993), for example, 'the Madrid in miniature that Almodóvar shows us can also be a model of the city which at times is difficult to find its own identity [sic]' (Gorostiza 2008: 45). But the architectural models in Almodóvar's films of the 1980s do a lot of other things, too. Perhaps most importantly, the models serve as a way of registering precisely the ongoing regional and municipal efforts, described above, to twist and pull Madrid's urban spaces, to exploit its plasticity. The mockups are also a way of introducing into the films a reflexive notion of urban scale: outsized family melodrama is made even bigger when Rebeca surveys a small-scale Barajas airport from above. This is a mise en scène positioned also as a melodramatic mise en abyme: Rebeca observes a toy-sized airport at the same time the viewer watches her in the airport; meanwhile, Almodóvar himself hides behind the maximal design of his cinematic dollhouses, the unseen architect of nested melodramatic worlds of excess.

The architectural replicas appearing in Almodóvar's films of the 1980s are scale models standing for the actual lived spaces that their Madrilenian protagonists inhabit. They are also icons of the urban as (1) constitutive or reflective of personal identity; (2) as a place that is inherently and constantly in a process of change and (3) locations for play and performance. If, during that time, Madrid itself was being modified by the somewhat less-visible efforts of politicians and investors, the authorship of change in Almodóvar's mises en scènes belongs to creative men invested with the power to move people around and to alter their cityscapes. The picture of Almodóvar's brother placing plastic dolls within a scale model of a housing block is evocative because this is what the El Deseo enterprise has always done: move bodies through postmodern plastic spaces.

Stapell describes how Tierno Galván ambitiously built a more livable city center around an improved transport system, new green areas, cleaner streets and rationalized processes of waste removal and disposal. Tierno Galván's aim to integrate diverse stakeholders in the political and cultural project of creating a Madrilenian identity was based on a politically progressive, at times utopian, imagination of social integration that relied on the participation of district councils, exhibitions and planning committees, the organization of popular festivals and the revitalization of popular cultural practices. But it was not without its costs, as the recent Spanish past was but one of the things that were lost to this egalitarian program anchored in transforming Madrid into a shining modern European capital.

Almodóvar is both a logical product of the plastic 1980s and their most eloquent defender. As one of the *movida*'s most enduring posterboys, Pedro's early Madrid films capture the dynamism and plasticity of Tierno Galván's progressive urban vision. The plastic lifeworlds that capitalist urbanism created for modern Spaniards became, logically and fruitfully, Almodóvar's playground. This is not to say that the past is completely absent from the Almodóvar universe. The rural world is figured in the films as an unchanging if distant *locus amoenus* where characters retreat when they need to find a temporal and emotional anchor. Geographic dislocation is often accompanied in his movies by a nostalgic yearning for a lost maternal-rural space, represented by the Manchegan towns appearing in *¿Qué he hecho yo para merecer esto!* (What Have I Done to Deserve This?!, 1984), *Matador*

FIGURE 12.3: Pedro Almodóvar (dir.), *Kika*, 1993. Spain. © El Deseo.

(1986) and ¡Átame! (Tie Me Up, Tie Me Down, 1989) (Amago 2013). Fittingly, *Kika* (1993) ends with its eponymous character (Verónica Forqué) confiding in a handsome hitchhiker, 'Eso es lo que necesito: un poquito de orientación' ('That's just what I needed: a little orientation'), as she leaves plastic Madrid behind.

NOTES

1. As we have seen across an array of global contexts in the wake of the killings of George Floyd, Ahmaud Arbery and Breonna Taylor, the past is never over, and history is still being written. In William Faulkner's terms, 'the past is never dead. It's not even past' (Faulkner 1951: 73). This is why it is so important to so many people that public spaces be reclaimed for the commons. Statues and other symbols situated in urban space are not history; they are pieces of the architectures of political power that continue to exert force in the present. This is why Tierno Galván and his contemporary heirs sought to take down statues of Franco and his minions.
2. The syringes were likely the result of illegal dumping by medical clinics. The urban cleanup crews averaged 16,745 kilos of trash per day (Anon. 1987c).
3. In an editorial column published later the same month, Lorenzo López Sancho criticized the Madrid government and Cogesep who, according to the author, *tercermundizan* ('third-world-ize') the city. López Sancho refers to a visit he made to two European cities whose cleanliness only made Madrid appear even dirtier. He also criticizes what he sees as the failure of the city's projects of *concienciación* ('awareness') when they clearly fail to keep

its streets clean (López Sancho 1987). I found at least two letters published near those dates in *El País* expressing similar sentiments, one authored by a Swedish exchange student (Gustafsson 1988) and another signed by elementary school students (Mata and Montejo 1987). They all lamented Spaniards' inability to dispose of their waste properly.

4. The bibliography on Spain's transition culture, its capitalist underpinnings and its omissions is ample. In addition to Stapell and Vilarós, Fishman and Lizardo, Duch Plana, Escudero Rodríguez, Burns Marañón, and Martínez-Alier and Roca are instructive.
5. Given its centrality to Almodóvar's filmmaking, it is curious that plastic merits only passing mention in the collected essays comprising the Vernon and D'Lugo *Companion*. Nevertheless, Pérez Melgosa's essay in that volume does devote important attention to the apparently trivial objects appearing in the filmmaker's movies, and which function to 'wrestle away from memory its power to dictate the present, and from trauma its ability to freeze the lives of those who are targeted as its victims' (Melgosa 2009: 181). Of the five mentions of 'plastic' in the Epps and Kakoudaki volume, three refer only to plastic surgery.
6. The worldwide proliferation of plastic waste has only increased with the global COVID-19 pandemic (Anon. 2020).

REFERENCES

Aguilar, Paloma and Payne, Leigh A. (2016), *Revealing New Truths about Spain's Violent Past: Perpetrators Confessions and Victim Exhumations*, London: Palgrave Macmillan.

Almodóvar, Pedro (1980), *Pepi, Luci, Bom y otras chicas del montón* (Pepi, Luci, Bom and Other Girls on the Heap), Madrid: El Deseo.

Almodóvar, Pedro (1984), *¿Qué he hecho yo para merecer esto!* (What Have I Done to Deserve This?!), Madrid: El Deseo.

Almodóvar, Pedro (1986), *Matador*, Madrid: El Deseo.

Almodóvar, Pedro (1988), *Mujeres al borde de un ataque de nervios* (Women on the Verge of a Nervous Breakdown), Madrid: El Deseo.

Almodóvar, Pedro (1989), *¡Átame!* (Tie Me Up, Tie Me Down), Madrid: El Deseo.

Almodóvar, Pedro (1991), *Tacones lejanos* (High Heels), Madrid: El Deseo.

Almodóvar, Pedro (1993), *Kika*, Madrid: El Deseo.

Almodóvar, Pedro (1997), *Carne trémula* (Live Flesh), Madrid: El Deseo.

Almodóvar, Pedro (2002), *Hable con ella* (Talk to Her), Madrid: El Deseo.

Almodóvar, Pedro (2006), *Volver*, DVD Extras, USA: Sony Pictures.

Almodóvar, Pedro (2011), *La piel que habito* (The Skin I Live in), Madrid: El Deseo.

Almodóvar, Pedro (2013), *Los amantes pasajeros* (I'm So Excited!), Madrid: El Deseo.

Amago, Samuel (2013), *Spanish Cinema in the Global Context: Film on Film*. New York: Routledge.

Anon. (1985a), 'Comienza en Madrid el primer encuentro ecologista de Amantes de la Basura', *El País*, 2 November, https://elpais.com/diario/1985/11/02/madrid/499782258_850215.html. Accessed 19 July 2018.

Anon. (1985b), 'La Comunidad de Madrid sigue adelante con sus planes para la instalación de vertederos', *El País*, 31 July, https://elpais.com/diario/1985/07/31/madrid/491657054_850215.html. Accessed 19 July 2018.

Anon. (1986a), 'El vertedero de Pinto entrará en servicio dentro de una semana', *El País*, 30 October, https://elpais.com/diario/1986/10/30/madrid/531059062_850215.html. Accessed 16 July 2018.

Anon. (1986b), 'Madrid genera cada año 64.000 toneladas de productos tóxicos y peligrosos', *El País*, 3 December, https://elpais.com/diario/1986/12/03/madrid/533996661_850215.html. Accessed 19 July 2018.

Anon. (1987a), 'Actualidad gráfica', *ABC*, 4 October, http://hemeroteca.abc.es/nav/Navigate.exe/hemeroteca/madrid/abc/1987/10/04/009.html and http://hemeroteca.abc.es/nav/Navigate.exe/hemeroteca/madrid/abc/1987/10/04/008.html. Accessed 16 July 2018.

Anon. (1987b), 'Reparto gratuito de 100.000 bolsas de basura en las carreteras madrileñas', *El País*, 2 May, http://politica.edicioneselpais.net/diario/1987/05/02/madrid/546953061_850215.html. Accessed 16 July 2018.

Anon. (1987c), '7.400 jefinguillas y 1.440.000 colillas, recogidas en un solo día en las calles del distrito de Centro', *El País*, 19 March 1987, https://elpais.com/diario/1987/03/19/madrid/543155066_850215.html. Accessed 16 July 2018.

Anon. (2020), 'Covid-19 has led to a pandemic of plastic pollution', *The Economist*, 3 June, https://www.economist.com/international/2020/06/22/covid-19-has-led-to-a-pandemic-of-plastic-pollution. Accessed 6 July 2020.

Bécares, Roberto (2006), 'La publicidad del Ayuntamiento sobre las obras desata odios y pasiones', *El Mundo*, 15 November, http://www.elmundo.es/elmundo/2006/11/15/madrid/1163605443.html. Accessed 16 July 2018.

Burns Marañón, Tom (2015), *De la fruta madura a la manzana podrida: El laberinto de la Transición española*, Barcelona: Galaxia Gutenberg.

Campoamor, José María (1987), 'Por un Madrid limpio', Cartas al Director (Letters to the Editor), *El País*, 28 February, https://elpais.com/diario/1987/02/28/opinion/541465204_850215.html. Accessed 19 July 2018.

Duch Plana, Montserrat (2014), *¿Una ecología de las memorias colectivas? La transición española a la democracia revisitada*, Lleida: Milenio Publicaciones.

Epps, Brad and Kakoudaki, Despina (2009), *All About Almodóvar: A Passion for Cinema*, Minneapolis: University of Minnesota Press.

Escudero Rodríguez, Javier (2005), *La narrativa de Rosa Montero: Hacia una ética de la esperanza*, Madrid: Biblioteca Nueva.

Faulkner, William (1951), *Requiem for a Nun*, New York: Vintage Books.

Fishman, Robert M. and Lizardo, Omar (2013), 'How macro-historical change shapes cultural taste: Legacies of democratization in Spain and Portugal', *American Sociological Review*, 78:2, pp. 213–39.

Fuente Lafuente, Ismael (1980), 'Generalísimo se convierte en paseo de la Castellana', *El País,* 26 January, https://elpais.com/diario/1980/01/26/madrid/317737456_850215.html. Accessed 19 July 2018.

Gabrys, Jennifer (2006), 'Media in the dump', in J. Knechtel (ed.), *Trash*, Cambridge: MIT Press, pp. 156–65.

Gabrys, Jennifer (2013), *Digital Rubbish: A Natural History of Electronics*, Ann Arbor: University of Michigan Press.

Gabrys, Jennifer, Hawkins, Gay and Michael, Mike (eds) (2013), *Accumulation: The Material Politics of Plastic*, London: Routledge.

Garcés, Marina (2019), 'From the politicization of life to the new politics', in Óscar Pereira-Zazo and Steven L. Torres (eds), *Spain after the Indignados/15M Movement: The 99% Speaks out*, Cham, Switzerland: Palgrave Macmillan, pp. 21–63.

Girelli, Elisabetta (2006), 'The power of the masquerade: *Mujeres al borde de un ataque de nervios* and the construction of femininity', *Hispanic Research Journal*, 7:3, 251–58.

Gorostiza, Jorge (2008), 'Backdrops and miniatures: The other Madrid built by Almodóvar', *Cine y... Revista de estudios interdisciplinarios sobre el cine español*, 1:2, pp. 35–48.

Gustafsson, Ylva (1988), 'El país limpio', Cartas al director (Letters to the Editor), *El País*, 17 February, http://www.elpais.com/articulo/opinion/pais/limpio/elpepiopi/19880217elpepiopi_4/Tes. Accessed 16 July 2018.

Kinder, Marsha (2013), 'Re-envoicements and reverberations in Almodóvar's macro-melodrama', in M. D'Lugo and K. Vernon (eds), *Companion to Pedro Almodóvar*, Malden, MA: John Wiley & Sons, pp. 281–303.

Labrador Méndez, Germán (2010), '"España, una mierda". Política, excrementos y poesía en la Transición', in L. Gómez Canseco (ed.), *Fragmentos para una historia de la mierda. Cultura y transgresión*, Huelva: Universidad de Huelva, pp. 221–46.

López, Isidro (2012), 'Consensonomics: la ideología económica en la CT', in G. Martínez (ed.), *CT o la Cultura de la Transición. Crítica a 35 años de cultura española*, Barcelona: Random House Mondadori, pp. 77–88.

López Sancho, Lorenzo (1987), 'El Madrid que no reluce', *ABC*, 29 October, http://hemeroteca.abc.es/nav/Navigate.exe/hemeroteca/madrid/abc/1987/10/29/034.html. Accessed 19 July 2018.

Manzano, Andrés (1984), 'Un vertedero con control sanitario absorberá la basura de los 785.000 habitantes de la zona sur', 15 October, *El País*, https://elpais.com/diario/1984/10/15/madrid/466691056_850215.html. Accessed 16 July 2018.

Martínez-Alier, J. and Roca, Jordi (1987/1988), 'Spain after Franco: From corporatist ideology to corporatist reality', *International Journal of Political Economy*, 17:4, pp. 56–87.

Mata, Laureano and Montejo, José Antonio (1987), 'Esto es basura', Cartas al Director (Letters to the Editor), 26 November, *El País*, http://www.elpais.com/articulo/opinion/basura/elpepiopi/19871126elpepiopi_8/Tes. Accessed 19 July 2018.

Merino, Eloy and Song, H. Rosi (eds) (2005), *Traces of Contamination: Unearthing the Francoist Legacy in Contemporary Spanish Discourse*, Lewisburg, PA: Bucknell University Press.

Pérez Melgosa, Adrián (2009), 'The ethics of oblivion: Personal, national, and cultural memories in the films of Pedro Almodóvar', in M. D'Lugo and K. Vernon (eds), *Companion to Pedro Almodóvar*, Malden, MA: John Wiley & Sons, pp. 176–200.

Scanlan, John and Clark, John F. M. (eds) (2013), *Aesthetic Fatigue: Modernity and the Language of Waste*, Newcastle upon Tyne: Cambridge Scholars.

Stapell, Hamilton (2010), *Remaking Madrid: Culture, Politics, and Identity after Franco*, New York: Palgrave Macmillan.

Vernon, Kathleen (1993), 'Melodrama against itself: Pedro Almodóvar's *What Have I Done to Deserve This?*', *Film Quarterly*, 46:3, pp. 28–40.

Vilarós, Teresa (1998), *El mono del desencanto: Una crítica cultural de la transición española (1973–1993)*, Madrid: Siglo XXI.

PART 6

THE VIRTUAL

13

Uncanny Urbanism and Generational Shifts in Carlos Marques Marcet's *10.000km* and *Anchor and Hope*

Leigh Mercer, University of Washington, Seattle

Trained at film schools in both Spain and the United States, Carlos Marques Marcet forms part of a novel young generation of Catalan directors who are equally at home in Spain as abroad, and who write and direct in Catalan, Spanish and English. Marques Marcet made his debut as a director in 2014 at the age of 30 with *10.000km*, a feature film for which he won the Goya Award for Best New Director. Set in Barcelona and Los Angeles, though filmed entirely in Barcelona on a $418,000 budget, *10.000km* is the Spanish-language film debut of actress Natalia Tena, known for her work in the *Harry Potter* series and *Game of Thrones*. According to *Variety* magazine, *10.000km* belongs to a new crop of Spanish films on the film festival circuit that were 'low budget films [...] with high ambitions' (De Pablos 2014: n.pag.). Since the success of *10.000km*, Marques Marcet has directed a historical telefilm for Televisió de Catalunya about Catalan president Lluís Companys's final days, *13 dies d'octubre* (2015); he has completed his second feature, *Anchor and Hope* (2017), a film inspired by María Llopis's 2015 book *Maternidades subversivas*, and shot entirely on location in London with an international and multilingual cast; and in January 2019 he premiered his third feature, *Els dies que vindran*, at the International Film Festival Rotterdam. Filmed in both Catalan and Spanish and his first feature fully rooted in the landscape of Barcelona, *Els dies que vindran* uses the real-life pregnancy of the lead actress María Rodríguez Soto and her husband David Verdaguer – the actor whom Marques Marcet had cast in both *10.000km* and *Anchor and Hope* – to explore the transformative experience of an unexpected pregnancy for a newly formed couple. Uniting all of Marques Marcet's film work, though perhaps not his foray into television, is a daring sense of play in casting and the construction of mise en scène, despite, or perhaps owing to, the crisis in the Spanish film industry and the nation's contemporaneous economic crisis, occurring just as Marques Marcet came onto the scene as a filmmaker.

For Marques Marcet, space and distance are the mediums through which he depicts drama and explores emotional stresses on human relationships. Describing his personal take on the seventh art, Marques Marcet has noted that 'at the end of the day, that's what cinema is, people and places; there's not much more to it than that. I'm interested in how space and all its facets have an impact on us: how we pass through those spaces and the distances that are created' (Rivera 2017: n. pag.). Filmed on the canals of England's capital, *Anchor and Hope* shows a side of London rarely explored in films previously set in this city. Marques Marcet has stated that, with this feature film, he became

> really interested in establishing a link between the people and the landscape: I wanted there to be a transfer of emotions between both things. I was keen to salvage that particular remnant of the industrial era: a project on an enormous scale, constructed the length and breadth of England, which, after 40 years, had become obsolete because of the advent of the train. I liked how people live in what remains of the industrial era, right on the fringes. That speaks volumes about the world we're living in.
>
> (Rivera 2017: n.pag.)

The distancing and dividing impact of space on human relationships is likewise front and center in Marques Marcet's first feature *10.000km*, which tells the story of two young lovers, one in Barcelona and the other now displaced from economic-crisis-era Spain to Los Angeles due to a photography fellowship, who communicate almost all of their domestic and urban experiences through online apps and computer screens. In this film's mise en scène, the cityscape of Los Angeles is revealed only through virtual photo sharing, Google Street View and Facebook posts, while the urban environment of Barcelona is hyper-present in its almost complete absence, with the exception of one crucial exterior balcony scene roughly halfway through the film. Although Marques Marcet's shoestring budget may have been the compelling factor in his choice to deploy the space of Los Angeles in the film only through virtual means, the economic limitations in place allowed Marques Marcet to explore online representations of landscape, highlighting the sensorial alienation of the protagonist couple's long-distance relationship.

An exploration of the relationship between people and places was of course a foundational element of cinema in its origins in the late nineteenth century. The earliest experimentations in film were frequently tied to emergent forms of urban space in particular. Point-of-view trolley and harbor boat films, city view films and urban actualities from the first decade of the silent era all confirm the connection between this novel technological and artistic medium and the era of expansive urban materiality into which it was born. For Giuliana Bruno, a new geography of visuality was being produced as film came into being. Architectural sites of transit, arcades, railways, panorama paintings and winter gardens, for example, were at the center of this transformation, with the dialogue between the urban and the light space of film leading to the creation of new haptic experiences (Bruno 2018: n.pag.). Likewise, as Geraldine Pratt and Rose Marie San Juan have noted, historically the materiality of the screen was likened to the urban street, as notions of movement, speed, continuities and discontinuities belonged to both (Pratt and San Juan 2014: 3–4). For these two critics, contemporary analyses of the encounter between cinematic and urban space have only grown increasingly complex in the contemporary era:

> Foremost is the understanding that the urban or cities are not most usefully conceived as mere context, content, setting or narrative support. The [...] interest is not so much in how this or that city is represented in film but in the more closely entwined workings of cinematic and urban space, within both films and the material spaces of concrete cities. [...] Film has [...] mobility and the capacity to create unexpected juxtapositions, and both film and the appearance of the urban within film can work on and with geographical imaginations in new and critical ways.
>
> (Pratt and San Juan 2014: 5)

Marques Marcet's statements on the transfer of emotions between urban places and the characters that populate his films clearly intersect with Pratt and San Juan's understanding of cinema as a vehicle for uncovering particularities of urban materiality and critiquing the human relationships enmeshed with city life in an unexpected fashion. They likewise recall Jonathan Raban's understanding of the 'soft city' as a site of illusion, myth, aspiration and nightmare rooted in the urban, but not captured in maps, statistics or in monographs on urban sociology or architecture (Raban 1974: 2). As François Penz and Andong Lu have argued in *Urban Cinematics*, the study of filmic urban spaces may offer us a particularly holistic venue through which to understand cities and this softer side of their articulation. For these critics, 'through the framing process and the subsequent screening, even the most anonymous and banal city location will be transformed from an unconsciously recorded space – or naïve space – to a consciously recorded space that becomes an expressive space' (Penz and Lu 2011: 8–9).

In what follows, I examine the distancing, decadent, virtual and residual spatial elements Marques Marcet deploys in his films, with the goal of highlighting how his peculiar portrayals of the urban consistently work to deepen our understanding of the affective relationships and cultural seismic shifts at the core of his films. The postindustrial landscapes of boat canals become the strangely outside-of-time mise en scène to explore the generational sea change portrayed in *Anchor and Hope* – what parenthood looks like for a present-day generation of 30-somethings who are questioning the inherited structures of the traditional Western family in the era of late capitalism. The film's title, though most obviously a reference to the eponymous canal-side pub depicted in the film, also suggests the anchored social institutions so prevalent in these young people's lives and their hopeful impulses to break free of them. In *10.000km*, the estrangement from city life and the mediated and alienating experience of urbanism depicted in this film likewise operate in parallel to the generational seismic shifts that the film explores, specifically how young adults can form affective bonds and deep romantic and potentially familial relationships in a postindustrial era that celebrates mobility and individualistic pursuits. Space, in Marques Marcet's usage, is Lefebvrian in nature, as it is not a contextual landscape but an active designer of social relationships. As Henri Lefebvre posited, space 'serves as a tool of thought and action; that in addition to being a means of production it is also a means of control' (Lefebvre 2001: 26). Thus, in both *Anchor and Hope* and *10.000km*, there is something subtly radical about the mise en scène, specifically the representation of bodies and urban objects in alienated or decadent space; this very commingling of people and places, in Marques Marcet's conception, becomes the site where he not only stages but moreover animates debates about adulthood, intimacy and parenthood in the contemporary era.

In *The Mise-en-Scène of Modernity: The French New Wave, Paris, and the Global 1960s*, James Tweedie has argued that French new wave cinema directors were the first to take cinema out of studio sets and into real urban sites, 'envision[ing] the urban environments around them as a stage where the modernization of France play[ed] out on the terrain of everyday life', where 'performance [...] competed with the spectacle of the city' and in which 'the border between cinema and the city [was] porous' (Tweedie 2013: 53). Marques Marcet's cinematic style pushes the exploration of city space beyond this mode of urban-cinema interface that came into being in the 1960s; by mining the virtual screens of contemporary urbanism or the alternative and neglected urban remnants of an industrial past that linger in the present day, he troubles the seamless relationship between urbanism and cinema in a way that is decidedly of this twenty-first-century moment. Embodied urban spaces are no longer the stages where contemporary processes of political and technological modernization play out, because the city, in his films, is always mediated or purposefully at a remove. Instead of a scaffolding for cinema or a counterpart held in tension with the cinematic, urban elements in both of Marques Marcet's films place viewers in the realm of the uncanny. Marques Marcet offers familiar landscapes made strange, especially as these urban sites resituate viewers outside of their present time or place and ultimately question the presentist projection of the play between cinema and urban landscape so often found in European film beginning with the work of the French New Wave auteurs.

As Marques Marcet has noted, the canals of London, just north of the heart of the capital's center and built in the nineteenth century to transport coal, timber and foodstuffs in and out of the city, are an urban site that was quickly abandoned with the advent of train transportation in England. In *Anchor and Hope*, the fluid landscapes of the canals take on the proportions of a fourth performance, beyond that of the couple, Eva and Kat, and Kat's sperm-donating friend Roger, whose triangulated baby-making relationship stands at the narrative center of the film. In first instance, these waterways and the constant unmoored nature of Eva and Kat's boat life (Eva herself will tell newly arrived Roger that they must move their boat every two weeks or risk their home being confiscated) seem the perfect backdrop for Roger's ejaculations, Kat's inseminations of Eva and the characters' fluid reformulation of the notion of family. And although the fluidity of the space in which the three protagonists move might recall the porosity between the cinematic and the urban that earlier film styles so richly enacted, Marques Marcet's film strives to visually contain and limit the three protagonists, who although buoyed literally and at times figuratively by their life on the water, are regularly stilled within or placed outside of the ebb and flow of the canals.

In *Anchor and Hope*, mise en scène, in conjunction with soundscape choices and Dagmar Weaver-Madsen's camerawork, focuses the audience on the static and the stagnant in these three characters' lives by framing them in contrast with the canals. The film's intro sequence is a perfect example of this distancing move and sets the tone for much of the interaction between bodies and the urban landscape in what will follow. The film begins with a black space that slowly reveals itself to be a lengthy tunnel under a bridge. From within this dark tunnel a distant view of the canal and its verdant banks appears, almost as through a peephole, a focal point that grows increasingly larger as we progress through the tunnel. This lush and inviting landscape with its dappled golden lighting contrasts sharply with the film's opening soundtrack, a rendition of the 1940s folk song 'Dirty Old Town', in which the singers acknowledge the drudgery and inescapable grind of life in a once-thriving industrial space. The lyrics – 'I met my love by the gasworks croft / Dreamed a dream by the old canal / I kissed my girl by the factory wall / Dirty old town / Dirty old town' – and the musical style of this song make us step back in historical time at the same time as they invite us to find a relationship between the dirty old town of the song and the images of the present-day canal. As the song momentarily cuts out and silence takes hold, a human shadow appears. A woman, initially seen from behind, turns to show herself in profile; Eva – her name resonant with that of the biblical first woman – slowly emerges from the darkness of the

FIGURE 13.1: Eva's cameo silhouette on the ship canal, Carlos Marques Marcet (dir.), *Anchor and Hope*, 2017. Spain. © Lastor Media, S.L.

tunnel, its rounded walls creating a dark oval shape at the borders of this scene. The visual result (Figure 13.1) is, on the one hand, reminiscent of a Georgian- or Victorian-era cameo brooch, and on the other, not unlike the shadow play scenes in the pioneering era of silent filmmaking or the oval-framing or peephole devices often deployed around female screen stars in that same period. Thus, from the start, Eva is marked as oddly outside of the time and beyond the place in which she is depicted, in early twenty-first-century London. As the canal flows beyond her, she is a fixed shadow, a two-dimensional layer superimposed on a watery background, contained for a moment by the oval framing that surrounds her.

As the film will subsequently reveal, what creates the rub between Eva and her time, as represented by her lack of integration and resistance within the film's canal-based mise en scène, is her yearning for motherhood and her deep connection with family. This will be expressed again in her discomfort with the ever-mobile canal boat on which she and Kat live, and her need, stated toward the end of the film, to live on *tierra firme*, or 'solid ground', with this expression notably serving as the Spanish-language title of Marques Marcet's film. Eva, with her braided-crown hairstyle, flowing dresses and nostalgic gaze toward her own mother and her mother's communal lifestyle in the 1960s, is not the only antiquated figure in the film. Like the alternative space of the canals or the gasworks croft later depicted in the film – spaces that have existed at the margins of the power, production and consumption of London's urban core for over a hundred years – the characters that inhabit this fringe space similarly exhibit outmoded forms of being and struggle to find alternative ways of existing in the contemporary world. Roger, for example, is a precariously employed hipster who comes across as something of an old-style drifter, and a cad who makes openly racist comments to a black lover while jokingly denying his racism. Although he is initially flippant about donating his sperm to his lesbian friends, and often forgets when Eva is fertile and expecting his donation, he becomes increasingly proprietary and asserts himself in a more patriarchal role once Eva becomes pregnant, hoping to participate in the ultrasound, helping her prepare the boat for the baby's arrival and taking her shopping for strollers.

Even Kat – who, as the 'captain' figure on the houseboat and a bartender at the canal-side Anchor & Hope pub, is the character most seemingly immersed in canal life – struggles to fit in to her contemporary environment. She engages in patriarchal posturing and cuts herself off from affective expression and deep emotional connection with her partner, most especially with the unborn child Eva is carrying. Kat's internal struggle is perfectly captured in the uncanny way Marques Marcet frames her in relationship to the canals. Although Kat imagines herself to be a free-spirited figure living a peripatetic existence beyond society's expectations, Marques Marcet does not link her character most closely with the boat's movement or the canal's fluidity. Instead, the film's camerawork and mise en scène consistently depict her in relation to the inescapability of these manmade waterways in their linearity and limitations. Multiple scenes focus on Kat as a runner who works out her emotional frustrations through movement, almost always by jogging along the paved shores of the canals; and though she compulsively pushes her body to utter exhaustion, she cannot break free of the prescribed routes of the canals. In the most telling of Kat's running scenes, she is captured in several sequential shots, running and panting, out of focus, along the manmade shoreline, until ultimately she stops and appears in a curious shot/reverse shot in which she is practically the only human figure present, just as she reaches the dead end of the Paddington Arm of the Grand Union Canal (Figure 13.2).

Unable to catch her breath and at a metaphorical end-of-the-line, feeling trapped by Eva's pregnancy and her own impending parenthood, Kat's relationship to the urban landscape metaphorically speaks to the realities of her generation, one that finds itself searching for fluidity in gender and familial roles, but that cannot move beyond the ingrained and imposed familial structures of generations past. Thus, even in the scenes in which Kat is depicted on the water, captaining her houseboat, she is either shrouded in the darkness of tunnels like Eva at the outset of the film, a shadow superimposed on the truly embodied contemporary life of London, or most notably, spinning the boat in a circle, again emphasizing this character's inability to escape the fixed channels of the canals. One such dizzying turnabout scene is set against the backdrop of a nineteenth-century gasworks croft, presently being remodeled into upscale loft apartments, and pointedly occurs just after Eva has miscarried the baby and left Kat to live alone on the houseboat (Figure 13.3). Here, as in other instances in the film, the

FIGURE 13.2: Kat, at the canal's dead end, Carlos Marques Marcet (dir.), *Anchor and Hope*, 2017. Spain. © Lastor Media, S.L.

urban mise en scène points to processes of gentrification, another strong undercurrent in this film that, though never openly discussed, appears in the two ideas of London competing for space along the canals throughout the film – one graffitied and subversive, the other architecturally chic yet sterile, and imposing in height and mass and a disruptive presence that is under construction. The neoliberal influences at work in the city space, like the traditional formulations of marriage and parenthood circulating around the film's leads, are inescapable forces that act upon the character's lives, despite their best attempts to carve new paths of marginal existence on the city's waterways.

The remix of architectural and industrial signposts that is present in this boat turning scene is particularly telling. The site of the gasworks croft recalls the lyric from 'Dirty Old Town' in the film's opening sequence, resituating us in this industrial remnant landscape, with a muted but unsettling soundtrack of nondiegetic

FIGURE 13.3: Kat spins in circles against the layered yet flat gasworks landscape, Carlos Marques Marcet (dir.), *Anchor and Hope*, 2017. Spain. © Lastor Media, S.L.

mechanical noise playing as the camera pans the height and breadth of the gasworks, the noise speeding up in rhythm until it sounds like the thumping of helicopter blades. Though this is the first close up offered of the gasworks, seen previously in the film in medium and long shots, mise en scène and soundtrack combine here to create a dissociative experience of this industrial relic. The soundscape of Molly Drake's 'Little Weaver Bird', which speaks to the urgent need to forget the past and build a home, rubs against the strangeness of the gasworks croft, a once-functional structure that at present is mere sculpture or neighborhood landmark, now being reconstructed as high-end condos. As Kat's boat spins in a circle in the midst of these layers of urban sediment, the camerawork shows depth of focus on the boat and Kat, and the flatness in the gasworks backdrop, perfectly distilling Kat's struggle to transcend inherited cultural mores and her awkwardness in trying to take on a role of power that pushes beyond the patriarchal as both a lover and potential mother. The subsequent scene, in which Kat seeks out Eva in her new apartment on firm ground, appears to be a direct result of Kat's spiral on the canal, a moment in which she is mobile against the urban spaces that surround her, distanced and never fully enmeshed in them, realizing that she must solidify her position in life. Ultimately, after Kat proposes a reconciliation to Eva, and despite the fact that Eva acknowledges she does not know what she wants from Kat or what she wants to do, now that she is pregnant again from an anonymous donor, the film's denouement suggests a hopeful future for the couple, in large part through mise en scène. In the film's final minutes, Kat and Eva's relationship to the urban landscape is presented in the inverse, with Kat shown captaining the boat, first as a cameo silhouette like Eva in the opening scene, and then slowly moving into the light, and Eva now depicted strolling, not running like Kat, along the canal pathway, her ambling keeping pace with the forward motion of the houseboat. As each character embodies the other's relationship to the urban canals, a promising middle ground has been reached.

Despite the temporally slippery, unexpected depiction of urban landscape in *Anchor and Hope* which locates us in a peripheral London, one lacking in monumentality and remote from the contemporary energies of this capital, the film is nonetheless always rooted in a realistic, albeit decadent and often obsolete visual discourse. This marginalization and the distancing effect of the film's mise en scène are frequently deployed in service of the narrative's exploration of the seismic shifts in romantic and familial relationships facing today's 30-something generation. Marques Marcet's first film, *10.000km*, proposes an even more alienated and uncanny relationship to urban space than *Anchor and Hope*. This story of two lovers, also in their 30s, who endure a long-distance relationship between Barcelona and Los Angeles in the midst of the Spanish economic crisis, deploys urban space almost exclusively through virtual or manipulated means, be it online or in Alex's photography, as a parallel to the manipulation of human thought and emotion that is part and parcel of networked and mediated life in the early twenty-first century. In this film, we are faced with Bruno's assertion that, in the contemporary era, 'our walls are becoming more like light spaces, and they are at times even turning into screens', as the visual architecture of our times is 'becoming increasingly fluid and mobile' (Bruno 2018: n.pag.). Though in the film Spain's economic crisis is only signaled through the lack of opportunities present for Alex, who must head to Los Angeles to find support for her photographic art, and Sergi's impossible board exams that leave him little hope of earning a permanent teaching position, transition and crisis permeate the whole emotional landscape of this film, and the spatial realms Marques Marcet depicts become sites for exploring the breakdowns in human communication and connection in the contemporary era. It is *10.000km*'s depiction of an inaccessible and consistently mediated urban landscape that most tellingly reveals the affective holes in this present-day generation's experience of intimacy and belonging.

There are three distinct narrative blocks in *10.000km*: an almost 23-minute continuous take of Alex and Sergi having sex, showering, cooking and eating breakfast together before the email news of her photography fellowship arrives; the almost hour-long middle section of the film in which Alex and Sergi carry out a long-distance relationship via Skype and social media, with Alex virtually sharing her growing understanding of her new home in Los Angeles; and the brief denouement of the film in which Sergi surprises Alex with a visit to her apartment in Los Angeles. In both the film's opening and closing sequences in which the two protagonists are based in the same city, the action is contained exclusively within apartment interiors, while curiously, it is the separated, but virtually connected scenes of Alex and Sergi's long-distance communications that portray exterior urban environments in most detail. While the heavy use of interior shots during the bulk of the film emphasizes the bubble in which the two lovers find themselves as they navigate both the profound closeness of their relationship (at the outset of the film, before their separation, they are trying to have a child) and the subsequent painful distance between them, the representation of exterior city spaces in the film highlights something quite different. These sequences offer a reflection on the real nature of intimacy, and an interrogation of how our human senses are being lost in the era of networked love.

Through Alex's videos of city scenes, her sharing of Google Street View captures and her own photography that focuses on the intersection of the technological with urban and natural landscapes, Marques Marcet explores a mediated version of urban life that works affectively in tandem with the version of mediated love that Alex and Sergi engage in during their almost seven-month separation. In *A Networked Self and Love*, Zizi Papacharissi examines the intersection of technology and romantic relationships in the twenty-first century, arguing that 'networks can only be as lively as the information and sentiments that flow through them. Without this flow, networks subsist as places where individual modes of egos coexist, but do not connect. They are dead spaces where distinct selves pass through but never bond, forever remaining strangers' (Papacharissi 2018: 1). Marques Marcet's portrayal of virtual landscapes mines this very sentiment, revealing the uncanny nature of networked and technologized spaces and their resultant dehumanizing force, while at the same time connecting these deadened technologized spaces to the dehumanizing forces present in contemporary technologies of love. As Dominic Pettman has argued, love itself is an essentially technological phenomenon, because it 'clamors to be expressed and communicated [a]nd it needs technology to do so' (Pettman 2018: 13). Furthermore, he suggests that 'love could be considered an exemplary case of 'techne', [t]hat is, an art or artifice that brings something new into the world; something deliberately fashioned. Modern love might thus be akin to modern technology' (Pettman 2018: 13). The film *10.000km* acknowledges this intermingling of love and technology in contemporary life, as its visual language explores their imbrication particularly with regards to cybernetic experiences of distance and connection, and landscape and the body.

A few examples of the uses of virtual urban spaces in the curious mise en scène of *10.000km* will suffice to demonstrate how Marques Marcet deploys the surreal, mediated depictions of urban life and technologized landscapes to communicate the disconnection and other emotional losses that *10.000km*'s protagonists suffer in the throes of a networked love relationship, a relationship that is, in Marques

Marcet's telling, all too representative of a generational shift in romantic expression in the digital era. Notably, the first depiction of an urban scene in Marques Marcet's film is the very first shot of Alex's new life in Los Angeles. Instead of the traditional cinematically rendered establishing shot that would orient viewers to the spatial and temporal leap in the narrative, from the closeness of Alex and Sergi's shared apartment in Barcelona, to Alex's new life in the United States, Marques Marcet brings us into this new mediated sense of reality with a grainy shot of what Alex declares to be Sunset Boulevard, captured by her poor-quality laptop camera. Alex's voice-over, describing her new environment, with accompanying pixelated images of her neighbor's patio, the cactus on her landing and her apartment door, all call attention to her framing of this space and the challenges of communicating closeness with only the aid of sight and sound. That Sergi and Alex's Skype conversation immediately switches from their discussion of these visual and oral presentations of landscape to the topic of smell only heightens this, with Alex commenting that the shirt she is wearing smells like Sergi, and Sergi responding that the apartment back in Barcelona 'apesta a ti' (reeks of you) (24:40). As demonstrated in the lengthy continuous take at the outset of the film, between Sergi and Alex's sex life, grooming in the bathroom as well as shared preparation and eating of breakfast, love has existed as a sensorial experience for this couple; now their interaction via screens only heightens their awareness of the loss of the tactile, oral and olfactory communication of love. For Pettman, 'love has always been a matter of negotiating the interface: of language, of signs, of bodies, of expectations, and so on' (Pettman 2018: 16). In the first days of their separation, Alex's deployment of these 'home videos' of an urban and domestic scenography strives to literally remap the interface of her love with Sergi, but the two-dimensionality and inconsistency of what is otherwise an intimate connection because of its immediacy only leaves the lovers longing for the bodily technologies of their prior love language.

This erasure of the body and true connection plays out in another scene in which Alex attempts to familiarize Sergi with her experience of Los Angeles through a shared online exploration of specific city locales on Google Street Maps and via particular image captures from Google Street View. Sergi's commentary as Alex shares these images with him is particularly telling, as he focuses on how the Google Street View landscapes she selects are often emptied of people. 'Aquello es un paraíso' (That looks like paradise), Sergi comments, adding that there are 'poca gente' (few people) and 'cuando tomes una foto no pasa nadie por ahí' (whenever you take a picture, nobody is ever passing by) (29:02). As this online conversation between the lovers occurs only one month into their long-distance relationship, Sergi's comments initially remain upbeat, marveling at the possibilities of both this real and digital space, and the ability of this online platform to bridge the distance between them. But their dialogue by way of these spatial apps quickly turns sour, as Sergi sarcastically jokes, 'Quiero ver famosos. ¿Hay famosos o no?' (I want to see famous people. Are there famous people or not?) (29:30). When Alex responds to this query, first by showing Sergi the site of a famous Stephen Shore photo of a gas station, and then by sharing a view from Hollywood Boulevard, where Alex offers a close up of the blurred faces of the pedestrians on that iconic street, it is clear that the young woman is curating a spatial expression of distance, imitation and unknowability for her lover. She looks at the present-day gas station from many angles, and is troubled that she 'quería sacar una foto para imitarla, pero ya no se puede, ha cambiado tanto' (I wanted to take a picture to imitate it [Shore's photo], but you can't anymore, it's changed so much) (29:49), in this way mirroring her growing feeling of remove from her partner and the impossibility of digitally reproducing the relationship they had once shared. So too, when Alex zooms in on the blurred faces of the young women in the Hollywood Boulevard Google Street View, and Sergi shouts that 'qué miedo da la increíble mujer sin cara' (the incredible faceless woman is so frightening) (30:18) (Figure 13.4), Alex will insist that they blur faces everywhere, and if Sergi cares to look, he'll find that they do it in Barcelona too. The lovers here again speak not *about* the landscapes and bodies they are viewing together, but *through* them; these digitally manipulated images

FIGURE 13.4: Corporeal erasure in the digital realm, Carlos Marques Marcet (dir.), *10.000km*, 2014. Spain. © Lastor Media, S.L.

address the blurred perceptions they are beginning to have of one another, and the loss of bodily presence and intimate knowledge in their present love technology.

As the geographical distance beings to weigh on the lovers, creating an increasing emotional distance between them, Sergi initiates another Skype session with Alex, some three months into their separation. In this scene, Alex juggles the use of multiple apps on her laptop simultaneously. Alongside her videocall with Sergi via Skype, she manipulates several open windows in SilverFast, a program for copying and processing images (Figure 13.5). Alex's connection to Sergi here is as flattened as all the other images she manipulates on screen, and throughout their conversation, she even hides Alex's face behind that of her landscape photographs, marking his dwindling real presence in her Los Angeles life. But it is what is depicted in these other images – the ones that compete with Sergi's face – that is most telling, as these photographs form part of Alex's artistic project on surveillance and technology masquerading as nature. Like the cell phone towers built to look like palm trees in one of the images, Sergi and Alex's virtual relationship imitates a real one, and may even look like one on the surface; but as these two lovers confess in several of their other Skype exchanges, smell and touch are intrinsic to their experiences of intimacy and cannot be simulated in this realm of distanced connection. Like the remote broadcasting news van with its telescoping antenna in another one of Alex's digital photographs on screen, remoteness and the need to report the news of their lives while apart is bringing a staleness to their relationship

FIGURE 13.5: Simulacra and surveillance in both landscape and love, Carlos Marques Marcet (dir.), *10.000km*, 2014. Spain. © Lastor Media, S.L.

through a fact-sharing discourse that, while continuing to connect them in some quotidian way, does little to provide true intimacy, especially in a forum in which their most intimate communication is haunted by the specter of digital surveillance.

Ultimately, Marques Marcet's filmmaking invites us to rethink the relationship between cinema and the urban. The characters in his films, just like the uncanny imbrication of cinema and city space he constructs, find themselves in flux between the familiar and the strange, navigating the implications of creating an alternative family or experiencing a virtual romance. In Marques Marcet's *Anchor and Hope*, the industrial-remnant landscapes of East London's boat canals become the outside-of-time mise en scène through which to express a generation's struggle to redefine family in the era of late capitalism. So too in *10.000km* does the estrangement from city life and the mediated and alienating experience of urbanism depicted operate in parallel to the generational seismic shifts that the film explores, specifically the challenges the first generation of digital natives faces in forming affective bonds and deep romantic relationships in a postindustrial era that privileges mobility and individualistic pursuits.

REFERENCES

Bruno, Giuliana (2018), 'Architecture and the moving image: A haptic journey from pre- to post-cinema', *La Furia Umana*, 34, http://www.lafuriaumana.it/index.php/67-archive/lfu-34/781-giuliana-bruno-architecture-and-the-moving-image-a-haptic-journey-from-pre-to-post-cinema. Accessed 8 June 2019.

De Pablos, Emiliano (2014), 'Cannes: Spain's low-budget pics come with high ambitions', *Variety*, 26 May, https://variety.com/2014/film/markets-festivals/cannes-spains-low-budget-pics-come-with-high-ambitions-1201183995/. Accessed 8 June 2019.

Lefebvre, Henri (2001), *The Production of Space* (trans. Donald Nicholson-Smith), Cambridge, MA: Blackwell.

Marques Marcet, Carlos (2014), *10.000km*, Spain: Lastor Media.

Marques Marcet, Carlos (2017), *Anchor and Hope*, Spain: Lastor Media.

Papacharissi, Zizi (2018), *A Networked Self and Love*, New York: Routledge.

Penz, François and Lu, Andong (2011), *Urban Cinematics: Understanding Urban Phenomena Through the Moving Image*, Bristol and Chicago, IL: Intellect.

Pettman, Domini (2018), 'Love materialism: Technologies of feeling in the 'post-material' world (an interview)', in A. Malinowska and M. Gratzke (eds), *The Materiality of Love: Essays on Affection and Cultural Practice,* New York: Routledge, pp. 13–24.

Pratt, Geraldine and San Juan, Rose Marie (2014), *Film and Urban Space: Critical Possibilities*, Edinburgh: Edinburgh University Press.

Raban, Jonathan (1974), *Soft City*, New York: Random House.

Rivera, Alfonso, (2017), 'Carlos Marques Marcet, director: How do we build an 'us' in today's world?', 11 June, Cineuropa, http://cineuropa.org/en/interview/342452/. Accessed 8 June 2019.

Tweedie, James (2013), *The Age of New Waves: Art Cinema and the Staging of Globalization*, Cambridge: Oxford University Press.

14

Dead to Capitalism: Zombified Territory and Junkie Spaces in *Cabanyal Z*, or How to Unleash Monstrous Creativity in the Urban

Stephen Luis Vilaseca, Northern Illinois University

> *When you will have made him a body without organs, then you will have delivered him from all his automatic reactions and restored him to his true freedom.*
>
> Antonin Artaud, 'To have done with the judgment of god'

The web series *Cabanyal Z* explores a new reading of the zombie as representative of dynamic activists rather than of mindless consumers. Participatory video, the aesthetic structure of *Cabanyal Z*, transforms the grotesque zombie into a largely metaphorical mode of thinking which questions consumption-based strategies of urban growth and design. Such a transformation is achieved by repossessing the zombie body, the empty body of exchange-value, with the spirit of use-value. That is, the value of capitalism is replaced with self-value in the form of art (in this case, participatory video), which moves the body to act in unexpected ways, much like affect in affect theory incites the body to action (Massumi 2002; Brennan 2004; Clough 2007; Thrift 2008; Labanyi 2010), or Félix Guattari's incorporeal universes in his mapping of subjectivity rouse the body to unplanned movement (Guattari 2013; Vilaseca 2014). By expanding the notion of territory as the interplay of built environment, body and mind, this chapter builds upon zombie theory (Fernández Gonzálo 2011; Giroux 2011; Harlan Wilson 2008; Juliet Lauro 2017; MacCormack 2008; Martínez Lucena 2012; McNally 2011), Bodies without Organs (Deleuze and Guattari 1987; Artaud 1977 [1947]), and the nomadic (Deleuze 1988; Derrida 1994; Foucault 1972, 1987). After first introducing the theoretical framework, I place el Cabanyal, the neighborhood in which the web series is filmed, within its social context. I then present the *Cabanyal Z* project and explore how it performs the relationship between creativity, city and self, and how participatory video as experimental art is a radical poetics through which to critique consumption-based strategies of urban growth and design.

Antonin Artaud, in the quote that opens this chapter, suggests that a body without organs, one that many would read as similar to a zombie, is a body full of agency, and, by contrast, a body with organs is actually one that responds to the world through automatic reactions. How can a zombie have more freedom than a person? Deleuze and Guattari view Artaud's affirmation as a 'kind of intensive state in thought' (Massumi 1987: xiv), one that they lift, recirculate and further theorize as the Body without Organs (BwO). Using Artaud's insights as a starting point, Deleuze and Guattari rethink what a body is and what organs are, and, ultimately, what a body can do in the context of predatory capitalism. For Deleuze and Guattari, a body is both physical and immaterial. More than an object, a body is a bundle of relations linking the material world, both self and built environment, with imagination. The organization of the organs determines how the organs relate to one another, to the world and to ideas. The organization can be a closed system (i.e. capitalism) in which binary oppositions like rich/poor and privileged/underdeveloped prevail or it can be an open system. A BwO is one whose organization is constantly changing and, as a result, is radically open to the world. In this context, a BwO is freer than one bound to fixed relations. Because of the pervasiveness of capitalism in the world in which we live today, D. Harlan Wilson argues that '[t]o be human is above all to be a productive capitalist' (Harlan Wilson 2008: 510). In other words, to be human is to be a body with organs functioning according to the organizing principles of capitalism. However, by functioning according to these principles, humans mindlessly consume much like zombies. Consumers are the walking dead. Patricia MacCormack contends that 'if the "human" describes the organized body – of subjectivity or politics – then perhaps the inhumanity in these humans is where we find salvation' (MacCormack 2008: 116). Nobody wants to be the zombies portrayed in film. Nonetheless, these rotting bodies do challenge the basic binary of alive/dead and thus relate to the world outside of fixed binary relations. The salvation of which MacCormack speaks comes from relating to the world like a zombie. I would add that the zombification of both self and built environment by consumption-based strategies of urban growth and design actually do not reproduce mindlessness in activists, but the opposite: newfound agency to resist the day-to-day symbolic and corporeal violence against them at the hands of capitalism. While Harlan Wilson contends that the revolutionary potential of Deleuze and Guattari's theory 'is limited to being realized by purely violent measures' (Harlan Wilson 2008: 511), I question his view that art as experimentation does not lead to new value systems and will argue exactly the reverse: that participatory video as experimental art performs a way of relating to the world that momentarily loosens the standardized ties of order. These ties will constantly be retightened, just as they will be incessantly loosened. This reality, according to Harlan Wilson, 'is as much an open range as it is a jail cell' (Harlan Wilson 2008: 530). We may be trapped, we may never escape, but, as Artaud reminds us, and as Brian Holmes articulates so well, there is freedom in 'the notion of process, as a value in and of itself' (Holmes 2008: 178) or, more specifically, in the process of creative experimentation.

In the participatory video web series *Cabanyal Z* there are ten episodes filmed over a period of five years (2012–17), and the premieres of eight of the shows (episodes 2–9) were projected against the walls of a neighborhood in Valencia, Spain, called el Cabanyal[1] on various dates from 2013 to 2016. The projected videos, for the length of the thirteen-minute episodes, became a form of temporary street art. The creators of the series, Gerardo J. Nuñez and Joan Alamar, taking their cue from street artists, wanted to take advantage of spaces in the city in order to reflect literally and figuratively on the city itself. In a personal interview, Escif, a street artist based in Valencia, explained to me the creative process urban artists undertake in order to determine what and where to paint. According to Escif, street art is always a compromise between what the street artist wants and what the wall needs (Escif 2009). In other words, space informs art, and the city becomes a cocreator of artistic content.

In order to figure out how to represent el Cabanyal and its neighbors in their web series, Nuñez and Alamar listened to the built environment. Characteristic of this seaside neighborhood are rows of nineteenth-century, two-story, contiguous houses whose façades, in order to keep the humidity out, are covered with plaster and then decorated with colorful tiles. The varied mosaics reflect the unique personalities of the residents. Because each home was constructed according to the personal tastes of each family, no two homes are alike (See Figure 14.1).

The singularity of the neighborhood earned it the Valencian Regional Government's designation of *Conjunto Histórico Protegido* ('Protected Historical Group Patrimony') in 1993. The Spanish Ministry of Culture decided to strengthen its protection in 1998 by granting the neighborhood the status of *Bien de Interés Cultural* ('Heritage of Cultural Interest') (Andrés Durà 2014). Despite these protections, however, in 1997, the Valencia Town Council announced an urban renewal plan to extend the Blasco Ibáñez Avenue to the sea, and in order to do so, 1651 homes in el Cabanyal would have to be destroyed (Plataforma Salvem el Cabanyal 2007). In preparation, the Town Council began to buy homes, brick them up or raze them, creating empty lots (see Figures 14.2 and 14.3).

FIGURE 14.1: 'Cabanyal (28)' by Santiago Lopez-Pastor is licensed under CC-BY-ND 2.0.

Through grass-roots associations, squatted social centers and experimental artistic practices, the residents of el Cabanyal were able to resist the prolongation of the avenue for thirteen years from 1997 to 2010 (Martín-Núñez and Sorolla Romero 2015; Plataforma Salvem el Cabanyal 2008). In 2009, the Ministry of Culture intervened and halted the urban renewal plan known as 'el Plan Especial de Protección y Reforma Interior del Cabanyal-Canyamelar' (PEPRI) (The Special Protection and Interior Reform Plan for Cabanyal-Canyamela') because it ruled that the project was violently appropriating cultural heritage. The Valencian Regional Government attempted to lift the legal ban, but the Supreme Court in 2010 upheld the Ministry of Culture's argument (Andrés Durà 2014). In response to this ruling, the municipal government, headed by then Mayor Rita Barberá, stopped giving permits to rehabilitate the buildings in el Cabanyal, and turned a blind eye to drug trafficking and drug use in the neighborhood. Both initiatives were conceived to speed up urban decay (Martín-Núñez and Sorolla Romero 2015).

FIGURE 14.2: Stephen Luis Vilaseca, 'Bricked-up Home', 2009. Digital photo.

FIGURE 14.3: Stephen Luis Vilaseca, 'Empty Lot in el Cabanyal', 2009. Digital photo.

The multiple empty lots and the crumbling buildings in the Cabanyal neighborhood inspired Nuñez and Alamar to represent these spaces in the web series as being overrun by junkies and zombies. In the first episode, after the eviction of squatters from a squatted social center, the Town Council sends Germán, a municipal cleaning services worker, to the building with an ax to destroy the bathroom and kitchen in order to dissuade the evicted squatters from returning. With his ax, he cuts up and dissects the building for marketable parts. The squatted social center suffers a monstrous destruction whose result is a transformation from use-value to exchange-value. The building, upon being bitten by the teeth of Germán's ax, becomes infected, and begins its cycle of becoming-capital, becoming-exchange-value, becoming-commodifiable good. In the middle of the transformation, a zombie hand emerges from the toilet. There is a blurring of the boundary between body and building. The fate of the building is that of the squatter. They both become empty bearers of exchange-value. They both become zombies. This squatter-zombie reaches out and scratches Germán, thus producing an exchange. The mutual contamination results in two becomings: the becoming-commodifiable good of the building (a monstrous transformation from the point of view of the squatters) and the becoming-activist of Germán (a monstrous transformation from the politicians' and capitalists' point of view). Subjectivity is thus conceived of as a dialectic of monstrosity, a zombie-dialectic, in which the production of self is a constant movement between two 'monsters': the zombie (be it the zombie-laborer – labor personified – or the zombie-ruler – capital personified) and the rebel-monster engaged in zombie thought, a metaphorical way of thinking that continually questions supposedly self-evident and closed systems of thought.

The birth of the two monsters in the first episode is doubled by a self-birthing of an accompanying website to the web series to which various parts – a Facebook page, a Twitter account, a YouTube channel and a WordPress blog – are stitched together to form a BwO. The website is like a rebel-monster or a BwO because it is not ordered by the set relations of capitalism, but, rather, by its own self-authored logic. Through the website, the *Cabanyal Z* project reflects upon its own birth as participatory video, a monstrous undertaking in its own right. Participatory video, as understood by Nuñez and Alamar and as realized in this project, is a process of disinterested, collaborative filmmaking whose aim is social change[2]. Their vision of participatory video rejects capitalism's imposed order of market-dependence and market-compulsion because each episode comes to fruition through self-financing, crowdfunding and the free exchange of creative talent. The acting, filming, make-up, visual effects, graphic design, music and editing are all provided as common goods instead of proprietary ones. That is, no one gets paid. The money raised is used to purchase hardware like cameras and lights, and material such as make-up. The majority of the main characters and zombies as well as the technical team are actual neighbors of el Cabanyal. They meet weekly in the squatted social center el Samurac to brainstorm ideas for future episodes. The logic of free exchange and openness informs the entire process. In other words, the on-screen zombies are both activists who engage zombie thought off-screen and zombie bodies as mindless bearers of exchange-value on screen. At the scale of the project itself, this would be common knowledge. However, at the city-wide, regional, national and international scales, this is made clear through extradiegetic narration in the form of blog entries and web pages found on the accompanying website. The metafictional commentary is essential to knock down the fourth wall and provide the necessary information to allow viewers to read zombie thought (or zombie as metaphor), one that questions systems of order like capitalism, as positive.

Because the *Cabanyal Z* project was completely self-financed and crowdfunded instead of bankrolled through a one-time loan, the ten episodes were filmed over a period of five years (2012–17). However, the actual storyline spans only a couple of weeks beginning with *las Fallas* (15 March–19 March) and ending during Holy Week (the week preceding Easter). Situating the web series during Valencia's annual festival *las Fallas* is not an accidental or trivial component of the plot, but an integral and calculated one. This cultural event, which celebrates the spring equinox through the burning of giant puppets, attracts hundreds of thousands of tourists each year. In fact, during the five-day festival, the city of 790,000 inhabitants more than doubles in size, and the partygoers generate hundreds of millions of euros for Valencia (Zafra 2017). Beginning in the mid-1990s, Valencian regional politicians, business owners and urban planners begin to hail culture instead of industry as the means to economic growth. This shift in strategy, a direct response to Barcelona's successful leveraging of the 1992 Olympics into sustained urban revitalization, leads to programs of urban renewal like the extension of the Blasco Ibánez Avenue and the pending destruction of the Cabanyal neighborhood. These programs often prioritize the desires of international investors and tourists over those of the locals.

In the web series, the celebration of the 2013 *Fallas* serves as the backdrop upon which, first, the terms of the zombie-dialectic are explored and defined, and, second, the constant movement between the zombie and the rebel-monster engaged in zombie thought is played out. During a televised interview with the mayor of Valencia in the public square in front of the town hall, various protesters display signs denouncing political corruption, and members of the Plataforma de Afectados por la Hipoteca (Platform of Those Affected by Mortgages) wave green and red cardboard shields protesting the *Ley Hipotecaria* ('the Mortgage Law'). Even though the name of the actual mayor of Valencia at the time, Rita Barberá, is never mentioned during the episodes, the actress playing the mayor bears a strong resemblance to Ms Barberá, and wears a frequent outfit of said mayor, a red power suit (See Figures 14.4 and 14.5).

Hence, the reference is unmistakable. The television reporter, acknowledging the protest signs, remarks to the mayor that there seem to be many antiestablishment people attempting to tarnish the festivities. The moment that she agrees with the reporter's categorization, a zombie emerges from the group of protesters, attacks, bites her and, thus, infects her. This timing suggests that, according to the mayor's perspective, zombies are equated with antiestablishment activists. They short-circuit conceptual order and mark its limits.

Initially, the images of the news report occupy the full screen. Slowly, the camera pans back to reveal the mayor (already physically changed from the infection) and her partner, Lourdes de León, watching the coverage on a monitor. The creators thus let us, the viewers, in on the filmmaking process. We are watching the mayor and Lourdes watching themselves. That is, we are complicit in the act of watching and in the capturing of their reactions to their own image-making. This formal, self-reflexive duplicity frames a doubling on the level of content: creativity and imagination may be used to serve the state

FIGURE 14.4: 'Proclamación Barberá como candidata del PP a la alcaldía de Valencia' by Eduardo Ripoll is licensed under CC-BY-2.0.

and/or capitalism (the image-making undertaken by the mayor and Lourdes), or may be harnessed to defy them (the web series itself). On the one hand, creativity and imagination as a continual process of becoming facilitates constant sharing and multiple connections and, as a result, challenges the fixed relations of capitalism. On the other hand, creativity and imagination that are tied to exchange-value are trapped within the confines of a specific aim, namely, the making of money. In this case, what matters is not the creative process, but rather the marketing campaign to incite consumption. In other words, creativity may be used to either manipulate or liberate. However, it is often difficult to differentiate a marketing campaign from artistic practice because they both share similar aesthetics.

The mayor and Lourdes are watching the newscast from the safety and protection of the Nou Mestalla bunker. After the outbreak of the zombie invasion in the Cabanyal neighborhood, the mayor, in order to assure political continuity,

FIGURE 14.5: 'La Jefe' by Diari La Veu is licensed under CC-BY-NC-SA 2.0.

FIGURE 14.6: 'Nou Mestalla' by anroir is licensed under CC-BY-NC 2.0.

decides to move the government offices to Nou Mestalla, a partially built soccer stadium located northwest of the city center, far from Cabanyal (see Figure 14.6). This real construction is a physical expression and reminder of the perils of remaining locked into consumption-based strategies of urban growth and design when they are no longer viable. Instead of leaving the failed ideological bunker of property speculation and the selling of place, the mayor and her political cronies double down into it. As Critical Art Ensemble, a US collective that explores the relationships between art and political activism, so eloquently puts it, even in crisis (be it financial or existential), 'it is so much easier to stay in the familiar bunker, where the issues (and the parameters of their interpretation) have solidified' (Critical Art Ensemble 1994: 122). To capitalize on Valencia's newfound success in the 2003 season of La Liga, Spain's tier-one soccer league, the team's club foundation believed that a new stadium would generate even more excitement and money for the team and the city. Betting that real-estate prices never fall, the foundation engaged in property speculation. The loan for the construction of the new stadium was secured using the projected profits earned from a future housing development based on the sale of the land on which the old Mestalla stadium sits. Construction began in 2007, but was halted in 2009 after the real-estate bubble burst in 2008. Because the club's main asset, the land surrounding the old stadium, plummeted in value, the loan would have to be paid with money the team no longer possessed. Thus, the project was suspended, and all that remains since 2009 is the concrete shell of the Nou Mestalla. It is to this abandoned construction that the show's mayor and fellow conservative politicians retreat.

In the show, the mayor, after the Supreme Court agrees in 2010 to suspend the extension of the Blasco Ibánez Avenue, releases the zombie virus in the Cabanyal neighborhood, thus initiating the zombie invasion. Some residents continue to sell their homes to the Town Council. These are the zombies from the perspective of those who are still resisting. However, the tendency to acquiesce to the mayor exists within every resident of el Cabanyal. Appalled at the imposed degradation of the neighborhood through the denial of building permits and the governmental permissiveness of drug use in the area, Alicia Fuster, one of the scientists who invented the virus and its antidote, steals the formula as well as the plant needed for the antidote, and joins the resistance movement in el Cabanyal. The antidote is a powerful, addictive psychotropic drug with two uses: (1) when injected in an infected body, it slows the body's transformation into a zombie, and allows the body to move freely among the zombies; and (2) when injected in an uninfected body, it gives the body an addiction-inducing high and also permits it to walk unnoticed among the zombies. To avoid creating more addicts in the resistance, a known junkie, Chusma, is asked to shoot-up and fight against the zombies (to fight against the spreading acquiescence in the neighborhood).

FIGURE 14.7: Chusma and the empty lot *before* transformation from 'Dimonis', Gerardo J. Nuñez and Joan Alamar (dir.), *Cabanyal Z*, 2014. Spain. Screenshot from *Cabanyal Z* is licensed under CC-BY.

In a particularly telling scene, Chusma injects himself with the antidote while seated on the ground in one of the multiple empty lots created by the mayor due to her policy of razing homes in order to clear a path for the extended avenue. The camera shot is a close-up of Chusma from the waist up. While waiting for the antidote to take effect, he lies down, falling into the backdrop of the crumbling building behind him, and out of range of the camera. Chusma's worn, drugged body – riffraff, as his name means in English – is equated with the urban ruins surrounding him. Riding the high of the antidote, he sits back up, and as he does, the empty lot behind him transforms into beautiful, nineteenth-century two-story homes with balconies typical of el Cabanyal (see Figures 14.7 and 14.8).

Chusma's altered consciousness allows him to relate to his exterior world in a radically different way. He is open to exploring new, unforeseen interactions with people, places, things and ideas. Chusma's drug-induced break from the imposed order of capitalism can be reproduced without a mind-altering substance through collaboration and the treatment of knowledge, language, technology, science and culture as common goods. The participants of the *Cabanyal Z* project perform this break as zombie thought, the separation from a totalizing way of thinking which views social relations as fixed.

FIGURE 14.8: Chusma and the empty lot *after* transformation from 'Dimonis', Gerardo J. Nuñez and Joan Alamar (dir.), *Cabanyal Z*, 2014. Spain. Screenshot from *Cabanyal Z*

Worried about her rapidly advancing transformation into a zombie, the mayor concocts a plan to recover the antidote from Alicia Fuster. She decides to send Roberto Castro Segarra, a self-obsessed, ambitious, young politician, to infiltrate the resistance movement in el Cabanyal and locate the antidote. To demonstrate that creativity is not inherently good or bad but may be channeled to either facilitate multiple connections between people, places, things and ideas, or to block them, 'fake' transformations are interspersed with true becomings in the web series. For example, Roberto must undergo a radical change in his appearance in order to successfully gain access to the resistance movement. Lourdes, the mayor's lover, but also leader of the search for the antidote, peruses videos of protesters to see how they dress and style their hair. In consultation with fashion experts, Roberto is transformed from a high strung, tie-wearing businessman with slicked-back hair into a laid-back, scarf-wearing activist with naturally messy hair. Roberto's cycle of becoming-activist is not a true transformation because his ways of relating to the world are still capitalist. While outwardly he resembles a protester, Roberto suffers no change in thought. He is just playing an activist.

The filmic cut from Roberto getting his hair styled to Lola removing blood, flesh and brain from Chusma's hair links and compares the two characters' situations. Chusma equates his 'fixes' with working because he is the one who goes out to redirect the zombies. He now has a 'job' and must look presentable; thus, his long hair is cut. However, Chusma is merely playing an employed, dependable person. He is still trapped in the body of a drug addict. Along the continuum of subjectivity, Roberto and Chusma move toward each other aesthetically (they have the same haircut), but this movement is the false movement of representation. Roberto's becoming-activist and Chusma's becoming-laborer are fixed by the limitations of expression. Their becomings go nowhere because representation restrains and reduces the constant movement of the production of self to one component: an image.

Both capitalists and anticapitalists leverage imagination to move bodies to act. Because they share the same aesthetics, it is often difficult to distinguish the two. Hence, we frequently are not able to read, recognize, see or identify the language of the market. Henry A. Giroux in *Zombie Politics and Culture in the Age of Casino Capitalism* contends that there is a new, growing illiteracy:

> The new illiteracy is about more than not knowing how to read the book or the word; it is about not knowing how to read the world. The challenge it poses in a democracy is one of both learning how to reclaim literacy so as to be able *to narrate oneself and the world from a position of agency.*
>
> (Giroux 2011: 91 emphasis added)

The neighbors of el Cabanyal must learn to self-narrate, and to combine the fragments of their imagination according to an auto-referential and auto-valorizing logic instead of according to the logic of the market. Eva, the young daughter of Germán, the municipal cleaning services worker who was bitten by a zombie in the squatted social center, imagines that her infected friend is well. They play doctor and she alone 'cures' him. Germán admonishes her by stating that only in collaboration with Alicia Fuster and the antidote can her friend be cured. The antidote, as the disguised Roberto professes, is self-management and autonomy. In other words, narrating one's own value different from exchange-value in collaboration with other people stops the spreading destruction of predatory capitalism.

Chimo Bayo, a real-life DJ and musician from Valencia, whose hits in the 1990s included 'Así me gusta a mí', 'Química', 'Bombas' and 'La tía Enriqueta', understands that imagination in the form of poetry, performance art, the plastic arts, graffiti, urban art, cinema and music (to name a few) has the potential to take hold of bodies and make them act in new ways that defy prescriptive models of being, valuing and signifying. In the web series, Chimo, playing himself, experiments with musical frequencies and rhythms that can control the zombies. His search for a song that will save the world is a nod to the power of affect to create social change.

His task is not an easy one because culture is oftentimes appropriated to serve capital. When place-making relies heavily on culture and events to stimulate economic growth, the results may be urban renewal plans like the extension of the Blasco Ibánez Avenue, or property speculation leading to abandoned soccer stadiums like Nou Mestalla. The Valencia Street Circuit, which once hosted the Formula One European Grand Prix for five years (2008–12), also lays abandoned. In 2005, Francisco Camps, president of the Valencian Regional Government, signed an agreement with Formula One chief Bernie Ecclestone to bring the European Grand Prix to Valencia. Camps promised that no public funds would be used to finance the project. As reported by the Spanish newspaper *El País*:

> The project that was going 'to put Valencia on the map', according to Camps, was meant to be funded through an ambitious property development in the area adjoining the circuit. A district filled with old factories would make way for modern canals and skyscrapers. But Spain's real estate crash put an end to those dreams, and these days there is no Formula 1 race and no development project here. Instead, trash is the only thing on view along the circuit.
>
> (Vázquez 2015: n.pag.)

Without the expected profits from the development project, the Valencian Regional Government owes hundreds of millions of euros, and dedicates no money to the aging urban circuit's maintenance. The urban landscape next to the port is an odd mixture of weeds, neglect, trash and desolation. It is near this wasteland, in the web series, where Chusma discovers Chimo conducting his experiments to determine what sounds and rhythms might potentially control the zombies. Lola, Chusma's junkie girlfriend, does not believe that Chusma actually met Chimo, and in an effort to prove his story, Chusma takes Lola back to the Valencian Street Circuit in search of Chimo's house. The camera frames the two of them walking along the abandoned track, and in so doing, their drugged bodies are equated with the urban ruins surrounding them, just as Chusma's cold and empty body was earlier equated with the empty lot in el Cabanyal (see Figure 14.9).

The defining characteristic of the zombie-ruler is the pathological need to reduce common goods to proprietary ones. By the ninth episode, the mayor's infection has progressed to such an extent that she even wants to patent the antidote. If the antidote is a metaphor for self-management and collaboration, patenting it means instrumentalizing social creativity for financial gain. McNally warns that in the present neoliberal climate, 'scientific investigation all too easily serves personal aggrandizement, not societal well-being' (McNally 2011: 91). The treatment of knowledge, language, technology, science and culture as divisible parts with price tags limits the potential number of connections to be made between people, places,

FIGURE 14.9: Chusma, Lola and the Valencian Street Circuit from 'Perduts', Gerardo J. Nuñez and Joan Alamar (dir.), *Cabanyal Z*, 2015. Spain. Screenshot from *Cabanyal Z* is licensed under CC-BY.

things and ideas. It foments a closed system in which the binary oppositions (rich/poor, privileged/underdeveloped) are solidified, not loosened.

In addition to the junkies high on the antidote, the members of a cult, los Hijos del Kaos y la Niebla (The Children of Chaos and Fog), are able to move undetected among the zombies. They think that they acquire this ability by drinking the blood of those who have survived the zombie invasion. However, it is not the blood, but the prescriptive way of relating to the world that makes them able to pass as zombies. They are no different than capitalists. They are monsters as well because, like capitalists, they suck the life out of people through the imposition of fixed rules.

In a last-ditch effort to destroy the Cabanyal neighborhood, the mayor seeks to coax all of the zombies out onto the streets to increase the likelihood of zombie attacks against the residents. During *las Fallas*, every day at 2:00 p.m. a loud firecracker and fireworks show known as *la mascletà* takes place. The zombies of el Cabanyal are drawn to *la mascletà* like the zombies in Romero's *Dawn of the Dead* are drawn to the shopping mall. Both *las Fallas* and the shopping mall are representative of the relentless and powerful compulsion to consume that empties us of agency. The residual effect of the daily *mascletàs* are increased hordes of zombies on the streets and heightened clashes with the neighbors.

Many of these clashes take place in the empty lot known as *el Clot* ('the hole') in front of an apartment building called El Bloc Portuaris (The Ports Apartment Block). This apartment building, one whose inhabitants since the 1950s have been a felicitous mix of working-class white and gypsy families, lays in the direct path of the planned extension of the Blasco Ibánez Avenue, and, hence, has suffered greatly from the Town Council's wrath. Fixing the missing and broken windows, the rusty and burst pipes, the rotting wood doors and crumbling façade is prohibited by the Town Council's suspension of construction permits. As a result, the physical degradation is advanced and unmistakable.

The battle scenes against the zombies with El Bloc Portuaris in the background are intercalated with the scenes in which Germán administers the stolen antidote to his wife María, whom he had previously, but unintentionally, infected. María's body is so diseased that her advanced physical degradation reminds the viewer of the apartment building's marked deterioration. Germán yells for María to return when he is giving her the antidote. His cry is shared by the residents of el Cabanyal who also want their neighborhood to return.

At the height of the neighbors' desperation, the zombies suddenly stop attacking and shuffle toward a bar from which emanates a heavy rhythmic pulse. Chimo Bayo is at the back of the bar mixing sound frequencies and rhythms that are controlling the zombies' movements. Once all of the zombies are inside dancing to the music, Chusma douses them with gasoline. Similar to *la Cremà* of *las Fallas*, during which the giant puppets are burned on the final day of the festivities, Chusma sets the zombies on fire. The whole place goes up in flames. As with the burning puppets, the flaming zombies indicate renewal and hope for social change. However, by framing Cabanyal's anti-property speculation movement within the temporality of an annual festival, Nuñez and Alamar emphasize the cyclical nature of resistance. The neighbors may have won the battle against the zombies, but there will always be more trials to come. For example, Alicia Fuster does not have the antidote any more, Germán stole the plant, and los Hijos del Kaos y la Niebla have taken Germán hostage. In other words, the mayor and the urban renewal plan may have been defeated, but there will be always new monsters on the horizon like los Hijos del Kaos y la Niebla.

On 24 May 2015, Rita Barberá was voted out of office after having served 24 years as the mayor of Valencia. The new majority consisting of councilors from the left-leaning parties Compromís, Partit Socialista del Pais Valencià and València en Comú abolished the urban renewal plan extending the Blasco Ibánez Avenue. The new mayor, Joan Ribó, in conjunction with the new government, has begun reinvesting in the Cabanyal neighborhood. The projected reinvestments using public funds has attracted the attention of foreign investors, so much so that 90 percent of the homes being sold in el Cabanyal are being purchased by foreigners who are betting that the public investments will raise property values in the future (Soriano 2018). Because of heightened interest in the area, rents are beginning to rise (Gabarda 2017). The recent investments are fueling a new challenge, gentrification and a new cycle of resistance. The final two episodes of the web series were being filmed during these changes even though the events depicted in *Cabanyal Z* take place during *las Fallas* 2013. The series serves, therefore, as a mirror to remind neighbors why and how to fight, and the website continually intensifies the *Cabanyal Z* project by acting as a volatile juncture at which various forms of social media constantly collide and, through such constant collisions, creates a continued awareness of the episodes as well as of the multiple projects in the neighborhood that collaborated together to produce them. The constantly repeating message is to embrace zombie thought, to rip out from one's body those organs that function according to the logic of capitalism and to be BwO. By being dead to capitalism, one's exhumed corpse consisting of self and built environment is able to move according to a different logic, that of free exchange and openness.

NOTES

1. All ten episodes can be accessed at http://cabanyalz.com/.
2. Previous work on participatory video and social change includes, but is not limited to, Milne's, Mitchell's and De Lange's *Handbook of Participatory Video* (2012), Sitter and Burke's 'Praxis with self-advocates: Exploring participatory video as radical incrementalism' (2015), White's 'Participatory video: A process that transforms the self and the other' (2003) and Sitter's 'Participatory video: Toward a Method, Advocacy and Voice (MAV) framework' (2012).

REFERENCES

Andrés Durà, Raquel (2014), 'El plan del Cabanyal, la obsesión paralizada de Rita Barberá,' *La Vanguardia*, 8 July, http://www.lavanguardia.com/local/valencia/20140708/54410872818/plan-del-cabanyal-obsesion-paralizada-rita-barbera.html. Accessed 24 May 2018.

Artaud, Antonin ([1947] 1977), 'To have done with the judgment of God', *Semiotext(e)*, 11:3, p. 61.

Brennan, Teresa (2004), *The Transmission of Affect*, Ithaca: Cornell University Press.

Clough, Patricia Ticineto (2007), *The Affective Turn: Theorizing the Social*, Durham, NC: Duke University Press.

Critical Art Ensemble (1994), *The Electronic Disturbance*, Brooklyn, NY: Autonomedia.

Deleuze, Gilles (1988), *Foucault*, trans. ed., Minneapolis: University of Minnesota Press.

Deleuze, Gilles and Guattari, Félix (1987), *A Thousand Plateaus: Capitalism & Schizophrenia*, Minneapolis: University of Minnesota Press.

Derrida, Jacques (1994), *Specters of Marx*, trans. ed., London: Routledge.

Escif (2009), in person interview, Valencia, 26 June.

Fernández Gonzalo, Jorge (2011), *Filosofía zombi*, Barcelona: Editorial Anagrama.

Foucault, Michel (1972), *The Archaeology of Knowledge*, trans. ed., New York: Pantheon Books.

Foucault, Michel (1987), 'Maurice Blanchot: The thought from outside', in Brian Massumi (ed.), *Foucault/Blanchot*, New York: Zone Books, pp. 7-60.

Gabarda, Guillermo (2017), 'El Cabanyal no teme al turismo', *El Mundo*, 21 August, http://www.elmundo.es/comunidad-valenciana/2017/08/21/59996fe8268e3eac088b45a0.html. Accessed 24 May 2018.

Giroux, Henry A. (2011), *Zombie Politics and Culture in the Age of Casino Capitalism*, New York: Peter Lang.

Guattari, Félix (2013), *Schizoanalytic Cartographies*, trans. ed., London and New York: Continuum Impacts.

Harlan Wilson, David (2008), 'Schizosophy of the medieval dead: Sam Raimi's *Army of Darkness*', *The Journal of Popular Culture*, 41:3, pp. 509–35.

Holmes, Brian (2008), *Unleashing the Collective Phantoms: Essays in Reverse Imagineering*, Brooklyn, NY: Autonomedia.

Juliet Lauro, Sarah (ed.) (2017), *Zombie Theory: A Reader*, Minneapolis: University of Minnesota Press.

Labanyi, Jo (2010), 'Doing things: Emotion, affect, and materiality', *Journal of Spanish Cultural Studies*, 11: 3–4, pp. 223–33.

MacCormack, Patricia (2008), *Cinesexuality*, London and New York: Routledge.

Martínez Lucena, Jorge (2012), *Ensayo Z: Una atropología de la carne perecedera*, Córdoba: Berenice.

Martín-Núñez, Marta and Sorolla Romero, Teresa (2015), 'La respuesta ciudadana ante la enunciación política en los contenidos informativos públicos de proximidad. El Cabanyal como caso de estudio', *Cuadernos Artesanos de Comunicación*, December, http://www.revistalatinacs.org/15SLCS/2015_libro/136_Martin.pdf. Accessed 24 May 2018.

Massumi, Brian (1987), 'Translator's foreword: Pleasures of philosophy', in G. Deleuze and F. Guattari , *A Thousand Plateaus*, Minneapolis: University of Minnesota Press, pp. ix–xv.

Massumi, Brian (2002), *Parables for the Virtual: Movement, Affect, Sensation*, Durham, NC: Duke University Press.

McNally, David (2011), *Monsters of the Market: Zombies, Vampires, and Global Capitalism*, Leiden: Brill.

Milne, E-J., Mitchell, Claudia and De Lange, Naydene (eds) (2012), *Handbook of Participatory Video*, Lanham: Rowan & Littlefield.

Plataforma Salvem el Cabanyal (2007), 'La resistència a perdre la paraula', *IX Edició: Cabanyal Portes Obertes – 2007*, Valencia: Martí Impressors, pp. 11–12.

Plataforma Salvem el Cabanyal (2008), *X Cabanyal Portes Obertes 08: El primers 10 anys [1998–2008]: Art, Resistència i Participació Ciutadana*, Valencia: Martí Impressors.

Romero, George A., (1978), *Dawn of the Dead*, USA: United Film Distribution Company.

Sitter, Kathleen C. (2012), 'Participatory video: Toward a Method, Advocacy and Voice (MAV) framework', *Intercultural Education*, 23:6, pp. 541–54.

Sitter, Kathleen C. and Burke, Amy C. (2015), 'Praxis with self-advocates: Exploring participatory video as radical incrementalism', *Catalyst: A Social Justice Forum*, 6:1, Article 6, http://trace.tennessee.edu/catalyst/vol6/iss1/6. Accessed 24 May 2018.

Soriano, Lola (2018), 'Burbuja inmobiliaria en el Cabanyal: los extranjeros compran ya el 90% de las viviendas', *Las provincias*, 14 April, http://www.lasprovincias.es/valencia-ciudad/burbuja-inmobiliaria-cabanyal-extranjeros-compradores-viviendas-20180409134940-nt.html. Accessed 24 May 2018.

Thrift, Nigel (2008), *Non-Representational Theory: Space/Politics/Affect*, Abingdon: Routledge.

Vázquez, Cristina (2015), 'Valencia's F1 Circuit: Left on the Curb', *El País*, 18 December, https://elpais.com/elpais/2015/12/18/inenglish/1450448301_243176.html. Accessed 24 May 2018.

Vilaseca, Stephen Luis (2014), 'Félix Guattari and urban cultural studies', *Journal of Urban Cultural Studies*, 1:1, pp. 137–44.

White, Shirley A. (2003), 'Participatory video: A process that transforms the self and the other', in S. White (ed), *Participatory Video: Images That Transform and Empower*, New Delhi: Sage, pp. 63–101.

Zafra, Ignacio (2017), 'El desconocido impacto económico de las Fallas', *El País*, 14 March, https://elpais.com/ccaa/2017/03/14/valencia/1489511830_881832.html. Accessed 24 May 2018.

Notes on Contributors

Samuel Amago teaches courses on modern and contemporary Spanish literary history, cinema, comics and culture at the University of Virginia, where he is a professor and chair of the Department of Spanish, Italian, and Portuguese. His chapter in this volume draws from his book *Basura: Cultures of Waste in Contemporary Spain* (University of Virginia Press, 2020).

María de Arana Aroca is an associate professor of architectural design in the School of Architecture of the CEU San Pablo University in Madrid. She is on the editorial board of the architectural journal *Constelaciones* and has taught architectural design at the Escuela Técnica Superior de Arquitectura de Madrid. She combines her academic career with professional practice and has completed a number of projects such as the restoration of the Monastery of San Pedro de Arlanza in Burgos and new building construction at the School of Psychology in Murcia.

Emeterio Diez Puertas is a professor at Camilo José Cela University and chair of the Department of Publications of the Royal Higher College of Performing Arts. He has taught courses and seminars at universities in Argentina, Colombia and Ecuador, and his research focuses on the history of media and performance, narratology and gender studies. His publications include *Arte, espectáculos y propaganda bajo el signo libertario (España, 1936–1939)* (Laertes, 2020), *Cine y comunicación política en Iberoamérica* (UOC, 2018), *El sueño de un cine hispano* (Síntesis, 2017), *Narrativa fílmica* (Fundamentos, 2006) and *Historia social del cine en España* (Fundamentos, 2003). He is a member of the Asociación de Historiadores de la Comunicación.

David Foshee completed his Ph.D in Spanish film and cultural studies at Texas Tech University and teaches at the University of Nebraska-Omaha. His research focuses on issues of modernization and the representation of childhood in Spanish popular films of the 1950s. His recent publications include 'Little monstrous "others": Recent trends in childhood representation in Spanish film' in the *Romance Quarterly* (2020, 67:4).

BENJAMIN FRASER is a professor of Iberian and Latin American cultural studies at the University of Arizona. He is the editor-in-chief of *Hispania*, founding editor of the *Journal of Urban Cultural Studies*, senior editor of the *Arizona Journal of Hispanic Cultural Studies* and founding coeditor of the Hispanic Urban Studies book series. He has published ten single-authored monographs, including the Eisner-nominated book *The Art of Pere Joan: Space, Landscape and Comics Form* (University of Texas Press, 2019), as well as *Visible Cities, Global Comics: Urban Images and Spatial Form* (University Press of Mississippi, 2019), *Cognitive Disability Aesthetics* (University of Toronto Press, 2018), and *Toward an Urban Cultural Studies* (Palgrave Macmillan, 2015). Among his more than 80 research articles are recent essays on themes of urbanism and architecture published in the *Journal of Literary and Cultural Disability Studies*, *Hispanic Issues Online*, *Transmodernity*, *European Comic Art*, *Journal of Spanish Cultural Studies*, *The Routledge Companion to Iberian Studies* and *The Barcelona Reader*.

JOSEFINA GONZÁLEZ CUBERO is an associate professor of architectural theory and projects at the Escuela Técnica Superior de Arquitectura of the University of Valladolid, Spain. Her research focuses on modern architecture and the cross-cutting relationships between architecture and other arts (the fine and visual arts, theater, cinema, photography and design). Since 2007 she has actively collaborated with the Architectural Studies research group of Centro de Estudos Arnaldo Araújo (FCT uRD 4041) in Portugal. She is also a member of the Portuguese FCT-funded project Photography, modern architecture and the Escola do Porto: Interpretations on Teófilo Rego Archive (FCT PTDC/ATP-AQI/4805/2012, 2012–2015) and the EU-funded research project MODSCAPES | Modernist Reinvention of Rural Landscapes (HERA.15.097, 2016–2019). She is currently involved in the R&D Spanish projects OEE CARTOTEA | Observatory of Scenic Spaces: Theatre cartography (BIA 2016-77262-R, 2017–2020) and PUH-RePlan (PGC2018-097135-B-I00, 2019–2021).

JORGE GOROSTIZA is an active architect and urban planner who has published numerous articles and books on cinema and architecture. He is the author of *Peter Greenaway* (Cátedra, 1995), *Directores artísticos del cine español* (Cátedra, 1997), *La imagen supuesta* (Fundación Arquia, 1998), *Constructores de quimeras* (València Generalitat, 1999), *Blade Runner* (Paidós Ibérica, 2002) and *David Cronenberg* (Cátedra, 2003) – the latter two with Ana Pérez – as well as *La profundidad de la pantalla, arquitectura + cine* (Ediciones Ocho y Medio,

2007), *Panorámicas urbanas: 50 películas esenciales sobre la ciudad* (Editorial UOC, 2016), *El intruso electrónico: La TV y el espacio doméstico* (Micromegas Ediciones, 2019) and *Construcciones filmadas: 50 películas esenciales sobre arquitectura* (Editorial UOC, 2019), among others. He was the director of the Filmoteca Canaria between 2000 and 2005 and has given lectures on architecture and cinema at institutions and universities in Spain, Chile, Costa Rica and Peru. He has participated as jury in many film festivals and curated a number of exhibits. His blog can be found at www.cinearquitecturaciudad.blogspot.com.

Juli Highfill is a professor of Spanish literature and culture in the Department of Romance Languages and Literatures at the University of Michigan. In her research, she focuses on the literary and visual production of the Spanish historic avant-garde, as well as popular film in the 1920s and 1930s. She is the author of *Portraits of Excess: Reading Character in the Modern Spanish Novel* (Society of Spanish and Spanish-American Studies, 1999) and *Modernism and Its Merchandise: The Spanish Avant-Garde and Material Culture, 1920–1930* (Penn State University Press, 2014). Her current book project addresses cinema, spectatorship, and politics: *Images in Flight: Popular and Political Affect in Spanish Film (1925–1939).*

Patricia Keller specializes in Spanish literature and visual culture. She is the author of *Ghostly Landscapes: Film, Photography, and the Aesthetics of Haunting in Contemporary Spanish Culture* (University of Toronto Press, 2015), which examines the relationship between image production, ideology, and spectrality. She is currently working on a new project titled *Photography's Wound: Exposing Belief in Times of Uncertainty*, a study of contemporary photography, ethics and structures of belief. Her research and teaching interests are located at the intersection of literature, cultural studies, photography, poetics, critical theory and cinema studies.

Susan Larson is the Charles B. Qualia Endowed Professor of Romance Languages at Texas Tech University, executive editor of the *Romance Quarterly* and coeditor (with Benjamin Fraser) of the Palgrave Macmillan book series *Hispanic Urban Studies*. She teaches courses in Spanish urban, film and literary studies, and her publications include *Constructing and Resisting Modernity: Madrid 1900–1936* (Vervuert/Iberoamericana, 2011) and the edited volumes *Language, Image, Power: Cultural Studies Theory and Practice* (Routledge, 2021), *Kiosk Literature of Silver Age Spain: Mass Culture and Modernity* (Intellect, 2016, with Jeff Zamostny), and *Visualizing Spanish Modernity* (Berg, 2005, with Eva Woods Peiró).

LEIGH MERCER is an associate professor of Spanish and adjunct associate professor of comparative literature, cinema, and media at the University of Washington, Seattle. Her research focuses on such areas as the modern and contemporary Spanish novel, early Spanish film, Hispanic urbanism, the Gothic tradition, Catalan identity and cultural expression, and tourism in Spain. She is the author of *Urbanism and Urbanity: The Spanish Bourgeois Novel and Contemporary Customs (1845–1925)* (Bucknell University Press, 2013), and is presently at work on a book project on technological display and technophobia in Spain's silent cinema era. In recent years, alongside her colleagues in the Department of Spanish and Portuguese Studies at the University of Washington, she has helped design and implement a new Ph.D. program with a strong public humanities component, and has a growing interest in film festival programming as public-facing scholarship.

NURIA RODRÍGUEZ-MARTÍN holds degrees in history and in journalism from the Complutense University of Madrid. She earned her Ph.D. in history in 2013 with a dissertation on the social and cultural changes in Madrid during the 1920s and 1930s which received the Distinguished Doctoral Dissertation Award from the Spanish Association of Contemporary History. She is the author of *La capital de un sueño. Madrid en el primer tercio del siglo XX* (CEPC, 2015), awarded as Best Book in Art and Humanities by the Nineteenth Spanish University Press Prize Committee. She held a position as *Lectrice d'Espagnol* at the Paris-Sorbonne University (2013–15), where she taught numerous courses on Spanish culture and history. In 2019, she joined the Department of Modern and Contemporary History at the University of Malaga as a postdoctoral fellow. Her research focuses on the processes of modernization in Spanish cities during the early twentieth century.

CARLOS SAMBRICIO was a professor of architecture and urban history at the Escuela Técnica Superior de Arquitectura de Madrid from 1986 to 2018. Select publications include *Madrid, vivienda y urbanismo. 1900–1960* (Akal, 2004), *Madrid: Ciudad-región. De la Ciudad Ilustrada a la primera mitad del siglo XX* (Dirección General de Urbanismo y Planificación Regional, 1999), *Territorio y ciudad en la España Ilustrada* (Ministerio de Obras Públicas y Transportes, 1991), *La arquitectura española de la Ilustración* (Consejo Superior de los Colegios de Arquitectos de España, 1986) and *Cuando se quiso resucitar la arquitectura* (Colegio Oficial de Aparejadores y Arquitectos Técnicos, 1984). His edited volumes include *El Urbanismo de la Transición. El Plan General de Ordenación Urbana de Madrid de 1985* (Ayuntamiento de Madrid, 2019), *Ciudad y vivienda en América Latina, 1930–1960* (Lampreave, 2012), *La construcción de la ciudad liberal* (Lampreave, 2009), *Un siglo de vivienda social; 1903–2003* (Ayuntamiento de Madrid, 2003), *La vivienda experimental: Concurso de viviendas experimentales de 1956* (Colegio Oficial de Arquitectos de Madrid, 1998) and *L'Habitation Minimun. Actas del II Congreso del CIAM* (Colegio Oficial de Arquitectors de Aragón, 1997). He has been a visiting scholar at the Getty Center for the Humanities in Los Angeles, Harvard University and the Centre for Canadian Architecture in Montreal as well as a visiting professor at the Bau und Stadtbaugeschichte of Hochschule für Bildende Künste in Hamburg, Germany and the Universidad Politecnica's School of Architecture in Milan. He was the Alisa Mellon Bruce Senior Fellow at the National Gallery of Art in Washington DC in 2013 and nominated in 2017 by the Consejo Superior de Colegios de Arquitectos de España for the Príncipe de Asturias Prize in Social Sciences.

VICENTE SÁNCHEZ-BIOSCA is a professor of film studies and visual culture at the University of Valencia and held the 2013 Chair of the King Juan Carlos I Center at New York University. Visiting professor and scholar at various European and American Universities, he is the author of a dozen books on topics related to art avant-garde and cinema and editing and montage in the arts. Since 1990, his research brings together film and history, dealing with topics such as the Spanish Civil War, the Holocaust and the Cambodian genocide. Over the last few years, he has led a research project on perpetrators of mass crimes founding a group called REPERCRI (www.repercri.com). His forthcoming book focuses on the production and circulation of 'perpetrator images', I.D., images produced by the perpetrators of mass crimes and genocide or their accomplices as a part of the violence exerted against their victims (Repository: http://roderic.uv.es/pers/G6106.html)

STEPHEN LUIS VILASECA is an associate professor of Spanish at Northern Illinois University and a co-associate editor of the *Journal of Urban Cultural Studies*. He is the author of *Barcelonan Okupas: Squatter Power!* (Fairleigh Dickinson University Press, 2013) and *Anarchist Socialism in Early Twentieth-Century Spain: A Ricardo Mella Anthology* (Palgrave Macmillan, 2020). He has also written articles in the *Bulletin of Hispanic Studies*, *Letras Hispanas: Revista de Literatura y Cultura*, the *Arizona Journal of Hispanic Cultural Studies*, *Transitions: Journal of Franco-Iberian Studies*, the *Journal of Urban Cultural Studies* and the *Journal of Spanish Cultural Studies*.

TOM WHITTAKER in an associate professor of film and Spanish cultural studies at the University of Warwick. He is the author of *The Films of Elías Querejeta: A Producer of Landscapes* (University of Wales Press, 2011) and *The Spanish Quinqui Film: Delinquency, Sound, Sensation* (Manchester University Press, 2020). He is also the coeditor of *Performance and Spanish Film* (Manchester University Press, 2016), *Locating the Voice in Film: Critical Approaches and Global Practices*

(Oxford University Press, 2017) and a recent special issue entitled 'Spanish Sound Studies' for *Journal of Spanish Cultural Studies* (2019).

ALBA ZARZA-ARRIBAS is an architect with a degree in the history and aesthetics of cinematography from University of Valladolid, where she was awarded a collaboration scholarship from the Social Council at the Department of Architectural Theory and Projects in the Escuela Técnica Superior de Arquitectura. Her research focuses on the relationship between architecture and cinema, and since 2018 she has been member of the Architectural Studies research group of CEAA | Centro de Estudos Arnaldo Araújo (FCT uRD 4041), taking part in the transnational collaborative research project MODSCAPES | Modernist Reinvention of Rural Landscapes (HERA.15.097). She is a Ph.D. candidate in architecture with an FCT Ph.D. grant (SFRH/BD/141720/2018) developed at the CEAA | Centro de Estudos Arnaldo Araújo and the Department of Architectural Theory and Projects, University of Valladolid.

Index

Page numbers in *italics* refer to figures.